THE LOST ADVENTURES OF JAMES BOND:
Timothy Dalton's Third and Fourth Bond Films, James Bond Jr., and Other Unmade or Forgotten 007 Projects
by
Mark Edlitz

Also By Mark Edlitz

How to Be a Superhero
The Many Lives of James Bond: How the Creators of 007 Have Decoded the Superspy

Dedication

For my wife, Suzie and my children, Sophie and Ben. You make me happier than you could possibly imagine.

Introduction

I never set out to write two books on James Bond. Nevertheless, the book that you hold represents my second book on the franchise, after *The Many Lives of James Bond*. Before I explain how this volume came into existence, it might be valuable to share my personal history with Ian Fleming's enduring creation.

I have been a huge Bond fan since I was seven years old and my mom and dad took me to a theater to see *Moonraker*. I was immediately enthralled by Roger Moore's portrayal of the extraordinary spy. From there, I was hooked.

I soon tracked down all the Eon Bond movies and I devoured Ian Fleming's novels and short stories. Over time, I discovered and reveled in the many absorbing Bond adventures that span across all media, from video games to television, radio dramas, comic books, comic strips, audiobooks, and continuation novels.

I have also been lucky enough to meet a few actors who have played Bond.

To my everlasting delight, I met Roger Moore at a black-tie event. Meeting Roger Moore while he's wearing a tuxedo can be disorienting. Your brain can trick you into almost believing that you are meeting the fictional character. Given the opportunity, I asked him a few Bond-related questions and he answered them in his characteristic witty and self-effacing manner.

Shortly before the release of *GoldenEye*, I attended a Bond convention where I asked Pierce Brosnan if he would mind introducing himself as Bond does, and Brosnan gamely played along. Later on, I briefly worked with him on an independent film, where I had the opportunity to share a couple of meals with him. On one of those occasions, a group of us were waiting for the next camera setup away from the set at a nearby restaurant. As we passed the time, Brosnan spotted two elderly women who were clearly fans of his. Brosnan discretely left our table, joined theirs, and sweetly listened to the women as they told him about their lives.

I first saw George Lazenby at a talk that Roger Moore gave for his memoir *My Name is My Bond*. I remember thinking about how thrilling it was to be in the presence of two different Bonds. The next day, I interviewed Lazenby about his single outing as Bond. Lazenby struck me as someone who is simultaneously extremely confident and appealingly self-effacing.

It is perhaps a fitting coincidence that I met my next Bond actor in Chelsea (a neighborhood in New York City), as Chelsea (England) is the location of 007's residence in Ian Fleming's novels.

Soon after my book *The Many Lives of James Bond* was published, I attended a screening of one of Daniel Craig's non-Bond films, after which Craig would be participating in a Q&A session. I desperately wanted to attend and present him with a copy of the book. But first I had to overcome a couple of obstacles.

The first hurdle was that the screening took place on a Saturday evening, which by long tradition is "date night" for my wife and me. It's the night when we leave our children at home in order to spend time alone over dinner. Saturday nights are sacrosanct for us, and I can't recall the last time either of us missed one to do something without the other. However, I explained the situation to her, and, without hesitation, she encouraged me to go.

The next hurdle involved my being able to get to Craig immediately after the Q&A, before he disappeared. I arrived at the screening early and when the doors opened, I ran to the front row of the auditorium. Although the first row is often the worst seat in the house because you have to crane your neck to see the film, it was also closest to the stage where Craig would be seated. After the movie, I sat nervously through the Q&A, eager to pounce quickly when it ended, with my book, wrapped in a red ribbon I purchased for the occasion, resting beneath my seat. When the Q&A concluded and Craig was making his beeline for the exit, I rushed to intercept him so that I could introduce myself to the actor and present him with the book, which features him on the cover. I heard him utter a little gasp of pleasant surprise. I can't remember exactly what I said because I was flooded with adrenaline, but Craig graciously accepted it, shook my hand, and said, "Well done."

With that, he left the building and slid into the backseat of the vehicle that was waiting for him. Due to the heavy downtown traffic, I suspected that Craig had a long trip ahead of him. In my imagination, he flipped through the book during his ride home.

It is highly unlikely that Sir Roger Moore, Pierce Brosnan, George Lazenby, or Daniel Craig remembered their encounters with me. But I will always cherish the memories of my brush with Bonds.

This brings me back to the reason for my second Bond book. When I began writing *The Many Lives of James Bond*, I assumed that one book on 007 would be sufficient. However, as I was working on what became the first volume, I cast a wide net and let my research carry me into any area of the ever-expanding Bond universe that sounded interesting. During the course of my explorations, I interviewed a variety of artists who were involved in the creation of Bond movies, books, television shows, comics, radio dramas, theme-park rides, and video games. While organizing the book, which had grown steadily into what would have been an inordinately large single book, it became apparent that my research fell naturally into two broad categories, each of which warranted a separate volume.

The first category consists of interviews with the myriad actors who have played 007 and with the various artists, such as writers and directors, who have interpreted the character of Bond in different media. Those conversations became the basis for *The Many Lives of James Bond*.

The second area of exploration concerns widely overlooked Bond adventures. This group of interviews is with the creators of "lost" Bond stories. That is to say, unrealized, out-of-print, or largely forgotten Bond tales. Among the unrealized exploits, I discovered fascinating and previously unreported details about an unmade movie that would have dramatized how Bond became a Double-O agent, the unproduced *Casino Royale* play by Bond novelist Raymond Benson, and different scenarios for Timothy Dalton's abandoned third Bond movie.

The Bond stories that I characterize as lost or overlooked include *James Bond Jr.*, the animated series about 007's nephew, which is not commercially available; "A License To Thrill," the shuttered 007 theme-park attraction which also featured a short Bond movie; the out-of-print, interactive Find Your Fate Bond books for children; the 59 Zig-Zag comic books that feature Sean Connery's likeness as the spy in both original and adapted stories that have never been published in English; and the cheeky beer commercial which inserts Daniel Craig's Bond into a Roger Moore-style escapade. I also interviewed Toby Stephens about playing Bond in a series of radio dramas, solved a long-standing Bond literary-mystery, and unearthed the story behind Sean Connery's lost Bond performance. These and other unmade or obscure Bond exploits make up this volume.

My goal in *The Lost Adventures of James Bond* is to draw more attention to these stories, to shed light on the fascinating work of these artists and their artistic processes, and to fuel the fantasies of other devoted Bond fans who also daydream about 007's unrealized and sometimes forgotten missions.

I hope you enjoy the book.

Author's Note

In different novels, Ian Fleming, who was not fussy about continuity, rendered Bond's elite section as "Double-O" (with a dash), "Double O" (without a dash), and "double-o" (in lower case). Similarly, in different media M, Bond's superior is styled with and without a period and *From Russia, with Love* is rendered with and without a comma. For consistency, I have chosen to use "Double-O," except when I am quoting Fleming or someone else who depicts it differently, to exclude the period from M, and to omit the comma from the title of Fleming's fifth novel. For aesthetic reasons, I have opted for "Eon Productions" rather than "EON Productions," and to identify animated series *James Bond Jr* as *James Bond Jr.* and the Bond film *SPECTRE* as *Spectre*.

All interviews have been editing for length and clarity.

Table of Contents

Section 1 – Timothy Dalton's Lost Bond Movies

Timothy Dalton's Unmade Third Bond Film

Bond 17: Another Unmade Third Dalton Bond Film

Dalton's Unmade Fourth Bond Film – *Reunion with Death*

Dalton's Unmade First Bond Film: James Bond's Origin Story

Section 2 – Roger Moore and Pierce Brosnan's Lost Bond Movies

Unmade *The Spy Who Loved Me*

Unmade *Moonraker*

Unmade *Tomorrow Never Dies*

Section 3 – Lost Bond TV: James Bond Jr.

James Bond Jr. Writer's Guide

Creating *James Bond Jr.*

Directing *James Bond Jr.*

Writing *James Bond Jr.* – Part One

Writing *James Bond Jr.* – Part Two

Novelizations

As Good As Gold

Lost Theme Song – "James Bond Jr."

Section 4 – Lost Bond in Print: Books, Comics, and Fanzines

003½: The Adventures of James Bond Junior

James Bond in Barracuda Run

The Secret History of Bond Comics

Zig-Zag Comics

A Silent Armageddon and *Shattered Helix*

"Light of My Death"

James Bond: 1942

Richard Maibaum's Bond essays

Section 5 – Lost Bond Productions

Raymond Benson's Lost Bond Play – *Casino Royale*

Theme Park Ride – *License to Thrill*

"The Chase"

Theme Song – "Never Say Never Again"

Section 6 – Lost Bond Performances

Radio Performance – Toby Stephens is James Bond

Dance Performance – Blair Farrington is (almost) James Bond

Film Performance – Sean Connery is James Bond

Appendix

Appendix One: James Bond Stories

Appendix Two: The Big List of Bond Actors

Appendix Three: Treatments for *A Silent Armageddon* and *"A Deadly Prodigal"*

Section 1 – Timothy Dalton's Lost Bond Movies

Timothy Dalton's Unmade Third Bond Film
Alfonse Ruggiero

Timothy Dalton, the fourth cinematic 007, made just two Bond movies, *The Living Daylights* and *Licence to Kill*. Yet, in his brief tenure, Dalton redefined the role and deepened the character. Like many fans, I was disappointed that Dalton didn't get the opportunity to make his third Bond film. While I would have loved seeing Sean Connery or Roger Moore don a tux one more time, their tenure felt complete. Even George Lazenby's legacy, due to his nuanced and vulnerable performance as Bond in his one appearance as 007, seemed fully realized. However, it feels as though Dalton's license to kill was revoked prematurely.

As Phil Noble Jr. observed in his essay "You Only Live Thrice," "Each Bond star's legacy seems to live or die on their third entry."[1] For many Bond enthusiasts, Connery and Moore's third films, *Goldfinger* and *The Spy Who Loved Me*, respectively, are their best. A third Dalton Bond film could have ingrained his distinctive performance as Bond into the public's consciousness and helped to fortify his legacy. A third film would also have answered the intriguing question: would Dalton's Bond have continued in the spirit of the cold-blooded *Licence to Kill* or would the franchise move towards the wonderful extravagances of the Moore era?

Dalton's first Bond film, *The Living Daylights*, is an excellent addition to the series and it quickly established him as an introspective, no-nonsense, conflicted 007. (Bond, "If he fires me, I'll thank him for it."). But many fans and critics at the time felt that his second mission, *Licence to Kill*, was too much of a departure from the established formula—that it was too grim. In it, Bond essentially feeds one villain to ravenous sharks and sets another one on fire. A third Bond film would have given Dalton a chance to fine-tune his already compelling portrayal and leave a deeper imprint on the Bond franchise. Dalton thoroughly inhabited Bond from the moment he was introduced in the pre-title sequence of *The Living Daylights*.

Of greater importance is that the next Bond film had less to do with what Dalton brought to the character than it did with Eon, which was going through a several-year period of experimentation and discovery, as it was deciding what kind of Bond film to make next. And it should be noted that Dalton was open to returning to the role for one last movie. According to the actor, he told Albert Broccoli, "I think that I'd love to do *one*. Try and take the best of the two that I have done and consolidate them into a third."[2]

A treatment for Dalton's third Bond film sheds some light on the answer. It was co-written by Michael G. Wilson and Alfonse Ruggiero and it was called "Bond 17 Outline." The 17-page document is dated May 8, 1990, and it was revised on May 10, 1990. Two additional pages include the cover and a short prefatory note stating that the "robotic devices referred to in this outline are complex and exotic machines designed," which are "designed for specific tasks and environments. They are not humanoid in form."[3] The outline is broken up into 84 numbered paragraphs.

The pre-title sequence, identified in the outline as the "Opening sequence," is not described.[4]

The story begins at a chemical weapons lab in Scotland, where a Bomb Squad is searching the building for explosives. An officer informs Nigel Yupland, "a young rising star in the Ministry of Defence," that the building is safe to enter."[5] But inside the lab "one of the robotic machines run amuck." Yupland and his men seek safety as the building explodes. Later, in the House of Commons, the Prime Minister faces acrimonious questions from the opposition about the safety of the British people. The Prime Minister pledges to have the explosion investigated.

At MI5 headquarters, Bond meets with M and Yupland, who tells Bond that because the "Double O section is outdated" he will recommend that it "should be closed down."[6] However, Yupland tells Bond that the Prime Minister wants his help. Yupland explains that he was at the chemical plant because "a letter was received threatening its destruction."[7] Yupland says that he tried but failed to prevent the explosion, and he adds that "experts have been unable to ascertain exactly how it was done."[8] Yupland also reveals that the government has received a second letter "threatening a serious incident in 72 hours at a government base in Hong Kong."[9] M informs Bond that he has 72 hours to determine who is behind the plot and to stop it.

In the Situation Room, Yupland tells Bond that they have no leads but that in addition to the plant in Scotland there have been a series of break-ins at other "high tech Government and military contractor facilities," yet nothing was taken from any of the facilities.[10] Bond is shown a photo of the intruder who penetrated the facilities, but the trespasser's face is blurry and none of the experts have been able to determine the culprit's identity. Bond takes the original surveillance video recording to Q, who will use experimental technology to identify the intruder.

Meanwhile, in Tokyo, a "Black Clad Figure" breaks into Kohoni Industries.[11] The figure removes one sub-assembly unit and substitutes a new one in a "robotic apparatus" that will be sent to Nanking, China. Outside, the Kohoni twins who are the "heads of the Kohoni Industrial Empire" order their men to capture the intruder.[12] Finally safe, the figure is revealed to be a beautiful American woman. in her early 30s. The woman recovers a microchip from the sub-assembly unit that she stole and hides it into her bracelet.

Back at MI5, Q has been able to identify the figure in the surveillance photo as Connie Webb. We learn that Webb is an "adventuress" and the daughter of a master cat burglar and a former CIA operative, who was trained by the agency "to penetrate high-security facilities...to plant bugs and gather intelligence" and who now works freelance.[13] Q also informs Bond that she is now in Tokyo. Bond is ordered to "make contact, gain her confidence, and find out who she is working for."[14] To support his cover story, Bond is given a superconductor that works at room temperature to use as "bait."[15] As they are leaving, Q shows Bond an Aston Martin DB V and he promises to get the car to Bond in Tokyo.

In Tokyo, Bond is introduced to Denholm Crisp, who is five years away from retirement from the service, and his "once hard edge has been dulled after twenty years in the Far East by age and duty-free drink."[16] Crisp, who is energized by Bond's presence, tells Bond that Connie is staying at a Japanese ski resort. Bond finds Connie at the resort and follows her. Connie spots Bond and tries to escape. A chase ensues, first by helicopter and then on skis, "the sheer recklessness" of which "exhilarates" Connie, who later reveals that she is an adrenaline junkie.[17] After a dangerous move, Connie is trapped beneath a snowbank. Bond digs her out and they agree to meet for dinner. After dinner, Bond and Connie go to her room. Bond shows Connie the "superconducting material" that Q gave him and asks Connie to introduce him to "the top man," and he promises her a finder's fee.[18]

The Kohoni twins and their thugs force their way into Connie's room and demand to know who Connie is working for. When she refuses to tell them, the Kohoni twins torture 007, using a taser gun. Bond turns the tables by using his own body as a conductor to transfer the electrical charge to one of the Kohoni twins. Bond and Connie fight their way out of the room. Once outside, Connie speeds off in her Lamborghini as Bond "manages to delay and evade the Kohonis in a wild chase scene" through the ski resort's torchlight parade.[19]

Connie contacts Otto Winkhart, a "bent Swiss lawyer."[20] She informs Winkhart that she still has Kohoni's chip and she also tells him about Bond's "high tech material."[21] Winkhart agrees to meet Connie and to look at the technology in Hong Kong.

Later, Winkhart goes through a "labyrinth of scientific laboratories" to meet his boss Sir Henry Lee Ching, "a brilliant and handsome...British-Chinese entrepreneur."[22] Sir Henry inspects the "graying brown cube" that Bond gave Connie. Impressed that "someone has finally discovered the elusive "room temperature" superconductor, Sir Henry instructs Winkhart to set up a meeting with Bond at a party that night.[23] Sir Henry decides to arrange a "little accident" at the Chinese atomic power plant in Nanking.[24] At the atomic power plant, one of the robotic devices (which resembles the "one we saw Connie tamper with" earlier) "runs amuck, smashing the rods" at the core of the reactor.[25] A "fire breaks out" and moments later the "whole building explodes."[26]

At the Kohoni twins' high-rise building, the brothers meet with Sir Henry, who offers to buy their company. Meanwhile, Sir Henry's henchman Rodin, who is dressed as a messenger and is wearing a high-tech motorcycle helmet with thermal imaging and a "heads up targeting display," enters the building and approaches the guards.[27] Targeting the men with his helmet, he activates a "futuristic gun" that sits "on its own gimbal independently aims and fires" at the guards, killing them.[28]

At the meeting, the Kohonis refuse Sir Henry's bid to acquire their company. Sir Henry leaves, and once outside, he signals Rodin. Rodin activates a seemingly ordinary "window washing scaffold," which he has rigged with a row of high-power flame throwers.[29] The scaffold is lowered to the floor of the Kohonis' office. The "spray gun tips of the washer" shoots a "ball of flame" and the "glass window begins to warp, sag, then finally explode; flames engulf the room," killing the Kohonis.[30]

Outside, Otto consoles Sir Henry about failing to reach a deal, which would have only led to legal and tax complications. His competition now eliminated, a coolly calculating Sir Henry counters, "Now we only have an estate problem. Make a deal with the widows." [31]

Bond and Denholm Crisp fly to Hong Kong. It is a "sight that Bond has seen many times but never tires of."[32] Once in Hong Kong, Bond and Denholm wait for a British military transport, from which Q emerges with the newly-equipped Aston Martin.

Bond is shown into his hotel suite by Mi Wai, an attractive Chinese assistant manager of the hotel. A photographer at the hotel takes Bond's photo and transmits it to Quen Low, "Bond's opposite number in mainland China."[33] Inside his luxury suite, Bond finds a naked Connie in an "environmental room," a steam room/sauna that, due to strategically placed flora and natural light simulators, gives "the impression of being in a tropical rainforest."[34] Connie greets Bond, "Welcome to the tropics, Mr. Bond." Connie informs 007 that his "sample impressed some important people" and that they have been invited to Sir Henry's party.[35] After drinking to a "merger," they make love.[36]

Later, Bond and Connie go to Sir Henry's party, which is being held in his highly secured building. An elite commando unit storms the building, but the attackers are quickly neutralized by "hidden machine guns" and "security robots."[37] Sir Henry explains that the attack was a staged demonstration, intended to show that the building is completely "automated, operated by computer" and that it is also "completely impregnable" to a terrorist attack.[38] At the party, a waiter gives Bond a fortune cookie, which provides Bond with the time and place of a meeting. However, the identity of the person Bond is to meet remains a mystery. As Bond, Connie, and Sir Henry are talking, Yupland arrives.

Sir Henry and Yupland talk and are revealed to be old and trusted friends. To Bond's astonishment, Yupland reveals to Sir Henry that Bond is an agent. Sir Henry now realizes that Bond is his enemy. Connie surrenders the microchip from her bracelet to Sir Henry and surreptitiously gives Bond another chip, which is labeled Kohoni Industries. Bond leaves and Rodin seizes Connie.

Bond goes to the meeting site provided by the fortune cookie, where he meets Mi Wai, the assistant hotel manager. Meanwhile, Sir Henry instructs Rodin to get their "stealth, robotic sports" car, which is essentially a "fighter plane" on wheels. Sir Henry "relishes the idea of pitting" his vehicle "against the best MI5 has to offer" and eliminating a threat.[39] A chase ensues, in which Bond's Aston Martin is pursued by Rodin's weaponized car, which is enhanced with stealth capability. Bond tries to evade Rodin but the "killer car is mirroring [Bond's] exact moves."[40] Using Rodin's technology against him, Bond deliberately drives off a cliff. Rodin's car is automatically forced to follow Bond's car, which goes "flying hundreds of feet off the seaside cliff."[41] Bond springs his car's ejector seats, which are equipped with parachutes, and he and Mi Wai glide to safety.

Out of danger, Mi Wai takes Bond to her superior Quen Low. Quen Low angrily tells him that "wherever James Bond goes death and destruction follow."[42] Quen confides that his government received a threat that has since been carried out, demanding that the Chinese declare Hong Kong a free and independent state or a disaster would befall one of their nuclear power plants."[43] Bond and Quen visit the destroyed nuclear plant, where Bond examines the remains of an out of control robot that led to the catastrophe and he sees that it was manufactured by Kohoni Industries. Bond realizes that "Sir Henry hired Connie to substitute his computer chip for the one originally in the Kohoni robot," which was now under Sir Henry's control.[44] Quen explains that Sir Henry's father was a disgraced General who eventually became a warlord in Burma. After Sir Henry's father was killed, Sir Henry went to Hong Kong and assumed a secret identity and built his private empire with plans to exact revenge on the Chinese for killing his father. Bond now has just 24 hours to stop Sir Henry from making good on his next threat. Bond and Quen realize that they have a better chance of bringing down Sir Henry if they work together, despite their fierce differences.

At the Far East branch of Universal Export, Yupland tells Bond that they've received another letter "Demanding the British withdraw from Hong Kong." When Bond points the finger at Sir Henry, Yupland defends him as "one of the most important suppliers of military equipment to Britain."[45] Yupland argues that given Sir Henry's English-Chinese ancestry "he is the perfect spokesman for the future of Hong Kong."[46] Bond counters that Yupland's "blind faith in Sir Henry" almost got him killed.[47] The obstinate Yupland orders Bond off the case, and a furious Bond, ignoring the order, responds by telling Yupland "to go to hell."[48] After Bond leaves, Yupland instructs security to arrest the defiant agent.

Sir Henry locates Bond's whereabouts by taking control of MI5's security robot, which has identified Bond. Sir Henry, who is standing next to a beautiful woman named Nan, issues orders to kill Bond. Bond meets up with Mi Wai and says he needs her help to stop Sir Henry. She informs Bond that Sir Henry's "control center is in the [sub-basement] of his building."[49] Rodin, who survived the car crash, follows their car on his armed motorcycle. Suddenly, a jeep with Royal Marine MPs appears and forces Mi Wai's car off the road. Using a portable missile launcher that is disguised as an ordinary document tube, Rodin fires a missile at the car, blasting it into the water. Mi Wai is killed, and Bond is temporarily rendered unconscious. Bond, who is presumed dead, comes to and sneaks away from the MPs.

Later, Q, Denholm, and Yupland arrive to survey the scene. They believe that Bond has died. Q "turns away, there are tears in his eyes."[50] Later at Denholm's home, Denholm and Q get drunk. Investigating a noise, they discover that Bond is alive. He tells them that officially he wants to be classified as dead so that he can complete the mission. "It is the only edge he has and he wants to keep it."[51]

Bond and Denholm attempt to breach Sir Henry's building via the "maze of sewers beneath the city of Hong Kong."[52] They wade through the waste and reach an open sewer pipe that is connected to Sir Henry's building. Leaving Denholm behind, Bond climbs into the pipeline, reaches its end, and uses an acetylene welding torch to breach and enter Sir Henry's stronghold. Once inside, Bond sabotages the fire pump, sets a timer for ten minutes, and evades a series of surveillance robots.

Bond finds Connie who is with Nan. Nan enters the room and, without saying a word, she punches Bond, sending him flying. Connie moves in, "grapples with her grabbing the top of her corset."[53] When Connie is tossed aside "the corset comes off in her hands revealing metal breastworks. Nan is a lethal security robot!"[54] Nan runs at Bond, who jumps aside, as Nan goes sailing through a window.

Bond and Connie try to escape, but Rodin and his men capture them. They are brought to Sir Henry, who is plotting in "his impregnable bunker immediately below the basement."[55] The villain boasts, "All navigation, communication, weapon and missile guidance systems in the world have critical components manufactured by one of Sir Henry's companies."[56] He adds, "Every military and commercial unit in the world can be instantly paralyzed from this room."[57] Sir Henry tells Bond that he will perform a demonstration in which he will activate a computer virus that will force a Royal Navy submarine to fire a missile at Shanghai.

The pump that Bond tampered with begins to flood the building. As Sir Henry's men panic, Bond and Connie escape. Rodin follows them, but the force of the water sends him flying and he is "swept to his death."[58] Sir Henry "dons Rodin's night vision helmet" and chases them. As the spy fights both the rising water and Sir Henry, Bond manages to blind Sir Henry with the welding torch and then he kills him. Bond and Connie escape.

The final scene or the "tag" is listed on the outline, but it is not described. These scenes usually involve a little exposition indicating that Bond has again saved the world and concludes with Bond kissing the leading lady.

The script, or as it turns out, the outline for Timothy Dalton's third Bond film is, for me, the Holy Grail of Bond script collecting. It provides a glimpse into Eon's mindset at a pivotal time as it approached the seventeenth film in the series.

It took years for me to track down Alfonse Ruggiero, who with Michael Wilson wrote the story for what might have been Dalton's third Bond film, and I was thrilled when he finally agreed to an interview. Ruggiero demonstrated that he can be as charmingly self-aware as he is elusive, for when I phoned him at the scheduled time, he playfully asked, "Are you surprised that I answered?"

* * *

How did you get hired to write what would have been the third Timothy Dalton Bond film?

I just went back to a high school reunion. I'm dyslexic and my mother went to her grave saying I wasn't. She would say you're hiding behind it. I would say, right Mom, I make my living as a writer but I'm hiding behind it. How does that work? She was very funny. She wanted to protect her children.

At school, I had a friend named Jim Sorrentino who had a wide back and was on the football team. Anyway, I would try to hide behind him, so I wouldn't get called on and be exposed. My reading was good, but I couldn't spell anything. I still can't spell words that I've written a thousand times. But now I've had assistants spellcheck and I have that all worked out. Anyway, I used to read all the Bond books behind his back so that the priest couldn't see me. I read them over and over again. So it was interesting that I came to be at least involved in the James Bond world. It's an interesting footnote to my love of the Bond. I still love Ian Fleming and James Bond.

How I got hired was surprising. I had done *Miami Vice* (1984-1990) and I was doing *Wiseguy* (1987-1990) at the time. *Wiseguy* was a bit of a darling for writers of the time. We had talented actors like Stanley Tucci, Kevin Spacey, Jonathan Banks, Kenny Wahl, Jerry Lewis, Deborah Harry, and Mick Fleetwood. More so than *Miami Vice*, *Wiseguy* was considered to be a writer's show. It was a breakout show for the writers who worked on it. We got a lot of kudos for that. A music manager that I knew used to have dinner parties, and [Bond producer] Barbara Broccoli came to one of them. I met her there. There was no talk of me writing a Bond movie. I wasn't auditioning at that point. When you're doing a show like *Wiseguy* you're not auditioning anyway. You are kind of in a position where you dictate what you want to do next. One day I got a call from my agent who said, "They're interested in you doing a Bond movie." I was ecstatic. At that point, Bond was going through a lot. It was still James Bond, but the public didn't know where it was going. Was it going to be the Roger Moore Bond or was it going to be the Timothy Dalton Bond? The audience itself was confused.

Barbara and I had a dinner meeting. We hit it off, and I threw out some ideas. I don't think it hurt that I was Italian when I met Cubby at the final interview. The Broccolis are part of the family that engineered broccoli [by crossing two vegetables, cauliflower, and rabe, at the turn of the twentieth century].[59] I had memories from my youth of my grandparents collecting vegetables at the side of the road. So I think that endeared me to him in a way. They made the deal with my agents at Creative Artists. I was excited. I wasn't sure what I was going to get into. I was going to be writing with Michael Wilson and I was wondering if he was going to be the 500-pound gorilla in the room because he's written how many of these things? He also produces them. I thought how much is he going to listen to me? When you're a writer and producer on TV, you get a lot more leeway than you do in a film. So I'm used to being more in the producer mode, but this is clearly a Michael, Barbara, and Cubby's thing. We started our meeting and Michael couldn't have been nicer or more giving as a partner. I was a little shocked at that. I thought he might be a little dictatorial because this is his and his family's baby and he's done so many of them. But instead, he was very collaborative and supportive.

We sat in the little room in MGM. It's a big modern slanted building. It's an odd building. At the time, MGM was going through something, which would later mess this project up. There was a lot of upheaval. We were in this giant building and we were the only people with offices in it. We used to come into this room and the rest of the building looked like Grand Central Station with no one in it. So it was odd. They had two of the greatest assistants. They were the most encouraging and nicest people. They really made me comfortable. Michael and I would sit in a room and just start to go through and figure out what do we want to do? What's the new story? And that's a process in and of itself. Not only have they done many pictures, but how many stories have they taken on and then discarded? So it was a long process figuring out what we were going to zero in on. The process was coming in there every day and sitting down comfortably in the room with our notepads and trying to come up with scenarios. That was fun for me. That's always fun. The great part about that is that on many days we would take a break from working on copy and we would go to lunch at Orsini's. I've been going there for years. The break in the middle of the writing day was the best. We would go to Orsini's, eat Italian food and Cubby would tell stories about old Hollywood, which were fantastic. Cubby had funny stories about George Lazenby. For some reason, he's always bringing up Lazenby. It was a lot of fun.

In that meeting what did you tell them you wanted to do with Bond?

I don't know but I guess it was the time for them to bring in somebody from a show like *Wiseguy* who had a different take. It was not a comical show. While Bond always had some humor running through it—and the Roger Moore films were surely more humorous—I was a big proponent and going back. I told Barbara [Broccoli] about the first time I saw *From Russia with Love* in Buffalo, New York on a cold winter day. My buddies and I saw this film, and we came out of it so jazzed. Bond is such an interesting character. He was so dialed down, but at the same time, he's in this glamorous world, which was outside of what we lived in. It made the experience so spectacular. I wanted our movie to be like those, with a dialed down Bond.

It sounds simplistic. But I wanted to make it edgier again. I want to go for hard crime and foreign lands. Fleming would always give you an education in something, whether it was gold, space, firearms, or fighter pilots with nuclear weapons aboard. So when you read a Bond novel or see a movie, you would learn something. Even with that strange movie *On Her Majesty's Secret Service,* you learned about genealogy. You learned something when you saw those movies. I said that's what I want to go after. I've nothing against the other movies. I don't want to diss them, but I thought it was time for a change. But I think that's what got it. I think that approach is where they said maybe we need to have him come in.

With the previous film, *Licence to Kill*, Eon was attempting to make a more realistic Bond, which the audience wasn't prepared for. For Dalton's third Bond, I wasn't sure if they were going to go back to the humor or continue with the gritty approach.

I don't think they were verbalizing a tone. They didn't say, "We failed here, I want to do something different." But I don't think they failed on any of them. They all made an enormous amount of money. That was the other thing I was aware of is that I could come in and tell them how to do a TV show because of *Wiseguy* and *Miami Vice*, but this was the most successful franchise up to that point. I would say that my job is to be as honest and to say this is what I believe in and try not to guess what the other guy is thinking about doing. That's my value when I come into something—I'm honest about looking at the story and giving them my unvarnished thoughts.

Can you talk more about the brainstorming session?

We looked at the different short stories that Fleming wrote that had not been made into movies. He wrote a bunch of Bond short stories that weren't full books. We brought those out and studied them and asked if we could make anything out of them? Is there a film in that? We talked and we went down that path for a while. We talked about [the first Bond continuation novel] *Colonel Sun* (1968) by Kingsley Amis. That's the one with the bad Chinese general. We went down that path for a while.

As we do with all these movies or TV shows, we just threw out a lot of ideas. We tried to come up with scenarios. What will this be about? Michael is great. He had a million ideas. He was fun to be in a room with and talk to. He's a sophisticated guy who has lived with the life of James Bond for many years. When we ended up doing the script, we wrote it at his house. I'll tell you about that process too. He would make a loaf of bread every morning. We would talk as he made the bread. Then he would put it in the oven and later we would use the bread for sandwiches for lunch. It was great; it was very homey.

He lived out in Malibu. It was inland so there was no one around. But it was great that Michael and I would write this cool way. Michael is a very good hiker. So we would hike, and we would talk. He would make his bread. He also has one of the best photography collections in the world. He was generous about that because my wife is a photographer. He would open his vault and talk to her about it. Buying photography was new at the time and my one regret is that I didn't offer to buy some then and ask him, which ones I should purchase. I didn't want to bother him, but at the same time, he loved that we loved what he loved. I still have that Eastern class mentality of I don't want to take advantage. But it was fun. It was great. His own photography is great. I only have good things to say about the Broccolis and the experience.

The two Dalton Bond films don't have a villain seeking global domination. The villains' plans were more modest in scope. Did you explore possible scenarios in which the villain seeks world domination?

Of course, we looked at that a lot. In the end, we did have a villain with a global plan. It's also one of the things you see now. When we were doing *Miami Vice* it seemed really about trying to stop drugs coming to the United

States, but now it seems superfluous. They seem to be thinking, "Are you really going to spend all that time catching drug dealers? Why don't you try to stop terrorists?" So if you write a plot about world domination or even just dominating England, then you've raised the stakes. That's why so many Bond films have that in them.

How did you start to zero in on this microchip idea?

I was thinking about it, and I know Michael added to this topic. I had just done *Vice* and I had a lot of good friends of mine who are into guns and they would follow weapons coming out of the military. We sell weapons all over the world. We sell to our allies. We sell to all sorts of people. We sell far more stuff around the world than anybody else. We sell missiles. But I thought, what if you could control them? What if you could sabotage them? What if you could send them to where they're not supposed to go? What if a mad man decided to start a war between, say, England and China? If he was a manufacturer, then he would be fully capable. I called him the Giorgio Armani of Arms Dealers. Remember, Michael and I were side by side so none of this is only me, it's always we. But this was something I recall that I was lobbying for.

This process is an interesting dive into who James Bond is. As a kid, I always thought it would be cool to be a CIA guy or a soldier. Bond is a secret agent with a license to kill, but it's England, so there is a whole class hierarchy, especially in the Fleming books. Bond is keeping the English status quo around the world. But you've got to put that aside because you've got to make him a hero. You can't say you're just there working for England. I don't know how much you know of the Bond books, but my memory is—and I haven't read them in years—that the villains, like Blofeld or Dr. No, had been slighted in their youth and they were thwarted as they got older. They wanted to cause havoc and they wanted to get back at those who oppressed them. They want to be more powerful than the system that held them down. We thought that about the Hong Kong switchover that was coming up, when [on July 1, 1997] England was returning control of Hong Kong back to the Chinese. And there was a lot of discussion about who's going to be mad about it. That was the fun of the Sir Henry character; he was part Chinese and part English and he was not fully accepted by either place. The two cultures that are not always accepting of the other. He was an outsider and people didn't accept him. This was going to be his revenge. He was going to start a war on the eve of the switchover and use his Giorgio Armani weapons to ignite it and do it slowly. Bond has to figure out his plan. Bond would be over his head with a guy who has all sorts of advanced technology. It's hard to remember all the technology we had back then but there was a lot of surveillance and there was a lot of robotics. We studied robotics and that became part of the opening that we did. Michael wrote the beginning and I think I wrote the rest of it. It was a fantastic opening.

What happened in the opening?

Michael wrote a hell of a sequence for it and I wrote the escape. Cubby came in and said, "This is the best Bond opening we've ever had." That's the best thing I've ever been told about my writing. I've been lucky enough to have been up for Golden Globes and Emmys and win the Edgar Award but when he said that's the best Bond opening we've ever had, I thought, "Wow. We're cooking."

What was the gist?

Bond is on his glider. Bond drops off from a glider onto what looks like a soap factory but instead, they are making munitions. The factory is guarded by robotics.

I think the sequence appears in the Davies-Osborne screenplay. In it, Bond fights a robotic defense system. The robot wounds him. Bond escapes but it looks like he has failed his mission. But we quickly learn that he has actually succeeded.

They took it from ours. It's a sequence that could look like it could have been in *The Terminator* or something because these robots were smart.

Who was the James Bond that you had in mind?

I was trying to write the James Bond that Fleming wrote but a modern version. He was a rough and ready kid. He didn't play [English] football, but he was a mountaineer. He didn't belong to the cool English clubs; he was an outsider. He didn't have a lot of money, but he had a fast motorcycle or a car. He wasn't from the upper class, but he was able to dress and move inside that society fully. He didn't have the privilege of a lot of people around. But he comes in and becomes the best secret agent that they've ever had. A lot of people like [William] "Wild Bill" Donavan who helped form the OSS, which later became the C.I.A., came from the upper class and wealth. But in my mind Bond was more of a street kid who moved elegantly in the world. He lived in it, but he was always an outsider. That's why he did most of his missions on his own.

What do you think he gets out of being a double agent? What's his motivation?

I think you must go back to Ian Fleming. I don't know how many people want to be in the CIA now but back when Fleming was doing this, a World War was going on and then a cold war. There were real risks. So the idea that you go in undercover and help stop this stuff was very heroic. It still is, but I don't think we always see it as such. With Jason Bourne, his own country is against him. That's the American take on it. But when Bourne joined, he wanted to do good.

If I had a complaint about the Daniel Craig Bond movies is that it's too much *Bourne Identity* (2002) and not enough James Bond. Bourne is angry. Bourne is fucking angry to be Bourne. The way Daniel Craig plays it is that even when he's with a girl, he just seems to want to get it over with and get a drink and beat somebody up. He doesn't look like he's having any fun. Connery's Bond loved women and took his time. He loved the seduction and he had a mink glove [that he used in *Thunderball* (1965) to massage a woman]. I'm not saying do that. But there was a seduction there. Some of the girls were trying to kill him, but he was enjoying it.

Don't get me wrong, Craig is great. But in this day and age, they migrated to something they thought would work and it has. But in my mind, I would like to see a little bit more of that sweeping music as you're coming over a bay or the Russian subway system, and you see something that you have never seen before. I'd like to have a little more of that feeling. A little bit more wonder at the places he's going. Bond used to be like Anthony Bourdain with class. He was enjoying himself. He would sit down and have a half bottle of wine that nobody else had. Or that scene in the novel *Goldfinger* where they would have these crabs with the sauce. He would say nobody today is eating better than we are now. Where I came from, who knew labels of wines? Who knew watches? I have a Bond watch. I went out and bought a Rolex before I even did Bond because when I was a kid, I read in *Casino Royale* that he put it over his fist and he killed someone with it. That was the kind of thing he used to do. But he was also smart and studied. I don't have a real complaint with Craig's Bond movies, they're great. But I miss a little bit of that "other land, other worlds."

There was also a character named Rodin who drives a high-tech car, which is described as a "killer car."

We did a whole chase sequence. Bond couldn't shake the car because of the robotics. It was a cool sequence.

Was it your idea to give the bad guy all the tools that Bond's Aston Martin has and see what happens?

Yes, but you need to remember that the guy who Bond is fighting against is the most sophisticated robotics guy in the world. Even the English and American scientists weren't as good; he was taking it to the next level. Plus, I had an inside source within our government who told me stuff that they have and we're working on, which really sparked a lot of ideas for the script. He wasn't supposed to tell me some of it. There's nothing in what we wrote that's a classified secret, but at the time I was thinking, "We've *really* got *this*? We can do *that*?" But it was cool.

Talk a little more about the villain's building.

It was a smart building. That was fun. I don't think they ever used that in a Bond movie. It was the coolest thing. Bond needs to defeat every surveillance trick in the world. Bond has to figure all that out to get through the building. It was great. It would have been a great film. It would have been very high tech. They could use any of this in future films. They own it. They paid me. They can do whatever they want with it. They can cannibalize it. They've done a pretty good job without my help if I do say so. But I would love to do another one.

The building floods.

The building is flooding floor by floor as he fights his way up. Eventually, it overtakes him, and then he still has to fight the robots and the bad guys to get out of there. We had some great sequences. It was a shame that it didn't get made.

Did you speak to Dalton about his ideas?

Yes. Dalton came in. I'm not sure exactly what the problem was but I felt like he wasn't happy being Bond at that moment. He wanted me to go with him to some Bondian island in the Caribbean and fish. He's a big fisherman. We would talk over the ideas. They didn't want me to go with Dalton to do that because of the tight schedule, but I thought, "How cool will this be? We will be like *Dr. No*. We will be on the beach, we'll find some Jamaicans, we'll drink some rum. We'll run, we'll swim, and we'll save the world."

You would be vacationing with Bond.

Yes, Dalton was great. He's an amazing actor. He looked the part. It just didn't sync up for them. Pierce came in and did a good job with what he was doing. But I was trying to convince them to find an unknown, someone you wouldn't have seen before, like Sean Connery. When we were kids Sean Connery was James Bond. He wasn't an actor from another film. He was James Bond. I was trying to impress on them how important that was at that time. Daniel Craig sort of did it but he was a little known. But Brosnan was known more when he became Bond. He's a great actor too.

I know you didn't get to go on vacation with Dalton, but did he tell you what he was hoping for?

He was hoping for a little more realism. That was my memory. He was a stage actor. I thought that this guy is for real. I also thought he was a great guy.

Did you turn your 17-page treatment into a script?

Do you only have the 17-page treatment? Yes, we wrote a script. A full script.

I've read a script that William Davies and William Osborne wrote that contains some broad elements of your outline. But you're saying you wrote a full script based on your treatment?

Right.

Wow, okay. I didn't know that. Then after you wrote the treatment did you then write the screenplay?

My memory is that after we wrote the treatment, which spelled everything out, we then wrote the screenplay. [Ruggiero said that he was uncertain that he could locate the script.] We went to Michael's, we made bread, and we worked in his office. I sat at one desk and he sat at another desk. The writing was easy, but the typing was hard. I remember thinking, You guys are going to pay me more if you're going to have me type more. Michael decided that I should type the script. I never typed up to that point. I used a number two pencil and I had an assistant for 20 years at the studio. I type now but I didn't then. So he made the computer code on this computer that he got from somewhere. It was one of the first portable computers and it weighed about 40 pounds. But it was a computer system that he installed. I'm not sure there was a Word program at that point. We were writing fast. There was a time limit, and I didn't realize that it was related to the lawsuit until after we were done. So we were writing fast every day, and I had to figure out the codes as I typed it. But I'm dyslexic. It was the hardest thing I ever did. But I did it. I was thinking, "How is this possible? Just give me an assistant to do the typing and I'll write with my number two pencil. Then we'll be done in a week."

How long was this process? From the pitch, to outline, to writing the screenplay.

I would guess that it was four to six months. Michael was pushing for the process to go quickly. He said, "I thought you guys in TV move faster." I said, "I didn't know we were in a race." His comment was absolutely not meant to be mean or critical in any way. On TV, you write shit right before you shoot it. Even if it means that you stay up all night writing. We're doing 24-hour days when I was in TV. I was thinking that I was going to get to luxuriate to find the story and the character because we're in the world of James Bond. I thought we could take six months to write a script. But I didn't know that they were gearing for the lawsuit. They didn't take me into their confidence about that.

Do you recall discussing possible film titles?

Yes, we were discussing film titles. *GoldenEye* was a possibility. I don't remember how it was brought up. I think Michael just said, I think *GoldenEye* would be a good title for this. Of course, GoldenEye is where Fleming's home was in Jamaica. It's where he lived and wrote. When Michael came up with the name I thought, That's cool. That's James Bond. We thought about *Colonel Sun*, which is also good. But once we had *GoldenEye*, I thought, we're off.

One of the rumors is that "The Property of a Lady," the Fleming short story, was in consideration.

I do not remember it, but it does not sound like a good idea. It feels like it should be an English drama and not a Bond film.

It sounds like you had a great experience.

It's fun going down memory lane. Once in a while, I'll sit around and tell stories about Cubby. It was a great time. Talking about the experience always brings back happy memories. It's a shame that I couldn't have done about four of those things and meet the Queen as I thought would happen. But who knew that the lawsuit would happen? Remember, the only reason that this movie didn't go forward was the lawsuit.

* * *

Assorted Observations

Some final thoughts about Ruggiero and Wilson's outline. Some reports speculated that the seventeenth Bond film would be about illegal drugs; that it might be titled *Property of a Lady*; and would feature a Terminator-like character. Let's look briefly at these three claims.

Because the film was co-written by Alfonse Ruggiero, a writer for *Miami Vice*, a series that routinely told stories about the drug-trade in Florida, that association is understandable. However, as Ruggiero explained in the interview, Eon's interest in hiring him had less to do with his *Miami Vice* background than it did with his writing contributions to *Wiseguy*, a nuanced and sprawling TV series about an undercover cop who infiltrates the mob, whose complicated story-lines, that extend over multiple-episodes, that pre-dated similar shows like *The Sopranos*.

Ruggiero dispels the myth that the film might take its name from Fleming's short story "Property of a Lady" (1963). Instead, Ruggiero offers *GoldenEye*, the name of Fleming's house in Jamaica and what would become the name of the seventeenth Bond film. However, Wilson and Ruggiero's "Bond 17 Outline" is a completely discrete story that seems to have nothing to do with the development of what would become Brosnan's first Bond film. Their only connection appears to be that Wilson was considering using the title *GoldenEye* for both projects.

The Terminator-esque character rumor does have some basis in truth. After all, Nan is described as "a lethal security robot!"[60] But the character Nan was not conceived with the intention of making a robot a central figure in the film; rather it was an attempt to dramatically expand on the premise that the villain plans to use cutting-edge technology to achieve his ends. In the outline, Nan doesn't talk, which is possibly an attempt to keep the film from getting too outlandish, like the invisible car in *Die Another Day*, and risk disrupting the audience's fragile suspension of disbelief.

I suspect that particulars of Nan's robotic nature were never intended to be spelled out to the audience. The writer's intention might have been more to suggest Nan's background, without explicitly explaining it. There is some precedence in the series for a preternatural character. Baron Samedi (Geoffrey Holder), the voodoo priest and villain, is apparently killed twice in *Live and Let Die*. In the first instance, Bond shoots Samedi directly in the head.

Yet, shortly after that, Samedi reappears, unharmed. Then Bond punches Samedi into an open coffin that is filled with extremely poisonous snakes, who bite him to death. However, Samedi returns yet again. This time in the final moments of *Live and Let Die*, he is seen holding onto a train and laughing maniacally.

In the first instance, Bond shoots Samedi in the head and torso. But Samedi doesn't bleed from the gunshot wounds, instead, his body breaks apart. Shortly after that, Samedi reappears, unharmed. Next, Bond punches Samedi, who falls into an open coffin and who is repeatedly bitten by poisonous snakes. It's his second death.

In our interview, Ruggiero didn't recall the exact details about this matter, but he believes that Nan was not intended to be an android. Moreover, the outline includes the disclaimer that the robotics depicted in the film "are not humanoid in form."[61] However, it is possible that the disavowal was a red herring, which was included to maximize our surprise when we discover that Nan isn't human, as we have been led to believe.

Since Eon hasn't repurposed the idea in the decades since the outline was written, it is reasonable to infer Eon decided it was a step too far. The idea should instead be considered for what it was, Eon's thinking at the time about possible ways for the Bond films to evolve. In any case, questions about the character shouldn't overshadow or highjack the larger discussion about the nature of this compelling outline. The outline suggests a gripping story that would have been made into an exciting Bond film, and one that would have been well-suited for Dalton's lamentably unrealized third appearance as 0

James Bond eliminating Sir Henry Ferguson.
Illustration by Pat Carbajal

Bond 17
William Osborne

After Michael G. Wilson and Alfonse Ruggiero completed their work on what would have been Timothy Dalton's third Bond movie, William Davies and William Osborne were hired to turn their outline into a screenplay.[62] What follows is a summary of the first draft of the 120-page script by Davies and Osborne, who also collaborated on the buddy comedy *Twins* (1988), for the untitled 17th film in the series.[63]

Although Davies and Osborne's script, which I refer to as *Bond 17*, is roughly based on Wilson and Ruggiero's treatment, their story can be considered a separate work, as their script departs significantly in plot and tone from the outline. The former is an irreverent action-comedy whereas the latter is a stylish thriller.

It's important to remember that this summary is for the first recorded draft of the screenplay, from which I quote, that it bears the names of all four of the above-mentioned writers, and that Davies and Osborne would write additional drafts.[64] If their work on the film had continued, further revisions would have been required, as is standard practice in the screenwriting process. So this summary of the Davies and Osborne script, dated January 2, 1991, should not be considered a definitive overview of Dalton's third movie. Instead, it should be viewed as a look at Davies and Osborne's early approach to the movie and as a springboard for discussion and debate, like the one that would almost certainly have ensued between the writers and their collaborators at Eon if the duo had continued on with the project and if the movie hadn't finally foundered due to various and protracted legal battles.

Summary of the Screenplay

James Bond is in a hotel room "looking very crumpled, almost hungover."[65] Bond has overslept and is late for a meeting. He goes into the bathroom and takes two Alka-Seltzer tablets to mitigate the effects of last night's debauchery. He looks in the mirror and, disheartened by what he sees, moans, "You're getting too old for this, Bond."[66] A beautiful woman beckons him back to bed and Bond figures, "On the other hand, maybe you're not."[67]

Then the Gun Barrel Logo sequence begins: Bond steps into frame, pivots, and shoots in the audience's direction at an unseen threat.

Bond is in Tunis and speaking in perfect Arabic to a young agent. The exasperated agent tells Bond that he has cited Bond's "sloppy behavior and appalling attitude" in his report to headquarters.[68] Bond chides the young agent, "When I was your age, I'd have been in my hotel room making passionate love to some over-sexed croupier."[69]

Bond and the young agent ride a powerboat along the Libyan coastline. Bond moves to the back of the boat and deploys a parachute, which he uses to glide onto the grounds of a nearby chemical plant. Bond has trouble picking the lock to the door of the plant and becomes frustrated with himself. A pack of Rottweilers closes in on him, but Bond picks the lock, barely escaping the guard dogs.

Once inside, Bond is immediately accosted by an armed guard. Bond introduces himself, "Oh good morning, the name is Bond, James Bond – I'm here to blow up the plant."[70] When the guard threatens Bond with his gun, Bond says, "It's obviously not a good time. I'll come back tomorrow." [71]Colonel Al-Sabra arrives with reinforcements. Bond swiftly snatches one of the soldier's rifles, uses it to knock out Al-Sabra, and dispatches Al-Sabra's security team.

Bond searches the plant and finds containers of deadly nerve gas. He sets up a bomb with a timed detonator to destroy the lethal chemical. A "Small Metal Robot" arrives.[72] The robot, which Bond addresses dismissively as "R2D2" tries to detain Bond by emitting a "BLINDING FLASH OF LIGHT and a HIGH PITCHED EXPLOSIVE SOUND."[73] Bond shoots the robot with his Beretta, insisting that he does not "take orders from tin cans." The damaged but still-functioning robot attempts to Taser Bond. Then a "lightweight UZI-like gun springs out of another compartment" and shoots at Bond.[74] Bond is unable to defeat or disable the robot, so he flees from the chemical plant. Bond looks at his watch and sees that the bomb should have gone off by now, but it hasn't. It seems that Bond has failed in his mission.

Troops chase Bond to the edge of a cliff. Bond looks at the steep drop and tells himself, "Forget it, Bond, for that you are definitely too old."[75] But when the troops fire at Bond, he has no choice but to jump into the water 200-feet below. The young agent reappears in a powerboat to pick up Bond and as they speed off, he chastises Bond for failing to blow up the plant. Bond says, "Everyone has off days, okay?" [76] The plant finally explodes before the agent can respond. Bond finishes his thought, "Fortunately this wasn't one of them."[77]

Elsewhere, a pilot steals a "High-Tech Experimental Fighter-Bomber" called a Scimitar from a United States aircraft carrier.[78]

Bond drives his Aston Martin Virage to MI6. At headquarters, Bond sees a "gorgeous" Moneypenny, who looks "like she had a complete makeover."[79] Bowled over by the new Moneypenny, Bond asks her out. He suggests that they go to "005's lodge in Scotland."[80] Unexpectedly, Moneypenny declines his offer, "I'm sorry James. But you're too late."[81] She shows Bond her engagement ring and says that she's going to be married to a structural engineer and they plan to "have lots of children."[82]

M calls Bond into his office for a briefing. The Junior Minister of Defense Nigel Yupland barges into their meeting. Yupland complains that Bond is "the single most expensive item on this department's budget."[83] M tells Bond that, "Two days ago the Scimitar, our top experimental plane, was stolen whilst on field trials with the US Navy."[84] Yupland adds that the plane, which has stealth technology, is significantly cheaper to produce than the US Version and is worth billions of dollars to England if they sell it. M's intelligence suggests that an American mob is somehow connected to the theft. Yupland says that the Vinelli crime family has a "warehousing operation in Vancouver" about "thirty minutes from where the plane disappeared."[85] He instructs Bond to begin his mission there. Before Bond leaves, Yupland tells Bond that there are "new department guidelines" about how money is spent in the field. If Bond wants to keep his job, he'll need to follow the "new rules and budgetary guidelines."[86]

Bond visits Q's lab and finds that it has been decommissioned and that all of Q's gadgets are in packing crates. Q laments that Yupland thinks his department is too expensive. Bond sees his original Aston Martin DB5 under a tarp. Q tells Bond that the car is scheduled for destruction. A dejected Q reveals that he's been forced to retire and he's not sure what he'll do without his job, confiding that "this lab has been my whole life."[87]

Once in Vancouver, Bond ignores Yupland's cost-cutting guidelines and rents a Ferrari. Bond visits the Vinelli's warehouse yard. He sneaks inside and finds shipping crates that were sent from "Nanking Shipping, Kowloon."[88] As Bond is investigating, he sees someone moving through the warehouse. Security guards also spot the figure, who kills them with expert marksmanship and deftly evades capture. Bond is impressed, musing, "Guy's pretty good."[89] Bond watches as the figure unmasks and is revealed to be a beautiful woman.

Sir Henry Ferguson is engaged in a violent fencing match with his instructor. Sir Henry, who is disproportionately disappointed by his opponents' ability to test his mettle, kills his instructor. He then gets on the phone with Connie Webb, the woman Bond spotted at the warehouse. Connie tells Ferguson that she found traces of the stolen plane's fuel at the warehouse. Ferguson, who is in Hong Kong, says that the plane has probably been moved to Las Vegas.

The next day Bond tracks Connie to a river where she goes kayaking. Bond obtains his own boat, paddles over to Connie, and introduces himself as "Baker, James Baker."[90] Connie tells Bond that he's "out of his depth" on the rapids,[91] which bounce him off rocks. Relying on brute strength rather than skill, Bond successfully makes it across the rapids. Although Connie is not impressed with Bond's "macho bullshit" she is charmed enough by him to accept his invitation to dinner.[92]

At dinner, Connie tells Bond that she is a former CIA agent who is now a cat burglar. Bond believes her, but then she insists that she was joking and that she's actually in the hotel industry. Amused by Bond, Connie suggests that they go back to her place so that they can have "mad, passionate, uncomplicated sex."[93]

When Bond wakes up the next day, he finds that Connie is gone. His back aches, presumably from the vigorous sex. Bond complains, "Definitely too old for this."[94] He finds a note saying that while she enjoyed last night, she doesn't expect to see him again. A surprised Bond notes, "She dumped me." [95]

Bond goes to Las Vegas. In his hotel, he encounters Jennings, an intimidating-looking Skinhead. Bond finds out that he is actually a West Coast liaison and an operative. Jennings, who is gay, enjoys flirting with a slightly "embarrassed" but genteel Bond.[96] Jennings instructs Bond to follow him outside so that they can spy on the Vinellis. Using hi-tech rifle equipment the two agents eavesdrop on Tony and Tiny Vinelli who are meeting their father Guido at a nearby hotel. Guido warns his sons not to get into the "arms trade" business and orders them to stick to "gambling, drugs, and prostitution."[97] The Vinelli brothers defy their father and insist that they plan to do business with Sir Henry.

Later at the hotel's health club, Colonel Al-Sabra, who has survived the explosion at the chemical plant, gets the drop on Bond. Al-Sabra's two female bodybuilder guards fight with Bond. Bond is no match for the women who batter him around like a ragdoll until Bond grabs a hand weight to knock out one of the bodybuilders and then gets his hands on Al-Sabra's gun and shoots him in the head. As the second bodybuilder lunges at Bond, he empties ten bullets into her torso. After she collapses, Bond marvels, "Gotta hand it to her...She went the whole ten rounds." Bond takes Al-Sabra's ID.[98]

Bond returns to his surveillance equipment and eavesdrops on a phone call between Tony Vinelli and Sir Henry. Bond learns that Tony Vinelli plans to sell the stolen plane to Sir Henry for $50 million. Vinelli and Sir Henry agree to meet that night. Bond hides in the trunk of Vinelli's car in order to be present at the sale.

The Vinellis go to a warehouse. Bond sneaks out of the trunk and finds the stealth bomber. Bond also spots wooden crates, which have Chinese markings on them from Kowloon shipping. Two mob soldiers capture Bond. The thugs deliver Bond along with Al-Sabra's ID to Tony Vinelli. Tony inspects the ID and mistakenly assumes that Bond is with Al-Sabra's organization and is Libyan. Bond plays along. Tony decides that because Bond is a Libyan spy that the American government, and not him, should kill Bond. He instructs one of his men to "take him to the [American] government."[99] The gangster knocks Bond out. When Bond wakes up, he's locked in a tank, in which Vinelli's men have secured him with the intention of having the U.S. government unwittingly kill him. He looks through the tank's eye slit and discovers that he is in the desert and that he's surrounded by decommissioned tanks that are being blown up. Bond escapes by jerry-rigging a bomb to blow the hatch off the tank.

Later, Bond and Jennings search the airfield for the plane but don't find it. Bond and Jennings decide to follow the Vinellis who have gone to a rodeo with the Chinese pilot who flew the stolen plane. Bond follows a cowboy into a dressing room, knocks him out, and dons his outfit. "Wearing full cowboy gear" as a disguise Bond explores the rodeo and bumps into Connie.[100] Connie warns Bond that for his own safety he should leave. When he refuses, she orders some nearby cowboys to force him onto a bucking bull. The Vinellis spot Bond and send their men after him. Bond jumps off the bull. Three gangsters surround Bond and, in a spaghetti Western-like standoff, all the men draw their guns. Bond draws fasters and kills them. More of Vinelli's men, as well as angry cowboys, now pursue Bond. He escapes in a monster truck. There is a high-speed chase through the streets of Vegas. Destruction follows in his wake as Bond escapes.

Later, Connie follows the Vinellis to the Hoover Dam. Bond, who has also followed the Vinellis, reveals himself. With a roundhouse kick, Connie knocks Bond to the ground and disarms him. Bond tells Connie that he spotted her in the warehouse in Vancouver. They are surprised when the stolen plane suddenly takes off from inside the Dam. Bond demands to know Connie's true identity but she knocks Bond out with a strong kick to his face.

Nigel Yupland arrives at the Chicken Ranch brothel, which turns out to be a front for the National Security Agency. Once inside, Yupland meets up with Bond. Yupland is furious because not only did Bond destroy "half of the city" in making his rodeo getaway but that he's also ruined the investigation and hurt Britain's relationship with their "most powerful security agency."[101] Yupland suspends Bond and tells him to go back to London.

The Vinellis travel to Hong Kong where they meet one of Sir Henry's men who explains that his boss is out of the country and will return the next day to meet them. Meanwhile, Sir Henry is traveling through China with a beautiful Chinese woman named Suzy. They meet General Han at an armored steam train. General Han tells Sir Henry that he wants the stolen plane. Sir Henry presents General Han with a ground-to-air missile launcher. After the General tests the deadly device on a hapless pilot and his plane, Sir Henry promises the delivery of two thousand more launchers.

At the Los Angeles International Airport, Jennings and Bond wait for a plane, which will carry the now-disgraced agent back home. A depressed Bond says that once he's back MI6 will "just have me sit around in London in suspension for a couple of months before Yupland can find an excuse for sacking me."[102] After considering his fate, Bond muses, "If I was half the man I used to be I'd be catching the first bloody plane to Hong Kong, finding that goddamn plane, and ramming it so far up Yupland's arse he'd never sing God Save the Queen again!"[103] Bond decides to fly to Hong Kong to stop Sir Henry.

In Hong Kong, Rodin, who is wearing a helmet and appears to be an ordinary motorcycle messenger, enters a luxurious apartment building. As he approaches Vinelli's men, an "infra-red sensor [on his helmet] identifies the heat outline" of his targets. Rodin touches a button on his glove, which activates a device on his hip pack, and "a miniature recoils rifle on a gimbal automatically UNFOLDS out of one side of the pack. In a fraction of a second, the gun INDEPENDENTLY AIMS and FIRES four quick bursts, taking out" all four men.[104]

In a conference room, the Vinellis meet with Sir Henry. Sir Henry proposes that the Vinellis work for him. Tony Vinelli rejects the offer. Sir Henry leaves the room and presses a button on a small device, which signals Rodin. Rodin presses a button on the control panel on his motorcycle's dashboard and the building's window washer platform descends until it's parallel with the conference room. Rodin activates another button and the spigots from the window washer "suddenly ignite in a ROW OF FLAME THROWERS."[105] The room is engulfed in flames and the Vinellis are killed. Sir Henry says, "Well, you know what they say...if you can't stand the heat, get out of the kitchen."[106]

Bond arrives at the Hong Kong airport and is met by his contact, "Chief of Section H" Gordon Denholm, who is a "great fan" of Bond.[107] Denholm tells Bond that he has "followed [his] career with interest for years"[108] and that even though Bond has been suspended he will help him. Denholm explains that the crates Bond discovered in Las Vegas belong to Sir Henry Ferguson's Nanking Shipping Company. Denholm says that meeting Sir Henry will be difficult because he "spends most of his time on a private island off the Kowloon coast."[109] Denholm also tells Bond that he has a "little surprise" for him.[110]

Denholm takes Bond to his Aston Martin DB-V, which has been flown over from England. Q emerges from the car and explains to a surprised Bond that "when I heard what a hash you were making of everything it seemed like every little thing would help, and besides, I'd rather you have her than turn her in for scrap."[111] Q tries to brief Bond on the technical specs of the car, which is "capable of speeds in excess of two hundred miles an hour," but an impatient Bond gets into the car and drives off.[112]

Bond goes to the Imperial Hotel and is greeted by a receptionist named Mi Wai, who was named after the Frank Sinatra song "My Way." On the way to the elevators, a Chinese agent posing as a wedding photographer takes a picture of Bond. The photo is transmitted to a "powerful-looking Chinese man" named Quen Low.[113]

Later, Bond takes a motorboat to Sir Henry's private island. Bond infiltrates Sir Henry's house, which boasts original paintings by Picasso, Chagall, and Van Gogh. Bond finds Sir Henry in his library where he is meeting with Connie Webb. Sir Henry orders Connie to take off her clothes. As Connie reluctantly starts to undress, Bond interrupts, introduces himself as James Baker, and tells Sir Henry that he's an art thief.

Sir Henry takes Bond to his gymnasium and says, "I admire your kind of desperate courage Mr. Baker, so I'm going to offer you a chance to get off this island alive... All you have to do is beat me in a fair fight."[114] The two men engage in a vicious sword fight. Although Bond is injured, he eventually wins and Sir Henry informs Bond that he can leave the island unharmed.

On a powerboat back to Hong Kong Connie tells Bond, who has still been posing as Baker, that she knows his true identity. Connie confesses that she's an American agent and angrily tells Bond that "it was *my* operation that you single-handedly destroyed in Las Vegas."[115] Connie adds that she was investigating "the most dangerous criminal organizations in the world," and she accuses Bond of "crashing around like a goddamn bull in a china store, putting my life and the success of this whole operation in jeopardy."[116]

Back on land, a despondent Bond is about to return home when Connie apologizes for her harsh tone. Bond tells her that he's returning to London because, "I cost too much, I'm out of date, and I'm in your way."[117] Connie points out that whereas it took her "eighteen months to penetrate the Vinelli organization" and nine months to find Sir Henry, Bond did it in just three days.[118] She praises him, "You had no support, you had no information and you still cracked the whole thing wide open!"[119] Connie tells Bond that she needs his help. Bond tells her to undress. Pressing against the hood of his Aston Martin, they kiss.

Later, and working together, Bond and Connie spot nine Nanking Shipping vessels. Bond surmises that the ships "Must be half Sir Henry's fleet – if every one of those ships is filled with the kind of stuff I saw in Las Vegas, he's got enough to start a war."[120] Connie believes that Sir Henry is working out a deal with the Chinese Government and that "since Tiananmen Square they've been cut out of the international arms trade market – they'd pay top dollar for anyone able to get them the kind of equipment Sir Henry's been acquiring. Get them a stealth and they'd give him anything."[121]

Bond is still not sure where Sir Henry is hiding the stealth plane. Connie teases Bond, "What is it about you and sex, James? Seems to dull your intellect."[122] Bond replies, "It's the people that keep hitting me that are dulling my intellect, sweet pea, and that includes you."[123] Connie suggests they investigate the Nanking Tower, a skyscraper in the business district that Sir Henry owns. Bond wonders, "What happened to all those girls I used to meet, the ones who looked great but let me say the smart lines."[124] Connie offers, "Like the dinosaurs, James, they just died out."[125]

Sir Henry calls Yupland and asks him to check on a British national named James Baker. Yupland, who greatly admires and trusts Sir Henry, reveals Bond's true identity.

Sir Henry sends Rodin, who is driving a "futuristic-looking, computer-derived" sports car, to eliminate Bond.[126] Rodin's vehicle, which is equipped with machine guns and missiles, is even more tricked-out than Bond's DB5. Bond tries to use countermeasures but he's unsure of which unlabeled switch to flip. Bond mutters to himself, "One day, Bond, you're gonna bloody well listen to Q when he explains all this."[127] Bond randomly flicks a series of switches until finally a "SERIES OF CLAYMORE MINES spill out onto the road." Although Rodin's car takes some damage, the chase continues.[128]

Rodin fires a missile at Bond who deploys a flare to send the missile off course. Rodin fires his cannon at Bond's car. The "rear BULLETPROOF SHIELD slides up" on Bond's car, but he knows that this countermeasure won't last long against heavy artillery.[129] As Rodin's car closes in on him Bond hits another button and "the roof flies off as [Bond] EXPLODES OUT OF THE CAR IN THE EJECTOR SEAT." Rodin, who isn't able to turn in time, "flies off the cliff" and "SCREAMS all the way down."[130] As Bond "glides gently down in his parachute" he reflects, "I hate to think what that's gonna do to his insurance."[131]

Bond takes a cab to the docks where Mi Wai gets the drop on him. He asks, "Why is it people always want to kill me?"[132] She forces him into a helicopter. Elsewhere, Suzy, one of Sir Henry's henchmen, tells him that "General Han's field HQ just called – the coup's been launched."[133] Sir Henry tells Suzy that Bond is too late to stop his plans.

Connie, Denholm, and Q race to Nanking Towers to search for the stolen plane. Connie figures out that the plane is hidden in the penthouse of Sir Henry's building.

Meanwhile, Bond is trying to warn the head of Chinese military intelligence, Quen Low, about Sir Henry's plot. Quen Low tells Bond that if the plane enters Peking air space, his government will consider it as an act of war and will launch missiles on London and Washington. He gives Bond one hour to stop Sir Henry.

Bond contacts Q and Denholm. Denholm tells Bond that the stolen plane is hidden in the tower. Bond tells Denholm to mobilize his troops. Under Quen Low's direction, Mi Wai transports Bond in her plane. Bond tells Mi Wai to fly to an apartment building, which is across from the tower. Bond climbs out of the plane, spots a pool on the roof of the building, and confesses "I'm really not getting a good feeling about this." He then "leaps from the speeding plane, arcs through the sky, and finally EXPLODES in the middle of the pool."[134]

Q and Denholm meet Bond on the roof of the building. A re-energized Bond proudly announces, "Did you see what I just did?... I *jumped*, out of a *speeding plane*, into a pool, *this* size (holds up two pinched fingers) ...can you believe that?"[135] Bond then attaches himself to a speed line and rides the line from one building to the next. "As he approaches the glass tower, he pulls out an [automatic weapon] and opens fire, SHATTERING A WINDOW as he explodes into the building."[136] Bond disables a guard and dons his uniform.

Elsewhere in the building, Connie knocks out one guard but before she can take on Sir Henry, Suzy steps in and gets the better of Connie.

Bond approaches a pilot on the Nanking Tower launch platform, knocks him out, and climbs into the plane. Bond flies the Scimitar off the roof and heads toward the British base on Kowloon. But the computer switches back to autopilot, arms the bomb, and locks onto its target as it enters Chinese airspace. Sir Henry explains to Connie that "The Scimitar doesn't need to be flown, its missions are all programmed in... And there's nothing the pilot can do to override them."[137]

Under Denholm's orders, his soldiers raid the tower and engage in a gun battle with Sir Henry's guards. Sir Henry tries to escape the building by using Bond's speed line to cross to the next building. As Bond struggles to regain control of the plane its "nose rod" rams "straight through Sir Henry's chest, ripping off the line, impaling him on the cockpit." Bond quips, "Touché."[138]

The plane crash-lands on the streets of Hong Kong, skids several blocks, and crashes through a government building before finally surging into Yupland's office. A grinning Bond remarks, "Good morning, sir – the good news is I found your plane."[139] Yupland fires Bond. But Bond gets the last word in by punching Yupland out.

Connie hugs Bond and playfully chides, "I suppose you think that kind of macho bullshit is gonna get you a date for dinner."[140] Bond replies, "I'm counting on it getting me a hell of a lot more than that."[141] Q marvels, "Even managed to impress me this time, Bond, to steal the plane, override the autopilot and then land it was enough, but pulling yourself out and disarming the nuclear warhead...that is genuinely impressive."[142] Suddenly, Bond looks worried. Connie says, "You did disarm the warhead, didn't you, James."[143] Bond begins to stammer out a defense as Connie, Q and Denholm run away.

Back in the United States, Bond and Connie are lying together in a sleeping bag in a forest clearing. Connie says, "If it hadn't been for me and Q, that bomb would have gone off."[144] She accuses Bond of sulking. He replies, "I'm not sulking, I was just under the impression we came up here for two weeks of passionate, uncomplicated sex in the great outdoors, not for daily analysis of my shortcomings as a secret agent."[145] She kisses him on the nose. He says, "I actually think I did a pretty good job."[146] She says that "being vulnerable makes you sexy." Bond asks, "Did I ever tell you about the time Blofeld dumped me in a pool of sharks?"[147] ...And then there was this chap Odd Job [stet], I was always underestimating him...And Goldfinger makes me look like a complete idiot..."[148] Connie bites Bond. Bond says, "God, you're a difficult woman."[149] She says, "And you like that?"[150] Bond replies, "I like that a lot."[151] Fade Out.

* * *

Assorted Observations

James Bond

The screenplay for *Bond 17* expands on the agent's attitude toward his profession that Timothy Dalton's Bond displayed in *The Living Daylights* and *Licence to Kill*. In those films, Bond expresses contempt for the spy game. In *The Living Daylights*, Saunders, a by-the-book colleague, chastises Bond for deliberately missing his target, an innocent musician. When Saunders threatens to report him, Bond replies, "Go ahead. Tell M what you want. If he fires me, I'll thank him for it." In *Licence to Kill*, M instructs Bond not to investigate the brutal torture of his friend Felix Leiter and the murder of his wife Della Churchill. Rather than comply and abandon what Bond considers a moral imperative, he resigns.

In *Bond 17*, the spy continues to question his life in the secret service. For instance, when Bond realizes that he has put Connie's operation in jeopardy, the dejected agent confesses, "I cost too much, I'm out of date, and I'm in your way."[152] When a group of enemy soldiers opens fire on Bond, he mutters, "God I hate this job."[153] Later, he vents that if the "penny-pinching, desk jockeys" just want their agents to follow the rules, then "they can bloody well go and find them somewhere else."[154]

In this script, 007 is not operating at the top of his game. In the pre-title sequence, he is worse for wear. He's "looking very crumpled, almost hungover" and he requires Alka-Seltzer tablets to fortify himself for the rest of the day. Later on, when Bond considers jumping off a cliff to attempt to elude enemy agents, Bond tells himself not to jump, "Forget it, Bond, for that you are definitely too old."[155] And after a night of passionate love-making with Connie, Bond concludes that he's "Definitely too old for this."[156] The "too old for this" theme of the script was included, in part, at the suggestion of Dalton who was wondering if he was too old to keep playing the part.[157]

This is a decidedly less confident spy than we have seen in the past. In one scene, Connie accuses Bond of sulking. Historically, Bond broods but he never sulks. Elsewhere, Bond is taken aback by the notion that Connie has "dumped" him.[158] And after a daring feat, Bond excitedly calls attention to his own audacity. "Did you see what I just did?... I *jumped*, out of a *speeding plane*, into a pool, *this* size (holds up two pinched fingers) ...can you believe that?"[159] Daniel Craig's Bond is also given to questioning his desire to continue working for Her Majesty's Secret Service. However, Craig's Bond and the Bond depicted in *Bond 17* play out differently. Whereas Craig's Bond has a crisis of conscience, this Bond seems to undergo a crisis of confidence.

As previously noted, this Bond is less proficient than the Bond we've come to know. While kayaking in a river, Bond is overwhelmed by the rapids, capsizes, and he emerges from the river coughing up water. It's an unimpressive effort by Bond who can usually master any vessel. At the story's conclusion, Bond saves the day by gaining control of the plane that's carrying a nuclear warhead and he kills the villain. However, he uncharacteristically forgets to disarm the bomb. It's a moment that is played for laughs and ultimately, no one is injured. Still, it's a major blunder for the usually capable agent.

I interviewed Bruce Feirstein, who co-wrote *GoldenEye* (1995) and *Tomorrow Never Dies* and wrote *The World Is Not Enough* (1999), for my book *The Many Lives of James Bond*. Feirstein told me that when he was working on a screenplay Barbara Broccoli and Michael Wilson would often pose the question, "How much do you wanna take the piss out of Bond?"[160] For the writers of *Bond 17*, the answer is an awful lot. By spoofing the character, however gently, the screenwriters seemed to be deliberately questioning Bond's relevance in pop culture as attitudes and mores are changing. Eon faced a similar challenge when they were devising the script for *GoldenEye* and questioning if the fifties-era Bond would still resonate with modern audiences. Feirstein also told me that he "brought to it an idea that the world had changed but Bond hadn't." The writers of *Bond 17* chose a different path. They experimented with the idea of a Bond who is struggling to adjust to aging and questioning his adaptability to changing times. The non-Eon film *Never Say Never Again* also explored these ideas.

Dialogue: Davies and Osborne give Bond some wonderful bon mots. For instance, when Connie comments on Bond's snobbery in his selection of a particular fine wine, 007 defends himself by explaining "there's a distinction to be made between snobbery and connoisseurship."[161] And when Bond is under fire and is unsure of which switch to flick on his newly equipped Aston Martin, he admonishes himself, "One day, Bond, you're gonna bloody well listen to Q when he explains all this."[162]

The script also gives Connie and Sir Henry some zingers. When Bond is uncertain of where to investigate next, Connie teases, "What is it about you and sex, James? Seems to dull your intellect."[163] And after Sir Henry kills his hapless fencing instructor by slashing his neck with a sword simply for disappointing him, the dispassionate villain coolly instructs his butler, "Get me another instructor."[164] Sir Henry is as droll and imperious as Hugo Drax in *Moonraker* who instructs his functionary, "Look after Mr. Bond. See that some harm comes to him."

Tone: *Bond 17* is an action-comedy that gives equal emphasis to both elements of the genre. Davies and Osborne's script contains thrilling set pieces, such as the high-speed car chase between Bond and the assassin Rodin and Bond's one-in-a-million jump from a plane in flight into a pool on top of a building. The script also contains instances of broad comedy. Take the scene in which Bond, who tracks the enemy to a rodeo, disguises himself in "full cowboy gear."[165] The image of the straight-faced Dalton dressed up as a cowboy would tickle some and irritate others who would wince at the sight of Bond dressed outlandishly.

Regardless, the Bond-dressed-as-a-cowboy sight gag wouldn't have been out of place in a Roger Moore-era Bond film. In *Octopussy*, Moore's Bond donned, not one, but two outrageous outfits—a gorilla suit and then a clown costume. Incidentally, and confirming his comedy credentials and impulses, Davies would later co-write the Bond parodies *Johnny English* (2003), which he worked on with Bond screenwriters Neil Purvis and Robert Wade, *Johnny English Reborn* (2011) with Hamish McColl, and, working alone, *Johnny English Strikes Again* (2018), all staring the comic Rowan Atkinson as the bumbling agent.

Jennings: Jennings, one of Bond's allies in *Bond 17*, is openly gay. An openly gay operative might have been a first for the franchise. Traditionally, gay (or bisexual) characters such as Pussy Galore from *Goldfinger*, Mr. Wint and Mr. Kidd in *Diamonds Are Forever*, *Skyfall*'s Raoul Silva, and Rosa Klebb in *From Russia with Love* are villains. Pussy Galore eventually becomes Bond's ally and, problematically for some, she also becomes Bond's lover. And, if it were handled with sensitivity, introducing an openly gay hero into the franchise in the early nineteen-nineties would have been progressive.

In the script, Bond is embarrassed when Jennings flirts with him. Later in the series, a similar scene between Bond and a man would play out differently. In *Skyfall*, Eon's twenty-third Bond film, after Silva hits on 007 and reasons that there is a "first time for everything," an unruffled, if not flirtatious, Bond counters, "What makes you think this is my first time?"

Q: Davies and Osborne provide Bond's allies at MI6 with nice character moments. Q's lab is being decommissioned in *Bond 17* and the armorer is being forced out of his job. A rudderless Q confesses that "this lab has been my whole life."[166] As written, it's a touching scene that would have given Desmond Llewelyn, who appeared in 17 Bond films, the opportunity to display greater depth and emotional range.

The script would also have allowed Bond to react differently towards Q. Usually, Bond pokes fun at Q's persnickety regard for his inventions. However, after hearing about Q's involuntary retirement, Bond is aghast and unreservedly appreciative and supportive of his colleague as he urges Q to fight to retain his job.

Miss Moneypenny: In the script, Bond decides to forgo the usual banter with Miss Moneypenny and finally asks M's secretary out on a date. To Bond's surprise, she's engaged to be married. The decision to have Moneypenny engaged, and therefore unattainable, reinforces the script's theme that time might be passing Bond by.

Rodin: The helmet-wearing henchman whose high-tech weaponry outmatches Q's gadgetry would have been a memorable foe.

Continuity: In the early nineties, the continuity of the series suggested that all the actors who had played Bond (Sean Connery through Timothy Dalton) were playing the same character at different stages of his career. *Bond 17* would have continued this practice. In the final scene, Bond briefly recalls his run-ins with Auric Goldfinger, Oddjob, and Ernst Stravo Blofeld. While it's a comedic exchange where Bond makes himself the butt of the joke, it unequivocally links Dalton's Bond to Connery's.

Legacy: Even though Davies and Osborne's screenplay was never filmed, it seems that their efforts had some enduring impact on the franchise. Some elements of their script might have been repurposed and used in later Bond movies. In *Bond 17*, Bond must escape a tank in a military graveyard before it's blown to smithereens. Similarly, in *GoldenEye*, Pierce Brosnan's Bond must escape from a decommissioned helicopter before rockets destroy it. The fencing match between Yupland and his instructor in *Bond 17* might have inspired the decision to stage a similar duel in *Die Another Day* between villain Gustav Graves and Bond.

Final Thoughts: It's important to reiterate that as polished as *Bond 17* seems, it is only the first recorded draft of the screenplay. In future drafts, the brief character moments where Bond is not in full possession of his powers – such as when he neglects to disarm the bomb–might have been rewritten to provide audiences with the self-assured and capable Bond that we had come to expect.

In the book *Some Kind of Hero*, Ajay Chowdhury and Matt Field conclude that the script "is very Bondian" and that it "would have made a terrific Bond film for Timothy Dalton. Had it been made, it would have secured Dalton's tenure as Bond and perfectly positioned 007 in the post-Cold War age."[167]

* * *

William Osborne, how did you and William Davies get involved in writing what would have been Timothy Dalton's third film?

Basically, we had been in Hollywood for three years by 1990, had enjoyed the massive success of *Twins*, worked on a lot of high-profile movies, sold two or three more spec scripts, and were coming off the end of shooting *Stop! Or My Mom Will Shoot* [1992] with Sylvester Stallone. History has much-derided this film as excruciating, but that fails to understand the studio politics and finances of Hollywood at that time.

In fact, *Stop* performed okay at the box office [$70.61 million] but hey, I really can't defend the indefensible.[168] Anyway, we were doing projects with Dylan Sellers and Fred Zollo, Barbara Broccoli's partner at the time, and he introduced us to Barbara and then to Michael Wilson and then Cubby and Dana. They got in touch with our agent Jeremy Zimmer and we went for a meeting. There was I remember quite a long period of dating with many dinners where we just talked Bond, ideas, anything. We looked at some of the most amazing Frank Lloyd Wright houses in L.A. as locations but it was also an excuse to see these buildings and there was a comfort zone established given our then track record and the fact that we were British and were felt to understand the whole Bond milieu.

Dalton was an excellent Bond, but his second film performed poorly. Was there a sense that the next Bond film could be the last if they didn't reinvent the formula?

Cubby and all of them loved Dalton and he was very close to them. They look after everyone who works for them in a truly unique way. But there was a sense of drift when we came on, particularly because the whole franchise was in this massive financial and legal gridlock with MGM run by this fantasist criminal Giancarlo Parretti [who was later charged with fraud], so there was no prospect of a film getting made any time soon, as was proved the case – a six-year hiatus that had never happened before or since.[169] So it felt even getting on board as though Bond was becalmed both as a character and film and as a business proposition.

What were your creative marching orders?

There was an outline from Alfonse Ruggiero [and Michael Wilson], which I think we basically threw out and came up with our own structure and story. I no longer have those outlines. Basically, we were given a lot of latitude to play around by some of the team, but there was also the need to conform to the expectations and traditions that Cubby and Dana were comfortable with. You have to understand that the franchise had been going for nearly thirty years by then—an unimaginable amount of time in Hollywood terms. We decided to give the whole thing a push towards modernity but also to acknowledge that in the classic Hollywood parlance, Bond was getting "too old for this shit." We were always high-action merchants and wanted to bring that weariness and fatigue into play as a counterpoint to the incredible stuff Bond had to pull off.

What were Timothy Dalton's ideas for Bond? What was important to him?

Tim was a classically trained actor, deeply serious but with an amazing twinkle in his eye. I think like many actors he longed for Bond to have a deeper back-story, some hinterland ["the land behind"] he could access, and he wanted to bring a bit more gravitas to the part. I'm afraid that as the script shows we did not service Tim's hope. But I believe he could have played the character beautifully as written.

In *Licence to Kill*, Bond is on a personal mission and he is disillusioned by his profession. What would have been going on in Bond's inner life in *Bond 17*?

We wanted to place Bond at this transitional point in his life where he is beginning to doubt his own abilities, losing a little bit his *joie de vivre*. I think looking back it was probably serendipitous that Bond didn't start again until all the incredible historical events of the early nineties had transpired.

Who was your Bond?

Bond is Bond, the narcissistic psychopath of the books softened over time by successive films and actors. Daniel Craig and Sam Mendes tried to hew it back and find some depth, but for me, that just seemed to be interminable scenes of him crying.

Can you describe the writing process?

When I wrote as a team with Will Davies back then it was an incredibly quick very high energy day where we would first break the story, then write a detailed outline, and then go to draft, hopefully writing ten pages a day – back and forth taking turns to type into very rudimentary personal computers. Coffee and cigarettes and Diet Coke all day till six or seven, then dinner. We were always getting fucked by either Word\DOS software or the actual hardware, floppy drives, and dot matrix printers. We sat and marveled at our first fax machine.

We worked unbelievably hard for the ten years we were together, averaging four to five projects a year which is pretty unheard of, but we didn't have much of a life outside work and exercise (or booze on my part). We made hay while the sun shined and every lunch or dinner would be with a producer, director, or piece of talent. Good times.

What direction were you hoping to take the series? How did you want to deepen the character?

I'm not sure we had such grandiose plans. We wanted to do a good job for the Broccolis, always, so they felt they had their money's worth. We would have loved to stay on but after three drafts they were locked into litigation and we had a ton of offers on the table, so we moved on. To be truly successful like [seven-time Bond writers] Neal Wade and Robert Purvis have been you have to dedicate your whole time to Bond and make it your life as they have done.

What did you learn writing a Bond script?

You learn something new from every script you write, but more importantly with a property like Bond it ultimately came down to the relationship you had with the Broccolis. They expect and reward commitment and exclusivity and this was something we couldn't ultimately offer them.

When you reflect on your overall Bond experience, what stands out?

Sitting inside Cubby and Dana's beautiful mansion off Sunset Boulevard, like something from a Bond movie itself, two young London chancers sipping tea from Meissen cups whilst talking story.

What were some of the titles considered?

I have only just noticed that the original cover page is typed as "Bond 18" not "17" – spooky.

Why do you think the script was ultimately not used?

When the litigation ended times had changed, the world of 1996 was completely different from 1990. In a way, our script was like a placeholder for the franchise whilst shit happened.

Any final thoughts?

I remain a true fan of Bond. I have a wonderful collection of original posters and the original books by Fleming and lots of silly memorabilia. In some ways, I regret that the timing of our involvement and where we were in our careers didn't allow us to invest more in the franchise and become a member of the Bond family, but that's life.

James Bond in disguise at the rodeo.
Illustration by Pat Carbajal

Timothy Dalton's Bond dressed up as a cowboy.
Illustration by Pat Carbajal

Bond squares off against the security robot.
Illustration by Pat Carbajal

Timothy Dalton's Fourth Unmade Bond Film:
Reunion with Death
Richard Smith

Bond fans love to speculate about Timothy Dalton's third outing as Bond. Dalton's brief stint as the secret agent was as powerful as it was unfinished. So it's only natural to wonder what might have happened if Dalton made more Bond films. However, a decidedly less popular topic than Dalton's third film is speculating on what form his *fourth* film would have taken. This chapter offers one possible answer to that question. But before I address the subject of Dalton's hypothetical Bond oeuvre, allow me to briefly touch-upon another fan-favorite issue—the speed at which Eon produces modern Bond movies.

For the first three decades of the franchise, Bond fans were accustomed to seeing a new film every one-to-three-years. In the '60s, audiences were treated to an impressive six Bond movies. In fact, *Dr. No, From Russia with Love, Goldfinger,* and *Thunderball* were released in four consecutive years. The '70s and '80s saw the theatrical distribution of five Bond films apiece. The schedule was undoubtedly grueling for the filmmakers but the public had demonstrated an unquenchable thirst for 007.

To the bitter disappointment of Bond's large audiences, after 1989's *Licence to Kill,* Bond's cinematic adventures were unexpectedly put on hold for six years. So when the script-development phase for the next Bond movie resumed in the early '90s, the producers and the studio were eager to ensure that fans wouldn't have to endure another long gap between films.

However, Eon faced a hurdle. Writing a tightly constructed screenplay that pits Bond against a formidable new villain and a surprising endgame is a time-consuming process. While Michael France was working on the first draft of the 17th film in the series, the producers wanted to get a head start on the development process for the 18th film. So they hired both Richard Smith, the co-writer of the Sylvester Stallone action-thriller *Lock Up* (1989), and who would go on to write the time-travel novel *Freezer Burn* (2010), and John Cork, who wrote the Civil Rights movement drama "The Long Walk Home" (1990), to separately write potential Bond movies.[170]

In a 1993 article for the trade magazine *Variety,* Charles Juroe, a spokesman for the producers said, "[Smith and Cork] are writing for future Bonds down the line, assuming [*GoldenEye* is] a success...When you get up to 17 in one series, you do things differently. You don't wait until 17 is a success to say, 'Oh, we better do another one. This two-year cycle does not give [the producers] the luxury to wait 10 or 11 months down the line to get started on the next one. They've learned that they have to be ahead of the game. When United Artists says they're ready to do another one, they're expected to have one ready."[171]

Let's return to the topic of Timothy Dalton's fourth Bond movie. When Richard Smith and John Cork were hired to write Bond scenarios, Dalton was, in Juroe's words, the "Bond on record."[172] So, if France was writing Dalton's third movie, Smith and Cork were independently working on what might have been the actor's fourth.

Hiring multiple writers was a prudent and forward-thinking idea but it didn't quite work out as planned. Neither Smith nor Cork's work resulted in a screenplay that was filmed. In an interview with the website *Commander Bond,* Cork explained that he "never worked out a story" that pleased the producers.[173] However, Cork's association with Bond didn't end there. Fans now know Cork as a leading expert in all things 007. He's the writer of *James Bond: The Legacy* (2002), with Bruce Scivally, *Bond Girls are Forever: The Women of James Bond* (2003), with Bond woman Maryam d'Abo (*The Living Daylights*), and *James Bond Encyclopedia* (2007), with Collin Stutz, as well as the writer-producer-director of numerous Bond "making of" documentaries and, with Dr. Michael L. VanBlaricum and Douglas Redenius, as the co-founder of the Ian Fleming Foundation, as well as the editor of its discontinued magazine *Goldeneye.*

While Cork's multi-facetted contribution to Bond scholarship is well-established, the particulars of Richard Smith's efforts are largely unknown, and it was my hope to bring greater attention to them. I tried unsuccessfully to track him down through direct means. Widening my net, I found a 1993 article in *Variety* which mentioned that Smith was also a make-up artist, actor, and producer.[174] I then contacted many make-up artists who shared Smith's unfortunately common name. That tack failed. I simultaneously approached a number of producers and actors who shared Smith's name. Still, no luck. I subsequently learned that Smith was never a make-up artist, actor, or producer. It turned out that the article had conflated Smith's credits with other artists who shared his name. Then I was saddened to learn that Smith had died in 2011 at the age of 48 from non-Hodgkin's lymphoma.[175]

However, I did manage to find Mariana Smith, Richard's widow. She was not only kind enough to talk with me about her late husband, whom she describes as a major Bond fan, she generously gave me a copy of Smith's unproduced treatment for his Bond film. And it's fascinating.

Smith's treatment, which is dated December 14, 1993, is titled *Reunion with Death*, and he rendered the title with a cursive font that makes it look almost as if it were handwritten. Under the title, he identified it as "Treatment for Future Bond Project."[176]

The opening scene of the 37-page treatment is set in New York, on the highest floor of a costly high-rise apartment building, which Smith describes as "like Trump Tower."[177] Inside, "master spy" Jacques Detroit is "making it" with his girlfriend when "suddenly, from out of nowhere, Bond drops into view outside the window, suspended from the roof by an almost invisible wire."[178] [Note: When Smith wrote the treatment in 1993, Donald Trump was a real estate developer and not a politician.]

Bond shoots the window, shattering it, and enters the apartment. Once inside, Bond chides, "Don't get up" and then he shoots Detroit.[179] Bond "coldly" addresses his now-dead target, "That's for 006."[180] When Detroit's girlfriend screams, Bond jibes, "Don't worry, darling. He wasn't your type."[181] Guards arrive and Bond flees. As he jumps out the window, a guard shoots and ruptures Bond's climbing wire. "Bond hurtles towards the ground. Death seems certain," but the agent pulls a previously hidden ripcord, a parachute deploys, and he floats to safety.[182] Bond lands at a nearby townhouse and crashes a party. When an attractive woman approaches Bond quips, "Sorry to drop in like this."[183] The woman introduces herself and Smith writes: "'Bond,'" comes the reply. "'James Bond.'"[184]

After the credits, the story picks up on a gloomy day in London. Bond drives to work not in an elegant sports car but in his Land Rover Defender 90. As Bond nears his office, he sees an empty parking space. But rather than "parallel parking like a normal person, he approaches it at high speed, and, at the last minute, throws the car into a controlled skid, sliding sideways into the spot, clearing the surround cars by mere inches."[185]

Inside his office, Bond is met by Loelia Ponsonby, his comely secretary from Fleming's novels. Ponsonby gives him a pile of paperwork, but "Bond hates paperwork, and will do almost anything to get out of it."[186] So he "flirts with Loelia to distract her, slips the papers into the outbox, then sneaks downstairs to the shooting range."[187] M goes to the shooting range and out of earshot to Bond asks the Armourer about Bond's shooting proficiency. The Armourer reports, "Best in the service, as usual."[188] M cautions the weapons specialist not to share that info with Bond, as it "wouldn't do to let him get a higher opinion of himself."[189] M interrupts Bond and asks 007 to accompany him to meet an old friend. Bond instantly agrees because even though requests might seem "casual" he understands that a "request" from M is "always serious."[190]

As the two men drive in M's car, a Rolls-Royce Silver Shadow, M tells Bond that they are on their way to meet M's friend Sir Robert Grey. Once at Grey's office, Bond and M are given a tour of the company and are told he's working on superconductors, which he explains are "the industry of the future. Worth countless trillions. But unless [MI5] can help, it will not be an industry of Britain's future."[191] Grey explains that his company is in a dire financial situation and that he might need to sell a portion of the company to a Japanese corporation called Asahi International. During a pause in the conversation, M lights up his pipe. Smith writes that the "smoke from the pipe drifts up and illuminates something strange; a laser beam coming from across the fields."[192] Bond realizes that the laser beam is actually a targeting device. Bond quickly alerts Grey of the danger and seizes M as he tries to get them to safety. But the missile "slams into the terrace" and kills Grey.[193] Bond is safe, but "when he gets up to survey the damage, he finds M has been critically wounded."[194] Barely alive, M is rushed to the ER.

Back at MI5, M's Chief of Staff Curtis Brown-Knoss tells Bond that a radical group known as the Malay Liberation Front assumed responsibility for Grey's death. Brown-Knoss instructs Bond to track down the group and advises 007 to go to Kuala Lumpur, a known whereabouts for the group. Bond tells his superior that he'd prefer to go to Rome because that's where he believes the killer is located. Brown-Knoss disagrees and wonders, "How in the devil Bond knows that?"[195] Bond explains, "It's the laser, sir. It was orange."[196] When Brown-Knoss argues that all lasers are orange Bond counters, "Not really, sir. They're mostly red. This one was orange, which makes it a Strontium-Agron laser. A frustrated Brown-Knoss tells Bond that, in that case, he should go to New York where the lasers are manufactured. Once again Bond disagrees. "If you recall, sir," Bond patiently explains, "Station R's report from last month... Three stinger missiles were stolen from the American Air Base near Rome."[197] And with that last bit of intel, Bond wins the argument. Smith's Bond is not flip or cavalier towards his superior. Instead, he "patiently" guides him through his reasoning, perhaps as a concession to M's precarious condition.[198]

Once in Rome, Bond is dressed as a tourist. He drinks espresso at the Tazza D'oro, "a famous old café next to the even older and more famous Pantheon."[199] Bond is approached by someone who appears to be a local artist. The artist asks Bond, "Signore, a picture of the Pantheon."[200] Bond replies, "I prefer portraits."[201] The man completes the code, "I have something you might like."[202] The "artist" explains that he is Enzo Martini, the local agent and that he's been tracking down a "triggerman" named Dante, who might have stolen the laser that killed Grey.[203] Martini adds that Dante doesn't have the "resources to plan a big operation," and he informs Bond that Dante's apartment can be found across the street from the café.[204]

Bond picks the lock and enters Dante's apartment, which he searches unsuccessfully for clues to his whereabouts. At first, Bond can't find any leads but then he notices that a book on the bookcase is "out of sequence."[205] He opens the book and discovers a series of photos depicting Grey's murder. As Bond studies the photos, Dante's girlfriend Grazia Bellochio enters the apartment. Because she is holding packages, she doesn't notice Bond. The "stunningly attractive" Grazia starts to put her groceries away when Bond says, "Here, let me help you with that."[206] At first, Grazia is startled to see a stranger in the apartment but Bond bluffs, "Is this the way you treat all of Dante's friends?"[207] Accepting Bond's impromptu cover story, Grazia vents, "He never lets me know when they are coming to stay." In his "most charming fashion" Bond responds, "Clearly, Dante doesn't appreciate you the way you deserve."[208] Intrigued by Bond, she asks, "How should he appreciate me?"[209] Bond replies, "I'd tell you but I worry what Dante might think."[210] Grazia explains that Dante is at the opera and isn't expected anytime soon. Given a green light, Bond says, "Then we have a few hours...However shall we spend them?"[211]

Later, Bond returns to Martini, his contact. Martini asks Bond where he's been for the last couple of hours. Bond replies, "Studying a foreign tongue."[212] Bond tells Martini that Dante is at the opera. Bond and Enzo go to the Baths of Caracalla, where the opera is being performed. They spot Dante who is meeting with a "mysterious

Chinese man" named Ng.[213] Dante expects payment for a job, but instead, Ng hands the triggerman an empty envelope. Angered, Dante kicks Ng in the groin, whereupon the unfazed Ng kills Dante. Bond and Enzo try to capture Ng, but Ng kills Enzo and escapes.

Bond returns to London where using MI5's database he cannot identify Dante's killer. M's Chief of Staff Brown-Knoss is pleased that Dante has been tracked down but he is not worried that Ng is on the loose. Smith explains that in "his mind, the case has been solved."[214]

Bond goes to the hospital to visit M, who is in an "oxygen tent, feeble. But stable."[215] M inquires about the case and Bond tells him that Grey's assassin was found. M suspects that Bond will not let the matter rest. When Bond responds that the case is "officially closed," M asks, "And unofficially?"[216] Bond replies, "Unofficially, sir, I have a meeting at Carrington-Grey in half an hour."[217] This brief scene unsentimentally shows Bond's respect for M, both for the man and his office.

Bond goes to Carrington-Grey, where he meets Byron Banning, who until very recently was the company's chief financial officer, and who in the aftermath of Charles Grey's death now runs the company. Banning shows Bond a note that is written on rice paper and which was kept in a safe. It reads: "If you want to know who killed Grey, wear a chrysanthemum to the Ashahi party. You will be contacted."[218] The note is cryptically signed "Dragon." Bond learns that the deal between Carrington-Grey and Ashahi International will be closed at the party.

Bond flies to Tokyo, where he poses as an attorney for Carrington-Grey. At the Tokyo International Airport, Bond is stopped in customs by an official. In a backroom, Bond speaks to a customs official who asks Bond, "Do you have a match?"[219] Bond replies, "I prefer a lighter."[220] The man counters, "Better still." The man wraps up the exchange with, "Until they go wrong."[221] The tension has been broken and the customs official introduces himself as Ryuichi Tanaka, the son of Tiger Tanaka, Bond's ally in *You Only Live Twice*. Bond aficionados will be reminded by the coded exchange between Tanaka and Bond of the same dialogue between Bond and Karim Bay in *From Russia with Love*.

After pleasantries are exchanged and Bond tells Tanaka that he looks like his father, the younger Tanaka informs Bond that Asahi is owned by the godfather of the Yakuza, Yasuhiro Nakasone. Tanaka explains that Nakasone effectively controls Japan and that Dragon might be a "mole in Nakasone's organization."[222] Tanaka gives Bond a chrysanthemum, which Bond requested in advance, and asks why he needs it. Bond replies, "Dragon fishing."[223]

Bond is met outside the airport by one of the representatives of Ashahi who chauffeurs Bond through Japan. When asked if he's been there before, Bond says that he has not. At this point in the treatment, Smith writes a note directly to the reader. Smith explains that Bond lied about being in Japan before because "he's been there many times and speaks fluent Japanese."[224] It's a little character note that wouldn't necessarily transfer to the screen but it informs the reader that this guy knows his Bond lore. On their drive to Asahi's office, Ohtsu gives Bond an impromptu tour and explains that cherry blossoms are an "ancient symbol of purity and evanescence and that the Kamikaze pilots used it as their symbol during the war."[225] Quoting a Haiku, Ohtsu says, "If only we might fall...Like cherry blossoms in the Spring." Bond "completes the haiku: So pure and radiant."[226]

Bond arrives at the party in the Ashahi World Headquarters. Amongst the Geisha girls and Kabuki performers, Bond spots Yakuza. Bond is brought upstairs where he meets Akutagawa, the attorney for Asahi. Befitting the Japanese custom, Bond and the attorney bow and exchange business cards. The attorney hands Bond the documents for the deal. Surprising Akutagawa, Bond refuses to sign them, demands to speak to Nakasone, and announces that he'll be at the party.

At the party, Bond sees two Yakuza in an arm-wrestling match. One of the Yakuza has a Dragon on his arm, so Bond naturally suspects that the man might be the mole who goes by the name Dragon. Bond and the man arm wrestle with Bond losing the contest. Bond soon realizes that the man is not the mole and leaves. Because Bond usually wins these sporting matches, it's a nice change of pace to see him come up short.

Nakasone arrives at the party with Michiko, his attractive wife. Nakasone introduces himself to Bond and asks why he has not signed the contract. Bond replies, "Things have changed."[227] Not wanting to conduct further business at the party, Nakasone invites Bond to his country home. Bond accepts the invitation. As Nakasone and Michiko depart, Bond notices that "underneath all of her traditional garments, Michiko is wearing a set of very hip, modern sneakers."[228]

Back at the hotel, the front desk attendant tells Bond that he has a message from his "mother" who said that he should "call her back at eight."[229] Bond enters his hotel room and signs into his computer. The password Bond uses is "Tracy," a reference, of course, to his late wife and true love from *On Her Majesty's Secret Service*. Bond then types in "PPK."[230] When nothing happens, he types in "Please."[231] With that, a side panel of the computer opens. Quickly getting past his annoyance with Q's attempt to teach him manners, Bond puts the parts from the hidden compartment together and assembles a gun, the Walther PPK. Bond knocks out one of the Yakuza who has been monitoring his movements and leaves the hotel.

Bond goes to the Ginza, which Smith describes as "Tokyo's main nightlife street."[232] Teeming with "neon signs, it is a parade of bars, restaurants, clubs, discotheques."[233] Bond enters a Karaoke bar called "Mother's" – the name explains the message at the front desk for Bond to call his mother. Once inside, Bond meets up with Tanaka and his sister Keiko. To Tanaka's frustration, Bond flirts with Keiko. Bond learns that Nakasone's wife Michiko used to be a "successful career woman" but after she married Nakasone, she became a "traditional wife."[234] Tanaka asks Bond about his interest in Michiko. In a brief but revealing character moment, Bond confesses, "I make a habit of pursuing unattainable women." [235]

Outside the club, Bond sees one of Nakasone's men. Bond chases after the man who "ducks inside an indoor hot spring."[236] Smith explains that "geothermal activity has created a popular bathing oasis right in the city. Underneath the huge roof are pools of naturally heated water, and steam/sawdust baths. Hundreds of men crowd the pools and the sawdust baths."[237] Bond catches up with the Yakuza. The two men fight. Using objects found in the steam room, including a towel, and the lid of a sawdust box, Bond kills the man by suffocating him. Smith seems to be making a concerted effort to place Bond in the specific cultural environment of Japan. He appears to be trying to get back to the early Bond movies where the locations were integral to the plot. It is perhaps worth noting that Smith's idea of staging a fight scene for Bond in a steam room would eventually occur in *GoldenEye*, which was being developed at roughly the same time that Smith was writing *Reunion with Death*.

Later, Bond is taken by jet copter to the Japanese Alps, which Smith describes as "majestic, high and snowy above the springtime plains."[238] Bond goes to Nakasone's home: a "castle – a remnant of Japan's medieval age – and a testament to Nakasone's wealth and power."[239] When Bond lands, he is met by Ohtsu, the man who picked him up at the airport, who explains that his employer is away now but will meet up with Bond later. Smith playfully writes: "For Bond, this amounts to an invitation to snoop."[240] Bond moves through the massive house and finds a private museum, which is a "shrine to the Samurai" and Nakasone's "private wing."[241] There he sees Michiko practicing Karate. She's both forceful and stunningly beautiful. She is also angry that Bond has interrupted her. He "apologizes in his best Japanese" and she's surprised by his fluency in the language.[242] Bond explains that he learned to speak the language at Cambridge. It turns out that Michiko also went to Cambridge and they bond (the pun is almost unavoidable) over their memories of the school. It's another nice character-revealing moment that, in this case, also advances the plot.

Their conversation abruptly ends when they hear Nakasone approaching the room. Bond leaves quickly. Nakasone asks if Bond was in the room. Michiko covers for Bond and lies. Nakasone "grabs her roughly and kisses her" but when his wife doesn't respond, he leaves.[243]

That night Bond attends a dinner with Nakasone and Michiko, and with Akutagawa, Ohtsu, and their spouses. At dinner Bond gains the "respect" of the other diners by eating a "potentially poisonous kind of sushi, the consumption of which is regarded as a test of courage."[244] Nakasone wants to know why Bond is trying to ruin the agreement and suggests that Bond "is trying to get a cut of the action and asks how much Bond wants."[245] Bond and Nakasone settle on a very high figure and agree to sign the contract in the morning.

Later, Michiko sneaks into Bond's room. Pleasantly surprised by her arrival, Bond asks, "Come to sing an old college song?"[246] As they flirt and kiss, their encounter is being captured by hidden video cameras. We learn that their passionate kiss is an act intended to mislead those monitoring Nakasone's surveillance cameras. Michiko reveals to Bond that she is Dragon, the mole in the Yakuza. Michiko gives Bond what appears to be a credit card and explains that it will prove that Nakasone killed Grey. When Bond asks her why she's helping him, Michiko explains, "He killed my father...I want him destroyed."[247] Nakasone enters the room. He believes the ruse that Bond was seducing his wife and threatens, "I suggest it would be wise to sign the contract and leave as soon as possible."[248]

After he signs the contract, Bond boards a jet copter, which will take him away from Nakasone's castle. However, once they are in the air, Ng, the pilot whose identity was previously concealed, presses a button that releases poisonous gas in Bond's portion of the helicopter, causing Bond to pass out.

Bond wakes up later to discover that he's tied to a chair and that Nakasone has found the credit card that Michiko gave him. Unsure of how Bond acquired the credit card, Nakasone has Ng torture Bond. On Nakasone's orders, "Ng snaps Bond's finger like a pretzel."[249] Bond defiantly asks, "You think that is going to make me talk?"[250] But Nakasone isn't going to be outplayed by Bond, and he replies, "Of course not. That was merely to make you yell. You have 255 more bones in your body. I feel comfortable in saying you will talk before we break them all."[251] When Bond still doesn't talk, Ng breaks another finger. The dialogue might be a winking nod to the famous exchange with Goldfinger: "Do you expect me to talk?" No, Mr. Bond, I expect you to die." The torture scene is tense and brutal. In the film and Fleming's novel *Live and Let Die*, Bond's fingers are similarly threatened by Mr. Big. However, in the film Bond bluffed (or seemed to bluff) his way out of that threat. In the novel, Bond is decidedly less fortunate.

While Bond is being tortured, Michiko enters the security room. She overcomes a technician that intentionally triggers alarms around the castle. Nakasone and Ng leave Bond to investigate the disturbance. When they leave, Michiko slips into the room and frees Bond. She explains how Bond can use Nakasone's "private escape chute" to sneak through the castle and make his way towards the river, where he can then escape by boat.[252] Bond takes the credit card, fashions a letter opener into a splint for his broken fingers, exits through the escape chute, and makes his way to the river, where he kills a guard guest with his "letter opener/splint," and steals a boat to make his getaway. Nakasone and Ng pursue Bond by helicopter, with the support below of men in five speedboats.[253] A chase ensues and Bond's boat crashes through the walls of the now-closed Seagaia Ocean Dome, an indoor waterpark that contains "Japan's largest indoor beach."[254] The Yakuza shoot at Bond and all "hell breaks loose."[255] Bond "grabs a towel and a sun hat from the Towel Boy, and donning them, disappears into the crowd."[256]

In Tokyo, as one of MI5's doctors is attending to Bond's hand, Tanaka and Keiko inspect the credit card, which Bond stole back from Nakasone. It appears at first to be a normal credit card, but Bond suggests that the card's magnetic strip might contain a secret and he asks if they can decode it. Once they do, they discover a "series of digitized photographs, identical to the ones Bond found at Dante's apartment in Rome."[257] This proves that Nakasone ordered Charles Grey's assignation. Bond learns that Michiko's father Satohara Ozawa was the head of a chemical manufacturing company called Ozawa Chemical. It seems that his company suffered through a "series of industrial accidents and was forced into bankruptcy."[258] Feeling shame, Ozawa killed himself. With this new information, Bond figures out the villain's scheme. Bond explains, "Nakasone sets his sight on a company...and drives it to the brink of bankruptcy through sabotage."[259] Bond and Tanaka decide to learn who currently owns Ozawa Chemical.

Bond goes to Nakasone's Asahi Tower to investigate. While perusing the company directory in the lobby, he sees both Ozawa Chemical Company and Fujiyama Fish Company, which are the only non-financial or industrial businesses in the entire building. Bond and Tanaka survey the Fish Company, which to Tanaka appears to be a normal business. But Bond points out that if they were simply a fish company then why do they need high-end digital locks, which are connected to "large steel doors" and are a part of a "very complex and expensive electronic locking system"?[260]

Bond and Tanaka return to the local agent's office only to find everyone dead. On one of the bodies is Bond's own business card that he gave Nakasone at the party where they originally met. Bond and Tanaka go to a safe house where they find Keiko who happened to be out of the office when her colleagues were gunned down by Nakasone's enforcer Ng.

At night, Bond breaks into the Fujiyama Fish Company with the help of a high-tech gadget from Q. Once inside, Bond discovers a lab, which is filled with superconductors. But before Bond can investigate further, the Yakuza arrive. Bond kills a few enemies with a few items that are specific to both Japan and the factory. "He buries one in a mountain of ice, spears another with a swordfish bill, tosses a third into a vat of crabs."[261] After trapping a few more Yakuza in a freezer, Bond quips, "That'll cool them off a bit."[262] Bond kills another Yakuza by throwing him into a fish-grinding machine. Bond "looks away, disgusted" and then notes, "That took guts."[263] It's a very funny line but perhaps a little close to a remark from *On Her Majesty's Secret Service*. In that film, when a bad guy falls into a snowblower that spits out red-colored snow, George Lazenby coolly remarks, "He had a lot of guts." After dispatching a number of Nakasone's men, Bond is finally cornered by Ng and a dozen Yakuza.

Nakasone has Bond tied to a "mass-driver, also known as a rail-gun. In less time than it takes to blink an eye it can accelerate an object to 400 feet per second in a distance of just four feet."[264] While Michiko helplessly watches, Nakasone tells Bond that he believes that his wife helped him escape from the castle but he cannot be sure. Nakasone tells Michiko to confess. When Michiko looks at Bond for help on how to respond Bond says, "Don't look at me for advice...I'm as alarmed as you."[265] Michiko grasps that Bond is telling her to sound an alarm. She sets off a nearby fire alarm, which the Yakuza quickly turn off. With that effort, Michiko has revealed herself to be Dragon. Just before Ng can kill Bond and Michiko, Tanaka, who heard the alarm, arrives with reinforcements and a gun battle starts.

Bond and Michiko escape with Tanaka in his car. Yakuza chases after them and Tanaka is shot in the shoulder. Bond drives to a waterfront and hides his car among the thousands of Toyota cars that are to be loaded onto the ships. By the time Ng finds their car, Bond, Michiko, and Tanaka have vacated it. However, the trio are quickly spotted by Ng as they escape to a Buddhist Temple called "The Temple of the Dragon of Heaven." Tanaka calls for back-up. Ng and the Yakuza pursue Bond into the Temple, where the wounded Tanaka, Michiko, and Bond hide. But they are soon discovered. Ng and the Yakuza corner Bond. It seems that they have no hope for escape, but Tanaka willingly sacrifices himself so that Michiko and Bond can get away.

Bond and Michiko jump into a car that is being driven by an agent who introduces himself as Watanabe. The Yakuza chase Bond. Working on instincts and not trusting the situation, Bond takes out his cigarette case and casually asks if the agent has a match? When Watanabe replies "I don't smoke" instead of "I prefer a lighter," Watanabe reveals himself as an enemy agent.[266] Bond and Watanabe fight while the car speeds down a hill and crashes through a house after rice paper house. Bond tosses Watanabe out of the car and remarks that "he's got a bumpy road ahead." Bond takes control of the wheel but the Yakuza are gaining on them. The chase takes them to a train station, where a freight train is beginning to pull out, and when Bond spots an "empty spot on the car carrier," he floors his car up an embankment and vaults his car onto the moving train.[267] Bond's remarkable move recalls the masterly parking maneuver that Bond performed while parking his car earlier in the movie when he was on his way to work. In this new light, the audience has come to understand that the first time around Bond wasn't simply thrill-seeking but rather that he was honing his moves and preparing for the possibility that a time might come when he would need to implement that dangerous maneuver in the line of work.

But Bond isn't out of danger yet. While piloting a machine-gun sporting helicopter, Ng catches up to the train car with Bond on it. It appears that Bond is trapped, but before Ng can open fire, his helicopter gets ensnared in power lines that in the excitement Ng had failed to notice. As they speed away, Michiko observes, "He looks angry."[268] Bond replies, "You know how he hates to be left hanging."[269] This scene, which depicts a character avoiding certain death, evokes similar apparent death scenes with a near-indestructible henchman, including the steel-toothed assassin Jaws, who survived multiple battles with Bond.

Bond's acting boss Brown-Knoss phones Bond at the Embassy in Tokyo to inform him that thanks to his efforts "the deal is officially nullified" and that the "Japanese authorities will finally be able to put [Nakasone] away."[270] Michiko makes plans to join Bond in London. Bond and Michiko make love.

Later, Bond is told that he has a call from M. On the way to take the call he spots a Geisha Girl arriving at the Embassy. A guard informs Bond the woman is the girlfriend of the deputy ambassador. Bond talks to M, who is still in the hospital but is on the mend. M tells Bond that the "Foreign Minister has recommended you for another knighthood" and that he suspects that Bond will "be turning it down again."[271] Bond replies, "Just doing my job, sir." M says, "And a damn fine job at that, 007."[272] A grinning Bond gently chides M with, "I believe your brush with death has made you sentimental, sir."

Meanwhile, the Geisha Girl makes her way through the Embassy. However, it turns out that the Geisha Girl is actually Ng in disguise. On his way back to his room Bond discovers a dead guard. Bond runs back to his room to discover Michiko who "lies dying on the bed."[273] Bond yells "for the doctor, desperation in his voice, but it is no use. He cradles her lovingly in his arms."[274] Bond's anguish for his dead lover is an interesting change in the Bond formula. At that point in the series, Bond was largely unaffected by the deaths of his romantic interests, whom Bond scholar John Brosnan describes in *James Bond in the Cinema* as "Obligatory Sacrificial Lambs."[275]

Bond calls M and asks for permission to go after Nakasone. Citing diplomatic concerns, M refuses. Bond tells M, "Then I'd like to put in for my leave right now."[276] While M isn't able to officially support Bond's mission, he wishes him good luck. Because Bond disobeyed orders in the previous film *Licence to Kill*, it's likely that if Smith were to turn his treatment into a script this narrow plot point would have to be altered. In that case, M would probably have had to give Bond permission to pursue Nakasone.

Bond and Keiko go to Nakasone's castle. Once there, Bond opens a crate that reveals a "one-man stealth Glider" that Keiko has borrowed from the local agency.[277] With the help of the glider, Bond sails into the villain's stronghold undetected. Bond overcomes guards and plants explosives as he makes his way through the castle. Ng finds the dead body of one of the guards with a card on it. The card reads: James Bond, Solicitor.

Bond confronts Nakasone in his office. Bond pulls a gun and forces Nakasone to watch as he detonates different parts of the castle. Nakasone tells Bond that he will simply purchase more castles and that Bond isn't hurting him at all. Bond coolly responds, "But to do that, you would have to be alive, wouldn't you?"[278] Suddenly, Ng enters the office. Bond and Ng exchange gunfire and Bond shoots Ng in the chest. In the commotion, Nakasone exits through his escape hatch. Bond goes after him. After Bond leaves, Ng comes to. It turns out he was wearing a bulletproof vest.

Bond searches for Nakasone and eventually finds him in the Samurai museum, which is catching fire. The two men battle. Wearing a suit of armor, Nakasone attacks Bond with a sword. Bond grabs a shield and a halberd (a fifteenth-century weapon which combines a spear and a battle ax). However, Nakasone's sword makes quick work of Bond's weapons. Bond grabs a kimono from the wall and throws it onto Nakasone, who gets tangled up in the garment. Bond slams Nakasone into a burning wall, and Nakasone's "kimono catches fire."[279] A still-burning Nakasone tries to escape but nearly falls off the balcony. Nakasone begs for help. Bond pushes Nakasone, who goes crashing to his death.

Bond tries to flee the castle. But his escape is impeded by Ng. During the vicious fight Ng chokes Bond, and "like a bulldog, he never lets go."[280] As he is about to blackout, Bond grabs a nearby cannonball and bashes Ng with it. The two warriors are exhausted by this extended fight. "Bond collapsed, barely conscious, gasping for air. For a moment, the two men lie there, trying to get themselves back together."[281] Bond and Ng steady themselves to resume the battle. Ng grabs a cannonball and raises it over his head. When Bond trips him, Ng loses control of the cannonball which comes crashing down on his head. Ng is finally dead. Smith describes the combat in detail. Smith's concept for the scene is that Bond engages in a rigorous and exhausting battle that leaves him exhausted, depleted of energy. Bond regroups sufficiently to escape the castle by rappelling down a wall.

In an epilogue, Bond and Keiko visit the cemetery so that they can pay their respects to Michiko and Tanaka. As they leave, the two "walk silently, together in grief, but together – sad, but giving us hope for the future. Around them, the cherry blossoms are falling. Smith gives Bond the final line of the treatment: "Today in flower," says Bond, quoting a Japanese poem, "tomorrow scattered by the wind."[282] End of treatment.

* * *

Assorted Observations

Richard Smith's storyline for *Reunion with Death* could have been the basis for an engrossing fourth Bond film starring Timothy Dalton. It was written to play to Timothy Dalton's strengths as an actor. Smith's depiction of Bond was tailor-made for Dalton's interpretation of the character. However, despite the potency of the outline, Dalton would not get a chance to play Bond in a third Bond film, let alone a fourth one.

I haven't been able to learn specifically why Smith's treatment wasn't used once Dalton left the franchise and Pierce Brosnan was cast as Bond. However, it's possible that timing might have played a factor. Presumably, Smith submitted his work to Eon around December 14, 1993, the date that appears on the outline. Four months later, on

April 12, 1994, it was announced that Dalton would retire from the part.[283] Two months after that, Pierce Brosnan attended a press conference on June 6, 1994 where he is heralded as the new James Bond.[284]

It's possible that once Brosnan was hired and the storyline to *GoldenEye* was fully formed, *Reunion with Death* no longer meshed with the direction that Eon was planning for the series. In fact, *Reunion* feels like it would be better suited for Timothy Dalton's more mature and steely Bond than Brosnan's suave, gentleman spy. Remember, Dalton was the "Bond of record" when Smith was developing the picture with Eon.[285]

It's also possible that the producers simply didn't want to set a film largely in Japan. If that was the case, it could have been a practical decision not to film in the country—due possibly to the lack of power of the dollar or pound or perhaps because the country wasn't receptive, or because after *You Only Live Twice*, it didn't seem fresh to set another film in Japan. The setting of Japan is inextricably woven into the *Reunion with Death* outline. As such, it would not have been feasible to take Smith's basic story and set it in another country.

Of course, it could also be that Eon didn't respond enthusiastically to the material. Maybe Nakasone's scheme to drive companies into bankruptcy and to corner the international market on superconductors, no matter how lucrative, didn't seem grandiose or diabolical enough to them.

When thinking about Smith's compelling treatment and questioning if it had any direct impact on any subsequent film in the series, one should be wary. It is not uncommon for writers working independently to come up with similar ideas. John Cork explained that "if I'm reading about satellite-guided missiles and technology that isn't quite there yet but is going to happen, you can bet everybody else is reading about the same thing too. The idea of manipulating a satellite that I had—none of that contributed to what *Tomorrow Never Dies* became. I know Bruce Feirstein, who wrote the first and last drafts of *Tomorrow Never Dies*, and there is nothing amongst the treatments that I came up with that works in a way he put together that script."[286]

Instead, let's recognize that Smith was attempting to take the series in a new direction. While Bernard Lee and, to a lesser extent, Robert Brown's fussy and temperamental M was always a beloved figure, Lee and Brown's function in the film was that of a tertiary character, a comic foil, and a functionary who delivered exposition and gave Bond his dangerous assignments. M didn't become a central figure until *The World Is Not Enough*, where the character, now played by Judi Dench, is kidnapped, and again in *Skyfall*, where she is the villain's primary target. Similarly, Ralph Fiennes, who assumed the role of M at the end of *Skyfall*, plays a vital role in *Spectre* (2015), where he joins Bond in the field. In one scene while attempting to apprehend an enemy agent who is trying to kill him, M inadvertently causes the operative to fall to his death. Long gone are the days when a stuffy and exacerbated M sits behind his desk and warns Bond about the dangers of "Jealous husbands. Outraged chefs. Humiliated tailors." It is noteworthy that as far back as 1993 Smith gave M's character greater agency, even if it was largely off-screen. (M was occasionally a more central figure in the novels. For instance, in Fleming's *The Man with the Golden Gun* (1965), where Bond is brainwashed to kill his superior, and in Kingsley Amis' *Colonel Sun*, the first continuation novel published after Fleming's death, when M is kidnapped.)

It is also noteworthy that Smith attempted to introduce Loelia Ponsonby, Bond's secretary in the novels, to the cinematic series. In *Moonraker*, Fleming describes Ponsonby as a "reserved, unbroken beauty to which the war and five years in the Service had lent a touch of sternness."[287] Ponsonby is "one of the most envied girls in the building" who has "access to the innermost secrets of the Service."[288] Whenever I reread the novels, I'm always struck by how much darn paperwork Bond is required to do as part of his job.

In *Moonraker*, Fleming writes that, for Bond, "Mondays were hell. Two days of dockets and files to plough through."[289] In the same novel, Fleming explains that it "was only two or three times a year that an assignment comes along that requires his particular abilities" and that the "rest of the year he has the duties of an easy-going civil servant."[290] Smith's decision to include Ponsonby is a small but pointed acknowledgment of Bond's less-glamorous responsibilities. In *Reunion with Death*, Smith seems to draw on another element of *Moonraker*. In both the novel and the treatment, Bond is identified as the best shot in the service and in both iterations that information is withheld from 007 under orders from M.

Smith's stark and elliptical ending, which I found effective, is perhaps better suited for a Bond novel, where an uplifting ending isn't always expected. Fleming's *Casino Royale*, *On Her Majesty's Secret Service*, and *You Only Live Twice* all have nuanced endings. The producers would likely have preferred not to end the film on a somber note. It is a widely held belief among Bond scholars that *On Her Majesty's Secret Service's* bleak ending, in which Bond's bride is killed, is largely responsible for that exceptional film's disappointing box office results.

However, Bond movies are not the work of one sole voice, working in isolation. The producers, if they wanted to, could have guided Smith into conforming to their vision. Later Bond films, like *Casino Royale*, where Bond falls in love with a woman who betrays him and is then killed, and *Skyfall*, where Bond fails to protect M's life, don't include neat and tidy endings. In those instances, the filmmakers found a way to create satisfying conclusions, even if they weren't "happy" ones.

Unlike William Davies and William Osborne's unproduced Bond 17 screenplay, Smith's treatment suggests that he was not writing an action-comedy. Instead, in the vein of *The Living Daylights*, while delivering both action and humor, Smith wrote a spy thriller that attempts to reveal more qualities of Bond's character, without undermining its appealing mystery. Bond's confession that "I make a habit of pursuing unattainable women" shows another aspect of his personality without offering a reductive explanation.

The line, which shows a sense of self-awareness on Bond's part, also recalls the moment in *The Spy Who Loved Me* when Roger Moore's Bond shows his vulnerability when the subject of his dead wife is brought up. It also echoes the sentiments of the not-yet made *GoldenEye*, when Bond's lover Natalya Simonova asks, "How can you act like this? How can you be so cold?" Bond replies, "It's what keeps me alive." Simonova counters, "No. It's what keeps you alone." All those scenes contain small moments that provide humanizing clues to Bond's inner life.

It doesn't appear that Smith's story ever went beyond the treatment stage. While she's not certain, his wife doesn't think it did. Mariana Smith explained, "I honestly don't know if he ever turned *Reunion with Death* into a screenplay. I don't have a copy or any evidence of it."

While there are many unanswered questions about the treatment, Richard Smith's love of and appreciation for James Bond come through. Smith's writing is brimming with wit and energy. In *Reunion with Death*, Smith sought to deepen Bond's character, reveal more of his personality, and give him a stronger emotional connection to both the mission and to his love interest.

James Bond visits the cemetery, as imagined by Pat Carbajal.
Illustration by Pat Carbajal

Dalton's Unmade First Bond Film:
James Bond's Origin Story

Casino Royale (2006) was not Eon's first attempt to tell James Bond's origin story. Long before Daniel Craig's Bond ordered his first martini in 2006, Albert R. Broccoli considered providing a very different account of Bond's early adventures twenty-one years earlier. The tale by Richard Maibaum and Michael G. Wilson, if it had made it to the screen, would have served as the basis for Timothy Dalton's debut as 007.

In the treatment, Bond is recruited by Her Majesty's Secret Service, nearly bungles his first mission, falls for a woman, gets brutally tortured, and eventually earns his Double-O status. While the plot shares some broad story elements with 2006's *Casino Royale*, the particulars are vastly different.

The following summary is comprised of Richard Maibaum and Michael Wilson's 35-page treatment that is dated November 8, 1985, whose working title was *Bond XV*.[291] Their outline is preserved in the Special Collections Department of the University of Iowa Libraries with the papers of Richard Maibaum.[292]

The film opens with a pre-title sequence set in Austria in 1972. James Bond, who is in his mid to late twenties, is naked in bed with a beautiful woman named Elsa. Post-coitus, she wonders, "Where have you been all my life? Who are you?"[293] Bond responds with his signature, "The name is Bond, James Bond."[294] During their conversation, we are informed that Bond is a Lieutenant in the Royal Navy and he's currently serving as the Assistant Military attaché to the British Embassy in Vienna. Unbeknownst to Bond, Elsa is the fiancée of Austrian diplomat Von Rahm.

Later, Von Rahm invites Bond to go hang gliding with him and when they are airborne, the outraged Von Rahm tries to kill Bond. There is a mid-air "dogfight" in which Von Rahm knocks Bond off his glider, sending him plummeting into Krimml Falls.[295]

That night, Von Rahm and Elsa go to the Vienna Opera House. Bond enters and, in a rage, punches out Von Rahm. A fight ensues where Bond also knocks out some of Von Rahm's bodyguards. Bond turns to Elsa and explains, "I never cared all that much for grand opera."[296]

After the main titles, we find Bond in the British Embassy in Vienna. The Ambassador scolds Bond for knocking "the living daylights" out of Von Rahm and tells Bond that not only has he been recalled but that he will also be court-martialed.[297]

In the next scene, Bond "returns to his ancestral home in the highland."[298] There we meet Bond's "spinster aunt" Charmaine and his "ailing" grandfather with whom he "shoots clay pigeons on the moor."[299] Later, Bond's grandfather summons Bond, whom he calls "Jamie," to his study to talk about Bond's future.[300] Bond's grandfather explains that they are running out of money but even if they had it, Bond would "gamble it away."[301] The grandfather references the family's coat of arms: "The world is not enough."[302] Bond admits that "I never knew what it meant."[303] His grandfather counters, "Someday I hope to God you will, Jamie."[304] The grandfather instructs Bond to see [305]an old suitor of Charmaine who frequents the Blaydes Club. [Note: In the novels, the club is spelled Blades, without the "y."]

At Blaydes, Bond meets an "impressive" man, who sizes up Bond as a "warrior type," and Bond laments "With no war to fight."[306] The impressive man corrects Bond by explaining that there is a "war that never stops. The covert war."[307] The man confides that he's the director of the Intelligence Branch and offers Bond a job. Bond declines. Even the man's offer to help postpone Bond's court-martial doesn't change his mind. As the conversation ends, Bond asks the man how he would like to be addressed. The man responds, "Depends on where we are. Here at the club, it's Admiral Messervy. In my office, it's M."[308]

Later, Bond holds a party at his house. The party, complete with girls and card games, is in full swing when Bond receives an upsetting call from Charmaine. In the next scene, Bond is at his grandfather's funeral. When he returns to his late grandfather's study, he calls M and says, "'I'll give it a try."[309]

In the next scene, Bond is piloting a DC3 airplane to Singapore. He lands in the airfield of Universal Exports, which is the cover name of MI6. There he meets Felix Leiter of the CIA and Q, MI6's weapons expert. Bond says that he's there to meet MI6 agent Bart Trevor. Bond is told that he will find Trevor at the Red Dragon Inn.

At the inn, Bond locates Bart Trevor, who is in his late forties and has a "once handsome face" that is now "ruddied and beaten up by years of hard-living, hard-drinking, and hard-fighting in a dangerous profession."[310] As Bond is about to sit at Trevor's table, Trevor stops him and advises Bond to sit with his "Back to the wall. Eye on the door."[311] Trevor is not impressed by Bond, quickly sizing him up as a "Wet behind the ears navy flyboy."[312] Trevor schools Bond with another rule, "Keep your cool. And while you're at it, keep your mouth shut. That's rule number two."[313] Bond is similarly dismissive of Trevor. For Bond, "This cloak and dagger bump. It went out with the Queen and Country sales pitch."[314]

Trevor tells Bond that their cover, Universal Exports, has a "shady reputation" as a company that "flies anything, for anyone, anywhere, no questions asked."[315] He tells Bond that he will fly Trevor and the crates containing machine parts to General Kwang, who is the "top dog warlord" and the "biggest heroin dealer" in the Golden Triangle, an area in Southeast Asia that comprises Thailand, Laos, and Myanmar.[316] Trevor advises Bond that he was chosen for this assignment only because "no one else was available and time is of the essence."[317] Yet Trevor doesn't trust Bond enough to reveal all the details about the mission. Trevor elaborates on his decision not to disclose further details, "There's an old Chinese proverb, 'The less you know the more you can't tell your torturer.'"[318]

Two "dangerous-looking Malaysians," Dai and Po, approach Bond and Trevor and instruct them to cancel tomorrow's shipment. Trevor explains that Dai and Po work for Kwang's competitor Ambong. Trevor and Bond try to leave but Dai threatens them with a knife. Bond makes a move to fight Dai, but Trevor stops Bond and offers another piece of advice, "Easy does it. Less wear and tear. Let's talk."[319] Dai and Po, thinking they have the upper hand, relax slightly. Trevor uses the momentary lull to his advantage and jumps them. A fight breaks out and Bond and Trevor defeat the men.

Back at the hotel, Bond spots Betje Bedwell, a stunning Eurasian woman wearing "chic Chinese "influence[d] attire" who is accompanied by her "enormous Chinese eunuch" named Kowtow.[320] Bond, who seems to be both attracted to and suspicious of Betje, follows her first to a small apothecary, where she buys a rhinoceros horn and then to a discotheque. Bond joins Betje on the dance floor.

Bond and Betje exit the club to enjoy more of Singapore's nightlife. They form an immediate connection, first dancing on the deck of a Chinese sailing ship and then eating local delicacies from a street vendor. Bond takes Betje to a jewelry shop and buys her a 22K gold covered iris orchid. They are followed by Kowtow. They return to Bond's hotel room where they go to bed together. Later, when Bond asks how they can stay in touch, Betje says that they can never see each other again.

The next day, Bond meets Trevor, Q, and Felix Leiter by the DC3 airplane that Bond will be piloting. They have the crates that they need to transport to Kwang, but they are missing the landing instructions. Betje and Kowtow arrive; she is carrying the box containing the rhino horn. Bond and Betje pretend not to know each other. Betje provides them with landing instructions.

Just then Po and Dai, each driving a truck, descend on them. Dai's truck is equipped with a flamethrower. Bond and company scramble to leave. Trevor shoots at the trucks while Bond rushes to the cockpit and flies the plane out of danger.

As it approaches Thai airspace, the plane is detected and takes on enemy fire before finding safety. While Trevor pilots the plane, Bond inspects one of the crates that they've been transporting and discovers that it contains guns for the Red Chinese army and not machine tools as Trevor originally told him. Bond doesn't understand why the weapons are being delivered to Kwang.

Bond lands the plane in a small hillside village. There they meet La Font, "a handsome, tough Frenchman, former major during the Indo-China war."[321] La Font, who works for Kwang and is in the opium smuggling trade, also "commands Kwang's five hundred men" army, which is comprised of "starving peasantry."[322] Soldiers unload the crate. Bond, Trevor, and La Font ride horses along a jungle path on their way to Kwang.

The trio reaches a Chinese fortress and meets Kwang who is "tall, in his early fifties, with a sensitive face and manner more like a poet's than a warlord."[323] Kwang is painting an image of a "ruined tomb-like structure with three pagoda-like rock formations behind them."[324] Betje, who is Kwang's concubine, appears holding the rhino horn from Shanghai. Betje presents it to Kwang. Bond tells Trevor that the Chinese people consider powdered rhinoceros horns an aphrodisiac.

La Font takes Bond and Trevor to his guest quarters, where they are told to wait. The agents remove Q's toiletry case from their duffle bag and sweep the room for recording devices. Trevor gives Bond rule number three: "Never take anything for granted."[325]

Near the gates of the compound, Bond and Trevor watch as another warlord Kim Feng and three of his men are admitted into the compound. One of Kim Feng's men pulls the pin from a grenade and Bond saves Kwang's life by getting rid of the grenade. La Font shoots Kim Feng's men. Kwang tells Bond that tomorrow he'll test the new weapons "on live targets."[326] Trevor suggests to Kwang that Bond fly over Kim's camp so that the warlord can personally oversee the plan. Kwang, who is grateful to Bond for saving his life, agrees.

Moments later, Trevor tells Bond that his mission was to kidnap or kill Kwang. Trevor explains that Bond interfered with the mission by saving Kwang's life. Trevor also discloses that "I carry a Double-O Section number, with a license to kill."[327] Trevor also informs Bond that British Intelligence and the CIA have joined forces to stop Kwang, who has made a deal with the communist Pathet Lao in Laos to "make the Golden Triangle a base to launch raids in Burma, Thailand, Malaysia..."[328] It dawns on Bond that he ruined Trevor's plans. However, Trevor said that there's still a chance to carry out their plan. Now that Kwang trusts Bond and has agreed to join them on their flight, they can kidnap him.

The next day, Bond readies the plane. He spots several concubines in the jungle. He follows them, discovers the golden orchid he purchased for Betje in Singapore, and locates her. They make love in the reeds. Betje tells Bond about her past. Her father was English and her mother was Asian. After her parents were killed by insurgents when she was just a child, Kwang took her in, sent her to school, and made the now teenaged Betje his favorite concubine.

Since he has recently begun to "lose his sexual prowess,"[329] Kwang sent Betje to Singapore to buy the rhinoceros horn. Betje tells Bond that if Kwang's men discovered that he is no longer virile, he would lose face and his power.

Later at the airstrip, Bond and Trevor are in the DC3. La Font, his soldiers and Song, Kwang's pilot, board the plane. Bond and Trevor realize that they are outmanned and have no choice but to go along with La Font's plan and wait for another opportunity to kidnap Kwang.

Bond flies them to Feng's camp where La Font's men capture Feng. They bring Feng to Kwang. Kwang, who never thought of Feng as an enemy, wants to know why he tried to have him assassinated. Feng says that the deal Kwang made will be the end of all the warlords in the area.

That evening, Kwang holds a victory celebration, where Bond and Trevor are his guests. Trevor sees that Kwang is wearing robes that bear the seal of the Manchu Dynasty. Trevor tells Bond about the Manchu Hoard, a lost cache of gems, gold coins, jewelry, and assorted other riches. Kwang offers Bond and Trevor one hundred thousand dollars if they fly him to a destination of his choice tomorrow. Bond and Trevor, who have been looking for an opportunity to kidnap Kwang, accept. Surreptitiously, Betje hands Bond a note that says that they must talk later that night. As the feast continues, Bond lifts the cover from the next dish to discover that it's Feng's severed head.

Bond goes to the concubines' quarters and finds Betje. She tells Bond that Kwang is leaving the Golden Triangle so that he can escape to South America. Betje, who doesn't want to spend her remaining days with Kwang, begs Bond for his help. Betje reveals that Kwang wants Bond to fly him to China where he hopes to acquire the lost Manchu Hoard, which Kwang intends to split with members of the Pathet Lao. Betje tells Bond that she wants to spend the rest of her life with him. Bond asks if it isn't really the hoard that she's after, but Betje protests that she wants to be with him even if it means living in a "peasant's hut on a bowl of rice."[330]

Unbeknownst to them, Kowtow has been standing outside the room, listening in on Betje's betrayal. Kowtow bursts through the door and attacks Bond. Bond picks up the rhino horn and the charging Kowtow inadvertently impales himself on it, "through an eye, into the brain, dying instantly."[331] Bond tries to escape but is captured by La Font and the guards.

Bond is brought to a cellar where Kwang announces he will kill both Bond and Betje. Trevor intervenes and tells Kwang that Bond might be a British secret agent and not just a mercenary. Trevor recommends that he torture Bond to extract information before killing him. Kwang agrees. In the torture chamber, Bond is beaten with a bamboo cane. Trevor, who is still maintaining his cover story, enters and offers to help torture Bond. But Trevor pulls out a gun that he had assembled from Q's faux-toiletry kit and shoots La Font's henchman. Trevor frees Bond and tells him that they need to escape. Bond says that he won't leave without Betje. Trevor asks Bond if he has feelings for Betje. Bond does. A disappointed Trevor admonishes Bond, "Never fall for a bird on a mission."[332] Trevor tells Bond that saving Betje could jeopardize the mission and says, "You'll never make an agent Bond. Your priorities are screwy."[333]

Bond and Trevor find Betje in a cell where she is being prepared for execution. They kill her captors and free Betje. Outside the courtyard, Trevor tells Bond, "Rule number five. Always look for a way out. I spotted it the day we got here."[334] Trevor shows Bond a way out of the compound.

In the jungle, Bond, who has been weakened by Kowtow, tells Trevor that he's not able to continue and that Trevor and Betje should escape without him. They are chased by four soldiers who are riding horses. Bond hands Trevor his gun. Trevor tells Bond, "Just remember the rules."[335] With that, Trevor makes a stand and allows Bond and Betje to escape. Kwang and La Font arrive on a horse and shoot down Trevor. Bond and Betje escape.

Later, Bond and Betje make love in the jungle. Afterward, they acknowledge that although they are temporarily out of harm's way, Kwang will hunt them down if they don't escape. Bond and Betje go to the airstrip where they see Song's men wearing Red Chinese army uniforms. Kwang and his men are going to fly to China, pose as Chinese government officials, steal the treasure, and depart. Bond sees an airplane, steals it, and uses it to follow Kwang on his way to China. Bond loses Kwang's plane in the clouds but locates him by spotting ruined tombs on the ground that look exactly like the ones that Kwang was painting when they first met.

Bond lands the plane and follows Kwang to the "ruined tombs of an old burial ground" where the hoard is hidden.[336] Posing as a Chinese government official, Kwang meets up with Pathet Lao's men who are wearing Red Army uniforms. Kwang and La Fond enter the catacombs, searching for the treasure. They eventually find the hoard, which is guarded by thirty-foot stone statues in the shape of Devil Dogs. The hoard contains chests with gems and jewelry. Gold coins are hidden inside the Devil Dogs. Kwang orders his men to take the gems and jewelry but to leave the gold from the Devil Dogs for the Pathet Lao.

Bond and Betje spot Kwang's pilot, Song, who is now at the plane and overseeing the transfer of the hoard. Bond and Betje capture Song and use the plane's short-range navigation equipment to inform Felix Leiter of their position and Kwang's plan.

Betje says that she and Bond should steal Kwang's plane and live "like kings" off the treasure.[337] Instead, Bond disables the plane by shooting at the controls. Betje, furious that Bond didn't just take the money, screams, "You lunatic! The world was ours!"[338] Bond quietly responds, "The world is not enough."[339] Betje is stunned to find out that Bond is a British agent and not a mercenary.

Bond and Betje make their way through the nearby burial grounds to get to the catacombs. Betje begs Bond to leave the area. But Bond spots Kwang in the catacombs, and, drawing his gun, goes after him. Betje spots a vanity table filled with jewels.

Bond and Kwang's men engage in a cat and mouse chase and then a shootout in the maze of the catacombs. Bond breaks a vessel containing thousands of gold coins, the coins spew out, and Kwang is buried under them. Betje grabs a sack full of gold coins and the two try to escape. Because the sack of gold is heavy and is slowing her down, Bond throws it away.

Bond and Betje reach their small plane but find that La Font is in it. Armed with a gun, La Font commands Bond to leave Betje behind and pilot the plane. Bond, afraid that Betje will be caught by the Chinese army, asks La Font to take her along. La Font refuses the request. Betje protests but Bond calms her down by repeating Trevor's advice from the bar. "Easy does it. Less wear and tear."[340] When La Font momentarily lowers his gun, Bond grabs for it. After a struggle, the gun goes off, killing La Font.

As Bond flies them away, Betje laments the loss of the fortune. Bond tells her that she needn't worry about money any longer, after all, she did manage to steal a forty-karat diamond from the hoard.

Back in London, Miss Moneypenny lets M know that Bond has arrived. M and his Chief of Staff welcome Bond. The Chief of Staff says, "I am delighted to inform you that you have been appointed to the Double-O section.[341] The Chief of Staff asks M what number they should assign him. M replies, "Why not Trevor's? Double-O-Seven."[342]

M turns to Bond and says that "your next assignment will be to investigate a man in Jamaica, Dr. No."[343]
End of treatment.
Revised Treatment: The November 8, 1985 treatment was not Richard Maibaum and Michael Wilson's only attempt to dramatize Bond's first mission. There are other drafts among Richard Maibaum's papers. There are also a revised 15-page treatment and a 19-page treatment, which are both dated October 25, 1986. However, those dates were handwritten on the documents, suggesting the dates could be approximate and possibly that they were added at a later time. Neither outline has a proper title-page. Instead, the initials RM (for Richard Maibaum) and MGW (for Michael G. Wilson) appear handwritten in black ink. There is also an undated and incomplete 19-page treatment which, if completed, would likely be roughly the same length as the 35-page November 1985 treatment. In

the undated 19-page treatment, Wilson's initials are rendered as "Mw G." There are assorted pages from other drafts but they also appear to be incomplete.

Although the treatments all tell the same basic story, each treatment provides new details, often through additional dialogue or different stage directions. For example, in the original November 8, 1985 treatment, Charmaine's character is not well-defined, but in the incomplete 19-page treatment she is depicted as a loving aunt. And when Bond first sees Charmaine, he "hugs her affectionately. She obviously adores him."[344] In the same outline, before Bond and his grandfather have their uncomfortable talk about how Bond is letting his family down, Charmaine brings them both a couple of glasses of whiskey and suggests that they "Drink up... It'll help you get on with it."[345]

The incomplete outline is also slightly more specific about why Bond was ejected from school. It states that he was "Expelled from Eton for some sort of trouble with a maid,."[346] Fleming referenced the incident with the maid in his novel *You Only Live Twice*. In the revised treatment, M also indicates that Bond went to his father's school "Fesse," and that he was also thrown out of it.[347] Fesse is presumably a typo and a reference to Fettes College, which is also established in *You Only Live Twice* as a school that Bond attended.

The new draft further paints Bond as a callow youth. M paints Bond as someone who lacks "commitment" and "dedication."[348] By the story's end, Bond will have been changed by the experience and he will become a more committed and dedicated man.

The draft also expands on the details of the party in Bond's flat. We know that "jet-set types" are in attendance and that two "party girls" flank Bond while he plays a game of "high stake hearts."[349]

In the October 25, 1986, 19-page outline, when his grandfather is lecturing him about his directionless life, Bond admits that "he knows that he let them [his family] down."[350] We also learn that as Charmaine weeps at his grandfather's funeral, "Bond's face is impassive."[351]

In this treatment, we are also told that when Bond is dispatched on the mission he is slightingly referred to as "Sub Agent Bond."[352]

In the November 1985 treatment, Bond orders a martini, shaken not stirred. In the revised treatment, he only orders the double martini and it's Trevor who adds, "Shaken not stirred, I hope."[353] When the waitress brings Bond his drink, he sends it back because it's "Not dry enough."[354]

In the incomplete 19-page treatment Bond shows his inexperience during the attack at the airport. In it, Trevor and Leiter play a more central role while Bond is more of an observer who has to "pick himself up" off the ground after the seasoned professionals neutralize the threat.[355]

In the revised treatment, Maibaum and Wilson elaborate on Trevor's advice that Bond stand down and not get into the fight at the bar. In the alternative version, Trevor instructs, "Let's talk to them. Less wear and tear on the nervous system."[356]

Bond's interest in cards is also given greater emphasis in the revision. He gambles at the party[357] and plays a game of solitaire while spying on Betje at his hotel.[358]

Bond's budding romance with Betje is also brought into sharper focus. When Bond and Betje spend time together in Shanghai the writers note that "Without actually hearing their conversations, what we have seen clearly indicates the growing fascination and physical attraction between them."[359] The sequence recalls the montage in *On Her Majesty's Secret Service* (1969) in which Bond and Tracy fall in love. And when Betje initially tells Bond that while she will always remember their time together, but they can't see each other again, Bond is "uncharacteristically moved."[360]

In the November 8, 1985, treatment, Bond and Von Rahm engage in a mid-air hang-gliding fight. In the undated and incomplete 19-page treatment, they go on a fishing trip, a considerably less dramatic choice.[361] While in a rowboat, Von Rahm tries to kill Bond by smashing him over the head with the oar and then tossing him into the river.[362] Yet, it should be noted that the writers had intended to flesh out the sequence and ratchet up the action. They write: "The following is only meant to suggest the locale and incidents of the action sequence we eventually hope to devise here."[363]

In the November 8, 1985 treatment, Bond kills La Font as they struggle for a gun while in the October 25, 1986 treatment, he dispatches the villain in a more brutal fashion. In that version, the gun-wielding La Font offers to spare Bond because he needs a pilot but insists that Betje stays in China. Bond seems to comply but then he "slides" a "bayonet out of his boot" and "stabs La Font in the belly."[364]

Maibaum and Wilson's script would have helped explain why Bond usually doesn't get romantically involved with women. In a 5-page addendum to the November 8, 1995 treatment, when Bond wants to save Betje, Trevor asks, "Don't tell me you love her." Bond's "silence confirms his suspicion." Trevor says, "You've just violated rule number one. Don't fall in love on a mission."[365] In another undated treatment, Bond offers to take Betje back to London to live with him. But Betje rejects Bond's offer because his salary wouldn't allow her to live in the style to which she's accustomed.

In the October 25, 1986 treatment, Bond "kills Kwang as he begs for mercy as he is being buried alive by the cascading gold coins.[366] Maibaum and Wilson suggest that scene is meant to be "reminiscent of the 'You've had your six' scene in *From Russia with Love* (1963)." The difference between the scene with Kwang and the scene in the Connery film is that Connery killed a defenseless man, and, in this treatment, Bond is providing a small act of mercy in an otherwise agonizing death. Of course, Bond fans know that the "had your six" line is from *Dr. No* (1962) and not *From Russia with Love*, but these renowned Bond writers can be forgiven for a slight slip. But what's interesting here is that Maibaum and Wilson wanted Bond to kill in cold blood and not in self-defense, as is usually the case.

Bond's History: In *Bond XV*, Richard Maibaum and Michael Wilson provide interesting details concerning Bond's personal life. From the treatment and from Bond's grandfather, we know that Bond was orphaned at the age of six when his parents were killed in a mountain-climbing accident, and he was brought up by his aunt. This version of his biography mirrors Ian Fleming's own accounts of Bond's backstory.

At his meeting with M at Blaydes, Bond's file states that he was expelled from Eton after an incident involving a girl, that he spent six years in Swiss schools, that Bond learned a wide variety of esoteric subjects on his own, and that he speaks "a smattering" of French, German, and Chinese.[367] All of these details roughly echo Bond's biography from Fleming's novels. However, in SMERSH's dossier on Bond in *From Russia with Love*, Fleming writes that Bond is fluent in French and German. Chinese is not mentioned in the novel but, in the movie *You Only Live Twice* (1967), it is established that Bond "took a first in Oriental languages at Cambridge."

The file also notes that Bond, who has a high IQ and a photographic memory, joined the navy, where he excelled in flight school and commando training, but was insubordinate and often AOL.[368]

In the undated and incomplete 19-page treatment, Bond's grandfather tells James that the entire Bond family is cut from the same cloth: "We've had our share of gamblers, womanizers and alcoholics."[369] Bond jokingly laments, "So it all comes to whose genes I inherited."[370] His grandfather dismisses that assessment and says, "It's not in the genes." and then pointing to his head and heart says that "It's here, and here."[371] In the same treatment,

Bond tells his grandfather that he's "never gone for all that Queen and Country stuff." and that he only joined the navy "because I didn't know what else to do. I still don't."[372]

In the November 1985 draft, we are told that Bond's family home is in Scotland, but in the undated and incomplete 19-page draft, the area is identified specifically as being "near Glencoe."[373] In the same treatment, Maibaum and Wilson put Bond behind the wheel of a Bentley[374], and not the Aston Martin. The Bentley is the car that Bond drove in the novels *Casino Royale* (1953), *Live and Let Die* (1954), *Moonraker* (1955), *From Russia with Love* (1957), *Thunderball* (1961), *On Her Majesty's Secret Service* (1963), *You Only Live Twice* (1964) and in the short story "*The Living Daylights*" (1962).

Trevor: In the 19-page incomplete treatment, Maibaum and Wilson change Trevor's first name from Bart to Burton.[375] We're told that he looks like a cross between Trevor Howard and Richard Burton,[376] who prior to Sean Connery's casting was one of the actors being considered to play 007. Connery would play opposite Howard in director Sidney Lumet's 1973 crime drama *The Offence*.

Much of Trevor's advice will form the basis of Bond's operational behavior in later missions. Most notably, Bond will rarely again fall for a woman while carrying out his mission. Trevor also teaches Bond that the best way to get out of danger is through talking. It's a technique that Bond relies on frequently. For instance, in *Goldfinger* (1964), when captured, defenseless, and is at risk of being cut in half by a laser, the fast-talking agent bluffs his way out of danger.

Bond's grandfather is fleshed out in the revisions. He is described as bearing a resemblance to the English actor Donald Crisp [*How Green Was My Valley* (1941)] and we are told that he speaks with a Scottish burr.[377]

Charmaine: Aunt Charmaine was a character created by Ian Fleming in the novel *You Only Live Twice*. Fleming spells her name as "Charmian." As in the novel, Charmaine takes Bond in and raises him.

The Mission: Richard Maibaum and Michael Wilson came up with a clever conceit for Bond's first mission—MI6 needs his skills as a pilot and not necessarily as a secret agent. While Bond has flown many aircraft in the previous movies, his piloting abilities have been ancillary to his main assignment. But, in *Bond XV*, Bond's aviator skills are the reason that he's been assigned to this mission.

Bond Women: There is essentially only one Bond Woman (Betje Bedwell) in the outline. The brief exceptions are his brief dalliance with Elsa in the pre-credit sequence and presumably his flirtations with the woman at his party. The treatment suggests that Bond actually falls in love with Betje or is at the least extremely taken with her. There are several scenes where their courtship is shown, including their time together in Singapore, where Bond buys her jewelry, an uncharacteristically romantic gesture for the cinematic spy. In one version of the treatment, Bond suggests that they live together. The Bond of the novels also formed relationships with women, including Tiffany Case, that would extend beyond the missions.

Pre-credit Sequence: The pre-credit sequence involves Bond battling an adversary while hang gliding. Hang gliding might not seem to be intrinsically dramatic. Nevertheless, I don't think Maibaum and Wilson had traditional hang gliders in mind when they wrote the sequence. Among the papers, was a doodle of what might have been high-tech hang gliders. Unlike traditional hang gliders where the operators are lying flat with their bodies completely exposed, the drawing depicts a figure who is sitting upright in what appears to be a motorized vehicle, almost like a helicopter.

Another thing to keep in mind is that the hang glider sequence would have been directed by John Glen, who orchestrated some of Bond's most iconic stunts, including the ski jump off the cliff in *The Spy Who Loved Me* and Bond's free-fall from an airplane in *Moonraker*. The writers seemed to have extreme faith in his abilities. In another treatment for the sixteenth Bond film, for an unrelated stunt, they write that the "action Bond takes against Sanchez will have to be devised by J. Glen, world's best action director."[378]

007: After successfully completing his mission, Bond is given his license to kill and is assigned the prefix of 007. In the last scene of the draft, we learn that Trevor was the previous 007. M's decision to assign him the same number appears to be practical, not sentimental. M doesn't seem to consider the idea that Trevor had become something of a professional mentor to Bond.

In Anthony Horowitz's continuation novel *Forever and a Day*, Bond is also assigned his name after a fallen agent. The difference is that in *Forever and a Day* (2018), Bond's first mission is to find out who killed the previous 007. In *Bond XV*, M gives Bond the code name but in Horowitz's book Bond selects the numbers himself, as a tribute to his predecessor.

Title of the Movie: I suspect that the working title for the treatment was *The Living Daylights*. Not only would Timothy Dalton's debut bear the title of Fleming's short story of the same name, but the phrase appears in the treatment. In it, Bond is scolded for beating "the living daylights" out of a superior officer. In the October 25, 1986 treatment, the living daylights also appears but it's used in a different context. In that version, Kwang commands that Bond be "put to the Living Daylights torture."[379]

Legacy: *Skyfall* (2012), the twenty-third Bond film, contains several plot points that echo scenes from the *Bond XV* treatment. For example, in the pre-title sequence in the treatment, Bond falls from a great height, and his fate unknown. In it, Maibaum and Wilson write, "We do not see whether Bond survives." Similarly, the pre-title sequence in *Skyfall* concludes when Bond falls off the train, shot, and is presumed dead.

In the treatment, Bond and his grandfather engage in target practice. In *Skyfall*, Bond and Kinkaid, played by Albert Finney, also shoot targets at Bond's ancestral home. In it, Kinkaid tells Bond, "Now remember what I taught you."[380] In both the treatment and *Skyfall*, Bond impressively hits his targets while his shooting mentor looks on admiringly.

Bond's grandfather in the treatment and Kinkaid (Albert Finney) in *Skyfall* seem to serve similar functions. However, Kinkaid is the groundskeeper and not a blood relative. While Bond and Kinkaid's relationship is familiar, the fact that they are not related is an effective way to keep Bond emotionally isolated.

Nevertheless, we shouldn't assume that the *Skyfall* filmmakers were drawing from Maibaum and Wilson's treatment when coming up with the plot for Daniel Craig's fourth Bond movie. While Michael Wilson was the writer of the treatment and a producer of *Skyfall*, it doesn't necessarily mean that he shared his discarded story with that movies' writers. It's possible that they came to these creative decisions independently. For example, although Bond's mentor Trevor was meant to wear a "scarf around his throat"[39], and Bond wears one in *Skyfall*, Jany Temime, the movie's costume designer costumer, told me in an interview that I conducted with her that she was thinking of World War II commander Bernard Montgomery when she dressed Daniel Craig in the scarf.

At the same time, neither does it appear that Eon completely disregarded Maibaum and Wilson's old treatment. While discussing the development of the screenplay for *Casino Royale*, Michael Wilson recalled that the filmmakers "really didn't rely much upon the work that I'd done with Richard Maibaum. This film [is] pretty much the ideas [of screenwriters Neal] Purvis and [Robert] Wade."[381] Given Wilson's statements, it is possible the treatment influenced *Skyfall* to some extent, particularly with regards to the creation of Kinkaid.

Licence to Kill: While Maibaum and Wilson's story about a pre-007 Bond was abandoned in favor of a more traditional tale for *The Living Daylights*, it seems that the writers returned to the story while figuring out the plot for *Licence to Kill* (1989), Dalton's second Bond film. A draft of the treatment for *Bond XVI* would also feature the character names of Betje, Kwang, Kowtow, and La Font. While Kwang would remain a warlord and Betje would still be his concubine, the overall plot for *Bond XVI* is different from *Bond XV*.

Still, some elements of the *Bond XVI* treatment survived. Both *Bond XVI* and *Licence to Kill* feature an unsavory villain by the name of Milton Krest. In *Bond XVI*, M instructs Bond to see if the philanthropist Milton Krest is actually involved in smuggling "priceless antiquities" out of China.[382] Later, Bond discovers that Krest's real scheme involves a scientific discovery for commercial superconductivity, which "would mean untold billions for whoever patents it first."[383]

However, the *Bond XVI* treatment hews closer to the plot of Ian Fleming's "The Hildebrand Rarity," which is about Krest's obsession with a rare fish, than *Licence to Kill* does. In both the 1960 short story and the treatment, Krest meets his end by suffocating on the fish that has been forced into his mouth. In the short story, Bond suspects that Krest's abused wife has killed him, but in the treatment, it is Bond who gives Krest his just deserts. Bond "jams the needle-sharp finned fish" into the villain's mouth and coolly reasons, "You caught it. You eat it."[384]

The 37-page treatment also revealed that Kwang and Krest were actually the same person and that for Kwang, Krest was merely a "convenient charade," a "cover to operate in the business world."[385] A variation on the ploy of the villain assuming a new identity was used in *Die Another Day*.

Continuity: The movie would then have ended with M ordering the newly minted 007 to investigate Doctor No in Jamaica, a clear reference to the first Bond movie. Nevertheless, it would be problematic to begin a new Bond actor's era with a mission that dovetails into Connery's first movie. It raises the question, what would Bond's next mission be? Would 007's future missions take place unchronologically but as part of Eon's previous films? The sequels could have been set between Sean Connery, George Lazenby, and Roger Moore's adventures. Alternatively, might *Bond XV* be the beginning of a separate but parallel timeline? Or would the series return to the established continuity and resume Bond's adventures immediately after *A View to a Kill* (1985), Moore's last mission? My guess is that the origin story would be a one-off experiment and not necessarily part of a new narrative.

Another potential issue is that Connery's Bond in *Dr. No* is already a proficient agent; although the Bond in the treatment learns a great many skills, he does not seem quite as capable as the Connery's Bond. So, the decision to make *Bond XV* an immediate prequel to *Dr. No* doesn't seem to add up completely.

Continuity aside, Eon would have other matters to address had they gone forward with Maibaum and Wilson's treatment. *Bond XV*, which is set in the nineteen-seventies but written in the mid-nineteen-eighties is a period piece. The period isn't central to the plot. The setting for this story was chosen in order to examine the youthful Bond's lack of experience and witness his growth. However, the choice raises some concerns. Would subsequent films also take place in the nineteen-seventies? Or would they resume being contemporary? If it's the latter—and even if it is a one-off experiment—it is likely to seem odd to an audience that the same Bond actor hasn't aged in a later decade.

One of the reasons that the script was not used was that Albert Broccoli believed that fans wanted to see the agent at the "height of his powers," not a novice. The Craig era Bond films adeptly handled this issue and addressed Broccoli's concerns by making Craig's Bond in *Casino Royale* as skilled and as lethal as any previous Bond but at the same time making his Bond the most emotionally raw. So Craig's Bond had room to grow emotionally from film to film.

It should be noted that the Bond in this treatment does develop as a character. He goes from being a directionless and callow lad to a man who learns to value more than his own immediate interests.

The Bond in these treatments is more emotionally vulnerable than audiences were accustomed to at the time. For instance, when Bond goes to his house in the undated and incomplete 19-page treatment, we're told that he's "oddly moved" to be in his ancestral home and that he "brusquely" attempts to conceal the emotions that are swelling inside of him.[386] In the November 1985 treatment, Betje asks Bond why Trevor sacrificed himself, "Why did he do it? For you?" Bond can only nod mutely.[387]

The torture depicted in the treatment would have been the most severe of any Bond film to date. Bond would not have recovered from it immediately, instead, its effects would be felt throughout the rest of the story. In fact, Bond would have been so severely damaged that he'd tell Trevor to "Take Betje and go on without me."

There are few Roger Moore-era puns. When Bond and Trevor are held captive in the Fortress, they open the window and survey the land for an escape route. Trevor tests the terrain by rolling a melon off the roof, which is "impaled on sharp spikes." Bond quips, "You've made your point."[388] Similarly, Betje's last name Bedwell (bed well) is a pun in the tradition of Holly Goodhead, Plenty O'Toole, and Pussy Galore.

In the November 1985 draft, Bond orders a "double martini, shaken not stirred." Ordering a "double" is a slight variation on 007's familiar drink of choice.

When Bond first introduces himself to Elsa, in the pre-title sequence, he says, "The name is Bond, James Bond."[389] In another draft of the treatment, Maibaum, and Wilson use the same line but they write it differently: "'The name is Bond,' he tells her, 'James Bond.'"[390] In this rendering, the writers highlight the natural pause in the line's delivery.

Final Thoughts: I am a huge admirer of Richard Maibaum and Michael Wilson's writing, and I believe that the treatments preserved in The University of Iowa library provide a fascinating peek into their craft. The treatments also reveal how densely plotted Bond films are. Their treatment doesn't rely on alluding to fan-favorite Bond moments, such as how Bond orders his drinks or how he introduces himself. Instead, the treatments are stripped-down blueprints for an unmade film. The story's impact is enhanced by the sheer velocity of the movement from one essential plot point to the next. While fans can participate in good-natured debates about the merits of their story and Eon's decision to abandon it, one thing is undeniable—Maibaum and Wilson's treatments are fascinating Bond artifacts for aficionados and scholars to study and enjoy, which offer a tantalizing glimpse into Bond's alternative cinematic history.

James Bond hang gliding, as imagined by Pat Carbajal.

Section 2 – Roger Moore and Pierce Brosnan's Lost Bond Movies

Unmade The Spy Who Loved Me
John Landis

Before making a name for himself as the director of anti-establishment comedies including *Animal House* (1978), *The Blues Brothers* (1980), which he also co-wrote, and *Trading Places* (1983), the genre-bending horror-comedy *An American Werewolf in London* (1980), which he wrote, and the Michael Jackson music video *Thriller* (1983), which he co-wrote, John Landis was a young filmmaker trying to establish himself in Hollywood.

He was given his lucky break when he was hired by Albert "Cubby" Broccoli to write the screenplay for *The Spy Who Loved Me* (1977). But when director Guy Hamilton, who had directed the three previous Bond films, left the project, Landis followed suit.

Landis told me that while he was working in London that he got a taste of Broccoli's legendary largesse. One day Broccoli stopped by Landis' office to see how he was doing. Landis playfully chided Broccoli that he was disappointed that while he'd been in England for a couple of weeks that he still hadn't met the Queen. When Broccoli apologized, Landis reassured the producer that he was only kidding. A short time later and without explaining why, Broccoli told Landis to stop working and follow him on an excursion. After Broccoli footed the bill for a quick wardrobe change for the casually attired scribe, Landis accompanied his employer on an undisclosed mission. At their destination, Landis took notice as the crowd parted to make way for Broccoli, as the purpose of their sojourn was revealed. There stood Her Majesty The Queen. To his shock, Landis was granted an audience with her royal highness. After a brief but engaging conversation, the two men took their leave and the young writer was left with the impression that Broccoli might be the unofficial King of England.

Landis' experience working on *The Spy Who Loved Me* was short-lived and little, if any, of his work made it into the finished film, which was eventually written by Richard Maibaum and Christopher Wood and was directed by Lewis Gilbert. However, the notion of the irreverent Landis writing a Bond film is a tantalizing "What if?"

***

How'd you get hired?

It was 1975 and I was twenty-five. I was working as a writer and I was doing all kinds of silly jobs. I'd made my first film, which was called *Schlock* (1973) when I was twenty-one and that made me a director. When you read bios of me, they say, "He made his first film at twenty-one." but they don't mention that between my first film and my second film was four years. During that period, I parked a lot of cars, did all kinds of menial jobs and [as a stuntman I] fell off a lot of horses. But I was also working as a writer. I was writing television and rewriting movies. It's one of those classic Hollywood stories. I wrote the screenplay for *American Werewolf in London* when I was eighteen. I wrote that in 1969, and I made the movie in 1981. But in any case, someone at Eon Productions read that script and liked it.

And then I know that I was called in one week. It was actually kind of heady. In one week, I had these three giant meetings. One with Cubby Broccoli about the new James Bond movie. One with Milos Forman about writing the screenplay for *Hair*. And one was with Dino De Laurentiis, who wanted to make what he called a big monster movie. This was the time of *The Towering Inferno* (1974), *Earthquake* (1974), and *Poseidon Adventure* (1972), all these big disaster films.

Dino wanted to make a disaster film, but he wanted the disaster to be caused by a big monster. I had this long meeting with him in his bungalow, in which I'd learned that he'd never seen *King Kong* (1933). He'd never heard of *Godzilla* (1954). He'd never seen *The Beast from 20,000 Fathoms* (1953). He was kind of unschooled in big monsters. He was thinking more about the Cyclops in *Ulysses* [than about classic movie monsters]. So I screened *King Kong* and *Godzilla* for him. I made a list of other movies for him to see. This went on for three or four days.

Then I went and met with Milos Forman at the Beverly Wilshire Hotel. Milos had *just* won his Oscar for Best Director for *One Flew Over the Cuckoo's Nest* (1975). The statue was literally on the coffee table in the suite at the hotel. When Milos first came to America from behind the Iron Curtain in Czechoslovakia, he saw *Hair* on Broadway. It was an incredible revelation for him, and he desperately wanted to make *Hair* into a film. He had been pursuing it for years and now that he was a major player, he was going to make *Hair*. So I met with him about *Hair,* but I'd never seen it. So I got the libretto and I listened to the album. I went in and had a good meeting with Milos, who I'd met years before at one of the first screenings of *Schlock*. Mike Medavoy and Donald Sutherland brought him. I was excited to meet this guy because he made *The Loves of a Blonde* (1965), and *Black Peter* (1964), and *The Fireman's Ball* (1967). I'd seen all those wonderful movies. He's a very charming and wonderful man. But I remember very well the death of my opportunity in that meeting. He's sitting there with a big cigar and his Oscar and he asked me if I'd seen his films.

I said, "Of course, Milos, I've seen I think all of your films." He asked me which one was my favorite and I said, "*Fireman's Ball.*" And he literally did a double take. He said, "*Fireman's Ball*?" I said, Yeah. He asked, "Why?" I said it was sweet and very funny, and I love *Fireman's Ball*. It's wonderful; it's about a small village in Czechoslovakia and the local volunteer fire department is having a ball to raise money. It's not grand; it's just a very funny comedy about what happens. But Milos was taken aback. He said, "Really? Well, what's your second favorite movie of mine?" I replied, "Probably *Black Peter* because it's a very dark comedy and I like that." He looked at me and asked, "What's your third favorite movie?" I said *Loves of a Blonde* is wonderful. Then he points at the Oscar and asked, "What about *Cuckoo's Nest*?" I told him I really loved *Cuckoo's Nest*. He said, "If you really loved *Cuckoo's Nest*, why is it four? Four? Those other movies are Czech." He was just appalled.

Then he points at the Oscar and says, "You didn't like *Cuckoo's Nest* as much as you like *Fireman's Ball*?" I told him truthfully that *Cuckoo's Nest* is from a classic novel by Ken Kesey that I adore. I loved the movie but it's different from the book, which I have a lot of emotional investment in. Anyway, it was a cordial meeting, and he's a wonderful man. But boy, I realized that I shot myself in the foot. So I didn't get that job.

But I met with Cubby. I remember going to his house off Sunset. But what I remember so well was driving up to the gate and then the gates open. It was like a chateau in France. I was going up this big drive and thinking, "Wow. Who knew all this land was here?" Cubby met me, and he was very nice. We had a very good meeting. He's a charming guy. And he's very warm. We talked about James Bond and other things. He told me they were doing *The Spy Who Loved Me*. Did you ever read the book?

Yes, the narrator is a woman, so it's told from her point of view. Bond is absent for most of it.

Right, it has nothing to do with the movie. He said, "Well, there's no movie there. So we want to come up with something original." We had a nice talk, and I made some stuff up. Then I had this whole bunch of meetings with Dino. So I was thinking, "I'm gonna write a big monster movie." But then I got a job offer from the Bond people. And within two days or so, I'm flying to London. First class.

It was quite something. It was all very exciting and glamorous. I was in London for around eight weeks. I've forgotten exactly how long it was. But when I was in London, there was a big trade announcement that Dino De Laurentiis is making *King Kong* (1976). And I thought, "You bastard! Wait a minute. I really felt cheated."

So that's how I got the job.

What do you remember about that first meeting with Cubby?

Just that he was warm and friendly and thoughtful and wanted to know my ideas.

Had you read the script at that point?

There was no script.

Not even a draft from a previous writer?

Not until a year after I left. I couldn't honestly tell you whose it was but when I got to London, Guy Hamilton [who was the original director on the film] and I talked about having a Captain Nemo type character in an underwater city. We also talked about having a submarine. I'm not sure if that came from Guy Hamilton or someone else but we were developing all those ideas. It evolved into what you see in the movie [with Karl Stromberg and his underwater base]. We didn't have Jaws, a giant guy with steel teeth. We didn't go to Egypt. But we did have a Russian agent. The movie that was made was not the movie I was writing.

After every few pictures, there seems to be a period of transition when Bond films are undergoing an evolution. It seems like that was one of those times.

What became very clear within a week of being there was that there was major tension. Not that I ever had a confrontation or anything, but it was very awkward. I was probably feeding off of Guy Hamilton's frustration, because he had been working on it for months, and he was getting really aggravated. He'd say, "They're not going to make this fucking movie." Because even though they were still partners at that time, Harry and Cubby were suing one another. So, it was difficult.

It's very interesting because I came along after they had done the George Lazenby movie. Have you seen it?

I love it.

Yeah, it's a very good movie, but the public didn't spark to Lazenby. He was foolish. He behaved badly and he alienated Cubby and Harry by being a jerk. Which, he admits freely now. I met George Lazenby two years later when I made *Kentucky Fried Movie* (1977); he's in the movie.

Did you talk to Lazenby about playing Bond?

Yes, I did. He said, "I was a fool."

Even then, in the late nineteen-seventies, he realized that he made a mistake?

Oh, my god, yes. Full of regret. [During the making of *On Her Majesty's Secret Service*] he suddenly felt he was a huge star. He was really foolish, but the big thing was his demands. By the way, I think he's not bad.

He's very vulnerable.

Yes, but the move has a bad rap. Did you see [Christopher Nolan's 2010] *Inception*? They copy the whole snow raid sequence from the end of *On Her Majesty's Secret Service*.

Straight from the film.

It was crazy. It looks like the same location. But Roger played it much lighter than Sean or Lazenby. Roger was sort of a light comedian. *Live and Let Die* (1973) is also a bizarre movie because it was a black exploitation film [disguised as Bond film]. There was the weird voodoo stuff. I mean like what the hell? It's a wacky movie.

The one thing I remember very well about working in London was that I had an office, which I shared with [*A Clockwork Orange* writer] Anthony Burgess for a while. But then he was let go. He was a fascinating man, and I enjoyed him tremendously. I had a treatment written by Tony Burgess that's on [the lightweight but durable] onion-skin paper on an old fashioned typewriter. He wrote this very dense treatment about the abduction of the pope. I was so amused by Cubby's reaction, which was "Are you crazy?" I had the treatment, but I just gave it to the Academy [of Motion Picture Arts and Sciences] library; I gave all my papers to the Academy.

What was Burgess's concept, that the pope was abducted?

SPECTRE or SMERSH abducts the pope. They make it seem like it's a normal kidnapping, but in fact, it became very complicated. A bomb was put in the Holy City, an atomic weapon. It dealt with the Vatican bank and with the US Treasury.

Sounds political.

It was political and it was outrageous. But more than that it was sacrilegious. And I think that was Cubby's objection. It was just too far.

What kinds of scenes were you writing?

I wrote many pre-title sequences. They became more and more outrageous. Guy Hamilton said a wonderful thing to me. He said, "The whole point of these sequences is to tell the audience, 'Right, put your brain under the seat, and here we go.'"

But I had an idea, and it was dealing with the fact that no matter what happened to Roger in his last Bond movie that his hair was perfect, and he never sweated. He never broke a sweat and you never felt he was in true jeopardy. So my idea was you fade up on a Latin American plaza, with a fountain in the middle, and a big church. It's somewhere in South America or Central America. It's Hispanic. It's a market day, so all the peasants are coming in, and there are fruit and vegetable stalls, and selling, pottery, and there's just all this stuff going on. They're going about their business.

You establish with the palm trees, and the heat and everything, and then, suddenly, Roger Moore staggers into the frame, and he's bloody. His clothing is torn and it's all fucked up, and his hair is a mess. And I wanted him to have a gash on his forehead with blood dripping down his face. So he's clearly in jeopardy and in trouble. He staggers into the fountain and throws water on his face. And then we hear kind of shouting, gunshots, and armored vehicles.

We hear trucks coming and horses. So he staggers, runs up and opens the big door of the cathedral, and goes inside. As soon as he's in the cathedral, these trucks, and jeeps full of soldiers and soldiers mounted on horseback—all of these guys come, the troops, the Federales—come pouring into the plaza. And they're brutal, and the commander is shouting out Spanish instructions, "Andale! Vamanos!" He's yelling and screaming, "Find him."

They're just ripping the place apart. They tear the plaza apart, and they're extremely brutal. And they knock shit over and toss things aside. They're just trying to find him. And they can't find him, and the peasants are being brutalized. Then the commandant looks toward the church, nods his head, and then we see those boots of the troops running up those marble steps.

Now we're inside, and it's an old Catholic Spanish cathedral. The doors open, boom! And the light pours in. And there's only one figure, and it's praying in front of a statue of the Virgin Mary inside the front of the church, and the troops go up and down every aisle of the pews with guns looking for Bond. They open the confessionals and pull out the priests and the people with guns in their faces, and there's this one woman with a black shawl. And they go to this figure, and they rip the shawl off, and it's this very elderly woman terrified. It's not James Bond,

They don't know where to look, and so they go, "Okay, he's not in here." And they all pour outside. And then the camera turns 360 degrees to the altar and moves in on a big Spanish altar. It's very Rococo and there's a giant crucifix with a large figure of Christ on the cross. And the camera goes up, and then around, and on the back of the crucifix is James Bond. Hiding. Crucified.

So I had this idea that Guy Hamilton was very enthusiastic about. He said, "I want you to pitch it to Cubby." I do all this pitch, and it's much more coherent, and I finish, and Guy's beaming. Cubby looks at me, he says, "So James is on the cross." I said, "Yeah, he's hiding behind the figure of Christ." Cubby said, "Are you fucking crazy?" Then I go outside, and I realize that Guy Hamilton kinda set me up. Guy, you motherfucker!

He knew that was a nonstarter.

Guy obviously knew it. I didn't know it; I liked it. I was just there trying to come up with stuff. I wrote a lot of stuff. I have no idea where it is or what happened to it. It was a long time ago.

But Cubby Broccoli was very warm and very generous to me. It was freezing in London, and I'm coming from Southern California. He said to me, "Do you have a coat?" I just had this light jacket. And he came in one day with a coat, a big heavy coat. He was nice. He was very lovely. I can't speak warmly enough about him.

I did not know Harry as well. I had two dinners with Harry, two or three lunches, and then three or four meetings. I was only in his office once. But that was it. I was not working in Harry's office. Harry was kind of a short guy and a little overweight. He wore outrageous colors. Very bright colors. He was nice too. I wish I had something salacious to say. I was well treated. It was sad because I would've liked to be involved more.

But Guy quit. He said, "I can't continue. They're not gonna make this movie." And it's true. They were distracted. Both of them. In fact, they didn't make the film for quite a while. What was the date of that movie?

It was released in 1977.

Right. I was there in '75. They had to resolve all their legal issues. Once they dissolved their partnership, then Cubby was free to just go ahead and make the movies.

In your pre-credit sequence, you wanted to put Bond through his paces.

I wanted him to be clearly in jeopardy and for the audience to see that there was a real threat. In *From Russia With Love*, which is I still think the best one; you feel that Robert Shaw's character is a formidable foe.

But now it's not as elegantly done as it could be. But at the time [during the pre-title sequence in *Goldfinger*], it was just such a wonderful idea to come out of the harbor with scuba gear on and take it off and reveal that he's been wearing a white dinner jacket. Then he fights with a stunt guy, Alf Joint, who I used many years later to gaff the stunts in *American Werewolf in London*. But when you work on British movies, there were these 12 stunt guys [that did all the stunts in a variety of different movies.]

I knew all the stunt guys in Hollywood. There was a scene in *Heat* where this armored car that transports money pulls up, and I saw that the driver was Rick Avery. Rick Avery's a stuntman who's gaffed several movies for me, and I went, "Uh oh. Something violent is about to happen." Having worked in Europe and with all the British films, it was like, "Uh oh, there's Eddie Powell. There's Alf Joint. Shit's about to go down."

There was a period in the nineteen-sixties and -seventies where if they cut to pedestrians, I would notice all these people were wearing sneakers. I thought, "Uh oh! Some car is about to drive through here." The stuntmen wear sneakers so they can leap out of the way. I just did stunts for a while.

Anyway, Alf Joint has a fight in *Goldfinger*. It's the scene where Bond goes into a club where there's a belly dancer and he goes back to her room. Alf Joint is the guy who attacks Bond. He's a broad guy and they have that brutal fight. Bond throws him in the bathtub, throws the heater in there and Alf Joint is electrified. That's him. Sean Connery's Bond was a brutal guy. Those fights had real jeopardy. Rosa Klebb, with that knife [affixed to the end of her shoe], was also scary. They've become less and less real. They've become more and more fantastic. *The Spy Who Loved Me* had a lot of fantasy elements in it.

What's very interesting is that as the Bond pictures evolve, they always try to be contemporary. They always try to go with the times. That's why they have whoever the hit person is at the moment, whether it's Madonna [singing the title song to *Die Another Day* (2002)] or Carly Simon [singing *The Spy Who Loved Me*]. But the most exciting stuff is when that genius Monty Norman music comes on. Dum-dum-dum-dum. The audience sort of sits up, it's like getting into gear. I think the old tropes are what work the best in Bond.

They didn't go into the internal life of Bond until the Daniel Craig films.

Well, no, that's very modern. That's Sam Mendes.

Did you ever think about Bond's personal life, or what motivated him?

Truthfully, I can't remember. I remember I did write a sequence where Bond is attacked by this machine; it's a killer machine. And it gets hairier and hairier for Bond. Bond [fights back and] is beating the shit out of it but the machine is [getting the better of Bond and is] about to kill him. It's literally about to kill him when suddenly it stops, then Q walks in, and we reveal that it was a training exercise. They said, "James, you died." So they take him off the case. They sort of did later [in the non-EON production *Never Say Never Again* and in *Die Another Day*]. But there've been so many writers and so many cooks. Everybody had input on those things.

You were working in the office.

I was in the office writing. I wasn't in production. They were two years away from making a movie. That was why Guy quit. There was all this Sturm und Drang and drama going on that I was not privy to.

After you left the film did you keep in touch with Cubby?

We weren't social or anything. But years later he offered me the opportunity to direct a Bond movie. What's the one where Robert Davi's the bad guy?

Licence to Kill

Licence to Kill. My agent got a call from Cubby and I'd already made a bunch of big movies and Cubby asked if I'd be interested. I went to his house and met with Tim Dalton, who is a lovely guy and very funny by the way. But I thought the script was lousy. I really did not like the script. It was corny and I just didn't think it was that interesting.

But there was also an issue that looking back I regret. I can't speak for what's going on now with Barbara and Michael Wilson producing but I know that Cubby kept tight control. And the director made the movie, but it was the movie Cubby wanted. And no Bond director ever got final cut.

Today the business has changed quite a bit. But in the nineteen-seventies and -eighties directors were treated with much more respect and because of financial success I'd had I was able to get final cut. So I had it on *Trading Places*, and four or five other movies. But even when you had final cut it was based on economic factors. If it went around 10% over the agreed-upon budget, then you lost final cut. And the truth is, 90% of the time, the director's cut is their cut anyway. But it's that 10% that's scary. And I've been involved in films where I didn't have final cut too and when the producer fucks up your movie. I had a terrible time on *Blues Brothers 2000*. The studio destroyed it; it was just horrible. But anyway, the bottom line is that at the time I felt very strongly that Cubby was not going to give me final cut. It's his movie. And that was an issue for me. And I think I was wrong.

Usually, there's no disagreement. But if there was a disagreement my agent proposed we would preview the producer's version and my version. Whichever tested better we'd use. Cubby said, "No. It's what I want." Which is his right to do. But the truth is I would've done it if I thought the script was good. The script was not interesting. It was just dumb. I didn't like it. And they were down the line. They had already cast [model turned actress] Talisa Soto. It was only like 10 weeks away or 12 weeks away from production. But the truth is, I regret it because I could've directed a James Bond movie. So that's when I saw Cubby. I was not close to him, but I was very fond of him. I really liked him.

Why has Bond endured?

I don't know. I couldn't tell you. But I think part of it is a class issue. I think there's this bizarre nostalgia for the Raj and when England ruled the world. It's this legend, this myth of British competence.

But the thing about Bond that was always so fun is that they always had the newest technology. But if you look back on a lot of the films, they're [unintentionally] funny. You look at *Goldfinger*, and they have a GPS device. But it's this little light and makes a "Beep, beep" sound. In a different Bond [*Live and Let Die*], there's a huge close-up on a digital watch. Because the digital watch at that time was new and fabulously expensive. It was this extraordinary thing. But within minutes digital watches were made out of the cheapest plastic [and stopped being exotic].

With Bond films, there's always this nostalgia for elegance. And the literary Bond is a snob. Ian Fleming was a snob. The weird misogyny of Bond is somehow attractive. And the way he treats women. He seduces women and everyone loves him. He seduces men and women all over the place. And every Bond actor gets to say, "Bond, James Bond." That's a fabulous line.

Did you ever see *Casino Royale*? The '67 [spoof] is fascinating because it's a mess. It's also a fabled disaster production and had multiple directors, including John Huston. It's so interesting that David Niven, who plays James Bond in the movie, was Ian Fleming's choice to play Bond.

Despite his ability to effortlessly play sophisticated wit, Niven is a bad choice for Bond.

Well, that's why I believe that you have to give Cubby credit. I believe the success of Bond was the casting of Sean Connery. And the way Terence Young molded him and took him to his tailor in Savile Row [in London]. That's all because Terence Young was a very upper-class guy. It's very interesting because Sean is this coal miner. He's a big rough Scotsman. He was a muscle guy. A weightlifter, and it's so interesting the way he's used.

Did you ever see *Darby O'Gill and the Little People* (1959)? It's really good. Well, what's great about *Darby O'Gill*? It's the Abbey Players [Dublin's acting troupe]. It's all Irish and British, and it takes place in Ireland. It's this fantasy island. But what's incredible about it is that it was shot in Burbank. But once they made it, they had a preview, and the American audience said, "What the fuck are they saying? The brogues were just too thick." So they had to go back and redub the whole thing.

But Connery is charming in it. Oh, he's totally different than Bond. He's charming, and what's interesting is a role he played before he played James Bond. He was the second bad guy in a Tarzan movie [called *Tarzan's Greatest Adventure* (1959).] A Tarzan movie! So I really think the casting of Connery was a masterstroke.

They made a Bond knock-off film with his brother, Neil Connery. It was called *Operation Kid Brother* (1967).

Yeah, he made several in Italy. The Italians, the Germans, and the French—everybody made James Bond movies. Did you ever see the Jean-Paul Belmondo movie *The Man from Rio* (1964)? I mean, they're *all* they're kind of Bondish pictures. If you look at what I've always thought was the father of the Bond movies. Not the books, but the father of the Bond movies is Hitchcock's picture *North by Northwest* (1959).

Absolutely.

Cary Grant is supposed to be an advertising executive, but [despite all the danger] he's so unflappable and elegant.

That's the Niven-Cary Grant style of sophisticated elegance. If Grant were Bond in *Dr. No* (1962)...

A young Cary Grant. Absolutely.

That would work?

Yes, but it would be different. What's interesting about *Dr. No* is the Fu Manchu stuff; it's "the Yellow Peril." There was darkness to it. The blind guys who murder people. But so much of it is the music. You should never get too far away from "Dum-dum-dum-dum." That's brilliant, genius music. And sometimes they stray too far, but the orchestration of it ultimately comes down to that electric guitar.

But the films had to keep getting more and more outrageous. There's that fight he does with those girls, Bambi and Thumper. And they did the silly car stunts. The Southern sheriff [who appears in both *Live and Let Die* and *The Man with the Golden Gun* (1974)] was in direct response to the *Smokey and the Bandit* movies. They're always trying to stay current. They always have to be current. And that's why some of them are kind of dated. Have you seen *Kingsman* [*Kingsman: The Secret Service* (2014)]?

Yes, a film playing up the notion of the "gentleman spy."

There were things I liked and things I didn't like. But one of the things I liked was the style. I mean, those bespoke suits and the way Colin Firth was dressed. What started happening in some of the Roger Moore Bonds is they dressed him in leisure suits, in those bell-bottom pants and acrylic. It's like, "*What!?*" It sort of strayed away from the style. And now, they have Daniel Craig in those too-tight tuxes. It's a fashion. They have the coats too tight now. Oh, that's going to look silly in 15 years, because it's a fad.

The BBC made an excellent three-hour documentary about the making of the *Spy Who Loved Me*. It's a candid, revealing, and very interesting look into the making of a Bond movie. In it, the actress Barbara Bach and director Lewis Gilbert, who by then had replaced Guy Hamilton, had a creative disagreement about what her character should wear. Bach said the outfits they wanted her to wear were not current. Gilbert said, "That's true, but we're *not trying* to be current."

Well, I think he was right. I can't speak to that argument, but that's true. But if Bond is dressed the way Colin Firth is dressed in *Kingsman,* he will always look good. He wore a bespoke Savile Row suit. Not some of the ridiculous stuff that Bond has worn.

There were some very funny ideas in the *Kingsman.* Ultimately, I didn't like it. But still, there were some very stylish things, and Matthew Vaughn is a very good director. There are just some stylish moments, and I love the conceit of it. In the opening title sequence of the TV series *Get Smart* (1965-1970), which is another James Bond parody, Maxwell Smart goes down the hallway, through a door, through another hallway, through doors, hallways, and more doors. Then he goes to the phone booth and drops through the floor. Well, there are always these hidden secret bases in the Bond movies. [In *You Only Live Twice*, M's office is hidden] in a submarine. It's always wacky. And what I enjoyed in *Kingsman,* is the conceit that the entrance to this super-secret extraordinary high-tech amazing weapons cache is through the fitting room. Off Savile. In a tailor shop. That's Ian Fleming. That was clever.

What's your relationship like with the family these days?

I've remained in touch with Barbara and Michael over the years. In fact, in my last film, *Burke and Hare* (2010) there's a scene at the Royal College of Medicine with Hugh Bonneville, Tom Wilkinson, and Tim Curry. They are all sitting around a large table. Well, the other doctors who are at this table are [stop-motion visual effects pioneer] Ray Harryhausen, [frequent Landis cinematographer] Bob Paynter, and Michael Wilson.

I didn't catch that.

Well, you wouldn't unless you knew him. But Michael's one of the doctors.

Ray Harryhausen is tagged at the end of that film, in a two-shot.

Yeah, with Bob Paynter. But Michael's one of them as well. [Wilson has also made cameo appearances in fifteen Bond films.] I'm very fond of him and Barbara. Barbara's a darling. They're both very, very successful. Barbara's produced Broadway shows [including *A Steady Rain* starring Daniel Craig] and all kinds of stuff.

I'm seeing Michael in two weeks. Michael and his wife Jane are coming for dinner at our house. My wife [Deborah Nadoolman Landis, a costume designer who worked on *Raiders of the Lost Ark* (1981)] was the curator of the Hollywood costumes show at the Victoria and Albert Museum. I made *Burke and Hare* there. We're in London a lot, so we see Michael when we're there. I think we've had two Thanksgivings at his house. And last Christmas, we were at his house.

Michael has a world-class photography collection. He's one of the leading collectors of photographs in the world. And it's quite something. He has this incredible collection that he loans to museums. They're both big philanthropists. They're very interesting people. It's funny because I've known them for so long. It's not like we're best friends or anything but we are social. I'm fond of them, and I wish them well.

They are intriguing figures. They took over Eon from Cubby and they've managed the seemingly impossible task of building on his singular vision.

It gets increasingly difficult for them to make these movies, and Bond is now competing with Bond knockoffs. Bond used to be unique because they were bigger and better. But then came all the Bond imitators, and you had the schlocky ones like *The Silencer* (1966) with Dean Martin as Matt Helm, *Our Man Flint* (1966), and all these movies. There were so many of them, millions of copies of them. Today there are the Jason Bourne movies, *Mission Impossible*, and *Kingsman*; they're all just James Bond movies. They now have to compete with their own legend.

Roger Moore's entrance in John Landis's version of *The Spy Who Loved Me*.
Illustration by Pat Carbajal

Unmade Moonraker

Cary Bates

One can't help wondering how a twenty-four-year-old with no screenwriting experience was able to sell an unsolicited treatment for a James Bond movie to Albert Broccoli and Eon Productions. Of course, Cary Bates was no ordinary aspiring artist. He was a precocious talent who broke into the comic book industry in his teens and became a prolific writer of Superman and Flash comics, but still...

* * *

How did you get hired to write the treatment for *Moonraker* (1977)?

It's not accurate to say I was 'hired.' Considering I was a twenty-four-year-old comic book writer at the time with no screen credits, it should surprise no one that neither Eon nor United Artists sought me out to work on a James Bond film. Here's how it went down, in 1972 I happened to see the actress Patricia Neal mention on a talk show that she and her husband Roald Dahl lived in Buckinghamshire, England in a town called Great Missenden. I had been toying with the idea of writing a Bond treatment on spec [without any assurance that it would be sold], but now that I had a general address for the scriptwriter of *You Only Live Twice,* I figured I had a potential "inside connection" to the Bond people. As unrealistic as this sounds in hindsight, it was that simple.

Because I got into comics to become a Superman writer at the age of eighteen pretty much the same way (blind ambition and blind faith against very long odds), I just figured if I was persistent, I could get lightning to strike twice. Sure enough, my package did find its way to Roald Dahl's doorstep. Even more improbable was the result: he actually read it and sent me a very complimentary letter saying he liked my treatment and thought Broccoli would too. That's what got the ball rolling.

At one point there was talk of Dahl turning the treatment into a screenplay, but for a variety of reasons that scenario never materialized. By this time, Dahl's main career as a children's book author [*Charlie and the Chocolate Factory*, etc.] was gaining momentum and he wasn't particularly eager to deal with suits and studio politics again. Also, by now Eon was occupied filming *Live and Let Die* and planning *Golden Gun.* So after a number of starts, stops, and delays, they finally purchased the treatment a year-and-a-half later in the fall of 1974.

What kind of guidance did Albert Broccoli give you?

None, since it was on spec. Because Eon's lawyers were extremely strict about letting Broccoli and Saltzman read unsolicited material, Eon bought my *Moonraker* treatment sight-unseen, which shows how much stock they put in a positive Roald Dahl recommendation.

I followed the usual formula of the era—a good girl, sacrificial girl, strange henchmen, action set-pieces, and so on. By this time I had been a DC comics writer for six years and had gotten to know Neal Adams [comic book artist]. He read the treatment and liked it enough to agree to draw several color storyboards for the action sequences, on spec. He also did a beautiful cover that mimicked the Bond posters of the sixties. Needless to say, his illustrations greatly enhanced the presentation.

What was the writing process like?

Just me and the blank page, as usual. I asked for input from a few friends along the way but obviously, I wasn't getting any notes from anyone in an official capacity.

What did you retain from the novel and what did you abandon?

The book came out in 1955 and was thoroughly out-of-date by the nineteen-seventies. The main plot had Hugo Drax, a secret Nazi, modifying a V2 rocket with a nuclear warhead on the pretense of defending England when in fact its first test launch was secretly aimed to strike London. Drax was a worthwhile villain, sort of in the *Goldfinger* mode, but otherwise, the book didn't offer much for a film: no exotic locations, unusual for Fleming, and a bridge game instead of the usual face-off over a baccarat table. Since the source material was so threadbare, I assumed any *Moonraker* film plot would pretty much be starting from scratch. So other than Drax and Gala Brand, I don't believe I used anything else from the novel.

What was the plot of your treatment?

Many of the details are fuzzy now, sorry to say. Since all this took place well before computers, the treatment only existed in hard copies. If there's still one laying around here somewhere, I haven't seen it in years. The main plotline had Hugo Drax as a lone mega-villain who sent his minions to steal a nuclear sub that was being serviced at HMNB Clyde, the British submarine base on the coast of Scotland. To the rest of the world it seemed like the sub "disappeared," but it was actually smuggled through an underwater channel in Scotland's coastline that led inland to Loch Ness.

This was a take-off on the geologically dubious theory that there was once such a channel that allowed plesiosaurs to swim into Loch Ness from the ocean, resulting in the Loch Ness monster sightings that have been reported for centuries. At any rate, once the sub was hidden in the loch, from that vantage its nuclear missiles could be launched to strike anywhere in Europe if Drax's demands weren't met, demands that not only involved money but some sort of hi-tech McGuffin—the exact nature of which I've blanked-out on.

You wanted to bring back the character of Tatiana Romanova, a corporal in Soviet Army Intelligence, from the novel *From Russia with Love*.

As I recall, the story presented her as a full-fledged Russian agent and sort of like what would become the Barbara Bach character in Spy Who Loved Me, who the Soviets had sent to investigate Drax. This put her on a parallel track with Bond, who had been dispatched by M to look into Drax as well. Drax's men eventually "acupunctured her to death" with needles applied to the so-called "death-touch" pressure points known to ancient martial arts masters.

Did you give Hugo Drax a henchman?

I gave him a pair of psychopathic twin bodyguards named Pluto and Plato.

Who would you like to have cast in the film?

Things never progressed that far. Daniela Bianchi's last film credit was in 1968 so odds are her role would've had to be recast. [Bianchi played Tatiana Romanova in *From Russia with Love*.][391]

Did you have a scene in which Bond has been captured and has to use his wits to escape the villain's clutches?

Working undercover, Bond got himself hired by Hugo Drax as a chauffeur, a job that required him to drive Drax around in a new (1972) Rolls Royce. Unbeknownst to Drax, one night Bond switched out his employer's Rolls for an identical model that had been "modified" by Q-branch.

Later, Bond's cover is exposed while he's driving Drax somewhere. Knowing that Drax, flanked by Pluto and Plato in the back seat, was about to kill him, he activates Q's secret modification, which allows the Rolls to literally split in half. As a bulletproof screen slides down behind the front seat, an extra set of small tires emerge from the split chassis, enabling Bond to drive off and leave Drax and his bodyguards in the inert back-half of the Rolls. An extended chase scene follows. Drax calls in reinforcements. To lose the bad guys chasing him, Bond drives the half-Rolls on to a nearby auto test track, where he loses them one by one by taking advantage of the banked curves and obstacle courses. [Bond driving half of a car brings to mind a similar scene in *A View to a Kill*. However, in that film,

Bond's vehicle doesn't break apart thanks to Q branch. Instead, Bond's car is split in half when another car crashes into it.]

What did you hope to bring to Moore's Bond and his interpretation?

I was going for a slightly more serious tone, closer to the still-to-come *Spy Who Loved Me* as opposed to the Moore Bond of *Live and Let Die* or *Golden Gun*.

Many Bond fans believe that you were one of many writers on *The Spy Who Loved Me*. But you wrote a treatment for *Moonraker*. Can you please clear this up?

I think the confusion comes from the fact my *Moonraker* treatment detailed a plot in which a nuclear sub was hijacked, and because a sub hijacking also became a key plot element in *Spy*, many people just assumed my pitch was for that film. When Broccoli bought my treatment in the fall of 1974, I'm not sure if they had decided on which title to go with after *Golden Gun*. They apparently liked the idea of hijacking a nuclear sub, but once they decided *Spy* was next, they chose to go in an entirely different direction.

As we know now, they decided to revisit the *You Only Live Twice* plot of "swallowing U.S. and Russian *space capsules*" to set off World War III by changing it to a giant oil tanker that was "swallowing U.S. and Russian *submarines*" to set off World War III. There's been some speculation the parallels might've been due to the fact Lewis Gilbert directed both films, but I can't say one way or the other.

Did anything from your treatment make its way into another Bond film?

The aforementioned nuclear submarine hijacking in Spy, pair of twin assassins turned up in *Octopussy* (1983), and a chase scene where Bond is driving a car split in half figured in the Paris section of *A View to a Kill*.

What idea from your story would you have loved them to use?

I was always psyched by the idea of a nuclear sub being smuggled into Loch Ness, which I think would've made an interesting location for a Bond film. The ruins of Urquhart Castle have overlooked the Loch for centuries and I gave Drax's forces a secret lair built under the ruins. His men would use mini-subs to go back and forth from the castle to the nuclear sub, which always remained hidden deep inside the Loch. I believe I suggested having the mini-subs tricked-out with an exo-shell that would make them look like "creatures" if anyone caught a glimpse of them from the shore.

Did you ever get a concrete reason about why they didn't go forward with your outline?

No.

Beyond the specifics of your plot, what were you hoping to bring to Bond films? Were you trying to push the films in any particular direction?

I wrote my version of *Moonraker* between the releases of *Diamonds Are Forever* (1971) and *Golden Gun*, but then, as now, I regarded *Goldfinger* and *On Her Majesty's Secret Service* as the quintessential Bond films. So I may have been trying to emulate those two films in my approach.

What is the most challenging aspect of writing a Bond film?

Just doing it. I think the phrase "ignorance is bliss" really applies here. If I knew back in 1972 what I know now about the harsh realities of the film business in general—not to mention all the additional hurdles specific to the most successful franchise in film history—I doubt I would have attempted it.

When you look back about your time writing Bond, what is your most vivid memory?

The best memories all have to do with the "Bond people" I got to meet along the way. Cubby Broccoli was always extremely kind to me. I initially met him on one of the New York locations of *Live and Let Die* and had a more extensive meeting several months later at the Eon offices in London. Roald Dahl was very gracious as well, and during my London trip he invited me out to his home in Great Missenden for a memorable dinner. Through Eon, I also got to spend a little time with John Barry. I've always been a big fan of his Bond music. I met with him both in New York and London.

Flash-forward to the late nineteen-eighties. Once again using my "blind faith against long odds" approach, I decided I was going to write a Superman movie. Admittedly, the odds were a little better this time around because of my DC Comics connection. At any rate, I submitted a spec treatment to an executive at Warner Bros. that eventually found its way to Ilya Salkind. Long story short, I ended up working as a story editor and writer on the Salkind/ Viacom syndicated *Superboy* series in 1988. Not long after that, I got the assignment to write the screenplay for what would have been *Superman* 5, starring Christopher Reeve. The main plot was directly out of my treatment, and we were calling it *Superman Reborn*. Unfortunately, by this time Warners was leaning toward doing their *Lois & Clark* TV series instead of a new Superman film. After some dicey negotiations, they doubled-down and bought back all the Superman rights from the Salkinds. Studio politics being what they are, my script was scuttled.

Final note: While *Superman Reborn* was still in the planning stages, the Salkinds hired me to be the third screenwriter on their 1992 film *Christopher Columbus: The Discovery*. Since I was writing the final production draft, I had to be at all the filming locations in Madrid, the Virgin Islands, Malta and I was working closely with the film's director, who was none other than John Glen. So as you might imagine, the subject of Bond came up. It was great getting a chance to reminisce about Bond again with one of the key members of the 007 team some twenty years after my own *Moonraker* adventure.

Unmade Tomorrow Never Dies
Nicholas Meyer

A fictionalized Chinese takeover of Hong Kong provided the backdrop to the original script of *Tomorrow Never Dies* (1997). However, when the imminent real-life changeover threatened to make the planned movie instantly out-of-date, and with production looming, Eon invited a cadre of writers to London to brainstorm new story ideas.

Among those enlisted screenwriters was Nicholas Meyer, the writer and director of *Time After Time* (1979), the time-traveling romantic-thriller that pits H.G. Welles against Jack the Ripper, *Star Trek: The Wrath of Kahn* (1982), which is widely considered to be the high-water mark of the series, and *Star Trek: The Undiscovered Country* (1991), a whodunit that bid farewell to the original cast. Meyer also wrote the novel *The Seven-Per-Cent Solution* bringing together Sherlock Holmes and Sigmund Freud, the great criminal detective and the great detective of the unconscious and which he adapted for the screen and directed.

For *Tomorrow Never Dies*, Meyer was joined by other writers, including Kurt Wimmer and Leslie Dixon (who collaborated on *The Thomas Crown Affair* with Pierce Brosnan), Robert Collector (*Memoirs of an Invisible Man*), and David Campbell Wilson (who later earned a story credit for the 2015 big-screen adaptation of *The Man from U.N.C.L.E.*).

* * *

How did you get involved with *Tomorrow Never Dies*?

Roger Spottiswoode, the director, is my brother-in-law once removed, and Jeff Kleeman, the studio executive [at MGM/UA] whose job it was to make these movies is one of my closest friends since 1985. Another reason I was brought on is that I had directed Pierce Brosnan in *The Deceivers* (1988) and Pierce and I remained good friends. So, I had three reasons or contacts for being summoned.

When Roger and Jeff were working on it, they got into a lengthy discussion and they had this idea that they were going to fly a whole bunch of writers that they liked and admired to London. The main thing that we were there to discuss was what does the villain want? But there were two things to bear in mind. One, over the course of the series the villain had already wanted the gold in Fort Knox (*Goldfinger*), control of the oceans (*The Spy Who Loved Me*), all the atom bombs (*Thunderball*, 1965), and everything in outer space (*Moonraker*). Two, keep it simple.

There were several of us, including Kurt Wimmer and Leslie Dixon. We were flown to London and put up at the Dorchester. As I recall, the Eon offices were just around the corner on Piccadilly. They wanted us to brainstorm on this issue and that was how I became involved.

My impression was that the idea of brain trusting with a bunch of screenwriters was a new one for Eon. It had been largely prompted by Jeff Kleeman and Roger and arguably by Pierce who said, "Gee, why don't we bring Nick over," and then for all I know it got expanded from there to, "Why don't we just bring over a bunch of guys and let them spitball and see what comes of it?" Given the budgets of these films, I think it was obviously not a very large amount of money that they were proposing to spend to have us hole up there for three or four days.

What idea did you have?

In a somewhat jet-lagged state, I went back to the hotel. I have smart days and stupid days, and for whatever reason, I had a smart day.

I went into the writer's room the next day and I said, "Oh, I solved your problem," and about thirty people were sitting in this room, all sort of very eager. I don't remember how many of us writers had been imported. There were six, maybe seven and there was Barbara Broccoli, Michael Wilson, and Roger Spottiswoode. Anyway, there were a lot of people who were all ears.

I said, "Well, here's the thing about James Bond. The way I see it the films have assumed all the formal rigidity of an English sonnet in terms of their structure. They always begin with the spectacular Bond stunt, followed by banter with Moneypenny followed by assignment from M, followed by stunt sequence, stunt sequence, stunt sequence until Bond actually meets Mister Big in his lair. Mister Big says, no Mister Bond it's not about the money, it's really about X."

So I said, "Now imagine that all of that has happened and Mister Big in his lair says, all the obstacle courses that you have negotiated were actually tests to see if you really were the man that I need you to be. Because I think when you get to know me really well, Mister Bond, you'll find that fundamentally I am a people person. But there's too many of them."

Then he flips a switch and all these monitors come on with every image of overpopulation that you can possibly imagine. Starving people in Ethiopia or wherever we're shooting. There's plenty of them, traffic jams where cars are immobile under these smog-laden skies in Los Angeles, and so on and so on and so on.

He says, "Mister Bond, even lemmings, even lemmings know what to do when they grow too numerous. I am willing to bite the bullet on the life and death issue for this planet that no politician will confront or face or mention ⌐there are too many people and the only way we can survive is to cull the herd. 007, that's some kind of license [to kill] isn't it? Tell me 007, how much game are you allowed to bag with that license? I'm imploring your help, sir, will you help me save planet earth?"

And at this point, they're all sitting there with their jaws hanging open and I continue. Bond says, "You're right. I will help you." So basically what Mister Big wants is to start a war between India and China, the two most populous nations on the face of the earth, and Bond says he'll help him.

Before anybody could raise an objection. I said, "Look, the people who know that Bond would never help him will just be hugging themselves with delight knowing he's not going to do it. The people who think he is going to do it will be surprised and say, 'Oh my god he didn't do it.' So you can't lose either way. And Bond at least would be up against a villain of real dimension. There's big stuff there that's real."

The best villains are the ones who are right, that you have to agree with. Then you really have to dredge up something real to deal with them, and so I left the room. My recollection is that they were like, stunned. But it fit the criteria because it hadn't been done before and it was simple.

I came back the next day and the idea was off the table and I couldn't believe it. I asked why? They said that it was too serious. I may have contributed a line of dialogue before I left, but that was basically my idea. I wrote some scenes but my feeling at the end of the day was that we were sort of coming at it from very different places.

Do you consider yourself a big Bond fan?

Bond is a little bit like the Strauss waltzes or Mozart piano concerti. I know there are twenty-seven Mozart piano concerti, and I pretty much love them all, but I'll be damned if I can listen to one and say, ah, yes this is fourteen or this is twenty-three. I was never really a big James Bond fan. It was a little too unreal for me and I preferred, for example, the Harry Palmer series with Michael Caine [the original three spy films were produced by Broccoli's partner Harry Saltzman]. I like my spies real, and the more real the better. What I love about John le Carré is that you felt like you were getting the real stuff. And Bond was sort of cartoony.

In order to stay true to his character, writers not only have to think about what Bond would do but they must also figure out what he would *not* do. And that can be a challenge.

I think that's true, but it also varies depending on which Bond you're writing. For example, there's a Roger Moore Bond movie [*Octopussy*] where he's dressed as a clown in a circus. But never in a million years would Sean Connery be a clown in a circus; he just wouldn't. So it's a different Bond.

What do you think motivates Bond?

It must be a nice thing to be an adrenaline junky who is paid to make love to beautiful women, throw people out of helicopters, wear a tuxedo, and do it all for king and country. What a sweet gig. If you said to Bond, "Oh, by the way, it's a wrap and we don't need you to do any of these things anymore," then what would he do with the rest of his life? And I think that's a good question and it is why I sort of liked my villain idea. I thought it would really put Bond on his mettle. There was no reason not to agree with this man; he was right up and down the line in what he was saying. So is Bond saying no to that and sticking up for what we'll refer to as a civilized code of conduct? Does he stick up for that code of conduct because he believes it or is it because he is doing it by rote? I don't know the answer to that.

What do you think is the trick to writing good Bond dialogue?

I thought it very easy to write Bond; all you have to do is think of a modified Oscar Wilde, a lethal Oscar Wilde.

* * *

Nicholas Meyer's plot was not the only unrealized element of *Tomorrow Never Dies*. Jeff Kleeman, who was the Executive Vice President of Production at MGM/UA in the mid-nineties, told me about two other intriguing projects. Kleeman recalled, "After the release of *Tomorrow Never Dies*, at UA we became very interested in making two spin-off movies. One would be a kind of prequel centered on Dr. Kaufman, the Vincent Schiavelli character. Think of it as our *Better Call Saul* [a well-regarded spin-off series that focuses on a supporting character from *Breaking Bad*.] It would have been a one-off movie. Something fun, unexpected, and a bit eccentric. The other idea was to attempt to launch an ongoing franchise based on Michelle Yeoh's character, Wai Lin. After a number of conversations, Barbara and Michael understandably felt they didn't have the bandwidth to produce either given the intense development and production schedule we were asking them to follow in order to deliver a Bond film every other year."

I asked Kleeman if Pierce Brosnan would have appeared as Bond in either film. Kleeman revealed, "We only had early-stage conversations on each. [Screenwriter] Dan Petrie Jr., who had created the Dr. Kaufman character, had a storyline he'd roughed out that led to a concluding moment when you knew Kaufman was on his way to encounter Bond and meet his fate. Pierce probably would have ended up having a cameo in the Wai Lin movie, but we never developed it far enough to determine." Had the Wai Lin film gone forward, Brosnan would have played Bond five times in the movies, instead of just four.

Section 3 – Lost Bond TV: James Bond Jr.

James Bond Jr. Writer's Guide

Bond fans don't agree on much. Ask a group of James Bond enthusiasts, "Who is the best 007?" and watch a fight break out. Other than their unbridled enthusiasm for the character, there is little consensus among fans about the "best" Bond actor, movie, theme song, Bond woman, quip, villain, or gadget. In fact, their eclectic answer can sound like it came from an off-brand game of Clue. "It was Timothy Dalton from *The Living Daylights* and Vesper Lynd from *Casino Royale*, fighting Jaws from *Moonraker* while listening to Adele's theme song to *Skyfall*, inside Blofeld's volcano from *You Only Live Twice*."

Still, there is one subject that the usually affably argumentative community will agree on and it concerns the least popular iteration of the character. Many will contend that *James Bond Jr.*, the 1991 animated series, was not the highlight of the venerable franchise. The animated series is not commercially available on DVD, Blu-ray, or via any streaming service, one might safely conclude that the Bond producers do not hold *James Bond Jr.* in high esteem. Eon would rather downplay the cartoon's existence than exploit it for financial gain. For the producers, the 65 episodes of *James Bond Jr.* were not, as Rita Coolidge put it in the theme song to *Octopussy*, "an all-time high."

Although *James Bond Jr.* might not make anyone's "best of" list, the producers' original aspirations for the show were far more noteworthy than the results. The producers, as revealed in the series bible, mapped out an ambitious and worthy plan to create an entertaining program for a young audience.

A series bible (or show bible), for those unacquainted with the term, is a document that is given to writers on a television show and it serves as their writers' guide. The series bible can also be used as a pitching tool and a way to get a network or financier interested in acquiring a show. The bible typically lays out the rules for the show, describes the characters, and outlines potential storylines. It meticulously describes the universe of the show. Along with the pilot script and guidance from the producers and showrunner, the writers often rely on the document for critical insight into the show. The show bible is particularly useful to the writers before a show airs and before the mythology of the show is firmly established. A reading of the bible for *James Bond Jr.* gives fans and Bond scholars a better understanding of the producer's original intentions and crucial background details about Bond Jr.'s biography.

Viewers of the animated series know that James Bond Jr. is a teenaged nephew of 007 and that he's enrolled in Warfield Academy, a boarding school. But audiences were never given James Jr.'s precise age or his grade in school. From the bible, we know that James is seventeen years old and that he's a junior.[392] I suspect that the producers wanted to make James old enough to be capable of holding his own on dangerous missions but young enough to have the enthusiasm and optimism of youth. Of course, as an animated character, James Bond Jr. would not have to age; he could have stayed seventeen for as long as the series ran.

The show's bible also clears up other long-standing questions about the show. In *James Bond Jr.*, the circumstances that brought James Jr. to Warfield and the whereabouts of his parents are hinted at but never expressly stated. The bible indicates that James Jr.'s parents are "missing" and that they are "obviously the victims of the notorious S.C.U.M. operation."[393] His parents are also given professions; his mother is an archaeologist and his father is a linguist.[394] The bible explains that James is enrolled in Warfield because of his parent's abduction and because of the "security risk posed by the nature of his uncle's work."[395] [Bond Jr.'s school took its name from Albert Broccoli's company Warfield Productions.]

The fate of James Jr.'s parents would have played a more central role in the series and is the reason for some of his adventures. Originally, what was "driving [James] on these missions is the hope that he'll locate his missing parents, whom he's convinced are being held captive by S.C.U.M. forces."[396] Having James search for but never find his parents could have added additional tension and stakes to the series. However, the notion of a teenager who is looking for his parents might have seemed to some network executives as too mature or upsetting for younger viewers. If that was their concern, they needn't have worried. A young protagonist, without parents, is a classic convention in literature and film. Books as diverse as *The Wizard of Oz, Lemony Snicket's A Series of Unfortunate Events, Harry Potter, Lord of the Flies*, and *The Catcher in the Rye* have all told stories where the parents are absent or dead.

The show bible also provides indispensable insight into James Jr.'s character. For instance, we're told that James possesses the "panache" and "the calculated disregard for the rules" but only "when they stand in the way of a greater good."[397] Bond Jr. doesn't have a "random disrespect for convention, but rather a strong sense of doing what he knows to be right regardless of any rules to the contrary."[398] James "has a passion for justice; he is incapable of standing by while an innocent party is being victimized—he is *compelled* to get involved and help out."[399] Significantly, the description of James Bond Jr. also perfectly encapsulates what motivates his uncle.

The document also provides valuable insights into the cinematic Bond's fraught relationships with his superior M. According to the bible, the rapport between James Jr. and Mr. Milbanks, the headmaster, is meant to evoke 007's bond with M. Underneath Milbanks's annoyance at young James there is also "grudging respect for a boy of unique abilities."[400] There was also discussion of having M., whose agency would have authority over the security of the Academy, making an appearance in the series.[401] However, that never came to pass.

The show bible also reveals that the creators had many ideas for *James Bond Jr.*, which were eventually abandoned. For instance, the creators originally envisioned including "an animated version of the classic silhouette in the iris" and a new arrangement of the Bond theme, the latter idea, given music royalties, could have been financially prohibitive.[402] The producers instructed writers that the "humour should be clever and there is no reason why much of it can't work on more than one level."[403] The producers were striving to "capture the sophistication and wit" of the movies to "translate it into kid-related references."[404] So the "fish with red wine" reference in *From Russia with Love* would be replaced with "I should have known – you're wearing *red* High Top (tennis shoes)."[405]

The Bond producers were also striving for a "very realistic style of design" and in lieu of wall to wall action, the producers were hoping to infuse the episodes with a great deal of suspense.[406] Even though the producers had comical villains, they were mindful that if the "jeopardies and threats are not portrayed convincingly, and sometimes even frighteningly" then they "will not be taken seriously, and the series runs the risk of deteriorating into a joke."[407] Given their concern, the humor in the show is probably broader and the tone is lighter than they had originally intended.

Other abandoned ideas include having a villain named Felony O'Toole, a play on Plenty O'Toole, from *Diamonds Are Forever*. Felony O'Toole is described as having "connections to organized crime, vice, drug traffickers, etc. throughout the world."[408] Considering the roughness of her background and the target audience, it's unlikely that the character's background would have been brought to the fore. Instead, she was indicative of the producer's desire to possibly introduce "standard" villains with less outlandish plans, into the series.[409]

There are several handwritten notes in the bible. For instance, after the typed list of villains, someone hand wrote that Dr. No and Oddjob's son, Oddjob Jr. could also appear. The handwritten addition of the two characters suggests that they could be last-minute additions. Or perhaps, in the pre-computer age, it was simply less time consuming, to handwrite a few ideas, than it would be to type an entirely new draft. Given that both Dr. No and Oddjob played prominent positions in the series and were both turned into action figures, it seems that irrespective of when they were invented, their inclusion in the bible was a meaningful one.

The bible also includes designs for most of the significant characters and several vehicles, such as James Bond Jr.'s tricked out sports car and a cycle. The black and white drawing of Bond is nearly identical to the final version, with one exception. Whereas in the final version, the patch on Bond's jacket is that of his school, in the bible, the patch displays the United Kingdom's national flag. Even Bond's scuba outfit would have featured the insignia. The inclusion of the Union Jack would have visually anchored the character to his English roots. Notwithstanding, I suspect the flag was eliminated in an effort to appeal to an international audience and, specifically, to children in the United States, where the show was heavily marketed.

In the original plans, the Union Jack would not have appeared on James Bond Jr.'s parachute gear. Instead, the image of a deployed parachute would have appeared on the badge. It's a curious decision to abandon the Union Jack because it is inseparably linked to the movie Bond's most iconic stunt – the breathtaking jump off the mountain in *The Spy Who Loved Me*. It would appear again during the opening ceremony of the 2012 Olympics when, in a filmed sequence, Daniel Craig appears as James Bond.

The document also provides critical advice on how the gadgets should be used in the series. As with the Eon movies, "Gadgets should *not* be specific or narrow in their application, only to have a situation in which they're needed "conveniently" arrive in the story.[410] The exception to this rule is if Bond knows "*ahead* of time" about the need for a specific device.[411] Given their instructions, if Bond were searching for hidden treasures, a high-tech Geiger counter would be appropriate. But they didn't want Bond to rely on the gadgets. Instead, the producers insisted that Bond "must use his *wits* or *improvise* with *existing materials* to extricate himself from a situation."[412] [Emphasis in the original.]

Most tantalizingly, 007 was to have a more significant presence in the series. The creators had planned on having James Bond contacting young James from time to time to inform his nephew of potential S.C.U.M. threats and to provide "news about his missing parents."[413] While the bible notes that "We never see 007 himself, but we can hear his voice."[414] If the producers followed through with their idea, it would mean that they would have to cast an actor to play the role of the animated Bond.

Though the animated series is mostly forgotten it could have had a small influence on the film series. According to the show bible, the villainous Pharaoh Fearo was supposed to have a pet cat named Jinx.[415] Jinx is also the nickname of Halle Berry's character Giacinta Johnson, in *Die Another Day*. It's possible that the name resonated with the producers and that it was repurposed for the 2002 film.

The show bible hints at the producer's plan for a more sophisticated and nuanced show. While the animated series might have fallen short of expectations, in my interviews with the show's co-creator Robby London, co-director Bill Hutten, writers Mary Crawford, Alan Templeton, Doug Molitor, Benjamin Pollack, story editor Bryce Malek, and theme song co-composer Dennis C. Brown, I was struck by how much thought and care the artists put into the creation of *James Bond Jr.* All the artists seem to recognize the importance of the opportunity to tell stories in the James Bond universe, and, given the limitations in front of them, tried to deliver the best work they could. Although *James Bond Jr.* was not an unqualified success, it's clear that the producers had higher aspirations for the series than that which were ultimately realized.

James Bond Jr.
Illustration by Pat Carbajal

Jaws
Illustration by Pat Carbajal

A *James Bond Jr.* gun barrel sequence, as imagined by Pat Carbajal.
Illustration by Pat Carbajal

Creating James Bond Jr.
Robby London

For Bond fans, the period between Timothy Dalton's last Bond film and Pierce Brosnan's first outing was an agonizing six years. It was during this fallow period that Bond producers experimented with an animated children's television show focusing on the exploits of 007's teenage nephew – *James Bond Jr.*

Along with Michael Wilson and producer Andy Heyward, writer and producer Robby London developed *James Bond Jr.* and wrote the "show bible" – the creative document, which delineates the characters, premise, setting, tone, and potential storylines for a television show. Although London was not involved in the production of the series, he was intimately involved in developing the show and he helped shape the foundation for all 65-episodes during its one-season run.

James Bond Jr. was launched in 1991, along with a toy line (including a red sports car equipped with a "spring-action ejector seat" and a Jaws action figure featuring "chomping jaw-crushing action," which I still possess), two video games, novelizations, and a comic book published by Marvel. Even though *James Bond Jr.* was not warmly embraced by Bond aficionados, it is a fascinating and rare example of the producers attempting to spin-off the character into television.

London has produced a great many animated shows, including *Alf* (1997-1998), *The Super Mario Bros. Super Show!* (1989), *The Karate Kid* (1989), *The New Kids on the Block* (1990), *The Wizard of Oz* (1990), *The Real Ghostbusters* (1989-1991), *G.I. Joe* (1991-1992), *Where On Earth is Carmen Sandiego?* (1994-1995), *Sabrina, The Animated Series* (1999-2001), and *Sherlock Holmes in the 22nd Century* (1999-2001).

* * *

You had been involved with the development and production of many shows based on popular properties. How did you get involved in *James Bond Jr.*?

I was Executive Vice President in charge of creative affairs at DIC Entertainment, which was the largest independent animation studio at the time, known for series like *Inspector Gadget* (1983-1985), *The Real Ghostbusters*, *Captain Planet and the Planeteers* (1990-1992), *Sonic the Hedgehog* (1993-1994), *Where On Earth is Carmen Sandiego?*, *Madeline* (1993-1994), *G.I. Joe*, *Super Mario Bros.*, and dozens and dozens of others.

The TV environment was such that it was simply easier to sell and place animation series based on already established properties such as live-action TV shows, celebrities, comic books, toys, and, in this case, feature films than it was to create a completely new property. Of course, the James Bond franchise was considered a "crown jewel" in this category. The CEO of DIC, Andy Heyward, got together with Michael Wilson – who, along with Barbara Broccoli, is the "steward" of the James Bond franchise – to discuss the possibility of adapting James Bond to an animated series for kids. I believe this meeting was orchestrated through our agents at the time, CAA.

A preliminary deal for a kid's animated version of James Bond was struck between DIC and Eon, Hasbro, as the toymaker, and Claster Television, which was Hasbro's semi-independent, in-house distributor of children's television, and was the premier syndicator of kids shows at the time. So all the great pieces were tentatively in place.

The only catch was that Michael insisted that Eon must own the copyright of the material generated – and specifically the written material for the development of the series. So that there could be no confusion or claim about this, he wanted Eon to hire and supervise the development writer – where this would normally have been the purview of DIC – and, in fact, of me specifically in my role as EVP. Which is to say I would have *hired and supervised* the writer – not written it myself.

But since I had an extensive background as an animation writer myself prior to my position at DIC (e.g. I was a major player in the creation of *He-Man* [*and The Masters of the Universe* (1983-1985)] and wrote its pilot script), Andy convinced Michael Wilson that I would be the perfect person to develop James Bond, and Andy offered to waive my exclusivity to DIC, and allow Eon to hire me independently for this one project.

I hadn't written anything in a couple of years (I was too busy being an executive and a producer), but I loved the property, felt this was a great creative fit for my sensibility, and I was up for the challenge.

So I negotiated a separate deal with Michael Wilson and signed a work-for-hire contract to develop the series – which meant writing the bible and a few sample stories.

Everyone was happy with this arrangement – *especially me*. I'd always loved James Bond and it was also really nice to step back from my executive responsibilities for brief periods of time to be a writer again. I couldn't possibly get any writing done at my office at DIC, so I often worked from home during the few weeks this lasted. Of course, I couldn't entirely abandon my producing and managerial obligations, so it was a little stressful, too.

Fortunately, Michael turned out to be a terrific "boss" and collaborator. I really enjoyed working with him and respected him creatively. He had written some of the Bond movies – so he brought a real writer's sensibility to the table.

Can you talk about the creation and development of the show?

I believe it was agreed by everyone from the beginning that we wanted to call the series James Bond Jr. It might have been my suggestion, but it wasn't exactly a creative breakthrough. The basic concept was to do a kid-friendly version of the iconic character. Of course, with the violence and sex toned *way* down so as to be deemed suitable for kids.

Once I consummated the negotiation to work temporarily for Michael, over the course of a few weeks I went to his office in Culver City for a series of meetings with him. The initial meeting involved him relating what was important to him – in terms of protecting and serving the franchise and what his general expectations and concerns were. I was reasonably knowledgeable about Bond and all its famous signatures, but I recall Michael going over a lot of that with me. It was certainly fun to hear it from the source.

We brainstormed about the series. I'm sure I would've pitched him a few different basic concepts at the first or, more likely, the second meeting – to see if any of them sparked him. The boarding school idea was one of them and he responded positively to that, so we talked about that some more and fleshed it out somewhat in these meetings. Then I likely went home and wrote up a brief treatment or "mini-bible," submitted it to him, got it approved, and then wrote the full bible.

How did it go from being a vague idea to a firm plan to put James Bond Jr. in a prep school, where he and his classmates would fight villains?

I think it was just one of several ideas I originally came up with to pitch and it was the one Michael responded to the best. I seem to recall that he liked the idea of James Bond Jr. having to find a way to sneak out of school each time, complete the missions, and get back with no one any the wiser. As I recall, there was an irritant character [Trevor Noseworthy IV] who always suspected that James was up to something and he was constantly trying to "bust him," but was always outwitted. A bit like the neighbor in *Bewitched*, for those old enough to remember.

And I think we both felt that a residential school was generally a rich environment for the story. Kids away from home – and sort of on their own. Of course, this predated Harry Potter by many years, but in my mind, it created the same sort of strength and appeal as the setting at Hogwarts (absent the magic, of course) – young people being away from their families and forced together in an insular community. No parents. Like summer camp in a way. Of course, this was mostly for "B" stories—the secondary stories and conflicts in the episodes—because we envisioned the "A" stories, the main plot of each episode, being big capers away from and unrelated to school.

What did you use from the Ian Fleming novels?

I have not read the novels, so the only material from the novels that had any influence on me would have been those elements of the novels that were used in the movies.

From the movies?

I was very familiar with the movies and Michael spoke to me about the various franchise signatures. I don't remember the specifics, but I'm sure I would've tried to weave in as many of these signatures as Michael would let me. Our goal, after all, was to take advantage of the familiarity of the movie franchise.

Can you talk about the decision to center the show around Bond's nephew and not a young Bond as they've done in the recent Young Adult novels?

I *think* it was the folks at Eon not wanting to raise the complication of James Bond having a wife, an ex-wife, or, certainly, a child out of wedlock. [They wanted to avoid] messing with the timeline if we made it a young Bond but set in the present and to avoid creating any potential inconsistencies or any limitations going forward. I think they didn't want the animated series in any way to dictate, reveal or change the backstory or lore of the James Bond of the films.

What were the self-imposed "rules" for the show? For example, Bond couldn't appear onscreen.

There were some. The example you raised would certainly have been discussed – and it is likely that I would have pushed for James senior [*the* James Bond] to make an occasional appearance and that Eon would've preferred that he didn't.

Talk about the creation and writing of the series bible.

Well, it came out of the meetings I had with Michael Wilson. Once we agreed on the basic concept it was up to me to flesh it out with support characters and villains—some derivative of previous movie villains and some brand-new ones. The animated series' version of SPECTRE was called "S.C.U.M." [Saboteurs and Criminals United in Mayhem]. There was also the nature and personnel of the school, the mechanics and tone of how the stories would work, and then some sample stories.

By the way, one of the most fun parts of writing the bible for me was coming up with the funny names for the new villains – sometimes by using double entendres—and some were probably not so "politically correct." I remember, in particular, people on the creative team at DIC and Claster Television got a kick out of some of my ideas. [Among these were Goldie Finger, Tiara Hotstones, Lotta Dinaro, and Marcie Beaucoup.]

Villains are always the most fun to create and write. Outlandish villains are particularly well suited to the medium of animation. That was one of the beauties of working with a franchise like James Bond. By its nature, it was way larger than life, which is what you always want in an animated action series. That was another reason I was so enthusiastic to work on the development.

I had written many bibles before, and while the *content* of every bible is different, the *format* is fairly standard. I think once Michael approved the bible, I turned it over to DIC and everyone there seemed *very* happy with it. I think our artists would've started doing some preliminary sketches to match my descriptions, and then we would've passed it on to Claster and Hasbro for their input and approvals. I had worked extensively with both Claster and Hasbro and knew their tastes, sensibilities, and concerns, and that was another reason I was a good candidate for developing the series. I felt pretty confident I'd hit the mark for them, too; and indeed, I recall that everyone was quite enthusiastic.

As development projects go, this one was extremely – I'd go so far as to say *extraordinarily* – problem- and conflict-free and straightforward. This was because the personnel – especially Michael and Eon – were all so reasonable, professional, and sane. That was *not* usually the case in the children's TV business. Some development writing gigs can be a total nightmare, but this one was a pleasure. At least from the *creative* side.

As it turned out, from the business side – not so much! Not to imply unprofessionalism, rancor, or insanity nor any scandal. And although I was not personally involved in those negotiations, as far as I knew, it was all cordial and amicable. But a "meeting of the minds" could not be achieved – the parties simply couldn't agree on final terms that worked for all of them. When the deal fell apart, and after several months of working under the assumption that we [DIC] would be producing it, it *was* a bit of a shock.

In terms of an unofficial backstory, did you sort out James Bond Jr.'s exact relationship to James Bond? Is James Bond Jr. actually the child Bond had in the novel *You Only Live Twice*? Or does Bond have a sister or brother that we don't know about?

You know, I can't remember for sure but I have the feeling we left it intentionally unspecified and vague for the reasons I mentioned previously. Understandably, the Eon team did not want the animated series to commit the Bond franchise to any facts about James Bond's backstory or lore so that they would never be in a position of having the movies contradict the cartoon or the toys, or worse, wind up having the "tail wag the dog," by having to make movie decisions based on the cartoon. The movies are the "golden goose." And they still are now 25-years later.

As a writer were you essentially writing James Bond Jr. as a young Bond rather than as a separate character?

Yes, in my mind, I was trying to get as close to a younger replica of James Bond as Eon would let me and children's television standards would permit.

But at the same time, while I intended him to be an extremely precocious and talented kid, he *was* still a teen. And so, realistically, he couldn't be as smooth, suave, confident, or competent as his uncle. Otherwise, he wouldn't play as a kid and he would be neither believable nor relatable as a surrogate to our audience.

Can you talk about the challenges of telling a James Bond story to a young audience? Was the aim always to make it a show aimed at a younger audience?

Yes, this was always definitely intended to be a children's program. So to answer this question would require a long treatise about the ins and outs of broadcast standards and practices and children's perception of media.

The best way to summarize this is the buzz phrase "imitable anti-social behavior," which is not permitted and is the general benchmark by which all script actions are evaluated. The word "imitable" is key here – because that's the "loophole" to getting around some of the restrictions. If the behavior or stunt is so fantastical, larger-than-life, exaggerated, and *unrealistic* that it is *literally impossible* for a young viewer to *imitate*, it was more likely to be acceptable. It was permissible as long as it wasn't "anti-social"—that is, intentionally hurtful or cruel. You can see where the challenge is in trying to write children's action series under this generic rule of thumb.

[To accommodate the constraints of children's TV, we avoided] certain kinds of violence, weaponry, and sexual reference or innuendo. I was *extremely* knowledgeable of children's television – and specifically the broadcast standards and practices: what was and wasn't allowed in children's television. After many years of jostling with network censors and exposure to developmental psychologist consultants and child advocacy groups, I was an expert in this. I knew not only the restrictions but also the thinking and research behind them. So I also knew all the acceptable ways, specific workarounds, and strategies to make action allowable and less likely to be detrimental to children. I knew right where the envelope was and how far I could push it. Michael hadn't had experience in this world, and to his credit, he realized this and was willing to rely entirely on my knowledge of these things.

Creatively speaking, what were the most challenging aspects of the show?

In terms of the development and bible and anticipating writing scripts for the series – I was a little concerned about the repetitiveness of always having to "break James Bond Jr. out of jail" school for every caper. I thought this might quickly get too formulaic – old, boring, and not credible. I don't know if it did, not having seen the series.

There are many references to the popular Bond characters, but the characters tend to have little in common with their on-screen counterparts. Can you talk about the reasoning behind that decision?

I don't remember for sure, but I strongly suspect much of this was probably an attempt by Eon to protect their movie franchise and keep some sense of exclusivity about it and retaining their characters' unique quirks, that could be seen *only* in a James Bond movie and not in our TV series.

How close was the final show to your original concept?

It will likely surprise anyone reading all this, but I honestly don't remember seeing even a single episode of the final series. Due to business differences between DIC, Claster, and Eon, DIC ended up not producing the series, so I had no further involvement in the production itself after completing the bible to everyone's satisfaction. During those years, I was in charge of approximately 200 half hours of original animation a year, spread across a number of networks, clients, and rights holders and responsible for all the problems and crises each series entailed. I was also developing a new series for the following year, plus aiding in international sales of our library, among other things. My life was largely putting out fires. I was working ridiculous hours – and to say I had my hands full is an understatement of magnitude.

Moreover, while I don't remember the deal falling apart as being terribly vitriolic or not amicable, it still was a little awkward. Once it fell apart, DIC was simply no longer involved. I had completed my contractual obligation to Eon, and I was, essentially, DIC, notwithstanding my good personal relations with Michael, Eon, Claster, and Hasbro. In fact, I was extremely flattered and gratified that Michael called me many months later to inquire if I was available to work on another TV project with him – which, to my eternal regret, I was not. The dissolution of DIC's deal was "just business" – it happens – and we went our separate ways, disappointed, but to my recollection without rancor, and certainly none on my part.

Although it wasn't "just business" in that I had a special attachment to this property. I felt I had bonded creatively with Michael. I remember he took me out to a celebratory "wrap' lunch after the completion of the bible, to introduce me to the legendary Cubby Broccoli – the "father" of the James Bond movie franchise. And I was really happy with the bible I'd created and would've loved to have been involved with the series. I would've been much more "hands-on" than I was with many of the other DIC series, in which I hadn't taken as large a role in creating.

I was pleasantly shocked to learn that I had been given screen credit on the series. There are no residuals in most children's animated series because, for the large part, animation writers are covered by a different union than the WGA, so there are no *financial* ramifications to writing credits in animation series. The studios can do whatever they want and tend not to be very conscientious or all that concerned about credits. They were not *required* to give me a credit even if they used my bible verbatim. And, since it was a competing company, I assumed I'd get no screen credit. I always wondered if my getting a credit was Michael Wilson's doing. He struck me as an honorable man. Anyway, as a longtime EVP at DIC and an exclusive Executive Producer of all of DIC's series, and being so firmly associated with DIC, it was bizarre in the extreme to have a screen credit on one of our competitor's shows. It was the only time it ever happened in my 22 years at DIC. But, alas, they misspelled my name [as "Robbie"]. Which remains the only one of my credits, which is spelled that way on IMDB. My personal legacy from *James Bond Jr.*

Advertisement for the series that appeared in a 1991 issue of *The Hollywood Reporter*.

Directing James Bond Jr.
Bill Hutten

With his business partner Tony Love, Bill Hutten directed and produced all 65 episodes of *James Bond Jr.* Hutten has worked in various capacities on over 100 animated television shows, including as an animator, supervising animator, supervising producer, and animation director. As an animator, he worked on numerous staples of children's television, including *The Flintstones* (1964-1965), *The Batman/Superman Hour* (1968), *The All-New Super Friends Hour* (1977), and *The Smurfs* (1981-1984). His directing credits include *Pac-Man* (1982), *Superman* (1988), *Police Academy: The Series* (1988), *The Toxic Crusaders* (1991), *Dino Babies* (1994), and *Chucklewood Critters* (1998-1999), which he created with Tony Love.

* * *

You've directed many animated shows and worked on scores of others. How did *James Bond Jr.* come your way?

The *James Bond Jr.* deal came about with a phone call one evening from Fred Wolf of Fred Wolf Films. Fred and I go way back to Hanna-Barbera Productions in the early sixties. Later, during the mid-seventies, Tony Love and I were well-established in our own animation service company [LHL, Inc.]. Fred called me and asked if I could take over and produce a commercial since he had no room to produce it at his studio. I agreed and produced the commercial for him. Later, during the *Ninja Turtles* production run [of the late eighties and early-to-mid nineties], my company Encore Enterprises performed production services for him.

My studio's animation serviced many studios over many years. Not only did our company contract animation to complete for other companies but my partner and I were also hired to work on large projects for other studios, including Hanna-Barbera, Marvel, DePatie-Freleng [known for *The Pink Panther* and a number of shows based on Dr. Seuss books], and Fred Wolf Films.

Over the phone, Fred outlined the 65 half-hour episodes of *James Bond Jr.* He asked if I would produce and direct the entire series and specifying that it needed to be completed with just a 12-month production schedule. My screen credit was to be: Produced and Directed by Bill Hutten. Fred wanted me to take over all of the show's elements that were not already committed. Story and scripts were previously assigned to a scriptwriting group. It was agreed that my partner would direct half of the programs. Having a co-director allowed me to also oversee all the programs in production and liaise with Eon's on-site supervisor John Parkinson.

The only matter to be worked out was the extra budget for my partner to join in as a co-director. Several days later a deal was made, and the production was scheduled to start the first workday of the new year in 1990. In addition to my responsibilities as a director, along with Fred Wolf and [the late] Tony Love, I was also one of the producers. It was an awesome responsibility.

Most people know what a film and television director does but fewer people understand the role of an animation director. Can you talk about your responsibilities as the co-director of all 65 episodes of the series?

My scope of work on the Bond show was script supervision, voice actor selection, working closely with the Eon supervisor and all production heads working on the series and reviewing the final edit of the episodes.

The director's job in animation can cover many different responsibilities, including animation director, timing director, supervising director, or just director. In this case, Fred Wolf hired me to oversee the entire series. Starting with the first draft of the script, I would review for content and identify any potential animation problems. Not all writers write scripts that are animation-friendly.

I also oversaw the main character designs and the designs of all incidental characters for each episode. All our material, including character model packets, [drawings of the figures] color style packs [which indicate the color palate], and background drawings would be compiled for each episode and presented to the producer and directors at a meeting. Once all the material was approved, then I would set a meeting with John Parkinson of Eon for his review. Then we shipped everything to the overseas animation company for the production of the animation, background, and cel painting [hand-drawn paintings on a transparent plastic sheet].

Each episode went through this approval process. Any changes would be made before the shipping date. Our goal was to ship on Fridays with assurances that the material would arrive on a Monday morning. This shipping arrival date was vital in making sure the corrected workprint would arrive back at the studio on time for our post-production to start.

During the period of pre-production, I would review each script and order changes when necessary. It is quite common for writers of half-hour animation shows to miss details relevant to the story. This happens more frequently when writers split scripts. Because we were producing 65 episodes in a [tight] time frame, many writers were needed. A bible of the series was created for the writers [so that they could immerse themselves in the names and traits of] the characters in the series. Story supervisors would be responsible for most of these areas, but things do slip by.

Catching last-minute mistakes was vital. Making changes during the review of the film workprint becomes very expensive and time-consuming. I always had department heads consistently check storyboards and other previously shipped materials for corrections. If a mistake was found after shipping, we immediately sent the corrected material to the oversees production company. The overseas supervisor had instructions to review all material they received and immediately notify the studio of any additional missing material. [Double-checking the material] saved valuable cost and time.

The director is responsible for all three areas of production—pre-production, production, and post-production. It was best to work in order of production, however, that rarely worked out. I could be wrapping up pre-production X-Sheets [a document that tracks all the elements of a scene, including the animation, dialogue, camera movement, and music] on one episode, pre-production approvals on model sheets for another show and making changes on the pre-production storyboards on another show and then go to my office in the afternoon to read a first draft script on another episode.

At times it was not unusual to have 10 to 12 active scripts sitting on my desk in various stages of production. After each script was approved, it was then turned over to the director who would give his notes to the production department. Also, during that time, the voice recording is scheduled and the dialogue scripts are created for the actors with the director's notes, if needed.

The overseas productions usually required 14 weeks to be completed. The work consists of layouts, finished animation, Xerox transfers and coloring, painted backgrounds, animation camera, and final workprint and negative.

The post-production stage begins with the 35mm workprint and negative going to the film editor. The editor trims the footage and cuts the episode into three acts. The director is then called in to review the show and be on the lookout for mistakes in the animation and camera goofs. If errors are spotted, then retakes are sent immediately back to the overseas production company, with detailed instructions on a retake sheet about how to redo the material. All retakes are given high priority. The returned retakes are cut into the edited workprint. Next, the producer-director reviews the episode to OK it and then it goes to the music and sound effects editor. The episode is reviewed before the sound mixing. If anything needs attention it is fixed before the final sound mix. It is very costly to re-edit after the sound mix. Now the episode is complete.

It sounds like a heavy load.

I estimate that creating 65 episodes would be like making twenty 80-minute movies in a year. It's the nature of the beast.

Can you further explain the purpose of X-Sheets?

During the production, the director's notes are well spelled out on the X-Sheets for the animators to follow. X-Sheets means "exposure sheets." The director times out each scene and even makes small drawings on the expressions of the characters to help the animators understand the director's intent during the scene. The animator's X-Sheet is usually a series of lines that form many squares. Each square in the column represents one frame of film. There are 16 frames for each foot of 35mm film. Each X-Sheet is five feet. For the director's timing purpose, every 24 frames of film are one second of real time. All around the world, animators use the same timing guide. This is how I can time each scene or sequence of animation to the exact timed-length. To figure out the length of scenes we count footage. Before sending material overseas each scene is charted so we know the exact length of the episode.

In the case of *James Bond Jr.*, I think we would have 40 feet or so for each episode. Broadcast delivery would be 2160 feet or 24 minutes. The director sits with the editor and cuts the show to length. Having some overage film allowed me to trim soft spots in each episode.

What is outside of an animation director's purview?

Anything relating to the content of the shows was covered prior to the start of the animation production.

What did you have to keep in mind when selecting performers for the show?

Due to budget restraints, it was necessary to choose some actors who have a broad range so that they could voice different characters for the show.

What was Eon's involvement in the show?

Eon's Michael Wilson and Barbara Broccoli appointed John Parkinson as their on-site contact. John's primary aim was to keep the Bond franchise separate from the cartoon series and to help keep the new young characters in *James Bond Jr.* from turning into more adult-oriented characters.

John would read all the final scripts and then discuss any questions with the directors. He also attended the recording sessions, reviewed master art, and episode model sheets; he always wanted to help. He was the eyes and ears for Eon Productions. *James Bond Jr.* was developed by another studio [DIC] before it went to Fred Wolf Films. I never viewed any of the material from their presentation.

Can you elaborate on working with Eon?

John Parkinson was our liaison to Eon. In the early part of the production, John reviewed the scripts and then forwarded them to England with both his and our comments. Eon would return scripts and material with comments ASAP. They were very aware of our production schedule.

I learned much from John Parkinson about how the family wanted to protect their franchise. I would meet with John in his office and over long lunches, we had discussions about looking for anything that could be detrimental to the program. For example, we needed to make sure that the artists didn't draw the girl characters too sexy or enhance any of their features. James Bond Jr. should never chase girls or speak to them in the same manner that Bond would in the movies. If we felt any aspect of the episode became too "salty," it was reviewed and changed. References to drinking were not allowed. To the best of my recollection, I do not think anyone referred to James Bond Jr. as "007 Jr." All of these elements were watched by Eon. This transfer of information worked out very well and Eon seemed pleased to have a good group of professionals working on their franchise.

Most of the important parameters for *James Bond Jr.* were ironed out before I came on board. I understand that protecting the James Bond brand was part of Fred Wolf's studio's presentation for *James Bond Jr.* These guidelines were given to the writers before they submitted their episode outlines.

***James Bond Jr.* was quite a departure from the Bond movies. Why do you think Eon wanted to make the show?**

At that time Fred Wolf was wrapping up the very successful 65-episode series *Teenage Mutant Ninja Turtles*. I don't remember being told but I suspect the Bond series went to Fred due to the *Turtles* success. It may also have had appeal as a successful merchandising venture. There was a good fan base out there and it probably seemed like a good project. Many companies were looking for the next *Ninja Turtles* success.

It's only my opinion, but I think Eon was drawn into the overall animated process and there was no risk that the *James Bond Jr.* characters would ever hurt the Bond movie franchise. Remember the series was geared to a targeted age group.

Later, after the series was completed Michael and Barbara had a wrap party for many of the people who worked on the series. During the event, he asked me to get together with him to discuss potential properties to develop for another animated series. We did meet but that's another story.

Did you think of James Jr. as a young 007 and not necessarily a separate character?

My take is that after the [events depicted in the series were] completed James Jr. would essentially be a young version of James Bond. There were many times when he had the look and style of the Bond movie character. But at the same time, I am sure that Bond Jr. appears to be a separate and distinct character.

How would you describe James Bond Jr.'s character?

One of the main goals was not to make him into a superhero.

What do you think the show did well and where do you think it fell short?

That's a tough question. When I finished the series and the last episode was finished it was a year and a week since we started. I met the deadline. I was not sure when the show would run on TV. It was out of my hands. So Tony and I headed back to our studio where we had some of our own productions to complete.

James Bond Jr. appealed to the young teenage audience that it was designed to attract. We all know marketing is the key to getting good ratings. I see comments on the internet and people still like it.

Personally, I don't think it came up short. It was entertaining and had audience appeal. I believe our production team did a great job. My belief is that if the distributors got all the required stations for broadcast then everything was done correctly. I still get e-mails and notes about *James Bond Jr.*

What are your fondest memories of making the show?

One of the better moments during the production is when John Parkinson arranged to have Michael Wilson, Barbara Broccoli, and "Cubby" Broccoli sit in a recording session for one of my episodes. I introduced the cast, voice director, and the others and then they watched the cast perform. After the cast left the recording studio Cubby said to me that he had no idea what it took to produce a cartoon film. Earlier that morning the group also visited the studio to see the entire production in action. Well over 60 to 70 people were working on the series.

During recording and editing, the sound guys liked to keep the outtakes of the sessions. Towards the end of the series, they gave me a cassette with very funny outtakes. But I think my most outstanding memory was being invited to Michael Wilson and Barbara Broccoli's home to celebrate the series wrap with cocktails and dinner. My wife and I enjoyed it greatly. Some other members of the show were also there. They were very gracious people.

James Bond Jr. and his Aston Martin, as imagined by Pat Carbajal
Illustration by Pat Carbajal

Writing James Bond Jr. – Part One
Mary Crawford and Alan Templeton

Mary Crawford and Alan Templeton co-wrote six episodes of the animated series *James Bond Jr.*: "Live and Let's Dance," in which Bond Jr. saves a ballerina from the terrorist Baron Von Skarin; "Dance of the Toreadors," wherein Bond Jr. rescues a kidnapped flamenco dancer and thwarts Von Skarin's plot to create a major blackout in England; "Mindfield," about a telepathic student; "There But For Ms. Fortune" concerns a glamorous villain's scheme to freeze the Colorado River to gain control of a major power source in the United States; "Appointment in Macau," in which Dr. No seeks to mete out vengeance on a Chinese triad; and "Killer Asteroid," which concerns Auric Goldfinger's plan to crash a gold asteroid into Earth.[416]

"Live and Let's Dance" and "Dance of the Toreadors" were adapted into novelizations, the latter of which was also turned into a comic book published by Marvel.[417]

In addition to writing *James Bond Jr.*, they also wrote for the animated series *Dennis the Menace* (1988), *The Care Bears Family* (1988), *Barbar* (1989-1991), *Young Robin Hood* (1991-1992), *The Legend of White Fang* (1992), *RoboCop* (1994), *Flash Gordon* (1996), *Watership Down* (2000-2001), *King* (2003-2005), *World of Quest* (2009), and the live-action shows *Earth: Final Conflict* (1997-2002) and *F/X: The Series* (1996-1998).

Crawford and Templeton offer this charming caveat about their joint interview, which was conducted via e-mail: "We're going back to '91 and we've written a couple of hundred scripts since then. But we'll give it a try. When we shift from 'we' to 'I' in our commentary, it's only to avoid sounding pompous."

* * *

Can you describe the process of writing an episode of *James Bond Jr.?* Were you assigned stories or did you pitch them?

Scripts weren't assigned. We were invited to pitch ideas by Jack Mendelsohn, the story editor on the series [who was also a co-writer of The Beatles animated film *Yellow Submarine* (1968) and an Emmy-nominated writer whose other television credits include *The Carol Burnett Show* (1967-78)]. We'd worked with him before on *The Adventures of Teddy Ruxpin* and I guess he liked our stuff well enough to invite a couple of Canadians onto an American series. For the time (and even now) that was unusual, unless the series was tapping Canadian funding. First up, I reread the Bond books, which I enjoyed all over again. Then we brainstormed six story ideas and sent them off.

Jack was generous with his knowledge about the cartoon game, and the first thing he told us was never present a story editor with a smorgasbord of ideas. He or she will cherry-pick, and the rest will be for naught. In this case, the Executive Producer at Murakami Wolfe asked to see what he had so far. All he had were our pitches, so we sold them all in one go.

We came up with the stories by starting with the villain. Then we devised a big Bondian plot to fit the villain's tastes. Next, we picked an exotic locale where the story would unfold. There were certain rote mechanicals we had to contrive. How do they get out of Warfield, what circumstances take them to the location, what's the subplot and so on. Then we just got down to writing.

The only variation on this approach was "Appointment in Macau." That story was triggered by Dr. No's revelation in the book and in the movie that he'd fallen afoul of a Chinese tong that subsequently tried to off him. He only survived because the heart shot failed to kill him because his heart was on the right side of his chest. We figured he had the right to seek revenge and followed the story accordingly.

First, we wrote an outline, beating out each scene—action teaser, three acts, and an epilogue. It usually ran ten pages or so and took two or three days. We'd fire that off to Jack by fax. He'd come back with notes and then we'd write the script. That usually took five days or so. That went off to Jack. As I recall, we usually wrote only one draft and Jack did any necessary tweaking. The whole process was fairly fast, as most cartoon gigs are.

Who was James Bond Jr. in your mind?

James Jr. was a kind of fantasy Bond for kids. He had to be. His uncle James had no siblings so he couldn't have a nephew. James Jr. was a vehicle to execute our over-the-top Bondian fantasies. He could just as well have been Matt Helm Jr. [The Matt Helm film series of the sixties were spoofs of the spy genre.]

Did you try to differentiate Bond Jr. from his uncle?

To be honest, the character wasn't much of a consideration. Action and smart-assed dialogue were the main drivers. Having James or IQ [Q's grandson] develop this or that crush on the Bond girl of the episode was about as far as character development went. There wasn't time, room, or inclination for depth. It just had to move fast, have good gags, and a few laughs. James Jr.'s character was based largely on Roger Moore's Bond incarnation and, as much I enjoy his movies, he didn't bring a lot of nuance to the character.

Goldfinger and Dr. No appear in "Killer Asteroid" and "Appointment in Macau," respectively. How did you approach reinterpreting classic Bond villains?

Let's face it, the original villains were already cartoons. We just took them as they were and sent them a little further over the top. In Fleming's *Goldfinger* novel, Goldfinger's plot didn't make much sense; something the screenwriters recognized. In the movie, Bond points out the impossibility of making off with all the gold in Fort Knox. It's then that Goldfinger shows his real genius – atomically contaminating America's gold reserves to drive up the worth of his own gold holdings. A far better plot development than Fleming offered.

Also, Dr. No and Goldfinger died in the movies. And even if Goldfinger hadn't died, can you imagine him siring an offspring [named Goldie Finger, as he did on the show]?

There were characters in your scripts with names like Mrs. Hotstones that are designed to amuse adults, but you are writing a children's program. Can you talk about finding the right tone for your episodes and striking the right balance with dialogue?

Even if we're writing for kids, we first write to amuse ourselves. Generally, we dislike dumbing things down more than a story editor deems necessary, and even then, we'll kick. Kids aren't given enough credit for taste and smarts. We wrote all 52 episodes of a series called *King* and packed it with satirical jibes at everything from politics to economics to environmental issues and so on. It was written to amuse both kids and adults and it was all done with the unwavering support of the producers. A lot of what you do boils down to what you're allowed to do and that depends on the wit and wisdom of the producer you're working with.

The only other thing we can offer about dialogue is – say it yourself aloud, and in the cartoon voice that you hear in your head. If the words don't fit real Kentucky in your mouth, it won't fit in the actor's mouth either.

In "Live and Let's Dance," IQ briefs James Bond Jr. about his newest invention, which IQ points out are "For your eyes only James." In the same scene IQ makes a reference to a few "optional extras" he added to Jr.'s van. I imagine a lot of the fun of writing for the show was trying to weave in references to the movies.

Yep, that was fun. So was coming up with an episode title that riffed on the originals. I guess my favorite Bond reference that I recall without access to the scripts was in "Killer Asteroid." That's the one that took our heroes to Iceland. IQ and James Jr. are locked in a cage about to be fried by erupting lava. Upon making their escape IQ makes some comment about their rough landing and James Jr. says something along the lines of, "Just be glad you're shaken not stir-fried."

In one episode, Bond and IQ are being held captive in a cage that is going to be submerged into an active lava pit. Bond narrowly escapes and remarks, "At least we were just shaken, not stir-fried." Do the story editors and producers make sure that a reference like that doesn't appear too frequently?

Yes, I imagine Jack made sure gags weren't overused. I like to think ours was the best take. Also, I think we got in first with the spin on that line.

Some of your episodes poke gentle fun at Bond movie tropes. For example, in "Appointment in Macau" after Dr. No's private island lair explodes, James Bond Jr. quips, "They just don't make artificial islands like they used to." Can you talk about your approach to affectionately sending up the series?

The movies, particularly the Roger Moore movies, were already sending up themselves. Using the tonal code lifted from *Close Encounters of the Third Kind* (1977) in *Moonraker* comes to mind. If we saw an opportunity for a line, in it went. No offense was taken.

Do you recall any ideas you wanted to use but were given some push back because they were too close to the cinematic Bond or because they violated the show's rules?

Jack never nixed much I can remember. Although in "Appointment in Macau" we gave the Raven Tong leader a different name, Jack wanted to call him Lo Fat. We thought that was a tad lame, and potentially slightly racist. But Lo Fat stayed. Since we only saw a couple of our own episodes, I can't really tell you what stayed or what was cut.

What do you remember about the day-to-day challenges of working on the show?

At the time, the Internet was nascent as were other communications options. At the time, scripts went to producers by courier. No one transferred data electronically, not even the other big companies we worked for like [the Canadian production company] Nelvana. When we got the Bond job, the first thing Jack asked us was "Do you have a fax machine?" The second was "Do you have a modem?" We had neither but went out and bought them pronto.

As I recall, the fax cost nearly a grand. I had a clunky old Toshiba laptop that used a five-inch floppy disk and a DOS boot disk. If we wrote an episode on the laptop, we had to transfer it to Mary's IBM, because that unit had the modem. Since our disks were incompatible, we had to use a gizmo called Lap Link to transfer files to Mary's IBM. It was hellaciously complicated and touchy. Jack Mendelsohn was an early adopter of computer technology. He set up his own Bulletin Board at his Son of a Beach production office and he had his own sysop [system administrator].

Once the file was on board the IBM, we had to dial into the Bulletin Board and upload our script. The whole operation was fraught, requiring several stiff drinks. The upload process took upwards of five minutes and was prone to shutting down in the middle of things. On one occasion, we lost an entire script off of our machine. Fortunately, it made the trip to Los Angeles.

It was also the first time we'd heard of scripts flying around the world before seeing paper. As I remember it, the script first went to L.A. From there Jack sent it to Eon in London. Then it went to New York and finally back to L.A. It made us feel all international.

Goldfinger's tractor beam in "Killer Asteroid" is called Skyhammer. I don't think the writers of *Skyfall* had your episode in mind when they came up with the name of Bond's childhood home, but when I recently watched your episode, I thought it was an amusing coincidence. Goldfinger's scheme to use the tractor beam to bring an all-gold asteroid crashing to earth feels like a particularly strong premise for the animated series. What do you recall about writing that episode?

We remember thinking, "Where can Goldfinger get more gold than he's ever dreamed of?" The idea of an asteroid popped to mind almost right away. That allowed us to give a nod to both *You Only Live Twice* and *Moonraker*, with the space shuttle hijacking scene at the beginning. The Iceland setting was prompted by Alan's backpacking days. In London, he stayed in a hostel used mainly by Australians. They traveled Europe for years, taking breaks to work lousy jobs for enough money to keep traveling. A lot of them went to Iceland to work in fish and cod liver oil plants. The job was lousy but the money was good. Alan almost gave it a shot, but second thoughts saved the day.

Bond Jr. dons a wetsuit in one of your episodes. Hasbro produced a line of action figures, including one in which James Bond Jr. is wearing a similar outfit. Practically speaking, how does it work? Were you asked to put Bond in a scenario where he would wear a wetsuit?

No one asked us to insert gizmos or get-ups that might see life in the toy line.

Do you have a favorite line from the show?

I'd say the one you mentioned. Although we did give a line to Baron Von Skarin in "Live and Let's Dance" that cracked us up. After the good Baron gets his just desserts he says to his dog, "Schnitzel, I think ve should haff stayed in Argentina."

Do you have a favorite script that you wrote?

Favorite would be "Live and Let's Dance." I thought the action was quite Bondian and I still love the idea of a Hawker Harrier Jump Jet chasing our heroes through the Mont Blanc tunnel. We checked the dimensions of both tunnel and jet and yes, a Harrier fits.

Least favorite?

Least favorite would be "Dance of the Toreadors." IQ's fishing lure tracker was too on the nose and the climactic action was a bit limp. It's one of the few episodes I saw. It looked much grander in our heads than it did on screen.

What were your thoughts about the show?

I had fun writing it. What I wanted to do was give kids the same Saturday morning jazz I remembered. Comic books had a page announcing the new season's upcoming cartoon shows and I couldn't wait. *Jonny Quest* [1964-65], *Frankenstein Jr. and The Impossibles* [1966-68], *The Herculoids* [1967-69], *Batfink* [1966-67], *Space Ghost* [1966-82], *Moby Dick and Mighty Mightor* [1967-68], and *Super President* [1967-68]. I even had the joy of writing for the Hanna-Barbera cartoon *Young Robin Hood* and sharing songwriting credits with those wonderful creators. I wanted to write a cartoon show that made kids as excited about Saturday morning as I used to be.

So every time we sat down at the computer, we'd start by riffing the movie's opening music and charge on from there with the intent of coming up with something juiced and fun. Being part of the Bond canon in any way was an honor. We're aware the series wasn't and isn't well received by those Internet trolls that feel the need to offer their dank basement opinions on a kids' show. Sadly, they're not kids and they're not likely to grow up soon, so to hell with them.

Admittedly, the animation in the few episodes I did see was wanting, but it was as wanting in all those Saturday morning shows that I loved. It was wanting in *The Flintstones*. So what? It's still aired everywhere. Kids fill in the blanks. *The Quick Draw McGraw Show* wasn't exactly *Bambi* but I did love Baba Looey. Sure I wish they'd thrown as much money at the production quality as they did in marketing and making the James Bond Jr. toy line but corporate bottom lines prevail. We live with it and take what we can get.

Writing James Bond Jr. – Part Two
Doug Molitor
Benjamin Pollack
Bryce Malek
Francis Moss

Doug Molitor wrote three episodes of the animated series *James Bond Jr.*—"Going for the Gold" "The Eiffel Missile," and "Shifting Sands." Two of Molitor's episodes, "The Eiffel Missile" and "Shifting Sands" were novelized by John Peel. "The Eiffel Missile" was also adapted into a Marvel comic book by writer Cal Hamilton.

Benjamin Pollack wrote two episodes of the 1991 cartoon—"Never Lose Hope" and "Canine Caper." "Canine Caper" was one of six titles that Caryn Jenner adapted into a children's book.

Bryce Malek was a story editor for eight episodes—"Earth Cracker," "Never Lose Hope," "The Emerald Key," "The Heartbreak Caper," "Far Out West," "Catching the Wave," Molitor's "Goldie's Gold Scam," and Pollack's "Canine Caper." Malek also has an unexpected connection to "Goldie's Gold Scam," which he reveals in this interview.

Francis Moss co-wrote two *James Bond Jr.* episodes with Ted Pedersen, "The Beginning," the first episode of *James Bond Jr.*, and "No Time to Lose." Moss was also an assistant story editor on the series.

In Doug Molitor's "Going for the Gold," James Bond Jr. travels to Spain to compete in a high school track meet and uncovers the dastardly plan by Auric Goldfinger's daughter, Goldie Finger, to steal all the gold from the Christopher Columbus Museum. In "Shifting Sands," Bond Jr. goes to Egypt, uncovers Pharaoh Fearo's plot to steal all of Egypt's oil. And in "The Eiffel Missile," Bond travels to France where he uncovers mad scientists Skull Cap and Dr. Derange's scheme to use the Eiffel Tower to launch a missile.

As was typical with the series, Molitor's plots generally follow the same beats as a Bond movie. His episodes include a pre-title sequence, a mystery which James must investigate, a scene in which Bond is trapped and must use his wits or a gadget to escape, a larger than life villain with a fantastic scheme, futuristic gadgets, elaborate action set pieces, and a teen version of a Bond Woman.

Molitor's episodes are replete with mission-specific gadgets, supplied to Bond by his friend IQ, grandson of Q. In the Paris-based "The Eiffel Missile," Bond is given a baguette that conceals a sword and landmine that is disguised as a beret. In "Going for the Gold," in which the students of Warfield Academy compete at a track meet, IQ gives Bond a vaulting pole that extends and a boomerang that's disguised as a discus.

In keeping with Roger Moore's later Bond films, Molitor, who would go on to write for the cult-comedy series *Sledge Hammer!* (1986-1988), packed his episodes with puns. In "The Eiffel Missile," Bond declines to take the sword with him because it's "A bit sharp for my tastes" and he declines to take a beret bomb with him to Paris because "That would blow my mind." The name of Bond's love interest, Marcie Beaucoup, is another play on words. In "Going for the Gold," Bond locks the muscle-bound Barbella in the steam room, and the angry villain demands to be let out. Bond remarks, "Why Barbella, you sound a bit steamed." When, in "Shifting Sands," a guard slips on some oil, Bond says, "Looks like we gave him the slip." Upon seeing a mummy, Bond says, "He's too wrapped up in his work." Before answering my questions about his work on the series, Molitor rewatched his three episodes, which he hadn't seen in years. He charmingly confessed, "I had forgotten so much of them. I hope it's not disgustingly immodest to say I laughed at gags I'd totally forgotten writing."

In Benjamin Pollack's "Never Lose Hope," James Bond Jr.'s new science teacher Hope Eternal, who also researches brainwaves, has been kidnapped by agents of the criminal organization S.C.U.M., short for Saboteurs and Criminals United in Mayhem. Bond tracks Hope to an island, which S.C.U.M. has been using to perform secret experiments. At the island, Bond learns that Hope faked her own kidnapping and had tricked Bond into tracking her there. It turns out that Hope is seeking revenge on 007, who she believes inadvertently killed her father while destroying S.C.U.M.'s lab. Hope straps Bond to her brainwave machine. But he escapes by employing his rocket-booster sneakers, which propels him into the insidious contraption, destroying it in the process. After James Jr. defeats Hope, it's revealed that Hope's father is still alive and that he has been in hiding from S.C.U.M.

In Pollack's "Canine Caper," England's top defense expert, Bernard Chaplan, is pursued by S.C.U.M. agents. Before S.C.U.M. kidnaps him, Chaplan hides the microfilm in his dog's collar. Bond finds the dog and discovers that the microfilm contains Scotland Yard's security plans. While trying to locate Chaplan, Bond meets Heather, who appears to have sinister intentions towards him. Later, Bond uses a homing device that IQ hid in the dog's collar to track Chaplan to an abandoned railway station. At the railway station, Bond learns that evil scientist Dr. Derange was planning to use the plans to destroy Scotland Yard with an acid bomb. Dr. Derange explains that when he couldn't locate the dog, he led Bond directly to him in the hopes that he'd bring the microfilm. After Bond defeats Dr. Derange, Bond finds out that Heather wasn't a threat, but a police officer and the daughter of Chaplan.

Pollack's episodes, like Molitor's, were also brimming with puns. In "Never Lose Hope," an angry clown chases Bond Jr. through a mall. After Bond changes the direction on the escalator and sends the clown flying, Bond says, "An escalator is no place for clowning around." Of the sneakers that enable the wearer to float, Bond says, "What an uplifting experience."

As a story editor, Malek was responsible for working with the scriptwriters of individual episodes, helping to facilitate the approval of their pitches, and ensuring that their scripts were consistent with the producers' vision for the series.

In Moss and Pedersen's "The Beginning," the evil S.C.U.M. Lord plots to steal 007's Aston Martin, which James Bond Jr. has borrowed from his uncle. James Bond Jr. thwarts the villain's plan but 007's vehicle is destroyed in the process. When Bond Jr. returns to his school, he learns that a very forgiving and generous 007 has gifted him with a new tricked-out sports car. [As part of the marketing campaign for *James Bond Jr.*, Hasbro sold a replica of the red sports car that was equipped with spring-fired toy missiles, a pop-out battering ram, and, of course, an ejector seat.]

In "No Time to Lose," Dr. No's inept goons mistakenly kidnap IQ, Bond's inventor friend instead of Q, IQ's grandfather, and their intended target. Dr. No seizes on the opportunity and forces IQ to build Q's aircraft dubbed The Vulture, the "most terrifying weapon in the world," so that he can use the aircraft to seize control of a major city. In the end, Bond Jr. and IQ stop Dr. No with the help of the "ultralight," IQ's own aircraft.

My interviews with Doug Molitor, Benjamin Pollack, Bryce Malek, and Francis Moss were conducted separately and I have combined them.

Can you describe the process of writing an episode of *James Bond Jr.*?

MOLITOR: "The Eiffel Missile" was my first episode, and it was atypical. The story editor gave me an approved pitch and the major beats of the story had been laid down. So I just had to figure out specific locales and gags and action beats and write all the dialogue. Usually, I'd come up with four or five brief pitches, send them to my story editor, Jack Mendelsohn, and he'd tell me which wouldn't work and why, and pick the one he liked best. I'd expand that into an outline, and if there weren't too many notes, and there rarely were when I worked for Jack, then I'd go straight to script. There would be more notes [from Jack Mendelsohn, the producers, or the partnering production companies, such as MGM Television], and I'd do the second draft; and then if need be, I'd do a polish, though I rarely had to do more than two drafts for Jack. On our last show together [*The Fantastic Voyages of Sinbad the Sailor* (1996-1998)], I was writing one script a week, a first draft, and done.

POLLACK: The writing process was very specific. One dry martini, shaken not stirred, and one fine imported cigar. By the end of the story, both would be gone. Sometimes there was a second cigar. No plots were given, I had to come up with all the scenarios. As I recall, I pitched the ideas and was given a green light the next day.

MOSS: We were handed some ideas but came up with others on our own, as did the freelancers who pitched to us. The show's bible had suggestions as well. Ted Pedersen and I had been writing together for a while, so our process was fairly smooth, working via phone and modem. First drafts took maybe three or four days. Based on the outlines we'd done, I'd write half the script, and he'd write the other half. Then we'd put them together and work out the kinks. It was the equivalent of joining the eastern and western tracks of the transcontinental railroad, but with less manual labor required. [As an assistant story editor,] my work on *James Bond Jr.*, like the other shows I edited, consisted of re-writing freelance scripts to conform to the arc of the show and the ways the characters spoke, and by adding action and humor.

What direction did the producers give you before you started writing your scripts? What were your marching orders?

POLLACK: There were no marching orders given when I was writing for *James Bond Jr.* The only direction I was given was "Don't do things like make the sun or moon a character that has lines." Given that as a guide, I re-watched as many James Bond films as I could to absorb the Bond universe and redirect it out for children.

Can you talk about the challenges of shaping the Bond universe for children?

MOLITOR: Pretty much the challenge of any cartoon action series is to do G-rated action with violence but no actual death or serious injury; with Bond, we also needed a hint of romance – but no sex. The story editor would simply rewrite anything that looked controversial, but that rarely happened with me.

POLLACK: Adapting the character for children was very easy as it was his nephew and not James himself. So he was a new character, one that had a set of rules already built in. Staying true to the narrative was also an important key. Children are smart but their attention span can be short.

MALEK: I think a lot of the interest in James Bond cannot be transferred to the young audience. James Bond is an adult, created for an adult audience. I mean, I liked the movies because of the women, the danger, including real death, and the adult aspects of the character. The plots may have been more juvenile and fantastic, but they were not childish. You have to strip all that out when you're doing a cartoon show. I'm sure the people who owned the rights wanted to make money from it, and syndicated cartoon/toy packages were the popular shows in those days. It can be fantastic and exciting, but it won't be adult. Perhaps Japanese anime would have been a better fit, who knows?

MOSS: I'd written for several kids' shows. Appropriate language, tone, and action were in my DNA by then – the good guys don't use guns; they make bad guys with guns fall down, and they make things fall down on bad guys. The good guys have the best lines, often the last lines. Nobody dies, at least not on-screen.

Were you trying to write a mini-Bond movie but in just 22 minutes and for children?

MOLITOR: Precisely. Though unlike the films, the opening stunt tied into the episode's plot. I no longer have my scripts. But as I recall it was a 3-act structure: Cold open, Act I, and Act II. And in those 22 minutes, you had to service the villains' plot, the Bond-and-Bond-girl plot, and often a tertiary plot, like IQ's feeling athletically useless in "Going for the Gold." And there would be the running gag where Trevor [Noseworthy IV, Bond's jealous school-mate] would have some goal and get his comeuppance several times an episode. And of course, at least one action set-piece per act.

POLLACK: It was a blend of Bond and something new that could stand on its own.

MALEK: Well, those aspects are what made the shows like "James Bond." You always have to plot for 22 min-utes, and you have to be concerned about the age of your audience. If we thought of these as feature-length films, we probably saved those ideas for feature films we wanted to write someday. They would have been too complicated, plot-wise, for a short time span. For some other shows, they might have been made into two or three-parters. The scripts were about 42 to 45 pages.

MOSS: The structure was more determined by the constraints of television: act breaks, length, age-appropriateness, etc. We used elements from the movies, but I at least had no intention of duplicating a Bond film.

What was the schedule like?

MALEK: The schedule was usually pretty brutal. Maybe one completed show per week.

I imagine trying to come up with 65 Bond capers was a challenge for everyone.

MALEK: That was the challenging part. Plus you had several other writers competing for stories. It's always hard to find new adventures that were not also used in the many, many cartoon series that were concurrently running. I do remember having some issues with writing dialogue for this show. Many writers wanted to write in an English accent or at least some kind of sophisticated voice. How should these characters speak, and how do we translate that in the dialogue? Ultimately, we wrote everything rather American, and let the actors revise their dialogue so that it would remain consistent.

Can you talk about Eon's involvement with the show?

MALEK: I never heard the name Eon until you brought it up. Perhaps they always said "MGM."

Conceptually, did you consider James Bond Jr. to be a young 007? Or did you think of them as two different characters and try to differentiate Jr. from his uncle?

MOLITOR: Obviously, he was far more innocent than 007. He didn't kill people. But he had the same smart-aleck attitude that Roger Moore displayed in the role. I could imagine him someday being a full-fledged spy, if not one with a license to kill.

POLLACK: They were the same in that James Jr. had to be honest and real, handsome, and modest, and true of heart. He also had to have some of the sense of humor James had. You must realize that the intended audience, little children, probably either never saw a James Bond movie or, if they did, probably didn't understand it as an adult would. So we had to create a character that could stand on his own.

MALEK: I generally thought of him as a separate character, as he was not James Bond himself, but his own man-boy. And he couldn't do a lot of things the older James Bond did, obviously, and didn't have a license to kill. But they were both master crime fighters who were erudite and elite without being pompous about it, never shrinking from danger, and always suave and somewhat sophisticated. But you always have to keep Junior a bit younger than the adults, so perhaps he's more impetuous. James Jr. also has a group of friends to help him solve crimes, whereas James Bond Sr. worked alone. I'm kind of surprised [the animation studio] Murakami-Wolf-Swenson didn't add a dog and a mystery van.

MOSS: I didn't think about James Bond senior much at all. The films were inspiring, but James Bond Jr. was a clever, resourceful teenager, loyal to his friends, and a fierce defender of right. He was not an 007-to-be.

How would you characterize James Bond Jr.?

MOLITOR: He was, like his uncle, a fighter for good. A defender of the realm. And like his uncle, the whole world seemed to amuse him. But unlike the elder Bond, young James had a circle of close friends whom he was always looking out for, which made him warmer and more reliable than the movie Bond. 007 has always tended to get the people around him killed. So you might want to be the Bond girl, but you didn't want to be the second-string Bond girl, like Jill Masterson (Shirley Eaton) in *Goldfinger*, or Rosie (Gloria Hendry) in *Live and Let Die*.

POLLACK: He was funny and clever. He was a winner and not just because of his family, but a true stand-up guy. He had to be street smart but also an A-student, as both would save his life.

James Bond was an only child and didn't have any siblings, so he can't have a nephew. Was there ever any discussion of how James Bond Jr. fit in the film canon?

POLLACK: Oddly, there was never any discussion of Bond Jr. and his connection with the films.

One of the original ideas of the show was that James Bond Jr.'s parents were missing and that young Bond must find them. Do you know why that wasn't included in the show?

MOSS: I recall mention of that, and I think a storyline was floating around, but such decisions were above my pay grade.

Let's discuss your individual episodes. Francis Moss, what do you remember about writing "The Beginning," the first episode of the series?

MOSS: I just re-read the script. It still reads OK, but I remember almost nothing. I wrote the sequence in the S.C.U.M. jet where James Bond Jr. and Tracy fight off Jaws [inside the large cargo hold] with 007's Aston Martin and narrowly escape the villain's clutches by parachuting away. As he does in the film *Moonraker*, Jaws jumps out of the jet without a parachute but miraculously survives.

What about "No Time to Lose," the episode where IQ is kidnapped?

MOSS: I just re-read it for the first time in years. I remember a few of the lines that I wrote. I was adept at snark and wisecracks, but how Ted and I came up with the storyline is lost in time. We sometimes got story suggestions or premises from Murakami-Wolf and/or the Broccoli people. This might have been a story from them. We had artwork for most of the props, but the plot details and dialogue were ours.

Doug Molitor, throughout the series, Bond introduces himself as, "Bond, James Bond, Junior." However, in "Shifting Sands," Bond simply says "Bond, James Bond." The Junior is uncharacteristically dropped. How did that come about?

MOLITOR: I believe that was a change made after the script left my hands. It did sound odd to me when I rewatched the show yesterday.

Was there ever any discussion of how James Bond Jr. and the villains fit in the film canon?

MOLITOR: Of course, Bond would have liked to fit any of these villains into a cannon and fire them over the next hilltop. As far as the canon, the show bible permitted us to use several classic Bond villains, like Goldfinger, Oddjob, Nick Nack, and Jaws. If I had a pitch for any of them, I've forgotten it, so I can't say how they'd have fit into the universe of the film. I presume Oddjob was just so darn tough that even getting fried at Fort Knox was only a temporary setback.

The bible also provided villains created for the show like Goldie Finger, Dr. Derange, Skullcap, and Barbella. Goldie inherited her villainy and her gold habit Auric. Barbella had plenty of butt-kicking antecedents in the films: Pussy Galore, Bambi & Thumper, and May Day. But we could also pitch our own villains. So in "Shifting Sands," I created Pharaoh Fearo, a kind of Captain Nemo who is obsessed with ancient Egypt.

Do you know why the villains often have little to do with their on-screen counterparts? For example, Doctor No has green skin and Jaws, the mostly silent killer, is fairly talkative.

MOSS: I don't know, but I can guess: our audience was younger than the audience for the films. No grownup would ever want to laugh at Dr. No or Jaws, but the prevailing wisdom is that kids want to see the bad guys be ridiculous.

Each episode contains numerous gadgets. In "Never Lose Hope," IQ gives Bond sneakers, which are equipped with jet boosters, a wristwatch that is capable of shooting a rocket, and a class ring that shoots lasers. In the same episode, IQ quickly fits Jr.'s skateboard with a device that supercharges it. In "Canine Caper," Q gives Bond a hologram ring (which sends holographic projections), a shortwave pocket watch, and an electromagnetic hidden in a belt. Can you describe your approach to writing the gadgets?

MOLITOR: Some were simply throwaways, good for a quip or used as a sight gag. For example, Trevor gets knocked over by the boomerang discus in "Going for the Gold." But at least once per episode, an IQ device would be crucial to Bond's triumph.

When Bond is chained to a missile in the "Eiffel Missile," he uses his watch, which is equipped with a saw, to free himself. And whenever I could, I let it fall into the wrong hands, like Goldie getting the Hyper-Helium in "Going for the Gold" or Trevor swiping the sonic-shovel in "Shifting Sands," to up the odds against our heroes.

POLLACK: All the gadgets that were in my episodes I created to assist James Jr. in the narrative. The approach was to create the gadgets so James could use them in a way you didn't expect.

Doug Molitor, I imagine that you enjoyed writing the show's numerous quips. After Pharaoh Fearo attempts to entrap and drown Bond in an oil pipe, Bond admonishes, "I find your methods rather crude." And when Bond Jr. returns to the United States following his Eiffel Tower bomb adventure, he describes the city as a "real blast."

MOLITOR: Most of those puns were pretty on-the-nose – our audience was young, after all. But then, the quips in the films were also dead-on. I never have to be encouraged to write puns. Quite the contrary. Two years ago, I won Worldwide Puns' first-ever Los Angeles area Pun-Off. It's a San Francisco-based event; it's what a rap battle is for rap. They haven't had a second one down here, so I take that as a tribute to just how outrageously contorted my puns were.

Benjamin Pollack, in "Canine Caper," a bad guy sprays paint on the window of Bond's sports car. As a countermeasure, Bond activates a high-powered water spray to wash the paint away, and says, "That clears up everything." When a dog jumps on Bond, covering him with kisses, Bond quips, "Even I know when I'm licked." Can you talk about writing the quips and puns for the show?

POLLACK: The puns and the quips were my personality coming through. I always put clues into the narrative that were directly a part of me, since James Bond Jr. was the only spin-off allowed by the Broccoli family.

Doug Molitor, what do you remember about writing "The Eiffel Missile?"

MOLITOR: Jack Mendelsohn handed me an approved pitch and asked me to turn it into an outline. It had to be about a missile hidden beneath the Eiffel Tower, and it had to have Skullcap and Dr. Derange and Marcie Beaucoup as the Bond girl, so I had less leeway than I did in the subsequent episodes. But I picked the other locales. How could I do a story about Paris and omit the Opera or the sewers? Four years earlier, I'd ridden the hovercraft from Calais to Dover, so I decided to stage one sequence on the reverse leg of that journey. Of course, I wrote the sight gags and the dialogue.

Long after the show wrapped production, I learned that DIC, a studio I had written a ton of shows for, had originally begun developing the series, then lost it to Murakami-Wolf-Swenson. I'd had no idea that Robby London, creative VP at DIC, originally came up with the plot for "The Eiffel Missile," which the new producers inherited. I felt bad that Robby didn't get a story credit, but nobody asked me.

"The Eiffel Missile" was adapted into a Marvel comic book and into a novelization called *The Eiffel Target*. Were you aware of it at the time?

MOLITOR: I was aware of it only later and found it funny. It still comes up in Google searches of my writing. They based it on my script, of course, but I was not involved beyond that.

In the episode, Bond is kissed by a Parisian student. Phoebe, one of Bond's friends, remarks that he looks, "Quite shaken." IQ corrects her, "Offhand, I'd say he looks not shaken but stirred." I'm sure it would be tempting to pack the episode with homages to the Bond movies.

MOLITOR: Puns and wordplay were very much encouraged, and it never hurt to refer back to the film series. Of course, there were limits: for instance, you definitely would not mention Honor Blackman's character in *Goldfinger*. And you wouldn't mention drinking alcohol. But using champagne to temporarily blind an assailant? No problem. "Not shaken but stirred" was not just a reference to adult Bond's martinis. Applying it to Bond after Marcy's kiss was a slight innuendo, not unlike the dialogue in Thirties movies after the Production Code came in. It had a perfectly innocent meaning, but I imagine older kids and parents not only caught the reference but smiled at the implication.

What do you remember about "Going for the Gold?"

MOLITOR: I was encouraged to be timely, so when I pitched an Olympics story for Spain, with the 1992 Games in Barcelona just a year off, Jack was happy to approve it. Originally, I just wanted to use Barbella in a sports-themed story, and I think when I sold the pitch, it was called "Iron Maiden." But Jack asked me to add Goldie Finger, which means the villains' object had to be gold; thus we added the museum robbery and the new title. Jack suggested adding Goldie Finger to the Barcelona story, and he was right. Villains work better in pairs because they tell each other what the audience needs to know about their plans. Though I confess, I found Goldie kind of a one-note character.

How about "Shifting Sands?"

MOLITOR: So much fun. I've always loved mummy movies and Indiana Jones-type adventures. But the real fun was Jack let me create Pharaoh Fearo and do 20,000 Leagues Beneath the Desert with his underground warship, the Subterranean.

Benjamin Pollack, what do you remember about writing "Never Lose Hope?"

POLLACK: The science teacher Mr. Pollack. The theme of forgiveness and not to pre-judge people. Close to my heart.

What about "Canine Caper?"

POLLACK: I love dogs, so it was only right that I made one the main character in a Bond film.

While 007 is sometimes referenced, it's usually just in passing. While he doesn't appear in "Never Lose Hope," 007 plays a central role in that his actions drive the plot. How did that come about?

POLLACK: The reason James Bond never had children, or a family was that he knew that they would never be safe. Our show overlooked that fact. This was an episode that took advantage of the connection between James and his nephew and explored what might happen if the real James Bond had a family.

"Never Lose Hope" is an interesting, meta-concept. In the Bond movies, the audience rarely gives thought to the faceless workers who work for the supervillain and who populate Blofeld's hollowed-out volcano or Drax's space station. So, when there is a giant battle and the workers perish, the audience doesn't over-think their deaths. This episode explores those concepts.

POLLACK: Death is not a thing we should be immune to spiritually. But I don't think anyone on the show gave that any thought, sadly.

Which of your two episodes do you prefer?

POLLACK: I like them both. I think "Never Lose Hope" was more meaningful.

A few episodes of the show were adapted into other media including novelizations, comic books, and a children's book. "Canine Caper" was adapted into a children's book called *Tunnel of Doom*. Were you aware of it at the time?

POLLACK: I had no idea. I ordered the book and got a really nice used copy. It looks pretty cool. There are lots of little teeth marks on the cover, so I think the original reader was pretty young. It's now sitting on my nightstand and when my son is old enough to read, I will give it to him.

Bond drives his car in both of your episodes. The car was turned into a toy, which I purchased and still have. Were you instructed to include a car chase so that they could spotlight the toy, or did you happen to include it in both of your episodes?

POLLACK: We just made stuff up as we went along regarding the car. No outline was provided that included the car that I recall.

Doug Molitor, do you recall any ideas you pitched but weren't used?

MOLITOR: Not really. Back then I'd send in five pitches at a time, so I might have developed as many as a dozen ideas that were not used. But I don't recall them, and they must have been lost in one of many computer upgrades. Jack picked the one he liked, and I'd do the outline of that one.

I am amazed, re-watching the show, how much violence we got away with. People getting slammed against walls, people hit with blasts of steam, laser guns, a nuclear missile launched at Moscow, and in general, a constant clear intent to kill. I've worked on a number of action shows since then that had to soft-pedal the violence. A year later, I caught a lot of flak for another nuclear terrorism plot in a *Captain Planet* episode, but that's another story.

Douglas Molitor, what were your favorite episodes?

MOLITOR: The most favorite is a tie between "Going for the Gold" and "Shifting Sands." I'd forgotten the part in "Sands" about the oil sheik, whom we lead the audience to think will stereotypically ride a camel, but then smash cut to him driving to Bond's rescue in his luxury limousine, blaring his horn and laughing his head off. I wrote him as if Akim Tamiroff from Orson Welles' *Touch of Evil* (1958) was going to voice him. And how can you go wrong, blending tomb raiders and mummies and Jules Verne?

"Gold," because of Barbella. I just loved that strong girl. It was so funny that Kath Soucie did both her voice and good girl Tracy's. Ironically, I'm having some success now with a series of comic novels called the *Time Amazon* book series—*Memoirs of a Time Traveler* and two sequels so far. The heroine is a gene-enhanced tourist from the future who's as strong as Barbella, only Ariyl [the heroine from the future] is on the side of good.

Least favorite?

MOLITOR: The least favorite is "Eiffel," but only because the original plot was someone else's. So I was less invested in the story.

What is your assessment of the show?

MOLITOR: I think the show did a fine job of recreating the dry wit of the Roger Moore Bond films. It had a ton of exciting action. I was glad I managed to get empowered female characters, both heroic and villainous, into the show. I do wish the animation had been better. I tend to look at it more like a comic book with the pages being flipped, than a cartoon.

POLLACK: On a scale from 1 to 10 I think the show, as a whole, was a solid 7. The actors were fine, the animation was lacking a bit, and the music was great.

MALEK: I don't think highly of the show. I think it was too much like all the other shows on the air at the time. Certainly, the style of animation was familiar, and it wasn't great animation anyway. Stories were a bit too simple, and I guess not very memorable, huh? Even my own! I didn't enjoy working on this show very much.

MOSS: Some people liked the show. I got an email from someone in a *James Bond Jr.* fan club in England. If *James Bond Jr.* was less than a hit, I think part of the reason might have been that not enough attention was paid to its origins. Maybe putting James Bond in an episode or two [might have helped]. Although, possibly budget, rights, or other factors played a part.

Was there ever talk of a second season?

MOLITOR: Not that I ever heard, alas. It was a fun show, and I would have loved to do more. But 65 episodes were the standard syndication order back then. Man, that was a heyday for animation writers – we had as much work as we could grab, and I didn't do more of *James Bond Jr.'s* first season only because at the same time I was also writing multiple episodes of *Beetlejuice* and *Bill & Ted's Excellent Adventures*, and writing and story editing *Captain Planet* for DIC. Those were the good ol' days.

An order of 65 episodes allowed TV stations 13 weeks of first-run shows in five-day-a-week syndication. Only a super successful show would get an order for more than 65—although *The Real Ghostbusters* did, I guess *James Bond Jr.* was not that.

What do you remember about working on the show?

MOLITOR: I just remember being delighted that I could write any crazy action – like Barbella braids two guards' gun barrels, then baton-twirls the guards over her head then shot-put them upside-down against a wall – and that's exactly what they'd animate. And great voice talent! Kath Soucie has voiced so many shows I wrote, including *Transformers: Rescue Bots* and *Captain Planet*, and Corey Burton was perfect as the dry younger Bond. I didn't realize until yesterday that we had a genuine Broadway superstar, Brian Stokes Mitchell, as Coach Mitchell.

Jack Mendelsohn was a great, great writer and story editor. He was my mentor, and he used me on show after show—*Camp Candy* (1989-92), *Ninja Turtles, Sinbad, Zorro* (1997-1998). The more hilarious the plot twists, the better he liked it, He said he never had to rewrite me. I took that as a great compliment since Jack was a genius at writing for kids – he did everything from co-writing [the 1968 Beatles movies] *Yellow Submarine* to a truly ground-breaking Sunday comic for kids called *Jacky's Diary* [the conceit of which was that a child wrote and illustrated it]. Like any show Jack ran, writing for *James Bond Jr.* was pure pleasure.

POLLACK: The late nights slipping into banks through skylights, slapping tracking devices on the backs of double agents, romancing beautiful women, and never losing a card game.

MALEK: I wish I had been more a part of the production team. It would have been much more fun and easier to do, but some studios just liked writers being cogs in the machine. At Disney, I got to direct the voice sessions and work with the artists on the look of the characters and backgrounds. I have a few vivid memories of the show. Without seeing much of the artwork or any of the footage, everything took place in my mind. And then, seeing the show, all of that is dashed like puzzle pieces when it doesn't look or sound like what you thought it might be. And so I don't remember what that looked or sounded like.

It wasn't my high point. Perhaps, I wasn't the best person for the job. I was nearing the end of my animation career. After *James Bond Jr.*, I wrote a couple of *Speed Racer* scripts and worked on a *Mighty Ducks* script for my friend, David Wise, who wrote one of these *James Bond Jr.* scripts for me, as well as several other shows I worked on. David also created and wrote most of the *Teenage Mutant Ninja Turtles* (1987-1996) for Murakami-Wolf-Swenson.

But by then TV animation was changing because of cable TV. Except for Warner Bros., most of the production was done in New York and written by the same person or a few people. There were no story editors like me after a while. I had to change careers, so I did. Now I'm a clinical psychologist with a private practice in Thousand Oaks, California.

MOSS: I'd worked with [story editor] Jack Mendelsohn on several shows, including *Teenage Mutant Ninja Turtles, Sinbad, Dennis the Menace*, and *James Bond Jr. James Bond Jr.* was one of the easiest shows to write for. Pretty much every story idea we pitched went to script.

Anything else I should have asked you?

POLLACK: You never asked me if I had any secret agent experience. Although I would have to kill you if I answered that question, I can safely say that the showrunners did their best to hire people with the right "experience."

In the rest of the interview, Bryce Malek reflects on his responsibilities and experiences as a story editor of James Bond Jr.

I was responsible for submitting completed scripts on schedule or as fast as I could, in this case. I was hired as an independent contractor, which was the first time for me, so I had to get my own writing staff, to pay them, etc. I submitted many premises in person or by modem.

All in all, I can only verify that I story edited eight episodes of the 65—there may have been a few more because I would have sworn there were almost twice that number, but I cannot confirm that.

And here's the dirty little secret of this show: I actually wrote one of the scripts myself! I used a nom de plume that a friend of mine liked to use—J.R. Morton—so "Goldie's Gold Scam" is all mine. I did it for the cash, and I wasn't sure it was any good at all, so I didn't bother to put my real name on it. I pulled out my off-the-air copy and started to watch it again. I couldn't remember a damn thing about it!

I was one of several story editors on this show, but I don't think I knew that would be the case when I was hired. *James Bond Jr.* came near the end of my animation career, which began in 1980 with Hanna-Barbera Productions with *Scooby-Doo and Scrappy-Doo* (1981), *The Little Rascals* (1982), *Monchhichis* (1983), several *Popeyes* (*Popeye and Son*, 1987) with various offspring, and other shows.

From there I went to Marvel Productions and story edited, with my partner, Dick Robbins, *Transformers: Generation 1* (1984-85) and *Defenders of the Earth* (1986-89)—both 65 episode shows. On November 21, 1990, Fred Wolf called me to ask if I would story edit *James Bond Jr.*, which elated me, as I needed the work. It wasn't until December 5 that I went in for a meeting and got the show bible and schedule.

My experience, as recorded in a daily calendar, is that I wrote and I worked with a small stable of animation writers to write story premises for the show. Over the following months, I submitted many, and most of them were rejected for one reason or another. That's probably another reason that I think I worked on more episodes than I really did. I was trained to work like a story editor and not a showrunner, meaning that I didn't originate the stories or write the scripts, except that one, but worked with writers I knew from past experiences and rewrote their work. I never liked writing many more premises than needed. I preferred and historically experienced writing fewer premises and getting most of them approved. So that experience was frustrating because nobody pays for unused premises. I was working solely with Walt at this time and started sending in more springboards, which he generally liked.

In January, I learned there would be more story editors, and I guess I can't blame them since production on my end was going slower than expected. I had a meeting with Fred Wolf and "an MGM guy John" and got more stories approved. I started working with Tony Love, a producer, who put some of the stories on hold. By the end of the month, I was rewriting scripts we had worked on and was getting paid. Finally. And that's the way it went on for several months.

On June 12, I was informed all story slots were taken, so we needed no more premises. Yay! There were still scripts to edit, and I wrote several inserts, brief scenes needed to fill the episode time, for completed shows, so it wasn't until August when my work with the series was finally done.

So, all in all, it wasn't a pleasant experience, and I probably didn't do as well as other editors on the show. I have a memory of visiting Murakami-Wolf-Swenson and visiting with Tony and Bill after most of the show was done, and we talked about it. Of all the episodes produced, they pointed out a few of their favorites—don't ask, I don't remember, and most of them were edited by me. So I felt good about that.

I had more exposure to the artwork at studios where I was on staff and had an office in the building, but *James Bond Jr.* was the first show I worked on from home, so I saw nothing until it was on television. It's always a shock, as the cartoon in your head is always a thousand times better than the one on the TV. And that was true for *James Bond Jr.*, too.

Marvel Comics adaptation of "The Eiffel Missile"
©1991, Eon Productions Ltd., MAC B, Inc. 19

Novelizations
John Peel

The robust marketing push for *James Bond Jr.* helped to generate awareness and build excitement for *James Bond Jr.*, the 1991 animated series about 007's hitherto unknown nephew. As previously noted, a wide range of Bond Jr. merchandise aimed at children appeared, such as a line of toys, comic books, video games, and a board game. But it wasn't until I was researching *The Many Lives of James Bond*, my book about how many artists have interpreted the character of James Bond in different media, that I learned that six James Bond Jr. novelizations had been published. It seems entirely fitting that *James Bond Jr.*—a spin-off show that was based on the film franchise that was adapted from a series of novels—would be adapted into a book. Still, I was more than a little surprised to discover six books set in the world of James Bond and featuring many of its iconic villains that I hadn't known of.

In 1991, Glidrose Publications (later Ian Fleming Publications) hired John Peel, writing under the pseudonym John Vincent, to write tie-in books for the cartoon's better episodes. Seeking to fill this gaping hole in my Bond education, I tracked down and read Peel's novelizations—*A View to a Thrill*, *The Eiffel Target*, *Live and Let's Dance*, *Sandblast!*, and *High Stakes*. Peel's books were released monthly in America and England, from January to June of 1992, and they were intended primarily for middle-grade readers. For those who are unfamiliar with Peel's James Bond Jr. books, I offer these encapsulated synopses.

In *A View to a Thrill*, the evil organization S.C.U.M. (Saboteurs and Criminals United in Mayhem) attempts to steal 007's tricked-out Aston Martin, which he has lent to his namesake, James Bond Jr., so that they can exploit the car's experimental technology in order to erase data on the computer systems in England's finance, civil defense, and law enforcement sectors, unless S.C.U.M.'s ransom demands are met. The book, in which the usually silent henchman Jaws speaks, was based on Francis Moss and Ted Pedersen's episode "The Beginning."

In *A View to a Thrill*, on a class trip, Bond Jr. discovers that S.C.U.M. agent Dr. Derange intends to fire a nuclear missile from beneath the Eiffel Tower. The book was based on the episode "The Eiffel Missile," which was written by Doug Molitor and was based on Robby London's plot.

In *Live and Let's Dance*, Bond Jr. escorts ballerina Marie Pleeay to Switzerland and uncovers the arms dealer Baron von Skarin's plot to kill her and King Zamora, for whom she is performing. *Live and Let's Dance* was adapted from Alan Templeton and Mary Crawford's episode of the same name.

In *Sandblast!*, James Bond Jr. is on a school field trip to Egypt where he discovers an evil pharaoh's plan to use the money from looted treasures and stolen oil to take control of Egypt and become its ruler. *Sandblast!* was based on Doug Molitor's episode "Shifting Sands."

In *Sword of Death*, Dr. No kidnaps Bond's classmate Tracy and steals a sword made out of a rare metal, which he intends to use to build powerful laser weapons in his quest for world domination. James battles the not-so-good doctor and his ninjas in Japan. *Sword of Death* is an adaptation of Ted Pedersen's "Sword of Power."

In *High Stakes*, S.C.U.M. operative Ms. Fortune and her stuffy, evil butler Snuffer steal a secret formula, which was invented by Q's grandson, Horace Boothroyd, that can quickly turn water into ice so that they can use it to rob a casino in Las Vegas. Alan Templeton and Mary Crawford's "There But Ms. Fortune" served as the basis for *High Stakes*.

The producers of *James Bond Jr.* gave their scriptwriters a few unbreakable rules, the most disheartening of which for Bond fans was that 007 wasn't permitted to appear on the show. Peel found a clever way around this dictate in his first book. In the opening passage of *A View to a Thrill*, Peel includes a top-secret cable from M to 007.

It reads: "EMP DEVICE HAS BEEN INSTALLED IN YOUR CAR. IT IS READY FOR YOU TO DELIVER AS INSTRUCTED."[418] In his transmission, Bond responds to his superior: "WILL DELIVER AS SOON AS POSSIBLE. TRUST THERE IS NO CONFUSION AS NEPHEW HAS BORROWED MY ASTON MARTIN TO GO TO HIS NEW SCHOOL."[419] 007 would not appear in any form in the following five novelizations.

In his books, Peel occasionally expands on the existing Bond lore. For instance, in *A View to a Thrill*, the author offers an explanation as to how Jaws, an assassin, got his choppers and acquired his alias. According to Peel, Jaws "had been shot in the mouth while robbing a bank. He escaped, but to save his life, the doctors had given him a set of metal teeth, and motors for jaw muscles. Now he was back in action, and his metal teeth had given him a new name – and a new weapon."[420] Elsewhere, Peel slips in a salient detail about 007's music preferences. While driving the Aston Martin, James Jr. discovers that Bond left a classic music cassette in the car's stereo system.

In *A View to a Thrill*, Peel also expands on 007's relationship with his nephew. According to Peel, James Jr. admired his father's brother. "People often told James how much he looked like his uncle, and James secretly hoped the resemblance went deeper than just good looks."[421]

Peel posits that 007 gave James Jr. some unique advice. In the opening passages of the novel, while driving 007's Aston Martin, James Jr. tries to evade unknown villains driving a Rolls Royce, who are trying to run him off the road. James Jr. has no choice but to jump his car over a brick wall. Peel describes the advice 007 gave his nephew, "Well, as his uncle always said, what you can't go around, go over ..."[422]

It also seems that 007 trusted his nephew implicitly: "[James Jr.] knew that his uncle, the James Bond he was named after – Double-O-Seven – was a famous agent of the British Secret Service."[423] Peel also suggests that 007 confided in his nephew details about some of his clandestine missions. Upon meeting the presumed-dead Dr. No in *Sword of Death*, James Jr. challenges the villain, "My uncle told me all about you. But he said you were dead!"[424]

Of course, Ian Fleming's Bond would not share trade secrets with his teenage nephew. However, given the conceit of the show, these passages seem like good-natured attempts to evoke the specter of the secret agent and to integrate him into the story.

And for those who enjoy a good pun, some of the chapter titles of Peel's books provide a few chuckles. In *Sandblast!*, the appearance of a mummy inspires the titles "Tomb It May Concern" and "All Wrapped Up," the book's final chapter. In *High Stakes*, the frozen victims set up "Ice Screams," in *Sword of Death*, the setting of Gnome Electronics give way to "There's No Place Like Gnome" and "Gnome Alone" and, in *The Eiffel Target*, Dr. Derange and the Paris-based provide the basis for "Derange Is In-Seine."

It should be noted that Peel's paperbacks were not the cartoon's only contribution to the 007 literary world. In 1993, Reed International published four books aimed at an even younger audience under their Buzz Books imprint in the United Kingdom. The four slim (as short as 24 pages) illustrated books, written by Caryn Jenner, were titled *Tunnel of Doom*, *Barbella's Revenge*, *Freeze Frame*, and *Dangerous Games*, and they were based on "Canine Caper," "Barbella's Big Attraction," "Weather or Not," and "Catching the Wave." In the same year, Reed also published *As Good As Gold*, an interactive gamebook by Dave Morris under their Mammoth imprint.

John Peel, an English author who lives in the United States, has also written novelizations inspired by other beloved properties, including *Star Trek* and two British series, the spy series *The Avengers* and the cult sci-fi show *Doctor Who*.

***

How did you get the writing assignment?

I was approached in June 1991 about the project by editor Leslie Morgenstein at Daniel Wess Associates. I'd worked for the firm before, and we'd all been happy with the results. They were a packaging firm – they would sell a series to a publisher and would provide all of the materials, including the cover art. Generally, they would then use several different writers working under a single pseudonym. In my case, however, they were certain that I could do all six books they'd been commissioned for, so they didn't talk to any other authors. The books were to be published by Penguin, and the copyright was held by Eon Productions and Mac B, who were making the series as Warfield Productions. What this basically meant was that I would be working with three layers of editing – Weiss, Penguin, and Eon. As you can probably imagine, they didn't all always agree on what I was to do.

There was one extra complicating factor, and that was the editor at Penguin – a young woman. I'd worked with her before on another project, and we didn't get along. In all of my decades of writing, she was the only editor I couldn't work well with. She thought I was arrogant, and I thought she was an idiot. For example, she had once told me that I didn't know how modern kids speak, and I should remedy that by watching more sitcoms. Leslie promised me he'd deal with her, and I wouldn't have to. It didn't work out quite that way, of course. However, the prospect of working on a James Bond franchise was so appealing to me that it outweighed the problems involved. I was eager to get to work, so I signed up for the six books.

For various reasons, several Bond authors, including Kingsley Amis (*Colonel Sun*), Samantha Weinberg (*The Moneypenny Diaries*), and Arthur Calder-Marshall (003½: *The Adventures of James Bond Junior*), have used pseudonyms. Why did you use one?

That wasn't my choice. I was told, though not by them directly, that it was Eon's decision. It was a rather odd choice, considering the fact that they wanted me on the project in the first place because I had started to make a name for myself in the field. As for the name chosen – they took a while to decide on it. I suspect somebody there thought "John Vincent" was a nice play on the popular ["The Power of Positive Thinking"] author, Norman Vincent Peale. Since the book was going out under a pen name, I added a dedication to the first one: "To John Peel, who helped fill in all the blanks."

What parameters did the publisher give you?

The main constraint was that since the books were licensed from Eon, we had the rights to use only elements from the movie Bonds. I was told that I couldn't use anything that had only appeared in the books because Glidrose owned those rights. For example, when I mentioned Universal Exports in book three, [someone] told me I couldn't use it because it hadn't appeared in any of the films. I told them to check out the credit sequence to *On Her Majesty's Secret Service*, and then they changed their minds and let me keep it in. It helped that I was a big fan of the films.

Leslie, however, suggested I tone down too many references to the films. I was told to stay away from all but the obvious references to James Bond. "While our readers will get the mention of 007, they won't understand Little Nellie." That was because I had wanted to put Little Nellie into one sequence, as I adored that part of *You Only Live Twice*. I was also told to tone down any romance, as the books were being aimed at 10-year-olds. That led to one of my problems with the books, because although they were *aimed* at 10-year-olds, I was certain that quite a number of the readers would be, like myself, older Bond fans, and I wanted to include material for them, too. Most of that – when it was caught – was cut.

They were constantly asking me to make the stories sillier, and the villains "badder." By that, of course, they meant more mustache-twirling and maniacal laughter, that sort of thing. Now, usually, I'm asked to take some of the jokes *out* of my books, not to add more, but I didn't want the books to be just plain silly. I wanted them to stand up as adventure stories, not cliché-filled nonsense. So there was a constant struggle between us all on that issue.

I was also told to stop asking questions. As a writer, I needed to understand the world frame I was writing about, and I needed a few official answers to questions like: "If James Bond is his uncle, why is he called *Junior*?" Their reply was: "He just is." So I wanted to say that there were two Bond brothers, and *both* of them were named James. They thought that was stupid, and I thought it would be very funny. They told me not to mention his family *at all*. Six books and our hero can't even *think* about his mother and father...

Was there a lot of oversight from the publisher or Fleming's estate?

There was certainly a good deal of oversight, mostly to cut any references I made to the mythos where it might cause problems with Glidrose. But I rarely received those comments directly. They would be aimed at the production company, who would pass them on to Leslie, and he would have to straighten me out. I did speak on the phone with representatives of the copyright holders from time to time, and they were always very nice, very polite – and very firm. I did feel sorry for Leslie, who was trying to please everyone – I didn't make his task any easier.

Did you have Fleming in mind while writing? What about the movies?

Well, I grew up reading Fleming and watching the movies, of course. That was the main reason that I jumped at the chance to do the books in the first place, a love of the Bond mythos. So, clearly, they were in my mind when I began – not to copy either, of course, but to pay homage to both. But I was very firmly told to cut all references to either books or films, as their "target reader" didn't know anything beyond the name.

Who was your ideal reader? Was it a Bond fan? Or a young reader with no knowledge of Bond?

I wasn't writing for any specific kind of reader. In general, I write pretty much the same way for 10-year-olds as I do for 30-year-olds – though, obviously, the choice of wording is a bit different, as well as the kind of things that might be bothering the main characters. But I always try to write for all ages, as it were, so that even an older reader should be able to enjoy my kids' books. And, as I said, I was certain that there would be plenty of older readers, as Bond fans would certainly pick up these books, so I wanted them to be able to enjoy the books as well.

In addition to the script, what other reference materials were you given? Did they share the "show bible," a guide for the writers and other creatives, with you? I ask because in your first book *A View to a Thrill* Bond's school, Warfield Academy, is referred to as High Risk High. I believe that the reference to High Risk High appears only in the show bible and not in the series.

They sent me quite a wad of material, which I still have, primarily the show bible and visual reference materials. They even sent me a batch of slides of the animation, but no episodes. The books had to be written so that they would appear at the same time as the TV series, so it's possible that at this point they didn't even have a completed episode. Or maybe they simply didn't want me to see one.

What was also interesting is that I had been shopping around an outline to publishers that I'd developed called *Spy High*. It was about a school for high-risk children – of diplomats, ministers, spies, that kind of thing – set up to protect them. Of course, kids like that see it as a prison and break out when they can. I had to retire that concept as it was too close to *James Bond Jr.*, but I did use some of the ideas I'd thought of in the Bond books. That's why I tended to like the "High Risk High" concept, though the production company asked me to downplay that.

As another example of the conflicting demands on me – the animation company wanted to downplay the High Risk concept (though they were the ones who came up with it), while Penguin kept urging me to be more creative in how James and his friends escaped school. I couldn't please them both at the same time.

Can you describe your writing schedule?

The books would be published monthly, so they needed me to complete each one in about three weeks. I wrote continuously but had to pause to revise earlier stories, especially the first one. For that, we were trying to find our footing, and everyone went over it very carefully. I had to basically rewrite that one almost entirely at least twice. Later books – once we had the format down, and I knew what was expected – tended to have a lot less revisions, so things sped up as we moved on in the series. I would be writing, say, book three, and at the same time doing revisions on book two and proofreading book one. It was a very intense six months of work, but I've had worse.

How did you approach adapting the scripts into books?

Well, there were several problems. The most obvious was that the TV scripts were only 30 pages long, so a good deal had to be added to them to make them into full novels, and it didn't have to look like obvious padding. So I would go through each script and identify places where I could expand on the story in some useful way before I started to write. One of the things I did was to round out the characters more. In a short script, they did tend to be stock characters, but in a book, they need to be more rounded and interesting.

One thing, in particular, I insisted on was that Tracy should be a lot stronger than she was on the TV. On TV, she was the damsel in distress, and that seemed short-sighted to me. So I improved her role to the point where they told me to tone it down – James is the hero, not Tracy.

The main problem for me, though, was that the scripts were horribly poor to begin with, and I could only make so many changes to improve them. When I complained about the quality of the scripts to Leslie – who was selecting them for the books – he just laughed. "Trust me," he informed me, "I'm sending you the best. You really don't want to see the ones I'm rejecting." That didn't console me very much. When I finally saw the aired episodes, I had a lot more sympathy for him. He had picked the best.

You see, you can get away with slipshod writing and a complete lack of any sense if you're doing a TV show. Let's face it, that happens a lot. Because the kids watching it can't go back and rewatch a scene, as they're already on the next one. But it's easy in a book to just go back a few pages and say "Wow, that doesn't make any sense." So I needed the stories to stand up, and the scripts weren't exactly helpful there. Besides which, I like to think of myself as a conscientious writer, and I won't write something poorly – at least, not intentionally.

This led to one of my inevitable clashes with the editor at Penguin. I was explaining to her about the problems with "Sword of Death." The entire script takes place overnight, and that includes James flying to and from Japan, from England, and having a fight and a meal in Tokyo, flying out to Dr. No's island, having another fight, there's also a volcanic explosion and another meal. Completely impossible, right? The editor's response was typical of her: she told me not to bother about such minor problems as "it's just for kids."

Now, that attitude is one that I absolutely hate – the idea that it's okay to write badly if it's "just for kids." To me, you have to be more careful when you write for kids, not less. Adults might dismiss something stupid, but kids will *believe* it if it's written into a book. So I believe you have to be accurate and careful and treat kids as discerning readers. The Penguin editor and the makers of the show had the exact opposite opinion, so we clashed a lot on this point.

Did you think of James Bond Jr., Bond's nephew, as a younger version of Bond?

No, not really, because Bond is a professional spy – with all the attitudes and morals of a trained agent. James Jr. was a talented amateur, if you will. He's a fairly regular teen – though brighter and stronger than most – so I couldn't allow him to do anything *too* unbelievable. He also has teen attitudes and concerns.

Would you have written James Bond Jr. differently if he were a young 007?

Definitely. I would have had to make him a lot harder.

How did you try to make him the same as Bond? How is he different?

Well, Bond is a loner – there's very little continuity in his life. He doesn't have friends as such – colleagues, certainly, and lovers – but he's not friendly with people. I mean, you can't picture him popping into the local for a pint with Bill Tanner, say, or a cup of tea with Moneypenny. And he is cold – he has to be in his line of work. For me, the line that sums him up the best is the final one in *Casino Royale* – "'Yes, dammit,' I said '[Vesper Lynd] was [a spy]. The bitch is dead now.'" And that's of the girl he was about to propose marriage to. For what he is, he can't be any other way.

James Jr., on the other hand, has friends. He's surrounded by people he likes and whose friendship he values. He is warm and sometimes silly with them. So he is a very different sort of character. He idolizes his uncle without actually being too much like him – thank goodness.

Their similarity, mainly, is that they're both incredible, inventive, able to sum up a situation quickly and think fast on their feet. They're both very action-oriented, and neither of them ever gives up.

In the books, you refer to the main character as James, as opposed to Bond. Were you instructed to?

Well, he's always "James" in the scripts and to his friends, so that was a given. It never occurred to me to call him anything else.

Unlike the show, Bond makes fleeting appearances in your first book, Bond appears via cables to and from his superior M. How did that come about? Why didn't you continue to use that in later books?

I did want to bring Bond himself into the books as much as possible, but I wasn't permitted to use him. I thought the cables would be a nice touch. The copyright holders didn't, and they instructed me firmly to drop them. They told me that they had made a one-time exception so I could use Bond and M cable exchanges one time only in the first book, and that was it. They also insisted on a line of acknowledgment in the credits for their use.

Even though he doesn't appear in person, 007 is a significant presence in the books. He casts a shadow on the stories, and he's frequently referred to. Was it important to you to keep 007 in the reader's mind?

Oh, very much so. I mean, Bond does overshadow everything, doesn't he? And as James Jr. idolizes his uncle it made perfect sense that he'd keep referring to him. Well, I wasn't allowed to talk about James' actual parents, but he needed to have an adult influence from someone.

James Bond kills Dr. No in the movie but he's a character in the animated series. In your book *Sword of Death*, you address that inconsistency. In it, you wrote: "Young James says, 'My uncle told me all about you. But he said you were dead.' Dr. No replies, 'The whole world thought I was dead. But, as you see, it's far from the truth. I am very much alive.'" Incidentally, this type of continuity error was common in the series. Was it important for you to address it?

Oh, so much. In the series, it drove me crazy. But that was certainly one of the worst for me – using characters that had been clearly killed off in the films. Much as I love the villains in the movies, I was hoping I wouldn't have to use any of them in the books. So when I was sent the script for that story, I wanted to address the "You were dead, you know" factor. That was as much as I was allowed to say, though.

Your books often have different titles from the episodes on which they were based. Were you involved in that decision at all or was that the publisher's call?

I had absolutely no say in the matter – it was purely the publisher's decision. I do prefer the book titles.

Can you please share any insight or memory for each of your six books? Let's start with the first, *A View to a Thrill*.

On this, my main memory was doing all of the rewriting. I got notes from everybody involved, of course, since it was the first book, and everybody had their own idea of how it should be. So I did several revisions to attempt to please everyone. It was a lot of work, disproportionately so. The later books were a lot easier, as we'd pretty much established in the first book the direction we were going to take. I did have a hard time swallowing the villains' name – S.C.U.M. I mean, who in their right minds would view themselves as scum? But the animators thought kids would find it funny, and I was stuck with it.

What about *The Eiffel Target*?

I hadn't had much of a problem with the plotline of the first book, because it was pretty straightforward, but this one drove me crazy. I mean – how could a bunch of villains manage to build a secret rocket base under the biggest tourist attraction in France? It made absolutely no sense to me at all. It was obvious that the writer of the episode had looked at the Eiffel Tower and thought to himself "Oh, it looks like a rocket gantry. Wouldn't it be funny if it was a rocket gantry?" And I was stuck with that. They didn't even *try* to make it make sense. For example, in the script, the rocket is fired up through the center of the Tower. There's a restaurant in the Tower, it's not hollow clear through. That was the level of writing I was stuck with, so I had to change the plot a bit to fit the facts.

In one of the other books, there's a bit where James and his friends have to get on a train traveling through the English countryside. And they keep referring to the "caboose." In England, there is no such thing – it's called the "guard's van." The animators made absolutely no effort to fact-check anything.

The villain was Dr. Derange, and since the plot made very little sense, I decided it would be rather fun if the villain didn't either. So I gave him a split personality, where the two halves were always arguing with each other – and losing, which was why he was always so angry.

This was another book where I had a problem with the Penguin editor's attitude. As he was in France, I wrote a scene where James goes to see an Offenbach operetta. Now, I *love* Offenbach, and I thought this would be a nice touch. The editor wanted to cut it, arguing that the readers wouldn't know who Offenbach was. I replied that this was the entire point, and that, maybe, if they read it in the story, they might want to go out and listen to some of his music – which is wonderfully kid-friendly, of course. It stayed in.

Live and Let's Dance came next.

I liked this title. *Live and Let's Dance* and *A View to a Thrill* were my favorites, as they were nice twists on the Fleming titles. And I felt a lot of sympathy for the wolf, as I'm a dog lover.

Then came *Sandblast!*

I can't remember anything about this one at all, except that by this point I was getting rather frustrated by the notes and comments I was getting from the editor at Penguin and the animators. The writing wasn't turning out to be as much fun as I'd hoped it would be.

Sword of Death?

This one was absolutely filled with complete nonsense. I've mentioned the bizarre time factor and the odd reappearance of Dr. No, but there were lots of other problems. The one that made me despair the most was when Dr. No aims to kill James by drowning him in lava *on the 35th floor of a skyscraper*. I mean – how do you even get lava up in the elevator?

High Stakes was the last one.

I'd given up all hopes of making any sense out of the scripts by this point, and I decided to simply be as silly as I wanted to be in this one. The main villains are Ms. Fortune and her butler, Snuffer. I'm a huge fan of *Thunderbirds*, so I immediately saw this pair as evil counterparts to Lady Penelope and Parker. I wrote the book with this in mind, even down to giving Ms. Fortune a pink Rolls Royce. I added in characters based on two elderly aunts of my wife and made my father-in-law a casino owner. It was way over the top. I had fewer notes on this story than on any of them. I suspect that everyone was glad it was the final volume and simply didn't care what I did anymore. Or maybe my level of silliness in this one was closer to what they had hoped for all along? But although they mostly caught all of my Bond references, they didn't know *Thunderbirds*, so they left all of those in.

In addition to Bond, you've written tie-in books for a number of properties, including *Doctor Who*, *The Avengers*, and *Star Trek*. When you were writing James Bond Jr., did you feel a sense of ownership? Or do you feel that because it's someone else's characters, you are limited in what you can do?

In retrospect, I wish I'd been able to simply create my own stories instead of being forced to adapt sub-par scripts. I've adapted *Doctor Who* scripts and loved it, but that was because I was working with excellent source material. When I did my *Outer Limits* novels, I adapted two scripts – but I was allowed to select the scripts and had a wealth of good stories to choose from. The *James Bond Jr.* scripts were all terrible. When the series eventually came out, it sank promptly, which didn't surprise me a bit.

I did feel invested in it enough to buy some of the merchandise. I still have the car and a James figure, and the comic books. They picked a couple of the stories I adapted, so I wanted to check out how they'd managed it. But I simply went on to my next writing project, which was a lot more fun.

How do you characterize the six books?

As my best attempt to have fun despite a lot of problems.

What did the books do well? In what areas were you not quite satisfied?

They're fairly decent adventure stories, but I felt from the start that they could have been much, much better. I think the biggest problem, honestly, was the "too many cooks" issue. I had three layers of editing – sometimes even more – and they couldn't all agree on anything. Leslie, at Daniel Weiss, was a good editor, trying his best with what he was handed. He was mostly on my side. The other editor at Penguin – well, she was exactly as much of a problem as I'd expected. She kept going around Leslie and complaining to me about the books. I believe she only lasted another year at Penguin and then became an agent. And the license holders didn't seem to be able to agree between themselves what I was allowed to do in the books. They were, on the whole, nice enough people. I talked with them on the phone a fair amount, but their memories of what they told me and mine tended to be quite different.

What sort of reaction did you get to the books when they were released? What about now?

At the time, I got zero reaction. I don't believe anybody ever reviewed them, and I didn't get any fan letters. Of course, this may simply be because none of them were ever forwarded to me. For a number of years, practically nobody knew I'd written them, which probably didn't help. Then, in the past few years, people have started to tell me that they enjoyed the books when they were kids. Maybe they're just being nice, but I do like to think that at least a few people had fun with them.

Where do you place your six Bond books in the canon?

In a deep, dark cellar? Well, perhaps not quite that far out, but certainly off the mainstream. Certainly not canon, whatever that may be, in any way, shape or form. An alternate universe, perhaps?

Looking back, what do you think of your entire experience? What does it mean to you personally to have written six Bond books?

The reason I agreed to write the books in the first place was that I loved the idea of having a small place in the Bond Universe. When I was a teenager, just starting to write, I tried to write a novel version of the movie *You Only Live Twice*. I never got very far. Then I tried to write an original Bond story – these days it would be called fan fiction, I suppose, but I didn't know about fan fiction in those days. I hand-wrote it in a notebook – long since gone, thank goodness. But writing Bond in some form was an early dream of mine, and these books were certainly a fulfillment of that dream.

The actual experience, though, was quite depressing, as I was constrained so much. It wasn't my worst writing experience ever – that has to be my only *Star Wars* novel – but it was pretty bad. I have had such wonderful experiences writing in other licensed universes. Having said which, if they offered me another go, even at James Jr...

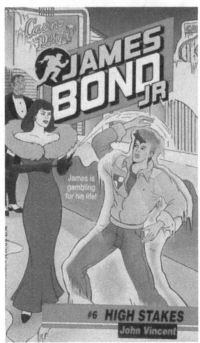

The first and last of John Peel's *James Bond Jr.* novelizations
©1991, Puffin

As Good As Gold

When Dave Morris was writing *As Good As Gold*, the *James Bond Jr.* tie-in book, the author was breaking one of the animated show's cardinal rules. As previously established, Eon decided that 007 could not appear in the series. As a result, the spy is not seen in any of the show's 65 episodes. Similarly, 007 does not appear in person in any of John Peel's six novelizations or in Marvel's 12 comics. Yet, 007 makes an unexpected appearance in *As Good As Gold*. In fact, the spy shows up twice.

Unlike Peel's books, *As Good As Gold* is not an adaptation of a particular episode of the animated series; instead, it is an original story. In it, on a school trip to London, young James encounters Goldfinger and Oddjob. James tracks the sinister villains to Egypt and discovers that Goldfinger has been stealing gold treasures from the pyramids and replacing them with miniature atom bombs. Goldfinger intends to trigger the bombs so that the resulting land-slide will change the path of the Nile river. The new course of the river will flow through the villain's newly acquired property. Goldfinger's endgame is to resell the property, at a significant premium, to the people of Egypt who re-ly on the river to provide food to the region. After learning of the plot, James puts it bluntly, "Goldfinger, you evil monster! You're profiteering out of a plan that will bring famine to millions."[425]

As Good As Gold is an interactive gamebook where young readers are asked to imagine that they are 007's nephew and they are instructed to make decisions that will determine the outcome of the story. The front matter of the book establishes that: "You are James Bond Junior... At the end of each page in this book, there is a choice to make. Decide what you would do if you were James Bond Junior, then turn to the page given in the instructions and continue your adventure."[426] Depending on the reader's picks, either James thwarts Goldfinger's fiendish scheme or James fails and the villain is victorious.

As noted, 007 has two cameos in *As Good As Gold*. In one instance, 007 surprises James by meeting him at an airport in Istanbul. James is thrilled to see his dashing uncle's smiling face. Elsewhere, James reaches 007 on the agent's car phone. Even though 007 is in the middle of a mission, he takes the call and warmly hails, "Ah, James... What can I do for you?"[427] Before concluding their chat, an unfazed 007, who is under fire from enemy agents, nonchalantly explains, "Ah, I'm going to have to dash now, James."[428]

In both occurrences, 007 is portrayed as a glamorous figure and a beloved uncle. The reader is left with the im-pression that their relationship is a loving one. If there is a downside to 007's appearances in *As Good As Gold*, it's that they signal the end of each storyline. For instance, when James informs 007 that he's stumbled onto Goldfin-ger's plot, the concerned spy instructs, "You [should] just go back to school and forget about it; it's out of your hands now."[429] In both circumstances, 007 doesn't want to see James placed in unnecessary danger and he sends his disappointed nephew back to the safety of the boy's home.

Dave Morris is a British writer of more than seventy books, as well as a video game designer.

Can you talk about the creation and writing of *As Good As Gold*?

I had just written a series of Choose Your Own Adventure-style books for Mammoth, the UK publisher of *James Bond Jr.*, and I was also known back then as the go-to guy for tie-ins with animated TV shows, having written *COPS* (1988-89), *Teenage Mutant Ninja Turtles*, and a few others. I think how it came about was over coffee with an editor at Mammoth about Bond. The movie series was then on a long pause after *Licence to Kill* and they men-tioned wanting to do a *James Bond Jr.* gamebook.

What are your most vivid memories about writing the book?

Normally when I was writing books based on a TV show, I'd start by watching the whole series, but Mammoth couldn't even get me one episode. I had the show bible and I just had to figure out the tone of the show from that. I started the story with a school trip to London because I wasn't even sure where James's school was located.

What about the title?

I wanted a stronger title. *As Good As Gold* sounded a little soft to me, but the publishers insisted and it was their project. I was just hired to work on it.

Do you recall any alternative titles?

I don't. It was too long ago, and I can't find anything about it in my computer archives, so I probably just scrawled a few suggestions on the back of an envelope. I remember that I wanted something more dramatic, something like *Gold Hearted*, for instance. *As Good As Gold* seemed to me to lack the impact of a good Bond title. But I was overruled.

It appears that the book was published in the United Kingdom but it was published in the United States. Can you confirm that?

My contract was probably just for UK publication, so if a US publisher had wanted to take on the book, they'd have had to get in touch with me. I'd have just as happily written regular novellas, incidentally; it was the publisher who wanted it to be a gamebook.

How long did it take to write *As Good As Gold*?

It's hard to remember, but the publishing schedule for movie and TV tie-in books tends to be pretty tight. I'd guess I had about a month in all to come up with the plot outline, get it approved, and plan and write the book. Then the editors would have had only days to okay it with the show's producers and get it to the typesetters. The book has to be in stores at the same time the show or movie hits the screen. In the case of the *Teenage Mutant Ninja Turtles* movie novelization, I had less than three weeks to write the manuscript and the book was on sale less than two months later.

How were Goldfinger and Oddjob selected to be the villains?

Goldfinger was the first Bond movie I saw, aged seven. It was all I talked about for weeks, especially the line, "No, Mr. Bond, I expect you to die." So when I got the chance to write this book, of course, Goldfinger and Oddjob were my choices of villains.

007 appears twice in your book but he does not show up in the animated series, John Vincent's novellas, or in the Marvel comics. How did that come to be?

That's one reason why I preferred to watch a whole season of shows before writing a tie-in book. If I'd seen the episodes, then I'd have noticed 007 was absent. But there was nothing about that in the show bible, so I gave him a couple of brief appearances. It was only after the manuscript was delivered that the editors at Mammoth remembered 007 wasn't supposed to feature in the series. They checked with the producers and because the deadline was so tight, and because there were only those two cameo appearances, they decided to let it pass. So that might be the only time 007 shows up anywhere in the *James Bond Jr.* franchise.

Were you given guidelines on how to depict 007?

No, since the editors had said nothing about including him. In my mind he will have been played by Timothy Dalton, though, I can tell you that much.

In the book, 007 is something of a foil in that when he arrives he takes over and ends the adventure for James. Of course, 007 is happy to help his nephew but he understandably doesn't want the teenager involved in his dangerous business. Did you consider other ways to incorporate 007 in the plot? Perhaps having 007 and James join forces and take on Goldfinger together?

I probably would have felt that took too much agency out of the hands of the reader. In kids' adventure books the trick is always to get adults out of the way so that the young protagonists have to solve everything for themselves.

But it's convenient to bring the adults back in when you need to wrap up the story. 007 served the same function there as Dumbledore in the Harry Potter books.

* * *

I often conclude my interviews by asking, "What else should I have asked you?" The open-ended nature of the query can take the conversation into unexpected areas of Bond history and lore. When I posed the question to Morris, he told me about an unmade Bond videogame of which I was previously unaware.

Morris recalled, "I was hired to do some narrative design work on a James Bond computer game for a UK software developer." This tantalizing bit of information piqued my interest and I asked Morris to reveal more about his experience writing the game.

Morris, who was working on the project in 1998, revealed, "It would have differed from games like [1997's hit] *GoldenEye* in being third-person, not first-person, and it would have been a lot cheaper to develop. It would have been more along the lines of a tactical game such as [1998's] *Commandos*, which had yet to be released but that I must have seen in my work at Eidos Interactive, who published it. The developer was a company called Ingames Interactive, that was negotiating for the rights. The idea was that each movie release was accompanied by a Triple-A game like *GoldenEye*, but that the market also had room for a more specialized tactical game covering the whole 007 series. Ingames's CEO, Russell Jamieson, hired me to write the design spec for a game whose working title was *BOND*.

Morris wrote a "concept document," which is dated February 2, 1998. The document provides enticing details about the videogame. *BOND* would have been designed for use on the popular game consoles at the time, including PlayStation and the Nintendo 64 and could be played by one or more players. He strived to retain the "style and glamor of the films" and to incorporate action, suspense, and creative problem-solving into the gameplay.

The premise of *BOND* is that the player is James Bond. Morris's document explains, "You will pit your skill and wits against the classic enemies of James Bond's past. Each level parallels the setting of one of the Bond films, and the finale of the level sees the player confronting the villain from that film. The guns and gadgets used are those that were available to 007. So in the first level, you could be using a Beretta or Walther PPK—in the final level it will be a fingerprint-triggered laser pistol."

BOND would have been designed for players fourteen and over and would have utilized a third-person perspective. A third-person view is a different approach from *GoldenEye*, a first-person shooter game, where the player "sees" the game through Bond's eye. Instead, in *BOND*, players would control an avatar of Bond and move him through different environments. Morris's document reveals that the "object of the game is to control Bond and one or more sidekicks, [to infiltrate] an enemy base with a combination of action and puzzle-solving, to eliminate the villain and destroy the base, and to get out in one piece."

BOND would have had 20 levels of gameplay. Eighteen of the levels would be based on scenes from the eighteen movies made to that point (*Dr. No* through *GoldenEye*). There would have been two additional levels—a training level in Q's lab and a finale battle that was not based on a movie. Morris also had an idea for a bonus level that was set on a train, where Bond battles a series of bad guys including Jaws, Red Grant, and Tee Hee. Some of the locations featured in the game include Dr. No's Jamaican-based center of operations (*Dr. No*), SMERSH's headquarters (*From Russia with Love*), Ernst Stavro Blofeld's lair (*You Only Live Twice*), Francisco Scaramanga's private island (*The Man with the Golden Gun*), Hugo Drax's space station from (*Moonraker*), Max Zorin's mine (*A View to a Kill*), General Georgi Koskov's Afghanistan-based airfield (*The Living Daylights*), and the laser satellite base (*GoldenEye*). The 2012 videogame *007: Legends* also utilize some of these settings. Whereas *BOND* would have included missions inspired from 18 Bond movies, *Legends* only incorporated six movies, one film from each Bond actor to date.

At the start of each level of *BOND*, M would brief Bond on his perilous mission and Q would equip the agent. Bond women would join 007 on the first leg of each mission. For instance, Honey Rider, Pussy Galore, Contessa Theresa di Vicenzo, and other Bond heroines would accompany the spy in the field. For Bond to succeed, he would have to rely on the women's unique skillsets. At some point, Bond would part company with his ally and he would complete the mission on his own.

In some missions 007 must assassinate the villain, his henchman and his stronghold and other assignments require an additional objective, such as freeing hostages (like the astronauts in *You Only Live Twice*) or retrieve a microchip. To succeed, Bond would have had to don disguises, follow maps that reveal the layout of the villain's lair, keep a watchful eye for double-agents, improvise traps and create distractions to confuse the enemy.

The structure of each mission would usually involve infiltration (stealthy entering the villain's stronghold), showdown (with the villain and his henchman), and escape. To complicate matters, M's intelligence would not always be complete; instead, it would be best on MI6's "best guess" and "based on their intelligence to date." As a result, Bond might be in store for some unpleasant and deadly surprises. The agent would have to learn the truth and act on his own initiative to complete his assignment.

Along the way, Bond would draw from armaments from the movies, including a Walther PPK, a throwing knife, dart watch (*Moonraker*), and he would need to be inventive and create impromptu weapons like the electric heater in a bathtub, as he had to in *Goldfinger*. Bond would have had the opportunity to step behind the wheel of the Aston Martin DB5 and the Lotus Espirit and surprising ones, such as the "dragon" from *Dr. No* and Blofeld's bobsled in *On Her Majesty's Secret Service*.

BOND was not designed to be wholly a shooting game, where the primary goal is for players to get the highest body count. While not skimping on the action, the game would also require strategy, puzzle-solving, and stealth maneuvering. Morris described the game as "thinking-plus-action" that incorporated "nail-biting strategic and tactical challenges." In Morris's estimation "007 is a surgical instrument. The opening sequence in *Goldfinger* is a perfect introduction to him in under five minutes – infiltration, stealth, sabotage, and thinking on his feet. Those are the hallmarks of the character for me. So in *BOND* the player definitely would have been dispatching lots of enemy agents, but it would have been "ninja" style – only taking out the enemies on a direct route to your objective, as any unnecessary bodies could be found by patrols. It's a very similar gameplay style to *Commandos*, where a lot depends on isolating any target and avoiding searchlights and sentry patrols."

Morris sought to draw on elements of Bond's abilities beyond his undeniable skills as an assassin. When possible, Bond must avoid combat. After all, Bond's "aim is not to get bogged down in a firefight against endless foes." So, to win, players must also use his stealth skills and rely on his "ability to improvise."

As Roger Moore noted in the *Happy Birthday 007: 25 Years of James Bond*, a 1987 television special designed to celebrate the silver anniversary of the film series, and as reported by Calvin Dyson, not only is 007 "licensed to kill, but he's also licensed to improvise."[430] Bond's ability to think on his feet was something that Morris intended to incorporate into the gameplay of *BOND*. Morris wrote: "Bond shoots a guard with a harpoon. The guard doesn't fall straight away (as he might from a Magnum .44 shot, say) but staggers for a few seconds first. If Bond closes towards him and there are other guards present, Bond automatically acquires the harpooned guard's gun and holds his body upright as a shield. If no other guards were present, Bond would instead catch the body as it fell to the floor, preventing it from making a noise." The 2004 video game *GoldenEye: Rogue Agent* would employ a similar fear, where Bond could use enemy agents as human shields.[431]

Had the game gone into production, it would have been necessary to cast an actor to voice James Bond's line. For the part, Morris had a surprising actor in mind. Morris recalled, "One idea was to get Bob Holness, a British television personality who was the second actor to play James Bond on radio back in the 1950s. However, by the time we got to recording voices for the game he'd have been in his seventies, so I'd need to have checked how well his vocal cords had held up. Some older actors can pass for younger on audio. Of course, each territory where the game was sold would have to localize the voice talent. For other parts, Morris hoped to draw in a familiar face from Eon's series. Morris explains, "I think we could have hired Desmond Llewelyn to play Q in the pre-mission sequences where Bond gets his equipment. That would have been a nice touch."

Because *BOND* would have been a third-person game, players would have seen an avatar of Bond. Morris revealed that the look of 007 would have been based on the then-current movie Bond. Morris explains, "Pierce Brosnan would be the obvious choice. At the time that *BOND* would have been released Brosnan hadn't been in the role long and it seemed likely he'd star in several more movies. But it depends on whether the budget would have stretched to paying for his likeness."

If producers were not able to secure Brosnan's likeness, Morris had a back-up plan. Morris indicated, "We'd have to have settled for an identikit [composite] look. If it came to that, I did have a fallback plan: to get the artists to depict Bond looking like the young Trevor Howard as he was in *The Adventuress* [1946, also known as *I See a Dark Stranger*]. Fleming apparently had him in mind [to star as Bond in a movie], but by the sixties, he was too old for the part. The great advantage of games is we can take decades off your age.

Despite Morris's comprehensive blueprint for the game, *BOND* was never created. Morris recalls, "I was juggling a lot of projects at the time so it's hard to remember now why the game never happened, but I think Ingames failed to raise the finance they were looking for to scale up to doing licensed games like this. Shortly afterward the company wound up, and by that time I was working full-time on a couple of games at Eidos HQ in London, so I lost touch with Russell Jamieson. A shame, I'd have so loved to work on this game."

Morris's vision of the video game was a compelling one. Even though *BOND* was never produced, Morris contributed to the wealth of Bond literature with his gamebook *As Good As Gold*, a book that unexpectedly featured two appearances by 007.

Advertisement for the James Bond Jr. book series.

Theme Song
Dennis C. Brown

In the already diverse catalog of Bond theme songs, "James Bond Jr.," the title track for the animated television series, is an outlier. Except for the alternate version of "The Man with the Golden Gun," which appears during the end credits of the movie, "James Bond Jr." is the only theme song that includes Bond's name in the lyrics. When referring to 007, only one song explicitly names him. Instead, they make oblique allusions to him or use pronouns like "he," "him," and "his" (as in "Thunderball"), or "you" (as they appear in "Moonraker," "For Your Eyes Only," "All Time High" from *Octopussy*, "Tomorrow Never Dies."

The notable exception is the ballad that Marvin Hamlisch and Carole Bayer Sager wrote for *The Spy Who Loved Me*, in which Bond is described as a spy. Defying convention even more boldly, the Burt Bacharach-Hal David tune for the 1967 *Casino Royale* mentions Bond's name numerous times, including in the intentionally daft lyric, "Have no fear, Bond is here." But since the spoof was made by a competing production company, the song deliberately defied Eon's established but unwritten rule.

Exceptions aside, including Bond's name in lyrics, simply isn't done. However, even when playing by a different set of rules and in a different medium, the Dennis C. Brown and Maxine Sellers-written theme song for the animated television series *James Bond Jr.* is a radical departure. The roughly 47-second song mentions James seven times, five times referring to the title character, Bond's nephew, and twice to the famous spy.

In one instance, Brown and Sellers create a gentle twist on Bond's familiar introduction, resulting in the lyric "Bond, James Bond Jr." In another, they use playful wordplay to establish James Bond Jr.'s relationship to 007: "He learned the game from his uncle James / Now he's heir to the name / James Bond."

Brown has also co-written the theme song for *Teenage Mutant Ninja Turtles* (1987-1996) with television-writer producer Chuck Lorre, with whom he has had a long and fruitful relationship. Brown has composed the theme songs for several of Lorre's sitcoms, including *Dharma Greg* (1997-2002); *Two and a Half Men* (2003-2015), which uses only two words – "men" and "manly" – but repeats them to comic effect; and for *Mike & Molly* (2010-2016).

In addition to writing the theme song of *James Bond Jr.*, Brown scored all 65 episodes of the series.

***

How did you come to co-write the music and score for *James Bond Jr.*?

The first animated series I worked on was a less than hugely successful series for Marvel entitled *Little Clowns of Happytown* (1987-1988). TV producer Chuck Lorre and I were writing featured songs for this short-lived series when our big break into animation came. One of the show's producers came to us with an opportunity to do a theme song demo for another project he was working on. The man was Fred Wolf, and the project with a title, which seemed pretty nutty at the time, was *Teenage Mutant Ninja Turtles*. Several attempts at creating a theme that met with everyone's approval had already been made, so we were very eager to win this one. We worked feverishly to create a theme and then spent all the demo money given us and even went into our own pockets to produce a recording that would knock everyone's socks off. We hit the bull's-eye, bringing the producers into a class A recording studio and blasting our theme on the big overhead speakers. The "socks" came off, and the theme was immediately accepted. Thus began my career with Fred Wolf Films.

After working with Fred on 187 episodes of *TMNT* [*Teenage Mutant Ninja Turtles*] and several other shows, I essentially became the Fred Wolf Films music department; it was a great relationship. Fred called me for every project that came along, and so it was with *James Bond Jr*. It was the fourth show I did for Fred Wolf Films. When the call came in, I contacted Maxine Sellers, a songwriter I had been working with, and we got started immediately on some theme ideas. Maxine was a great and clever lyricist who could tell a story well, and with me being more of a music guy, I enlisted her help. We recorded the theme at the studio of Larry Brown, who later helped in scoring the show.

In terms of the title song, what were your creative marching orders? Did you work with Eon?

I had to look up Eon to see what that is. Yes, Cubby Broccoli's name was mentioned frequently, but I knew nothing of EON. As far as marching orders, well, "Give us a great theme song" was about it. Fred trusted me enough to realize that I'd know what would work.

There was a warning, however, and though it was also Fred's concern, it seemed that this came originally from Cubby. We were told to be very wary of copyright infringement. There is a motif in the original Bond theme that became a Bond signature. It was even used as the guitar riff in the Johnny Rivers's hit "Secret Agent Man" (1966). So it has become a spy/intrigue motif in general. It's a supporting line consisting of three pitches, which would be B, C, and C# [C Sharp] in the key of E minor (the original Bond theme key). In its original use, the chromatic line was played mainly by French horns and vibes [vibraphone] and ascended and descended through the intro and as an accompaniment to the guitar line. Even though the line may go unchallenged in other contexts, because our use would be in a James Bond context, we had to be very careful to avoid the line. Whatever the concerns, we treaded lightly and held plagiarism avoidance as a top concern.

Can you talk about the development and creation of the song?

Our first challenge in creating the theme was finding a way to pay homage to the Bond sound without using the forbidden motif. As a guitarist, I didn't find it too difficult. In the original Bond theme, after the legato intro using the chromatic line, the edgy, galloping guitar line enters with another identifiable Bond figure. I came up with a galloping guitar line similar in nature but not close enough to raise an issue. Following [guitarist] Duane Eddy, [who performed Henry Mancini's theme music for the TV series] *Peter Gunn* (1958-1961), and even the guitar in *Bonanza* (1959-1973), the Bond theme solidified using an edgy guitar—sometimes galloping, sometimes driving—as a symbol of action, adventure, and intrigue. I feel my opening guitar line captured the Bond sound perfectly.

Another part of the original Bond theme was the very jazzy, high brass line that appears right after the guitar plays. The first four notes of that line (bum bah dah) sound like a fanfare of sorts, evoking thoughts of danger, intrigue, or some big-screen action. We took that as the outline for the "James Bond Jr. chases scum" melody. We use seven notes instead of four, but there are enough similarities to give our line the same jazzy feel. Listening to both lines back to back, you might be able to hear what I'm talking about; or maybe you'll *feel* rather than *hear* the specific points. The original starts on the root of the key, begins to outline the minor chord, and then jumps up to the major 7th (a pitch not in the pure minor scale) and drops back down a half step. Our line starts on the root of the key, goes up the minor scale, and then peaks at the minor 7th before it drops back a half step to the major 6th (again, a pitch not found in the pure minor scale). It's those color pitches outside the scale that give the lines their jazzy flavor.

Finally, the high guitar lick that comes after "James, James Bond Jr." employs the technique of dropping down a half step to the major 6th. That major 6th is the top of the forbidden line I mentioned, so we used it as much as possible to substitute for not using the ascending/descending line. It infused the theme and score with a good deal of Bondian flavor. I think of that 6th as the "intrigue tone."

What were you aiming for? Artistically, what was your goal?

The foremost aim here, as with most animated shows, is to get as much of the premise of the show introduced in the short time allotted. Of course, the Bond franchise is well-known, so not much explanation was needed; we just needed to put a youthful spin on things. The producers always want the title clearly stated, so we start with "Bond, James Bond Jr." We also wanted to express that there would be plenty of action, so we kept the music driving, urgent, and bold.

What aspects of his character were you trying to capture?

His boldness and derring-do with a splash of youthful vitality are what we wanted to accentuate.

What were the challenges of explaining the show's premise in the song while also incorporating the show's title?

The fact that James Bond was already a known entity made explaining the premise relatively easy. And using the title in a Bond catchphrase—Bond, James Bond Jr.—even emphasized that we indeed have a character much like his uncle. Also, the fact that the character's name is also the name of the show allowed us to get the title mentioned several times. The pieces of the puzzle fit together smoothly.

Can you pick a couple of lines from the song and explain their origins?

I like the two lines that set up the peak of the theme when the singer is at the top of his range. The two lines are "He learned the game from his Uncle James...Now he's heir to the name," which brings us to "James Bond (James Bond Jr.)." The pitch of that "James" is a tenor's high C, a note for which Pavarotti gets compliments. Our singer nailed it.

We wanted something strong leading up to that high C, and I think the two preceding lines encapsulate the show. We needed to make it clear that this is not James Bond's son, and just the mention of Uncle James does that. Being "heir to the name" announces that young James has big shoes to fill, but he "learned the game," so he's up to the task.

With "James" with "game" you use what Stephen Sondheim sometimes calls a "near rhyme." How did you come up with the rhyme? Did you try to rhyme the word "Bond" with anything?

Well, that's a good question to follow what I just said. "Game" is an internal rhyme (not at the end of a line), so I don't think it needed to rhyme at all. The main rhyme in those two lines is actually "James" and "name," but that is also an imperfect (near) rhyme. I generally use the term "imperfect" for any rhyme that is not exact. But simply adding an "s" to the end of one word is a minor imperfection. I also don't automatically view imperfect rhymes negatively; popular music is full of imperfect rhymes, some more imperfect than others. There are many examples of a writer taking a much greater poetic license. One example is the huge hit "More (Theme from *Mondo Cane*)" (1972), which has the refrain "I know I never lived *before,* and my heart is very *sure* no one else could love you *more.*" This is like our theme in that the first and last rhymes are perfect, but the second isn't. This one feels awkward to me, and my brain wants to hear "shore" instead of "sure." Incidentally, we have another imperfect rhyme in "girl" and "world."

Since I brought up the internal rhyme, I'd like to mention that our use of it helped drive those two lines leading to the high C. The song feels more urgent there because the rhymes come more quickly, heightening the payoff. We haven't set up a rigid rhyme or phrasing scheme, which helps make the song more exciting. If a song is constructed of all rhyming couplets and symmetrical phrases, it can get singsongy and bland. Maxine mixed things up well with these lyrics. Perhaps not being locked into a pattern is why we never needed to rhyme "Bond." If we had, it likely would have been an imperfect rhyme since there's no magic "wand" in the show.

Do you recall any unused lyrics?

Yes, there was one unused lyric. In an effort to find some Briticisms, we did some research, and Maxine came up with something we liked. The line "while he rescues the girl" was originally "while he chats up the girl." I don't think we played that for anyone, but we decided on our own that maybe the line wasn't strong enough. At least we'd gotten the girl mentioned, but we thought it was better to have James rescue her so as to keep with the action and adventure of the show. We also thought the line might not be accepted by the American audiences—better not to get too tricky. I thought the original line was clever, but the change to "rescues" was probably warranted.

Can you talk about the choice of a singer?

We wanted a very strong and intense vocal, but not necessarily macho. It needed to be youthful and energetic, and we hired the right guy, a studio singer named Rand Bishop. Rand could cover many styles, having a good rock sound but not a rough-edged one. That's just what we needed, and I'm still impressed by his strong high C.

I imagine that scoring a show with 65 episodes is different than scoring a movie or a single, self-contained TV episode. Can you describe the process of scoring 65 episodes?

Scoring a 65-episode series may not be as difficult as you think. Animated shows tend to stick pretty close to a formula. After 13 episodes, you've written and produced just about enough music to cover all 65 episodes. Early on, I do as much of the writing as possible, and once the sound of the show is established, I sometimes call in another composer to share the load. The theme was recorded at Larry Brown's studio, so I turned to him to help with the score. When I collaborate on a score, I'll usually do act one myself and then assign some of the longer act two cues and chases to the second composer. Most of the chases have a similar sound, so the basic cue template just needs to be adjusted for timings. What you want to do is make the music sound as if it comes from one writer, so we both work with the same palette of sounds, cue templates, and musical motifs.

I'm rarely given much time to prepare the music for an episode (maybe a week or so), so it \helps to share the load. After 13 episodes, it's time to call in a music editor. Once the show gets rolling, episodes start coming due at a faster pace, and a good editor can turn a show around in 24-hours in an emergency. I can't, however, detach from the show at that point. Every episode will have a few scenes for which we have no music that would adequately cover the action. So I am still writing, but the editor is busy cutting together existing music to fit the standard scenes. It's good to have some fresh ears join in anyway, and I'm often quite pleased and impressed when an editor finds a way to use an existing piece of music in a way I might not have.

Sixty-five episodes is a big job, but I estimate it's only about twice as much work as doing 13. I still supervise everything and have to keep the producers happy, but things are a lot easier once you get through the first 13 episodes.

Looking back, what are your thoughts about the finished song?

I can't imagine changing anything. I still love the theme.

Section 4 – Lost Bond in Print: Books, Comics and Fanzines

003½: The Adventures of James Bond Junior

There are two mysteries associated with *003½: The Adventures of James Bond Junior,* the 1967 children's book about 007's young nephew James Bond Jr. The first mystery unfolds over the course of the book, which is completely unrelated to the animated series *James Bond Jr.* In *003½,* young James must uncover the truth about the new owner of a nearby estate, who employs ferocious guard dogs and erects barbed wire fencing to ward off pesky intruders. After learning of a robbery of two million British pounds in gold bullion, James Bond Junior wonders if the owner of the estate is somehow connected to the theft. To quickly dispatch with the first mystery, I can reveal that the estate's owner was the mastermind behind the robbery. Case closed.

The second mystery is: Who wrote: *003½: The Adventures of James Bond Junior*? The answer to this question is deceptively complicated. According to the cover of the book, the author is R.D. Mascott. However, Mascott is not the writer's name; it's a pseudonym. *003½*'s true author has been a long-standing question in the Bond community. 007 Forever, a now-defunct fansite, described it "as a frustrating and perplexing question. For a Bond fan, it was an intriguingly elusive mystery, like asking, 'Who killed JFK?'"[432] Similarly, Jake Rossen observes in his article "No One Knows Who Wrote This James Bond Novel," "For Bond fans, what started as a passing bit of trivia grew into a literary forensics cold case."[433] The cold case dates back to the nineteen-sixties.

After Fleming's death in 1964, Glidrose Publications (now Ian Fleming Publications) posthumously published *The Man with the Golden Gun* in 1965 and the short story collection *Octopussy and The Living Daylights* in 1966. However, after those books were released, Glidrose wanted to guarantee that Fleming's creation remained in the public consciousness and in print.

To that end, Glidrose helped develop a genre of books called continuation novels, in which further stories featuring a popular character are written by someone other than its creator. Sherlock Holmes is a notable example of a character who has lived on through continuation novels long after Arthur Conan Doyle's death in 1930. The intimate involvement of the author's estate in this process helps to ensure that the new work is in keeping with the author's original intent. Moreover, continuation novels can also help preserve the estate's copyright.

Since their inception in the sixties, Bond continuation novels have been a success. Starting with *License Renewed* (1981), John Gardner wrote more original Bond novels than Fleming—fourteen original novels and two film adaptations. Since Gardner retired from the series in 1996, other authors have sent the literary Bond on missions, including Raymond Benson, Sebastian Faulks, Jeffrey Deaver, William Boyd, and Anthony Horowitz (who has also written continuation novels for the Conan Doyle estate).

Over the years, Bond's literary adventures have taken many forms. *The Moneypenny Diaries,* three spin-off novels by Samantha Weinberg explore the life of Miss Moneypenny, M's dutiful secretary. In 2006, Westbrook also wrote the short stories "Moneypenny's First Date with Bond" and "For Your Eyes Only, James." Glidrose has also authorized seven novelizations of Eon films, *The Spy Who Loved Me* (1977) and *Moonraker* (1979) by the films' screenwriter Christopher Wood, *Licence to Kill* (1989) and *GoldenEye* (1995) by John Gardner, and *Tomorrow Never Dies* (1997), *The World Is Not Enough* (1999), *Die Another Day* (2002) by Raymond Benson. Glidrose has also published a fictional "authorized biography" of James Bond aptly titled *James Bond: The Authorized Biography of 007* (1973) by John Pearson.

However, long before their success, Glidrose made two significant decisions to make sure that the Bond literary canon kept expanding. After an unsuccessful attempt by Geoffrey Jenkins, Glidrose hired Kingsley Amis, who wrote *The James Bond Dossier,* an insightful analysis of Fleming's writing, to write the continuation novel *Colonel Sun.* In Amis' book, Bond must rescue M who has been kidnapped by the sadistic Colonel Sun Liang-tan of the People's Liberation Army.

For the most part, Eon has avoided adapting elements of the continuation novels into their film series. Nevertheless, there are notable exceptions. *Die Another Day*, the twentieth Bond film, slyly alludes to *Colonel Sun* by naming one of its villains Colonel Moon. The brutal scene in *Colonel Sun*, in which Sun tortures Bond by inserting a skewer into the agent's ear canal inspired a similar scene in the film *Spectre*.

Even though 1968's *Colonel Sun* remains one of the most beloved Bond continuation novels, it was not the first publication set in 007's cloak and dagger world. The first book to carry on Fleming's legacy, as you might have surmised, is *003½: The Adventures of James Bond Junior* published a year earlier. *003½* is an adventure book that is squarely aimed at young readers. The spin-off book is not unlike the Hardy Boys mysteries book series, in which the teenage brothers get embroiled in adult-sized mysteries. (The Hardy Boy books employed the pseudonym of Franklin W. Dixon for the myriad authors who have contributed to the series since its inception in 1927.)

It's worth noting that *003½* is more nuanced and adult-themed than a typical adventure book. For instance, James Bond Junior discovers that Sir Cuthbert Conningtower, an esteemed member of the community, is having an extramarital affair. Additionally, despite his efforts in recovering the gold and bringing the villains to justice, young Bond walks away with only a limited victory. In the end, the adults do not give young James the credit he deserves for solving the case. Instead, the philandering Sir Cuthbert takes the glory.

Even though James Bond Junior isn't recognized for his bravery or his help in bringing the criminals to justice, Mascott gives the boy high praise: "The way this school-boy had bucked everyone in this blind drive to find what was hidden in [the estate] was as good as anything that precious 007 had done."[434]

003½ takes liberties with 007's ancestry. In the novel *On Her Majesty Secret Service*, Bond tells a genealogist that he has "no relatives and no children."[435] In the obituary for the presumed-dead agent that appears in Fleming's *You Only Live Twice*, M writes that the agent has "no relative living."[436] Whereas 007 is an only child in Fleming's work, Mascott extends the spy's family tree by giving him a brother, Commander David Bond, a sister-in-law, Mrs. Bond (no first name is given), her sister Penny, and, of course, a nephew who is named after him.

Young James laments that he never met 007 and that his parents never saw him either; it appears that 007 "was always on some mission or other."[437] The fact that young James never sees his uncle might have been included to explain why 007's brother and his family are never mentioned in Fleming's work.

Throughout the book, different characters tease young James about his famous uncle. Even the housemaster at his school in North Yorkshire, England inquires about the association. "'Tell me, what's it like, James, being overshadowed by 007?'"[438] Bond is famous in the book, even though the identity of a secret agent shouldn't be known by school kids. It's worth noting that the 1991 animated series *James Bond Jr.* employed a similar conceit in that the identities of 007 and his nephew James Bond Junior were known to the villains and junior's classmates. Because the target audience of *003½* and *James Bond Jr.* was adolescents, it's sometimes best to take these matters at face value.

Nevertheless, there are other instances in the franchise when 007 steps into the public spotlight. Among them, in Fleming's novel *You Only Live Twice*, the presumed-dead agent's obituary appears in the newspaper, and we learn that Bond briefly appeared on television newscasts in both John Gardner's novel *Icebreaker* (1983) and Raymond Benson's short story "Live at Five" (1999).[439]

Bond producer Harry Saltzman, whose interests weren't exclusively limited to producing Bond films, reportedly considered adapting the book for television. The July 22, 1967 edition of *The Book Seller* announced that Saltzman "plans to make a series of television feature films based on the book."[440] Even though those plans did not come to fruition, *James Bond Junior* set the stage for other spin-off adventures set in Bond's world. In 1991, Eon produced *James Bond Jr.*, the animated TV series about 007's nephew, which was also adapted into a series of books and comics. Similarly, the *Young Bond* novels, written by Charlie Higson and then Steve Cole, are a series of nine books published over a twelve-year span that explore 007's exploits as a teen. The first novel, *SilverFin* (2005), was later adapted into a graphic novel. Dynamite Entertainment, commonly referred to as Dynamite Comics, published *James Bond Origin* (2018-2019), a twelve-issue series about seventeen-year-old Bond's adventures in World War II, from his time as a student at Fettes College to his service as a Lieutenant in the Special Branch of the Royal Navy. The stories concluded long before Bond rose up the ranks to Commander, let alone becoming a Double-O agent.

Traditionally, a publisher doesn't advertise the fact that a pseudonym has been used. But Glidrose let the cat out of the bag in the "About the Author" section of the book. In it, they reveal that "R.D. Mascot is a pseudonym of a well-known British writer." R.D. Mascot would not be the last time that Glidrose would use a pseudonym in a Bond continuation book. Kingsley Amis wrote under the name Robert Markham and Samantha Weinberg used the moniker of Kate Westbrook while writing *The Moneypenny Diaries* trilogy.

There are different reasons that pseudonyms were used in the Bond continuation novels. The conceit of *The Moneypenny Diaries* is that Miss Moneypenny actually existed and that Fleming fictionalized some of her adventures in his spy novels. *The Moneypenny Diaries* trilogy, *Guardian Angel* (2005), *Secret Servant* (2006), and *Final Fling* (2008), include passages from Jane Moneypenny's "actual" diaries, as well as journal entries from her niece, Kate Westbrook. So including Westbrook's name on the cover helped maintain the fiction that the books were about historical figures. But the Robert Markham pen name for *Colonel Sun* was utilized for different reasons. Markham was supposed to be a pseudonym that multiple writers would use if additional continuation novels were published.[441]

For *003½*, the Mascott pseudonym might have served dual purposes. If Glidrose wanted to continue with additional James Bond Junior tales with different authors, it would have given Glidrose a way to create a consistent brand. Additionally, revealing that the book was written by an unidentified, yet popular author is also a shrewd marketing move, as it invites the readers and press to guess at the popular author's true identity. If that's the case, the plan worked. Over the years, many well-known authors became suspects. Kingsley Amis and Roald Dahl, the beloved author of *Charlie and the Chocolate Factory* and the screenwriter of *You Only Live Twice*, were thought to have written *003½*.

However, the list of subjects has shrunk over time and it's been a long-held suspicion that Arthur Calder-Marshall, a critic, biographer, essayist, and novelist wrote the book, but that's never been confirmed. In Andy Lane and Paul Simpson's comprehensive *The James Bond Files*, the authors observe that despite the fact that "a case has been made that" Calder-Marshall is the author "there is no documentary evidence for this."[442]

To determine once and for all if Marshall wrote the book, I contacted his grandson Tom Burke, an actor, and his daughter Anna Calder-Marshall, an actor and a painter. In my interview with her, Anna Calder-Marshall confirms the true identity of the author of *003½: The Adventures of James Bond Junior*.

* * *

Tell me about your dad, Arthur Calder-Marshall.

From what I've found out, Dad has been proposed as the author of the James Bond book. It was proposed that he should write it. He wrote it when I was twenty. He had written two other children's books [*The Man from Devil's Island* (1958) and *The Fair to Middling* (1959)]. He always believed that when you wrote books for children that you wrote them in an adult fashion. You never talked down to kids. You treated them like adults. He had a wonderful turn of phrase. Most of his novels and his best work is characterized by beautiful details of characters and nature. When he does that, your heart sings.

There's interest in turning one of his works into a musical. He's dead now but I wish he knew the interest that some of his novels have created. When we were brought up, he was pretty penniless, and times were very hard. I wish I could call him and say, "Someone phoned me about *003½*." [Laughs].

He never boasted much about *003½*. But he did talk about it. He also spoke about meeting Cubby Broccoli and Harry Saltzman. He was very tickled, and they showed him into their office. On their desk were these gadgets for the latest James Bond film and they were more interested in playing with these gadgets than really talking about the venture, which tickled him.

Do you know why he used a pseudonym? Other Bond authors have used them for various reasons.

I think he wrote it under a pseudonym because it wasn't especially the kind of thing he normally wrote. It was a bit out of his normal work. But I think he used a pseudonym because he wasn't creating something original. [Calder-Marshall used the name "William Drummond" when he wrote film novelizations.[443]] If he was creating something original, he would use his name.

I found it interesting that a pseudonym was used yet the publisher reveals it's a pseudonym in the book.

I read this very interesting article about the book and the writer said, "I need to find out who the hell he was." It's like a detective story. The article said that it's very well written. They wondered if Graham Greene wrote it but then they decided it must have been Arthur Calder-Marshall. [Anna Calder-Marshall is referring to an article by Nick Kincaid on the website 007 Forever. The article "The Search for R.D. Mascot" examines the writing styles of different authors, including Greene, to determine who could have written *003½*. Ultimately, the website concludes that Calder-Marshall most likely wrote the book.]

People don't realize that you don't need to talk down to children. There's a lot of adult themes in *003½*. For example, some of the adults in the novel are having illicit relationships with each other.

Dad always believed that children should be treated with great respect and that we had brains. We used to have children's books delivered in great big boxes, which he would review. We were allowed to read them and give comments. Some writers try to pass off a history lesson in a dull way. He also thought there should be a bit of a history lesson, but dad always believed in a bit of magic and a bit of invention. He was a very gifted writer. There were a few bits in the book where I thought Dad got a bit stuck. But this is me, as his daughter. I am a painter as well as an actress and I know that if I have to do something that someone asks me to do it's not the same if it comes from me. But his writing is exquisite.

You said that your dad met with Broccoli and Saltzman. I've read rumors that Saltzman was considering turning the book into a series of television movies. Do you know anything about that?

No, but in our childhood, there was sometimes talk of those kinds of things. I remember that Orson Welles adapted his novel *The Way to Santiago* (1940). I remember we got a phone call about the rights. We got terribly excited, but nothing happened with that. James Mason wanted to do *Occasion of Glory* (1955). There were these things that fell into the letterbox. He didn't make money. It was a hard life. If only one of those projects had come off, it would have helped him. I don't remember an offer for James Bond. But they could still do it.

It's logical that Broccoli and Saltzman would want to meet the writer of a James Bond book. Was there a specific purpose or was it just a meeting because they were all part of the James Bond family?

Dad went to Hollywood and wrote a lot of film scripts for MGM. None of which were taken. Maybe they knew about Orson Welles and James Mason's interest in his work and thought maybe they could find a way to work together.

Do you recall how long it took to write?

I imagine it would have taken him seven, eight or nine months to write.

Part of the fun of the lore of the book is trying to figure out who wrote it. I can understand that upon its release. But do you know why it's taken so long for your father's name to come out?

I don't know. I can't pretend I know. Because I don't. But it would be wonderful if it starts a thing where there is more interest in his other work. They should make a film of it or a cartoon. Dad did have something.

What do you make of the interest?

I'm absolutely chuffed with it. I really am. It gives me deep joy. We adored him. My great grandfather William Calder-Marshall was a sculptor who did a little bit of the Albert Memorial [created at the direction of Queen Victoria]. His father was a cold and hard man who didn't give him any money. My father spent his entire life writing novels, biographies (*Lone Wolf: The Story of Jack London*, 1961), essays, and children's books. Towards the end of his life, he was still writing an autobiography. He was trying to understand his dad who was a miserable old sod. My mother would say why are you bothering with that man anymore. But there's this compassion, curiosity, enthusiasm for people that he kept all of his life, to the very end. Whenever I get an inquiry, I just wish I could phone him up.

I have a copy of *003½* on my bookshelf. Do you still have one?

I found the book in the corner of his studio and I felt so pleased.

Arthur Calder-Marshall's copy of *003½: The Adventures of James Bond Jr.*
Courtesy of The Calder-Marshall Family

French edition of *003½: The Adventures of James Bond Jr.*
Courtesy of Clinton Rawls

Italian edition of *003½: The Adventures of James Bond Jr.*
Courtesy of Clinton Rawls

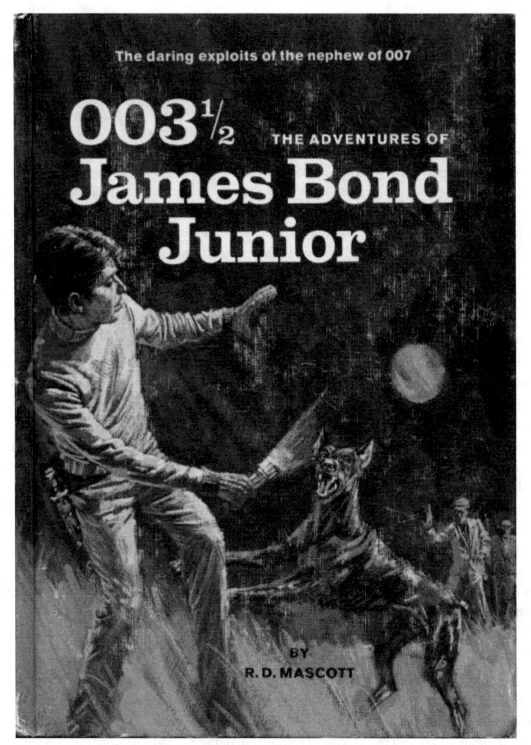

Italian edition of *003½: The Adventures of James Bond Jr.*
Courtesy of Clinton Rawls

James Bond in Barracuda Run
Steven Oftinoski

007 dies in the book *James Bond in Barracuda Run* by Steven Oftinoski. For fans, it's a shocking yet surprisingly accurate statement. It's important to note that James Bond's death is not a ploy to confuse his enemies and it's not another agent who was assigned the designation. Nor is it a cheap trick to fool the audience that gets reversed later in the story when it's revealed that the hero escaped in the nick of time. No, Bond actually perishes in *Barracuda Run*. In fact, he dies *repeatedly*. In various storylines in the book, Bond is burned by active lava, devoured by sharks, drowned in a water-filled submarine, and he is blown to smithereens. Bond's demise is an unexpected but consistent element to this tie-in to 1985's *A View to a Kill*.

One curious and somewhat forgotten contribution to Bond's literary legacy were the book tie-ins to Roger Moore's last outing as Bond. Aimed at young readers, the other three titles were *James Bond in Strike it Deadly* by Barbara and Scott Siegel, *James Bond in Programmed for Danger* by Jean M. Favors, and *James Bond in Win, Place or Die* by R.L. Stine, the prolific author of the popular *Goosebumps* series.[444] Cliff Spohn's striking cover art for the four books resembles posters for unmade Bond films, and his evocative pencil illustrations depicting key scenes are interspersed throughout.

Book tie-ins aren't unusual for Bond movies; *The Spy Who Loved Me*, *Moonraker*, *GoldenEye*, *Licence to Kill*, *Tomorrow Never Dies*, *The World is Not Enough*, and *Die Another Day* were all novelized. However, *Barracuda Run*, *Strike it Deadly*, *Programmed for Danger*, and *Win, Place, or Die* were not novelizations. They were interactive books, published in the Find Your Fate series, in which readers would help dictate the direction and outcome of the plot by making numerous strategic decisions for the protagonist.

In Oftinoski's *Barracuda Run*, when a scuba diving Bond is attacked by a shark, readers are given a choice to make for Bond – fight or flight. If they choose to have Bond battle the ravenous shark, they are instructed to turn to a certain page. However, if they want Bond to refuge inside a nearby sunken ship, they are directed to turn to a different page. Each decision can lead one step closer to Bond completing his mission, but one wrong choice might result in failure.

In Stine's *Win, Place, or Die*, May Day, the villain's loyal enforcer, tells Bond that her boss has implanted microchips into men, giving them superhuman strength. His goal, she claims, is to build an "army of these monsters."[445] Readers must then decide if they believe her fantastic tale. If they determine that Bond should trust her story, he can thwart the villain's plans. But if they decide that Bond should remain suspicious, he is captured and is forced to undergo surgery that will turn him into a soldier in the villain's army.

Because some choices don't lead to a successful completion of the mission, the story can end with Bond failing. In that respect, the Find Your Fate books are unique among Bond stories since Bond readers are accustomed to Bond succeeding in the end. However, as previously noted, the Bond depicted in the Find Your Fate books often dies. In Stine's *Win, Place, or Die*, Bond might be blown up after opening a "locket that was booby-trapped and planted on 009,"[446] assassinated by the KGB after his experimental "laser-blaster ski pole" fails to work because "Q never got a chance to test" it[447], or trampled by a horse that performs "a little tap dance – on [Bond's] face."[448] The novel's front matter lays out the stakes and explains that if the spy fails, "the golden legend of James Bond will become a tarnished memory of the past."[449]

Another atypical element of the series is that even though Bond is the protagonist, the novels are written in the second person. So, the readers are addressed as if they are Bond. The conceit is explained before the story begins, "You are about to go on a secret mission as James Bond, secret agent 007...As agent 007 of Her Majesty's Secret Service, you must choose your actions and decide your fate..." Readers are also instructed, "Be on your guard, James Bond."[450]

In a brief interview with me about *Win, Place, or Die*, R.L. Stine recounted, "I wrote that James Bond kids book many years ago...It was at a time when I was writing many Choose-Your-Own-Adventure type books. Kids loved those multiple ending books. Then they just died." Stine felt that his creativity was dampened by the parameters of writing a tie-in book. Stine recounted, "They insisted that I use the story for that book. I wasn't allowed to invent anything or create anything new. It was a challenge, as I recall." While his book hews closely to the film on which it was based, Stine manages a few liberties, including outfitting Bond with a flying car. It's a fantastical invention, even for Bond.

Stine joins Roald Dahl, screenwriter of *You Only Live Twice*, as a popular children's author who has contributed to the Bond franchise. Of course, Fleming also made his contribution to children's literature (and flying car narratives) with *Chitty Chitty Bang Bang*, which was adapted into a film by Dahl and director Ken Hughes, with additional dialogue by Bond screenwriter Richard Maibaum.

Jean Favors, who died in 2018, relished the opportunity to contribute to the series. In an interview with me, her husband Ed Favors recalled her delight at being approved by Fleming's estate to write the book and said that she likened the process of devising the interactive plots to puzzle solving. Ed told me that Favors studied architectural engineering and mathematics and that she was a mathematical analyst for the United States government. She also wrote several Harlequin Romances. Favors is the first African American woman to write a Bond book.

Scott Siegel shared with me some of the unexpected pleasures he had in co-writing *James Bond in Strike it Deadly* with his wife Barbara. Siegel explained:

"It isn't often that a writer is given the opportunity to tell a story about a character so iconic as James Bond. It can be intimidating, of course, but in this case, it was exhilarating to be able to come up with our own plot and throw James Bond into it. The challenge was to see if Bond (and my wife, Barbara, and I) could get him out of [jeopardy] with his usual aplomb. It was fun. I have one unique memory about this book, but it has nothing to do with actually writing it.

First, please understand that writing books is a lonely endeavor. If you're a theater actor, or a singer or a comedian, you get instant feedback. People see what you do and they applaud or laugh immediately upon the moment of your work. But writers? You put the book out there and crickets. The process, itself, is so slow. The book might not come out for six months to a year after you've written it. The point is, you write in a vacuum, never getting the satisfaction of literally seeing your work consumed. Oh, you can see it on a bookshelf in a bookstore, but that's usually the best you can hope for. Except for this one time...

I live in New York City. I walk a lot. One afternoon, while out doing an errand, I saw a teenage boy ahead of me, walking and reading [*Strike it Deadly*]. I couldn't believe it. An actual person, in my sights, reading something I had written. It never happens. I followed him. One block, crossing the street, turning down another block, still following him. And he's turning pages, continuing to read, fully engrossed. Yes, this was a little bit creepy, because, well, I was stalking him. But I couldn't believe I was seeing someone reading one of my books. I followed him for six blocks until he turned and went into a building; I lost him. I never talked to him. Happily, he never saw me. Except for occasionally looking up to see where he was going, which I resented, his head was inside the covers of the book the whole time. I marveled at what had just happened, realizing how rare it was to see someone actually reading one of your books. And that experience explains why it was not too long after that that I started producing, writing, and hosting live entertainment events."

Three of the Find Your Fate books echo pivotal plot points from *A View to a Kill*. *Strike it Deadly*, about a "mad computer genius," *Programmed for Danger*, about a new "micro-energy source," and *Win, Place, or Die*, about a secret device that can fix horse races," contain elements taken from Roger Moore's final Bond movie, which was written by Richard Maibaum and Michael Wilson.

Although Steven Oftinoski's *Barracuda Run* draws on some elements of *A View to a Kill*, including Dr. Hans Glaub, who was a supporting character in the movie, and a brief appearance of the film's villain Max Zorin, the book is essentially a brand-new Bond story.

In *Barracuda Run*, Bond is called back from vacation by M, who tasks him with investigating Glaub, who was last spotted in Greece. There, Bond uncovers Glaub's scheme to steal the Barracuda, a top-secret supersonic submarine, equipped with a nuclear missile. Despite the familiar set-up, the book is decidedly more fantastic than the typical Bond novel. In one outlandish subplot, Glaub, who has been experimenting with cross-species brain-transplants, captures Bond and attempts to replace Bond's brain with a tiger's brain, which is designed to give 007 superhuman strength and turn him to the enemy's side.

In addition to altering the nature of a typical Bond yarn, Oftinoski also provides new biographical details about Bond's past. In one passage, Bond has a fleeting childhood memory falling down a chute at a carnival playhouse.[451] In another, Bond is again reminded of his childhood when holding a seashell to his head, a sensation that he "used to love."[452] Readers also learn that Bond studied under a Japanese sword master named Aki, who also taught Bond how to kill a shark by piercing it through the eye with a blade. It's possible that the character of Aki is a reference to the ninja agent of the same name in the film *You Only Live Twice*.

Although the four Find Your Fate Bond children's books are not considered to be part of the canon by most Bond aficionados, they are noteworthy experiments.

*　*　*

How did you come to write *James Bond in Barracuda Run*?

I had been hired the previous year to write another Choose Your Own Adventure-type book for Parachute Press, a packager in New York City. Packagers in book publishing are hired by publishers to put together books, especially series, for them – hiring the writers, editing the manuscripts, etc. In this case, the publisher was Scholastic, one of the largest publishers of children's books for the school market. The first book I was hired to write was part of a series called Twist-A-Plot and was called *Midnight at Monster Mansion*. It was after that book that Parachute Press approached me to write *Barracuda Run*, part of a similar series published by Ballantine Books called Find Your Fate.

What instructions were you given?

We're talking more than 30 years and many, many books ago and I frankly remember little. I may have well been given an outline about *A View to a Kill*, the movie my book was based on, but I can't recall for certain. As usual with these types of books, I was given some guidelines on tone, number of endings, and number of storylines. I may have been given some guidelines for handling the character and situations, but I can't recall. I probably was given a rough plot outline or set up by my editor at Parachute and then went from there.

Did you work with Ian Fleming Publications or Eon?

I had no contact with Fleming Publications or Eon. I would have followed any guidelines I was given about Bond and the series, but having done a number of these books already, I knew the general setup, style, and format.

The other three Find Your Fate books were more closely tied to plot points in *A View to a Kill*. While there are some connections to the movie, your book is largely a new adventure. How did that come about?

It would appear that they couldn't cannibalize the film any further and gave me a different plotline, but I can't say for sure. I did see the film around that time and thought it was one of the better Bond films, but if I saw it before I wrote the book, I doubt it had much influence on my writing.

Were you instructed to use the submarine storyline and the cross-species brain transplant plot?

Again, the memories are long gone, but I would think I was given the submarine storyline, especially since it figured prominently in the title. I'm not sure but I would think that they gave me the brain transplant to work with as well.

You gave Bond several new gadgets from Q branch. They included a calculator that holds a small gun, shoes that release knockout gas that is activated when Bond pulls on the laces, and a voice-disguising necklace. What do you remember about creating these gadgets?

There's a very good chance I was given these gadgets by the packager to include in the story with other guidelines.

The Bond in your book was taken from Moore's films. Which aspects of his character did you want to depict?

Sex was kept to a minimum, given our audience, and the emphasis was on action and a certain amount of humor to soften some of the deadly endings. I recall the editors added a few more double entendres to capture Bond's wit.

What motivates the Bond in your book?

Maybe the same thing that motivated me to write the book – a paycheck.

What aspects of writing the Bond book did you find the most challenging?

What I always find challenging in these multiple-adventure books – keeping up the plot lines straight and filling in all the pages. It's a challenge and the only way I find I can do it is to make a visual map of the book and make sure all the pages are filled appropriately. A few times I've finished the book and discovered to my horror that I have a blank page that needs to be filled. The whole house of cards collapses, and I have to go back and work it out.

The format of the book is that readers must decide what Bond must do next and not all decisions lead to the successful completion of his mission. So, theoretically, the book can end with Bond failing. In that respect, your book is unique among Bond adventures. The Bond we know always succeeds in the end. Do these "failures" change Bond's character?

I don't think so. This is standard in all these types of books and makes for fun reading. When you reach a dead-end, you go back and pick up the story by making another choice. Children have found them addictive and still do. The genre has proved remarkably robust for each generation of readers. In the last few years, I have been writing books for Capstone Press's series "You Choose" that are called "interactive history adventures." In this series, I've given the multiple-story spin to such historic events as The Sinking of the Lusitania, the Building of the Transcontinental Railroad, and D-Day.

You had to dream up a wide range of outcomes in which 007 fails his mission. You could have chosen to write that Glaub gets away and that M summons 007 back to London or that Glaub kills Bond. Were you given guidelines on how to depict Bond's fate?

Good question. I can't recall exactly, but the deaths couldn't be too grisly and usually had a dollop of humor to make them acceptable. And I know James couldn't die in every ending. That would have been a bit much for our audience and a bit predictable.

You killed Bond in a variety of ways. Was coming up with inventive ways to kill Bond part of the fun of writing the book?

That is always a fun part of writing these multiple-adventure books. Even more fun is tricking the reader into thinking that one path they choose will be safe and another riskier and then reversing it, so the safe path leads to the reader's demise.

The Bond of the movies and the adult books, of course, never dies. What was it like to "kill off" Bond?

While I've always enjoyed the Bond movies, I was never a devotee of the character, so killing him off didn't get personal for me. He was just another character in a multiple-adventure book that had to die.

What are your thoughts about adding details such as learning how to kill a shark with a blade and his fond memories of his visit to a carnival as a child to Bond's history?

I don't recall whether I got the details from the packager or not. I do think giving personal details like these to a fictional character, especially one as two- (or even one)-dimensional as James Bond helps to humanize the character for the reader. We've certainly seen that happen in the most recent Bond films with Daniel Craig.

What do you think a Find Your Fate Bond book offers the reader that a typical Bond novel doesn't?

For young readers, there's the fun of the reader becoming the central character – in this case, James Bond – the challenge of making choices in the story that determine what path it takes, and the adventure of following a number of storylines.

Where do you place *Barracuda Run* in Bond's literary legacy?

I wouldn't place it too high, but I think it does show how appealing the character has been over the years to both adults and children. In that regard, he must rank right up there with Sherlock Holmes and Batman.

Cover for *James Bond in Barracuda Run*. Art by Cliff Spohn.
© 1985, Eon Productions Ltd./Glidrose Publications Ltd.
Courtesy of Clinton Rawls

The Secret History of Bond Comics
Alan J. Porter

"There's been more original James Bond stories told in comic's format than in any other medium," pronounced Alan J. Porter, the leading authority on the illustrated Bond. Porter made this astonishing observation to *James Bond Radio*, a podcast founded by 007 super-fans Tom Sears and Chris Wright. While most Bond fans think first about the movies and the novels, comic books and comics strips have been the most robust area of Bond storytelling. Yet, for a variety of reasons, which will be explored in this section of the book, the comics have gone largely unnoticed by all but the most dedicated Bond fans. In the following interview, Porter provides an overview of the often-overlooked history of the illustrated Bond.

Porter is the author of *James Bond: The History of the Illustrated 007* (2008) and *The James Bond Lexicon: The Unofficial Guide to the World of 007 in Movies, Novels, and Comics* (2021), which he wrote with Gillian Porter.

* * *

There have been a greater number of James Bond stories told in comic form than in all other media combined. How is Bond particularly well suited to the comics?

Bond is a visual experience, even the prose novels have a very cinematic feel, and comics are the perfect medium for this type of storytelling. Comics are the only visual medium that still allows a reader to add his own interpretation and imagination to fill in the gaps. They say the best stuff in comics is what happens between the panels. Given Bond's mixture of high adventure, travelogue, great-looking people, fantastic vehicles, larger than life villains, and more than a touch of wish fulfillment, it's a sub-genre all of its own that has all the right ingredients for bringing out the best in comics.

Who is the illustrated James Bond?

There isn't any single incarnation of Bond that could be described as "the illustrated James Bond." Just as there are different versions of Bond in the novels and the movies, the same can be said of his various appearances in comics. The character of Bond was a combination of the writer/artist on a particular strip, the venue, and even the country where the story was published. Perhaps the longest-lasting comics incarnation was the British newspaper strips which started out as direct adaptations of Fleming's Bond stories and kept that darker, "blunt instrument" tone when it moved on to its own original stories. But if you want the lighter Bond, or the slick gadget-laden super-spy, or even a comedy Bond you'll find him somewhere in one comic or another. As an aside, when we were writing *The James Bond Lexicon* encyclopedia, we identified at least twenty-eight distinct different incarnations of Bond across the novels, movies, TV, and comics.

How is the illustrated Bond different from the Bond of the novels and movies?

In many cases, the comics stories are direct adaptations of the novels and, to a lesser extent, the movies. In most of those cases, the adapters focused more on the plot than the characterization leaving the illustrated Bond lacking nuance. One of the problems with writing Bond in any medium is that he is just basically a plot device that the story revolves around, rather than driving the story. This makes him an almost avatar-like character that the reader can project themselves into, but it does make developing that level of nuance that an actor brings to the role on the screen difficult.

The one writer in comics who really made Bond his own character was Jim Lawrence who wrote the majority of the newspaper comic strips that appeared in the *Daily Express*. In fact, Lawrence wrote more original Bond stories than anyone. His Bond built on the foundation of Fleming but over the years Bond's craft developed more, with Bond becoming as much detective as a spy, and he also becomes a more rounded character with deeper emotions and showing more empathy with those caught up in his adventures. Lawrence's Bond was also the first to try different gadgets and devices, many of which later ended up in the movies.

What aspects of Fleming's creation don't translate well to comics?

You would think that it would be the quiet more introspective moments, like the extended card games in *Casino Royale* and *Moonraker* that wouldn't translate well, but a skilled sequential storyteller can make these just as compelling as they were in their prose versions. Probably the one area that the newspaper strips failed to capture was the travel aspect of Fleming's work. Restricted to a small black and white strip as a canvas each day it was difficult to evoke the feeling of new 'thrilling cities' or vistas and the cultures of unfamiliar countries. This was less of a problem in some of the later comic books, especially some of the more modern ones where painted backgrounds and a broader canvas allowed the artists to build more compelling environments in which to place Bond's adventures.

Fleming was initially reluctant to allow Bond to appear in comics. Why do you think he ultimately relented? Was it just the money or was there more to it than that?

You're right, the general consensus is that Fleming was reluctant for Bond to appear as a "strip cartoon," as he phrased it. Reading his published note on the subject it appears that he was concerned that it would affect the quality of his writing and dilute Bond to the point where his stories "will lose their point." From this, it seems that when he was originally approached it was with the assumption that Fleming himself would write new stories for the proposed newspaper strip.

At some point, the idea switched to adapting Fleming's original stories instead, and he agreed on the principle that the stories be adapted by the *Daily Express's* literary editor, Anthony Hern, as he approved of the serialization of a text Bond story that Hern had previously worked on. The fact that Fleming received a nice check for the rights to each story also probably helped. In the end, Hern worked only on the initial *Casino Royale* adaptation, before regular writers Henry Gammidge, and later, Jim Lawrence took over.

The look of the illustrated Bond is quite different from the Bond Fleming originally envisioned. What did Fleming's Bond look like and how that changed for the comic strip?

At some point, Fleming commissioned an unknown artist to draw a portrait of Bond, presumably to assist the comic strip artists. That picture shows a hero very much in the pre-war 1930s mode; slim angular features, with slicked-back hair, piercing eyes, hawk nose, and a stiff-backed posture. Fleming always said his model for Bond's look was actor-composer/bandleader Hoagy Carmichael. Instead, artist John McLusky developed a Bond that, even though it predated his casting by four years, invokes something of Sean Connery; a more rounded face, tousled hair, tough almost menacing stare, a cigarette dangling from the corner of the mouth, and a prominent scar (described by Fleming but never appearing on any Bond screen actor).

The *Daily Express* published fifty-two original and adapted Bond tales. Talk a little bit about the kinds of Bond stories that appeared in the newspaper.

Bond made his comics debut in the *Daily Express* adaptation of *Casino Royale* in July 1958 and was followed by the adaptations of the rest of the novels in order. The early strips were subtly different from the novels in that the stories had to be suitable to a wider audience, including children (myself among them), so some of Fleming's harsher and edgier scenes were toned down or restaged so that the action took place off panel. The *Express* format dictated a three-panel strip each day ending with a hook sufficient to bring readers back the next day.

It was also decided that each story should run for a specific number of weeks, in some cases this led to very protracted plots with two stories taking over six months to complete. An early attempt was made to make Bond the narrator of the strips but that meant he had to have prior knowledge of events he shouldn't have and that undermined any real sense of mystery or suspense. With the end of any Fleming material to adapt the decision was made to move on to new original stories. The new stories ranged from real science to almost science fiction, from straightforward espionage to the more esoteric, yet through it all, they maintained the central tenet laid out by Fleming that while his surroundings and opponents may appear fantastic Bond himself was always a serious character, something the movies often forgot.

In many ways, the strips pre-empted many of the tropes and staples that we have come to expect from the Bond movies, in fact, some of the strip panels now look like early storyboards from some of the movie scenes. The newspaper strip was where the Bond/Moneypenny byplay started, and it's where we first see Bond use a hang glider and several other gadgets that made their way onto the silver screen.

Over the years many different publishers have licensed the character. Not all of them were faithful to the source material. What are some of the most bizarre departures and storylines?

The ones that immediately spring to mind were the four Japanese manga "adaptations" from 1964 [of *Live and Let Die, Thunderball, On Her Majesty's Secret Service* and *The Man with The Golden Gun*]. I use the word adaptation in the loosest sense as the Japanese publishers only really used the title and a few of the character names from each story they licensed and then spun them off into their own strange adventures (a precursor to the way that the movies were developed many years later.) The Fleming estate quickly pulled the license, so the manga studio kept telling its own violent, graphic, sexy stories of the world's top spy under the title *Gogol 13* – when you read them it doesn't take much imagination to make the Bond connection.

Some of my favorite stories were from the Scandinavian publisher Semic that was granted the rights to create its own original Bond stories in the eighties. While they published some good straightforward spy thrillers, they also produced some stories with definite "what did I just read?" moments. Some of my favorites include Bond and Felix Leiter tracking down the bad guy by talking to a realtor that specializes in finding hideouts for bad guys. "Excuse me, but did a bald guy with a cat rent a volcano from you recently?" or the moment Bond tries to help stranded aliens get home, and probably the best moment is when the Millennium Falcon from Star Wars makes a cameo appearance.

What illustrated Bond story best captures the spirit of Fleming's Bond?

My personal favorite James Bond comics story and the one that I think comes closest to invoking the spirit of Fleming is *Permission to Die* a three-issue miniseries by writer/artist Mike Grell (Eclipse Comics, 1991). Grell is an old-school Bond fan who knows Fleming's novels in detail. His story is both a homage to and updating of Fleming's world, to the closing days of the cold war. It's a tense, atmospheric traditional East vs. West Bond story grounded in reality. Unfortunately, there was a year's delay between the second and third and final issues being printed, and during that gap, the Berlin Wall came down meaning the series suddenly went from being current to anachronistic. However, rereading it now it still holds up very well as a taut cold war thriller and a solid addition to the James Bond legacy.

What illustrated Bond story best captures the spirit of the Cinematic Bond?

Without a doubt that would be *Serpent's Tooth*, another three-issue miniseries, this time by writer Doug Moench and artist Paul Gulacy, which was published by Dark Horse Comics in 1993. While some would argue that he comes close to parody with the inclusion of flying saucers and a villain who looks like a human lizard, Gulacy's distinctive art and his stylized take on the world of Bond make it an almost movielike experience. It's a fun, fast-paced read and the slickest looking of Bond's comics adventures. It is perhaps for this reason that despite its flaws for the Bond purist it is the most widely reprinted Bond comics story.

With the exception of the United States, Bond has been very popular in comic strip form all around the globe. Why didn't American comic book fans embraced Bond?

Excellent question, and there's no easy straight answer. I believe it's a result of bad timing, misunderstanding of Bond's appeal, lack of consistency between publishers and creative teams, all underscored with a different publishing model that failed to provide the foundation that built an audience in the other markets.

That changed when Dynamite acquired the publication rights to Bond comics. What has Dynamite done differently than other publishers of Bond comics? Can you put their run into a historical perspective?

In 2014, Ian Fleming Publications announced a surprise new deal with American publisher Dynamite Comics. This time around, the Bond comics achieved great success in finding an audience with Bond fans and a new generation of comics readers thanks to their clear respect for, and appreciation of, the franchise and the realization that Bond can be both a nostalgic indulgence, as well as a vehicle to tackle the issues of a modern world.

The availability of the stories in multiple formats from traditional magazine-style comics, to digital versions, and beautifully produced hardback collections available in bookstores and libraries has also helped widen the audience. So far Dynamite has followed three distinct takes on the Bond franchise, a series featuring a contemporary Bond, a historical origins series, and a planned sequence of graphic novels adapting the Fleming novels.

The *James Bond Origin* series is an interesting experiment set prior to the timeline of the Fleming novels and featuring a teenage Bond during World War II as he starts to become involved with the Secret Service.

Only two of the promised Fleming novel adaptations have been published to date with *Casino Royale,* in 2018, and *Live and Let Die* in 2019. Both are excellent adaptations, with the *Casino Royale* one being especially notable for some employing some interesting visual storytelling techniques to present insights into Bond's thoughts and motivations.

However, the highlight of the Dynamite run of Bond comics has been the consistently excellent series of contemporary stories that, in my opinion, are the best Bond stories being told today in any medium. The tone was set by the team of award-winning writer Warren Ellis and artist Jason Masters, who launched the new Bond series in 2015 with a dark gritty tales of international intrigue, violence, drugs, and betrayal. Interestingly they also went back to Bond's comic book origins for inspiration as Ellis pointed out that the reason their "Bond doesn't strongly resemble any of the actors, by the way—Jason worked from Fleming's own description of Bond, the sketch Fleming commissioned ... and the adaptation of that sketch by the first Bond comics artist, John McLusky."

They also established a new take on Bond's supporting cast of M, Moneypenny, Q, and Felix Leiter. After the initial two stories by Ellis and Masters, Dynamite has employed a changing roster of writers and artists for the various follow-up stories, each with their own distinct style, yet all true to the spirit of Bond.

The different stories have so far covered arms dealers, invasive technology, counterespionage, bioengineering, plus an encounter with updated versions of Goldfinger and Oddjob.

These modern series have reached a level of awareness for Bond in comics not seen since the days of the original newspaper comic-strips and bought a new audience to the world of Bond comics.

What place does the illustrated Bond have in the character's rich and diverse history? Is it just an interesting footnote? Or does it help build on the legacy?

I often refer to the story of the *Illustrated Bond* as his secret history. It is often overlooked, but I believe that it's a foundational part of Bond's legacy and worldwide appeal. Particularly in the case of countries where local translations and repackaging of the newspaper strips introduced Bond for many audiences. In the period between the publication of *Colonel Sun* and the first John Gardner novel, *Licence Renewed,* the comics provided the only source of new Bond adventures between the various movies. The newspaper strip almost single-handedly kept the Bond literary franchise alive throughout the nineteen-seventies. It has been interesting how many Bond fans I've heard from since the publication of *James Bond: The History of the Illustrated 007* who were unaware of the various comics interpretations and are discovering them for the first time.

Zig-Zag Comics
Germán Gabler

If you're a Bond fan, it pays to know different languages. If you're fluent in only one language, as I am, you will miss out on a wealth of foreign language Bond adventures. For instance, Chris Moore's novelizations for *Octopussy* and *A View to a Kill* were published only in Dutch,[453] and many Bond comics are available only in myriad foreign languages.

Comic expert Alan J. Porter estimates that Bond comics have been published in over 23 countries.[454] These illustrated tales include Takao Saito's Japanese manga and Semic Press's Swedish 45 issues, 42 of which were original Bond stories.[455] In many Latin American countries, Bond comics are available only in Spanish. Nevertheless, the foreign-language Bond comics that I most wanted to read were published by the Chilean publisher Empressa Editoria under their Zig-Zag label. These fifty-nine comics, published in the late-sixties and early-seventies, have never been released in English.

Zig-Zag comics feature eye-catching and colorful artwork by Germán Gabler, among others, and places Bond, using Sean Connery's likeness, in adaptations of Ian Fleming's novels and short stories, as well as in original tales. Gabler wrote the scripts for fifty-six of the fifty-nine comics and he also created the artwork for many of the issues. Because the comics were published solely in Spanish, non-Spanish-speaking Bond fans were unable to enjoy them.

The comics became more accessible when *Comics Royale*, a website featuring English translations of foreign-language Bond comics, including Zig-Zag, debuted in 2018. *Comics Royale* is run by Bond enthusiast Clinton Rawls who, when not working as an instructor in the Department of Communication and Media at a university in Texas, painstakingly translates foreign-language comics into English.

Bond devotees who visit *Comics Royale* or download the complete untranslated series from the Spanish Bond website *Archivo 007* will discover that Germán Gabler's adaptations were often largely faithful to Fleming's short stories and novels. Gabler's fast-paced tales often feature Fleming's plot points and details that were omitted from Eon's films. For instance, in the comic "Dr. No," Bond battles a giant squid; in "You Only Live Twice," 007 fights his way through Ernst Stavro Blofeld's Garden of Death, and in "The Man with the Golden Gun," the brainwashed spies attempt to assassinate M. "In Fatal Crossroad," when Bond is strapped down and is in imminent danger of being sawed in half, Gabler illustrates the circular blade described in Fleming's *Goldfinger* but not the laser beam that appears in the Eon movie.

When Ian Fleming sold Eon the rights to adapt his novels into films, he stipulated that they could not use the plot of his experimental novel *The Spy Who Loved Me* (1962), which is broken up into three sections (Me, Them, and Him), which is told from the point of view of the novel's protagonist Vivienne Michel. As a result, except for the title, Roger Moore's third outing as Bond, in the 1977 film, bears little in common with Fleming's book. However, Gabler's adaption of *The Spy Who Loved Me*, is truer to the novel. In it, Vivienne (now Mitchell) is held hostage by a trio of hoods. Although Bond eventually arrives and saves her, much of Gabler's comic, like Fleming's novel, focuses on Vivienne and relegates Bond to the sidelines.

There are amusing exceptions to Gabler's fidelity to Fleming. For instance, in the adaptation of "Risicio," Bond unsarcastically orders spaghetti, hardly fine-dining.[456] Yet in Fleming's short story, the gourmet agent orders "Tagliatelli Verdi with a Genoese sauce."[457]

Gastronomy aside, there are a few more substantial departures from the source material. In the novel *Casino Royale*, Vesper Lynd commits suicide after betraying Bond but, in Gabler's comic, Vesper is not disloyal to the besotted spy. The novel *Moonraker* ends with Bond forlorn that Gala Brand, a policewoman who he has developed feelings for, abruptly ditches him and returns to her fiancé. Bond fares better in Gabler's version. In the comic (now named "Sabotage"), Bond and Gala walk off arm in arm. In the final frame, Gala suggestively tells 007, "I am entirely at your command, Commander Bond."[458] Whereas the novel *You Only Live Twice* ends when Bond leaves Kissy Suzuki, who unbeknownst to him is carrying his child, Gabler revises the story so that Suzuki is not pregnant.

The novel *From Russia with Love* ends inconclusively, with Fleming suggesting that Rosa Klebb's poison-tipped-blade may have killed Bond. But in Gabler's adaptation, Bond is unequivocally victorious in his final confrontation with the Russian assassin. Fleming deliberately left Bond's fate ambiguous because he wasn't sure if he would continue to write Bond novels. Because the comic book adaptation was issue twenty-two in an ongoing series, Gabler's changes are understandable.

In "Doctor No," Gabler replaces the gloved hands that in the novel conceal No's mechanical appendages with hooked hands—a visually more striking choice. Gabler's modification predates Tee Hee's metal claw in Eon's *Live and Let Die* by about four years.

Gabler's Bond contends with a variety of deadly animals. In "The Silk Chord," Bond is bound and suspended over a pit, which holds a nest of poisonous snakes; in "Deadly Safari," Bond fends off two vicious leopards with a tree branch, in "The Crows," Bond is attacked by a murder of crows, and in "Queen of the Bees" he evades a bloodthirsty shark. But it is the animal attack depicted later in "Queen of the Bees" that nearly undoes the usually unflappable agent. In it, Bond's captors release a pack of wild rats into the room where he is being held prisoner. The vermin "swarm" and overwhelm Gabler's Bond.[459] During the first wave of their strike, the agent freezes in terror. The caption explains: "Bond transforms himself into a sad imitation of the courageous agent who has faced thousands of dangers with a smile on his lips."[460] But Bond doesn't succumb to his fears. Instead, he suppresses his emotions: "Suddenly, something deep within his subconscious rebelled against the illogical terror that dominates him."[461] Batting away the rodents, Bond fights back and saves himself.

Gabler gives us brief glimpses of Bond's domestic life in multiple issues. In "The Condemned," readers find him at home, in bed, wearing striped pajamas, and with an open pack of cigarettes on his nightstand. In "Mystery on Television," Bond unwinds with a book in his living room, in "A Beauty in Distress," Bond is awoken from his slumber by an intrusive late-night phone call, and in "The Crows," Bond, wearing an ascot, begins his day by reading the newspaper. In "Deadly Gold," Bond relaxes in bed, wearing his red bathrobe and smoking a cigarette, with a drink on his nightstand. Later in the issue, readers learn how Bond recuperates after a bruising mission, "Nothing quite like a hot bath for an aching body!"[462]

Gabler's original titles are playfully pulpy—"Death is Amused, "Danger at Dock 4," "Inferno in Sicily," and "Hand of Fate." Other titles paint a vivid picture, "Death is Amused," "Beach of Flowers," and "The Golden Dolphin." Still others, such as "The Prince and the Dragon," "The Queen of the Bees," and "Yeti!" are a bit more sensational.

The missions send 007 globetrotting to different locales, including the Himalayas, Berlin, Marseilles, the Arctic, Sicily, the jungles of Africa, and, closer to home, a discotheque in London. In "Rally of Death," Bond's assignment takes him to an auto-racing track. Although the sight of Bond in racing gear and donning a helmet, as he is depicted in the comic, might initially be a bit jarring, Fleming had toyed with a similar concept. When Fleming was developing an unrealized 007 television series in the nineteen-fifties, he concocted several plots, such as the one in "Murder on Wheels," which were set in the world of car racing. (Bond continuation novelist Anthony Horowitz used elements of Fleming's treatment for his first Bond book *Trigger Mortis*.)

Some of Gabler's comics seem to take cues from the movies. For instance, in a couple of issues, villains fly around in jet packs like the one worn by Sean Connery in the pre-title sequence in *Thunderball* and the weaponized cigarette from *You Only Live Twice* figures in the plot of "Gold for Le Chiffre." From the same movie, Bond's line to femme fatale Fiona Volpe, "Oh, the things I do for England," is reshaped in "Queen of the Bees" to "Oh England! The things I do in your name!"[463] In *Thunderball*, a SPECTRE. agent undergoes surgery in order to pose as a French pilot to hijack two atomic bombs and, in *From Russia with Love*, "Red" Grant, a SPECTRE assassin, garrotes another agent who is wearing a convincing Bond mask. In Gabler's "Doubles," an enemy agent has his face surgically altered in order to look like 007 so that he can pose as Bond and penetrate the secret service. In the issue's highlight, Bond battles and defeats his doppelganger, providing readers with a double dose of Double-O Seven.

In other comics, Gabler dramatically departs from Eon's and Fleming's sensibilities. In "Flowers on the Beach" Bond infiltrates a band of "flower children." Upon meeting Bond, the hippies immediately strip off his clothes and playfully throw the agent into a vat of wine. After tasting the drink, Bond pronounces it "a little soft for my taste."[464] Later in the comic, when a flower child informs Bond that he has been "accepted" into their "society," Bond replies "Groovy."[465] It is likely that this is the only instance of the agent saying "Groovy" in a licensed Bond comic. 007's deliberately uncharacteristic response helps him to insinuate himself into the group.

Some of Gabler's comics are even more unconventional. In "Yeti!," Bond encounters what appears to be a race of dangerous Yetis. In one full-page sequence, a Yeti attempts to strike Bond down with its huge claws. But Bond's reflexes kick in, and he dodges the attack and fires his weapon at the monster, scaring it off. Later, Bond discovers that the Yetis are nothing more than men in disguise, designed to keep the locals away from the villain's stronghold. Bond fans are accustomed to occasionally seeing their hero dressed in unusual outfits (for instance, Roger Moore's clown costume in *Octopussy*). But Bond's most outrageous getup likely occurs later in "Yeti!," when 007 dons a Yeti costume to gain access to a guarded room in the villains' lair. In "Queen of the Bees," a beautiful operative and her agents fly around in jet packs while wearing bee costumes to bring down airplanes with their high-tech weapons. In the comic, to ingratiate himself with the Queen Bee, Bond slips on his own bee suit. Bond, who isn't happy with his new threads, frets, "How ridiculous I feel... James, you've fallen into an insane asylum."[466]

Part of the fun of the Zig-Zag comics is that Sean Connery's Bond has been inserted into Bond novels that would eventually be turned into movies starring Roger Moore, whose performance as the spy was substantially different from Connery's. As such, Spanish-speaking Bond fans get a taste of what *Live and Let Die, The Man with the Golden Gun, The Spy Who Loved Me, For Your Eyes Only* (1981), and *A View to a Kill* might have appeared if they had starred Connery rather than Moore. And readers who are familiar with the image of Roger Moore, tied and being dragged over a reef, as he is *For Your Eyes Only*, instead see Connery being tortured in the adaptation of *Live and Let Die*, from which the scene was taken.

Similarly, and depending on which artist is illustrating the stories, the characters of M., Moneypenny, and Goldfinger are often based on Bernard Lee, Lois Maxwell, and Gert Fröbe, the actors who played the characters in the Eon movies. However, the mustachioed armorer character looks nothing like Desmond Llewelyn's Q and Le Chiffre, who was played by Orson Welles in the 1967 parody, was usually the visual basis for the villain in the *Casino Royale* prequel "Child's Play," which was drawn by Hernan Jiron. However, when Gabler illustrated "Top Secret" and "Child's Play," he redesigned Le Chiffre's look.

When Zig-Zag's run of Bond comics came to an end in the early nineteen-seventies, Gabler reshaped his old Bond scripts into a new comic book line called "Killer," about a British secret agent named Jack Killer.

* * *

How did Zig-Zag get the rights to the Bond comics?

Zig-Zag got the rights from Albon International, Inc. I don't know anything about Albon. But the information comes at the bottom of a page in each issue. [It states in the copyright section of the comics that the comics were printed "by agreement with" Albon.] Unfortunately, the head of the comic department, Elisa Serrano, died some years ago [2012] and the company known as Zig-Zag is no longer operating in Chile. I guess Zig-Zag had an old connection with the James Bond franchise, since, in the nineteen-fifties, they published the UK comic version in a weekly magazine called *Okey*. Each issue carried two pages of 007 stories adapted from *The Daily Strips*. The magazine folded in the mid-sixties. I think the interest in the character was renewed after the success of the movies. Before that, except for the ones who read Okey, myself included, most people in Chile didn't know anything about James Bond and Ian Fleming.

The comics were published in Chile, Argentina, Paraguay, and Peru? Anywhere else?

I guess the comics were published in many more countries in Latin America, but the company never told us about it, maybe to avoid extra payments. I know this because one day in the comic publishing director's office, I found a Sunday edition of a Panama newspaper that had an insert consisting of a complete black and white 007 issue. The issue was completely done by me, including the cover. Confronted with the situation, the director, a woman named Elisa Pérez, who wrote a couple of novels under the name Elisa Serrano, explained to me that they needed to cover additional markets in order to finance the cost of the publishing rights. I never let others know what I found. I didn't want to start a controversy. I was happy with my job and had a very good relationship with her. She was nice to me and after all, she was the one who appointed me as responsible for the project. That, I felt, was an honor.

[Note: Since conducting the interview, I have learned of additional territories where the comics were published. The cover of later issues indicates that, in addition to Chile, Argentina, Paraguay, and Peru, the comics were also published in Bolivia and Uruguay.]

How did you come to work on the Bond comics?

I started working for Zig-Zag in 1965 while I was still in college. First as a writer of sci-fi stories. Then I slowly graduated to writer and artist of various comic genres: fantasy, westerns, car racing, etc. By mid-1968, Ms. Elisa called me into her office and gave me the news. They had acquired 007 rights and needed to know if I, as both writer and artist, could handle the project.

There were only three novels translated [into Spanish] at the time—*Dr. No, Goldfinger*, and *From Russia with Love*. It helped that I could read English without a problem. Besides this, I was younger than most of the other writers, so I assumed they thought I was more up to date with the new trends. Well, I dressed the part, at least.

When I look at the comics, it appears that you contributed to many of them. However, the credits are not clearly listed. Do you happen to know how many of the fifty-nine comics you wrote? Or how many covers or splash pages or interior art you created?

Except for three stories, I adapted and created the rest of the fifty-nine comics.

Do you know the publication dates?

The first number was published on November 1, 1968. The last one, issue fifty-nine, was published on March 16, 1971.

What was the schedule like? How long did it take to write and illustrate a typical comic?

I drew about twelve pages a week approximately. We worked under pressure and to some extent that affected quality. We could have done it better, but in my case, I also had to draw other stories, mainly for a car racing magazine called *Ruta 44*. I wrote the stories myself, too. Some artists did only the pencil work and would have another artist ink them. Lettering and color were done by other people. It took me about ten days to write a script. To do that I created the plot during the workweek and I typed the whole issue during the weekends.

Were you reading Fleming's book in Spanish or in English?

I read the material in its original language. I didn't trust Spanish translations. After I was appointed to the job, I went to a bookstore specialized in foreign language material and bought the complete collection of novels written by Ian Fleming. It was the same place where I bought copies of *Playboy* and *Mad* magazine.

What was your approach to adapting the material?

In adapting Fleming's novels, I tried to be as close to the story as possible. I avoided unnecessary descriptions. In some cases, I used the basics of the story and enlarged it by adding additional sub-stories, as I did in *Goldfinger*. I dedicated a few pages to set up the purpose of the mission and then came the action. The novels were intended for grown-ups. The comics, mostly for teenagers.

What makes Bond stories well-suited for comics?

Big criminals and fiendish plots were crucial. We were not talking about gangsters or burglars. We were confronting people trying to dominate or almost dominate the world. Our 007 stories were more direct, and the pace was faster compared with the English comic version. Moreover, you needed to have it all resolved in one magazine. Fleming was very descriptive about places and other things. Well, we had to accomplish the same thing with just one image.

Unlike the Fleming books, the comics began with a pre-title sequece, which is a popular element from the movies. How did that come about?

The first sequence, related or not to the main plot, caused a big impression with the movie viewers. So I thought that it would be cool to use the same trick. We were trying to be closer to the movies than to the novels and that was the reason to use Sean Connery's face. Anyway, starting with a scene before the credits had been used many years ago. I remember "Beau Geste" [the 1939 Gary Cooper film] used it too.

After reading your wonderful adaptations of "Risico" (1960), "Hildebrand Rarity" (1960), and "For Your Eyes Only" (1960) on *Comics Royale*, I was inspired to re-read Ian Fleming's short stories. Your stories are very faithful adaptations. Were you a fan of Fleming? What part of his writing were you trying to capture?

As they were short stories, you didn't need to abbreviate very much. That's the reason why they are very close to the originals. Very good stories indeed. I knew the Bond character from the English comic strip. Then I became aware of Ian Fleming once *Dr. No* was on the screen. I remember the story about the influence of President Kennedy in Ian Fleming's popularity when he told the press that he was reading one of Fleming's books [*From Russia with Love*].

In Chile, we didn't know anything about the writer before that. I liked the first movies and all the books of course. But I would say that my favorite spy novels writer is John Le Carré. After seeing "The Spy Who Came in From the Cold," I bought all Le Carré's available novels. Returning to Ian Fleming novels and movies, what impressed me about Le Carré's novels is that evil and crime could be very elegant and sophisticated.

Did Glidrose, who published Fleming's novels, need to approve stories or provide oversight?

There was no contact with them at all.

In addition to adapting the books, Zig-Zag used a variety of ways to create stories. Some comics, like "Deadly Gold", were "prequels," set before Fleming's novel *Casino Royale*. Other comics were adapted from a chapter or an incident described in a Fleming novel. For instance, "Mission in Mexico," was suggested by the opening chapter of *Moonraker*. Other comics, like "Vacation for a Spy," "Bait," and "Cry of Freedom" were original stories. Please talk about this unique approach.

Zig-Zag had nothing to do with this since it was I who controlled the whole writing procedure. I had to write one story in just two weeks, besides my drawing schedule. It was easier to adapt and harder to create a new story, so I had to be constantly thinking about different alternatives. I guess I had read easily two thousand or more books and seen a similar number of movies by that time. And I'm not bragging. When I was a teenager, I used to read a book —short ones—daily during my summer vacation. Westerns, war, FBI, CIA, adventure. Between books, I practiced my drawing skills. I got out of bed no later than 8 a.m. With my older brother, I went to cinemas that projected two or three flicks in a row at least once a week, or even more if it was a fine package.

The inspiration came from different sources. There is a story ["The Hand of Fate"] where James Bond goes to find a Nazi scientist hidden in the jungle where he meets an Israeli commando with the same mission as Bond and then a Russian agent. The idea came to me when I read in the newspaper that a real Nazi could be living there. How could 007 get involved with that? Read the issue. "In Vacation for a Spy," the approach was different. Bond needed a vacation of course, but it couldn't be a regular one. No, sir. He needed to get involved with a group of criminals. And so on. My head was and is, full of stories. You have a lot of ingredients in your brain. You pick something from here, something from there, and there you go. It's just like cooking.

Can you talk about the challenges of creating new Bond adventures?

The first challenge is to write a story that the reader may consider suitable and acceptable for the character. Bond is an intelligent, strong, and audacious man. But he's not Superman. So the incidents in the plot must be credible. You must put some chicks in it. They must appear naturally and be connected in some way with the plot. I had some fun writing the stories and I think some of them could have been good for a movie. For example, the one with the Nazi criminal. And others too. But I lived in a very distant country and remained anonymous.

What aspects of Bond's character did you want to convey?

Courage, intelligence, dry sense of humor, manhood.

What do you think motivates 007?

Loyalty to the cause of the free world. Where are you now, James? Loyalty to his peers. A strong sense of duty. The determination to carry on with his mission regardless of the personal cost. Kindness to the victims of the criminal's plot.

In what ways is your Bond similar to Fleming's? How is he different and unique to your personality?

I think it's the same guy. I believe I got the essence of the character. There are other stories of course, but when I was conceiving the plot l always asked myself: What would James do in a situation like that? Trying to imagine Bond as a different kind of person would have been treason. Like James Bond, I'm with the good guys. I love democracy. I think people can do whatever they want if it does not interfere with other people's rights. The reds are no longer the enemy, at least for the time being. But new threats are coming from religious intolerance and terrorism. We need a lot of James Bond now.

How did your Bond stories differ in any way from the English originals in order to resonate more effectively with his Spanish-speaking audience?

The recipe was simple. More action, fewer words. My Bond acts like Sean Connery in the first movies. That's the way Chilean moviegoers loved the character. Cool, calm, collected when necessary. Mean and violent when the occasion made it necessary. And with a hint of irony in every situation.

Does Bond share any qualities that are specific to your countrymen? If so, what?

In a word, resilience. We are used to suffering strong natural disasters, like earthquakes and floods. But we keep going.

Let's move on to the art. The Zig-Zag comics feature your rendering of Sean Connery as Bond. How did it come to be?

Using Sean Connery's face came out naturally. After all, he was the guy people connected with the character.

Was there any talk of drawing a Bond based on his look in the novels?

In the novel, Ian Fleming depicts the character as looking like the American orchestra director Hoagy Carmichael. Well, nobody in Chile knew the guy.

What did you want to convey with your illustrations of Connery?

At first, I tried to make him look like he looked in *Dr. No*. When he was thin. Then I started to put some extra pounds on him, just as Sean did. I liked the *Dr. No* version better.

What's the most challenging part of successfully depicting Connery?

I had problems with getting the face at first. Zig-Zag provided a few pictures, but it was not enough. That's the reason that I was able to start drawing the character only in issue #6. [In the first five comics Hernan Jiron drew the inside art and covers. In subsequent issues, Gabler, Jiron, and artists Abel Romero, Luis Avila, and Lincoln Fuentes also illustrated the comics.]

While the stories were often based on Fleming's books, the look of the characters was often based on the films. Can you talk about mix and matching the two media?

Ian Fleming's novels were not familiar to the Chilean public. *Okey* magazine, where Bond looked like Hoagy, had folded and nobody remembered the characters except fans like me. So using the faces of the actors in the films was a natural thing to do. The films were very successful. The novels were not. At least, not at first.

Of the fifty-nine covers, there are only two where Bond is smiling with his teeth bared. Neither of which you drew. Similarly, when Bond smiles inside the various comic books, we generally don't see his teeth either. Why is that? Beyond preserving the character's mystique, is it also a technical issue?

Most of the cover shows Bond in perilous situations. There's a time for smiling. Regarding teeth, the problem is that when you draw you use black ink. If you show the teeth, you have to draw a line of separation between them. But that looks bad. Maybe you could use that when you are portraying a mean character or an old one. But never the hero. Never beautiful women. When painting a cover the situation is different. You could insinuate separation with a soft colored line.

The final page of the comic was often a bonus page. They were called "Weapons for a Secret Agent," "Planes for a Secret Agent" or "Automobile for a Secret Agent." How did that come about?

It was Hernan Jiron's idea. He was the guy who started drawing the first issues while I was dedicated to writing at least eight scripts in advance. After a while, I took over the task. The idea was to add some "cool" extra features. I also included "Motorcycles for a Secret Agent."

Let me ask you about a few individual issues – three originals and three adaptations. Your adaptations were often faithful to Fleming's stories. But there are two notable exceptions. In the novel *Casino Royale*, Vesper betrays Bond and commits suicide. In your comic, they wind up together. Why did you make the change?

I love women. So I wish the best for them. I sympathized with the character, so I decided to save her, maybe for a rainy day.

The novel *You Only Live Twice* ends with Kissy Suzuki pregnant with Bond's child. In the comic, she's not pregnant. Why did you change it? Was it a cliffhanger that you knew you couldn't pay off in a later issue?

Bond shouldn't have a child at all, considering the nature of his work. Besides, leaving behind a pregnant woman would have been considered awful behavior by our rather conservative society in those times.

Next is "The Spy Who Loved Me." Your comic, like the novel, puts Bond on the sidelines for much of the story. Instead, it focuses on Vivienne, a woman who is being held captive by three hoods. Did you have any concerns that Bond wasn't the sole focus?

I was in doubt. It was a different kind of story. But I didn't dare to make a drastic change and tell the story from Bond's point of view. After all, it was Ian's story.

There are three original stories that I had questions about. Can you talk about the idea behind "Yeti!" in which 007 investigates the possible existence of Yetis.

Since I was a kid, I read stories about the Yeti. I was starting to prepare a new script when a new Yeti spotting appeared in the newspaper. I decided it was a good idea to take advantage of the myth but – as I am a rational kind of man – it had to be a fake.

Can you talk about the idea behind "Queen of the Bees," in which a beautiful operative and her agents fly around while wearing jet packs, dressed up in outfits that resemble bees, and shoot down airplanes with their high-tech weapons?

My older brother Guillermo gave me a hint. He was very fond of sci-fi novels and both of us started working at Zig-Zag for "Rocket Magazine." On some occasions, I had the idea and wrote the script; in others, he provided the idea and I developed the story. Maybe he was anticipating the "human feminist movement." Another contribution from my brother appears in "The Crows." He imagined the mechanical birds and how they could be used for evil purposes. I put Bond in the middle of it. I guess my brother was anticipating the invention of drones.

What was the idea behind "Beach of Flowers," in which Bond encounters "flower children?"

There was a lot of talk about the hippie movement in those days. We knew about Woodstock, and as a dedicated *Playboy* reader—yes, I *read* it—I was very curious about it. Besides that, my main hobby is music. I loved Jefferson Airplane, Hendrix, The Doors, and the rest, though [Bob] Dylan in the sixties was the best of all of them. I sympathized with the movement, except for the use of drugs. Maybe I would have liked to participate in it, but I didn't have the guts, of course. My mind could have been traveling but my feet were stuck to the ground. So I decided that Bond would have the experience that I wanted but didn't dare to experiment with.

What was your favorite Bond adaption?

"From Russia with Love." Great novel, great movie. I guess in just thirty-two pages I got the essence of the story without leaving aside anything important.

Do you have a favorite original story?

Definitely "Death is Amused." After a mission in Scotland, Bond pays a visit to his friend Inspector Gillespie, whom he met in "Sabotage." The policeman is investigating the killing of a British Lord, found dead in the library of his mansion. The suspects are his wife, his nephew – who happened to have an affair with the woman – and the butler of course. The three of them have good alibis and incriminate others. A fourth version is provided by a burglar who happened to be outside the mansion to break in. It has mystery, some humor, and a surprising end. A little bit apart from Bond's usual experiences but very funny. Some years ago I wrote a movie script with the same story, replacing Bond with a rookie who had just arrived at the police department and added some more humorous situations to have some dark comedy.

What is your favorite illustration of Connery as Bond?

Cover twenty-one. [The cover for the comic "A Beauty in Distress" features Bond in a black scuba suit, standing in front of a yellow background. In an insert image, a figure (possibly Bond) scuba dives in an orange suit, similar to the one Connery wore in *Thunderball*.]

How were the comics received?

People loved the comics. They sold in great quantities in Chile and in the Latin American countries. Only the comic magazine "Tio Rico" (Walt Disney's Uncle Scrooge) sold more than 007. Fifty years later, I still meet people who remember the magazine and my name.

Zig-Zag produced fifty-nine Bond comics. Why did they stop making them?

When [Marxist] Salvador Allende was elected president [in 1970], Zig-Zag's worker's syndicate went on an illegal strike that forced the owners to sell the company to the government. Socialists and their communist allies wanted to control Zig-Zag because it was the main printing and editorial company. That way they could control what was published. They could influence people's minds.

I read an article on MI6, a Bond fan site that argued that when Allende was elected "the political climate drastically shifted in Chile and James Bond went from celebrated hero to a symbol of Western fascism, causing the publication to fold instantly."[467] What are your thoughts?

James Bond was anathema to the leftists. I had anticipated what was coming on and created a Soviet agent (Prochenko) who interacted with James Bond in some adventures and started a new threat: "The Man Without A Face," about a South African, expelled from his country looking for revenge against the western countries, which he felt were responsible for his disgrace. I was trying to alleviate the pressure in the boiler. But it was not enough.

They branded the magazine as fascist and stopped publishing. By that time I was appointed as director of the new *Children Magazine*. The new executives accepted me, though they knew that I was on the right—yes, the *right* —side of the political scene. But they wanted me to write socialist stories. So I packed up my things and left the premises.

Fortunately, I had a university chemical degree and got a job in a big company. I was married, had two children, and faced a dim future. Money was tight, the economic situation was bad, and soon you couldn't find anything except in the black market—an incipient Venezuela. I managed to survive without too many problems by combining my chemical work with adaptations of great novels into comics for an Argentinian publishing company. I did "The Three Musketeers," "The Portrait of Dorian Gray," "Ivanhoe," "Tom Jones," and others.

How did the ending of the Bond comics lead into your next series, *Killer*? What elements of Bond did you keep?

I was determined to get back to the comic business and started a joint venture with the people from Argentina. *Killer* was a kind of James Bond. I even used some of the scripts I wrote for 007. I drew the character with a face resembling Charles Bronson, as he was very popular in my country in the nineteen-seventies. The magazine sold in good amounts but the economic situation in the first year of the military government was awful. Printing costs grow higher and higher with every number. In just 9 bi-weekly magazines, we got to multiply the price by seven. There was no way to keep going with the magazine. *Killer* will be published in the USA in the near future.

How would you like your Bond comics to be remembered?

As an honest effort to entertain people.

* * *

A note about the methodology. My observations about Gabler's first four issues—"Operation Risk," "The Hildebrand Rarity," "For Your Eyes Only," and "Deadly Gold"—were informed by Clinton Rawls's English translations and commentary on his website Comics Royale. My thoughts about the subsequent issues, which I found on the website Archivo 007, are based on my own translations.

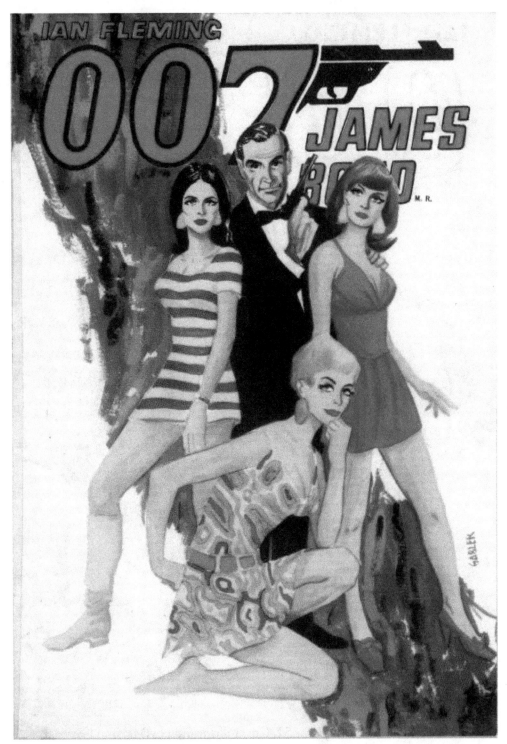

"A Beauty in Distress," Zig-Zag Issue 25, Cover illustration by Germán Gabler

"The Saboteurs," Zig-Zag Issue 51, Cover illustration by Maximo Carvajal

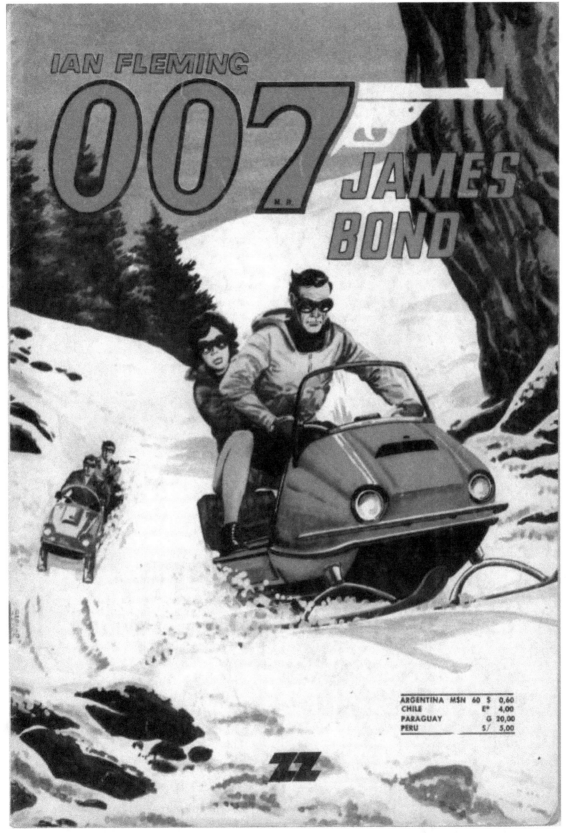

"Mercenary," Zig-Zag Issue 53, Cover illustration by Germán Gabler

"Death is Amused," Zig-Zag Issue 42, Cover illustration by Abel Romero

"Intrigue in Berlin," Zig-Zag Issue 15, Cover illustration by Abel Romero

"Bait," Zig-Zag Issue 44, Cover illustrator Unknown

"The Saboteurs," Zig-Zag Issue 51, Cover illustration by Maximo Carvajal

Interior page. Illustration by Germán Gabler
"Intrigue in Berlin," Zig-Zag Issue 15
Courtesy of Peter Lorenz

Single panel. Illustration by Germán Gabler
"Intrigue in Berlin," Zig-Zag Issue 15
Courtesy of Peter Lorenz

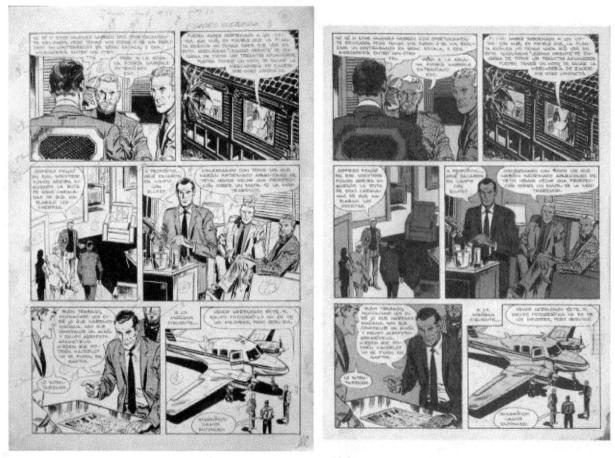

Gabler's in-progress work (left). The finished comic (right).
Zig-Zag Issue 55, Illustration by Germán Gabler
Courtesy of Peter Lorenz

007 seems to battle a Yeti!
Zig-Zag Issue 55, Illustration by Germán Gabler

Bond dons a bee uniform to ingratiate himself to the Queen of the Bees.
Zig-Zag Issue 29, Illustration by Germán Gabler

In Germán Gabler's adaptation of "Casino Royale," Bond is not betrayed.
"Casino Royale," Zig-Zag Issue 25, Illustration by Germán Gabler

Surfs up for 007 in "The Beach of Flowers."
"The Beach of Flowers," Zig-Zag Issue 36, Illustration by Germán Gabler

Overly-enthusiastic flower children greet Bond in an unorthodox fashion.
Zig-Zag Issue 36, Illustration by Germán Gabler

A fairly risqué illustration from "A Pleasure Trip," in which Bond finds romance while on holiday.
"A Pleasure Trip," Zig-Zag Issue 52, Illustration by Germán Gabler

In this splash page, The Grim Reaper chases Bond (on the left) and
M interrupts the slumber of a pajama-wearing 007 (on the right).
"The Condemned," Zig-Zag Issue 59, Illustration by Germán Gabler

A glimpse of Bond's domestic life and May, his Scottish housekeeper.
"From Russia with Love," Zig-Zag Issue 22, Illustration by Germán Gabler

Bond closes out the story with a wink to the reader.
"Top Secret," Zig-Zag Issue 06, Illustration by Germán Gabler

A Silent Armageddon and Shattered Helix

Simon Jowett

Bond comic books and comic strips have been an important part of the franchise since its inception. In fact, the first adaptation of Ian Fleming's spy was not the 1961 film *Dr. No,* it was the 1958 comic strip *Casino Royale*, which was written by Anthony Hern and illustrated by John McLusky and appeared in the British newspaper *Daily Express*. The success of *Casino Royale* proved that Fleming's hero could succeed in the illustrated form, and it set the stage for a long run of Bond comic strips.

The *Daily Express* published graphic adaptations of Ian Fleming's novels and short stories, as well as Kingsley Amis's *Colonel Sun* and many other original Bond adventures with eye-catching titles, such as "The Harpies" (1968-69), "The League of Vampires" (1972-73), and "The Nevsky Nude" (1974). After the *Daily Express* completed its run in 1977, first the *Sunday Express* and then the *Daily Star* continued to publish original Bond stories until 1984. The combined run of all three newspapers amounted to an impressive twenty-five years of Bond comic strips.

More recently, Dynamite Comics has met tremendous success by publishing comic books that depict the exploits of the legendary spy. One of the keys to Dynamite's achievement is their willingness to experiment with the kinds of stories that they tell and how they are told. For instance, whereas some of their comics weave a narrative that unfolds over the course of six separate issues – among them *VARGR* (2015), *Eidolon* (2016), *Black Box* (2017), *Hammerhead* (2016), *Kill Chain* (2017), and *The Body* (2018)—others, such as *Service* (2017) and *Solstice* (2017), conclude in one stand-alone comic.

Some of Dynamite's comics focus on Bond's colleagues, such as *Felix Leiter* (2017), *Moneypenny* (2017), and *M* (2018), and others, such as *Casino Royale* (2018) and *Live and Let Die* (2019), are faithful adaptations of Fleming's novels. In 2019, Dynamite, launched two different series—*James Bond Origin*, set in World War II, before Bond became a Double-O agent, and *James Bond 007*, focusing on Bond's tenure at MI6. In 2020, Dynamite published *Reflections of Death*, an anthology containing six stories by different writers and artists.

Whereas the aughts have been a fertile time for Bond comics, the late nineteen-eighties and -nineties were a fraught period. A revolving group of publishers held the rights to publish Bond comics for what turned out to be a short duration. Moreover, those Bond publishers faced various setbacks. For instance, Eclipse Comics published the first volume of Mike Grell's three-part epic *Permission to Die* (1991); however, due to a production issue, parts two and three of *Permission to Die* were released nearly two years apart. The delay made elements of the story less timely, dulled the impact of the narrative, and negatively affected sales. In 1995, Topps Comics published the comic book adaptation of *GoldenEye*. Yet despite the popularity of the movie, only the first issue of three was published.

Dark Horse Comics published a slew of stories, such as the graphic novels Doug Moench's *Serpent's Tooth* (1992), Simon Jowett's *A Silent Armageddon* (1993), and Jowett's *Shattered Helix* (1994), as well as the Bond adventures "Light of My Death" (1993) and "Minute of Midnight" (1994), which were included in their anthology series that also featured storylines from other licensed properties such as Star Wars, Godzilla, Alien, Predator, and RoboCop. "Minute of Midnight" was included on a double bill with an *Aliens vs Predator* tale. In "Light of My Death," 007 reunites with his old flame Tatiana Romanova from *Russia with Love* and it was published in four parts. Like Topps and Eclipse, Dark Horse also faced frustrating production challenges. "Minute of Midnight" was planned to be a multi-issue comic, but only the first part was completed. Similarly, *A Silent Armageddon* was intended to be a four-part comic, but only the first two issues were published.

At first glance, "Minute of Midnight," which was written by Doug Moench and illustrated by Russ Heath, appears to tell a complete story. In the comic, Bond accomplishes his mission to investigate a terrorist organization and to assassinate one of its key members. However, in the final frame of the story, the remaining members of the terrorist group plot to kidnap M. The dangling plot thread suggests that Moench wasn't finished with his tale. I contacted Moench who confirmed to me that, while he didn't recall the specifics of the story, the villains would have successfully kidnapped M and "Bond would have had to go through hell to save him." Moench, who wrote part one of his story overnight, also explained that whereas his three-part *Serpent's Tooth* was inspired by the Roger Moore Bond movies of the time, that "Minute of Midnight" was his tribute to Ian Fleming's writing.

A Silent Armageddon was written by Simon Jowett and John Burns created the cover art and lush interior illustrations. In it, Bond is assigned to protect Terri Li, a 13-year old computer genius, from the criminal organization CERBERUS, which wants to kill Li and unleash a computer program known as OMEGA that can seize control of computers around the world. Although Bond comes to feel protective of the young girl, he initially finds himself unsuited to the task. He confides to his colleague Major Boothroyd, "I'm not much of a babysitter, I'm afraid sir." Boothroyd counters, "If you had a child of your own, you might have had a better idea of how to come with her... Most fellows your age have already started families. Having a child does a man no end of good..."[468]

The comic book features an artificially intelligent computer and a relatively early prominent use of the Internet and virtual reality in fiction. And drawing on Bond's past, the story also gives us henchman Erik Klebb, the son of *From Russia with Love*'s Rosa Klebb.

The book also features an artificial intelligent computer, an early appearance of virtual reality and the Internet, as well as the introduction of henchmen Erik Klebb, the son of *From Russia with Love*'s Rosa Klebb.

In a brief interview with me, John Burns, the respected English comic book artist, revealed how he came up with the look of his Bond. Burns recalled, "When I was asked to draw and paint the James Bond books, I pictured Sean Connery with a touch of Timothy Dalton. My James Bond was created with these actors in mind." Burns further explained that his interpretation was also informed by Connery's on-screen persona, which was occasionally cruel, and by Dalton's good looks.

Bond comic book historian Alan Porter calls Burns's artwork a "fully-painted delight" that combines "excellent panel layouts, deceptively simple inking, and trademark color washes."[469] Still, Burns beautifully painted illustrations took more time to create than pencil drawings, the more common method. Burns explains, "I do everything from the layout to the finished art. In step one, I read the script a couple of times to get a feeling of what the episode requires. Two, I do the layout of the pages. Step three is the composition of frames and small thumbnail sketches. Four, the thumbnails are sketched full size on the layout page. Then, they are drawn up to the finished pencils. If there are any last-minute alterations, they can be carried out on the layout page. Five, using a light table, the finished pencils are transferred to an artboard. Then, they are redrawn and painted."

Despite the potency of his art and, for reasons that will be further explored in this chapter, Burns did not complete his work on *A Silent Armageddon*. Burns revealed, "I don't recall a signed contract. When the storyline about the world of computers began to take me out of my comfort zone, I felt that I would not be able to do the work to my satisfaction. So I stopped. I guess Dark Horse felt that I was slipping behind as well. I also felt the amount of work I put into the page was being lost in the reproduction size of the comic."

Another contributing factor to the collapse of the series might have been the artist's grueling schedule. Burns remembered, "At the same time that I was drawing James Bond, I was also drawing a national daily strip [*Girl Chat* for the *Daily Mirror*], six strips a week, and any little job when necessary."

Fortunately, both issues of Jowett's other Dark Horse comic, *Shattered Helix*, were published. In *Shattered Helix*, with art by David Lloyd and David Jackson, Bond travels to Antarctica in the hopes of stopping CERBERUS, which threatens to release a deadly computer virus that "would be carried across the globe in a matter of days"[470] unless the world meets its ransom demands. In the two-part comic, Bond enlists the help of Serena Mountjoy, a scientist and the daughter of an old friend, and battles Bullock, an oversized brute who is essentially bulletproof due to surgically "implanted body armor."[471]

Regrettably, neither Jowett's *A Silent Armageddon* nor *Shattered Helix* are in print today.

* * *

When Dark Horse hired you to write a James Bond graphic novel, what direction did they give you? What was most important to them?

To be a hundred percent accurate, I wasn't hired by Dark Horse, but by London-based comics publisher, Acme Press. Acme held the license to publish original Bond stories in the U.S.-style comic book format. Acme and Dark Horse had a co-publishing agreement, but I'm not entirely sure how much of a veto this gave Dark Horse over creative hirings and firings.

Acme's Editor-in-Chief had expressed interest in an idea I mentioned during a conversation with him at UK-CAC [United Kingdom Comic Art Convention], the annual London comic convention, long since superseded by larger and more glamorous affairs. As is very common in the comics industry, this conversation took place in the bar. I suggested that an AI, an Artificial Intelligence—in my pitch, a highly sophisticated computer virus that had grown so complex that it had achieved self-awareness—would make for a very different kind of Bond villain. Virtually impossible to trace, it could infiltrate and influence the computerized systems used to run global stock markets, air traffic control, the launching of nuclear missiles. This conversation took place in 1990 and 1991—long before terms such as 'hacker' and 'cyberspace' entered the mainstream.

Interested, but not sure how this idea might work as a Bond story, the editor asked me to work up an outline, which he read and liked, and which he passed on to Dark Horse for their notes.

I should point out that, at this time, I had precisely two professional credits, for strips featuring Dr. Who and Young Indiana Jones, which had only been published in the UK. I was a completely unknown quantity to Dark Horse, who, very sensibly, wanted their Bond titles to be written and drawn by names that were immediately recognizable to comic buyers.

Which is why it is totally understandable that they showed no interest in my outline until a pitch from a more established writer was rejected by Fleming's literary estate, who retained final approval over every story, every script.

Happily, my outline was approved, and *Silent Armageddon* was hustled onto the previously locked-down schedule. As far as I was aware, Dark Horse's primary concern was that it hit the already-established publishing dates. Ironically, the artist proved unable to stick to the deadlines, which resulted in the book being pulled from the schedules when only half-complete. [Only two of the four parts were published.] If I recall correctly, *Shattered Helix*, my second Bond title, was slotted into the schedule in its place.

How did you come up with the story?

The germ of the idea behind *Silent Armageddon* came when I set to work up an outline from my convention-bar pitch, and it was informed by years of informal reading—mostly in the pages of *Scientific American*—around the subjects of computer design, complexity theory, and the earliest attempts to model, in both hardware and software, the behavior of the human brain.

As I worked on the outline it became apparent very quickly that my AI would make a very poor villain. Faceless, emotionless, and with very little concept of the human world, it would offer very little for Bond to kick against. However, the AI's ability to pull the invisible levers that operate the modern world would be catnip to the kind of global criminal conglomerate that Bond had encountered in SPECTRE. With the AI under its control, SPECTRE could become the secret controllers of the world.

There was, however, one catch. Due to a since-resolved contractual dispute focused on the novel and script of *Thunderball*, SPECTRE was off-limits. If I wanted a global criminal conglomerate for Bond to do battle with for the emergent soul of the Artificial Intelligence, codenamed Omega, and the fate of the world, I was going to have to come up with one of my own. Hence CERBERUS, named and structured after the giant three-headed dog that guards the gates of Hades in Greek myth. [The crime syndicate operates on three different fronts—espionage, enforcement, and extortion.]

Fleming's literary estate approved CERBERUS and I placed them on one side of the board with Bond on the other, assisted by the only human to have had deliberate two-way contact with the AI: a thirteen-year-old paraplegic computer genius. I fully expected a note requiring that I rework the character into a more usual Bond girl, but Fleming's estate gave her the green light and *Silent Armageddon* was a go.

Shattered Helix came together in a much more straightforward manner. I was halfway through writing the scripts for *Silent Armageddon* when I was asked if I had an idea for a two-part story. It occurred to me that, as my first Bond concerned the completely unnatural and artificial, it might be fun to look around for something more natural, but also utterly deadly. A disease, manipulated by science, seemed a good fit—a soft horror compared to the silicon-based threat of *Silent Armageddon*'s AI. And since I had gone to the trouble of creating CERBERUS for *Silent Armageddon*, it seemed only sensible to bring them back for this story. The story itself—which pits CERBERUS against Bond in a race to secure a bio-weapon of appalling destructive potential that had been sealed away in a high-tech lab in the heart of Antarctica—came together very smoothly, including the addition of a much more traditional Bond girl, albeit one with vaguely Oedipal undertones, and it went through the approval process on rails.

For someone with very little experience writing comics, *Shattered Helix* and *Silent Armageddon* were an invaluable storytelling boot camp. There may be moments in each of them that make me wince, but I am immensely proud of them and hugely grateful for the chance to write them.

Who is your Bond?

When I started work on *Silent Armageddon*, it had been some time since I had read a Bond novel or seen a Bond film, so my take on the character was a messy admixture of the Bonds of two mediums, incorporating my unreliable memories of reading my mother's paperback editions of the novels and watching the Connery films in TV reruns. Fleming famously referred to Bond as a "cardboard booby" and "blunt instrument" which I think, allows for a writer to bring his or her own vision of the character to the fore. It may also explain why the films' audience has been so willing to accept such a wide range of different actors in the role—in terms not only of how they look but also in how they play the part. [Fleming self-effacingly referred to Bond as a "cardboard booby" in a letter to his editor.[472]]

What did you take from the cinematic and literary Bonds?

Bond is such an embedded part of popular culture that I think it's almost impossible not to draw on both the cinematic and literary strands of the character. It felt important to surround him with a solid and convincing a story world as possible; I worked hard on my version of M, for example, and on developing CERBERUS and its operatives into a credible set of adversaries who, I hoped, could run through a number of stories. I had several stories at various stages of development when Dark Horse pulled the plug on the Bond books. I also enjoyed bringing the name Klebb back into a Bond story. But mostly, I just tried to write the best Bond of which I was capable.

In *A Silent Armageddon*, Bond must protect the life of Terri Li, a 13-year old computer genius and a math prodigy. In issue two, M encourages Bond to consider fatherhood. M tells Bond, "Most fellows your age have already started families. Having a child does a man no end of good. He sees the world through a fresh pair of

eyes..." The story puts Bond in a paternal role. What did you reveal about Bond through this normally unexplored dynamic?

It felt like a fun way to confound expectations. Bond's relationship with women was well known. I thought that having to protect a girl, and one that was his intellectual superior, at that, would put him off his game and also give us a chance to show a new facet of his personality. I don't subscribe to the idea that Bond must be some kind of sociopath; he has chosen, for whatever reasons, to live and work through a limited set of psychological states—shoot, shag, survive—but the potential to interact with the world on a more empathic level must be in there, somewhere.

What would have been Bond's emotional arc by the end of the story?

Over the course of the story, he goes from having no interest in Terri, and no idea of how to relate to her, either for the sake of his mission or on a purely personal level, to feeling genuinely, paternally protective of her. It turns out that M is right. It does him no end of good.

What do you recall about writing the outline?

I remember taking a week to research and then a week to write the document, which then sat on the desk of an editor at Dark Horse until Glidrose (now Ian Fleming Publications) rejected a pitch from a more established writer.

Bond stories have been told more times in comic strips and graphic novels than in films and novels. In what way is Bond particularly well suited to comic book form?

Ironically, given the character's origins in novels, a visual medium gives him—and those creating his stories—the chance to "go widescreen." Now we see the exotic locales. Now we see the mad science with which the villain plans to conquer/extort the world and we see the devastation it causes before Bond stops him. Bond lives in a violent, immediate world of punch and counterpunch, and a visual medium gives the reader that same immediate hit.

Also, unlike movies, the comics medium offers the storyteller an unlimited special effects budget—the only limits are the imaginations of the writer and artist—so the opportunity exists to take the visual extravagance—and the immediate hit—up to eleven.

What are the difficulties of translating Bond to comic strip form?

I don't remember any difficulties that were particular to creating a Bond story as a graphic narrative beyond the tyranny imposed by the page count of the then-standard twenty-two-page comic book. I believe the mainstream page count has since been reduced. There's little or no room for lengthy exposition; the pressure is on the storyteller to pack all the information in as quickly and efficiently as possible. The text does one job, the art another and, when it works, the two elements complement each other in a way that is particular and unique to the comics medium: the comics-only buzz that keeps the reader reading and, in my case, the writer writing in the hope of hitting the same pitch in the next issue.

What are the challenges of telling a Fleming Bond story when much of the audience will primarily be familiar with the movies and not the books?

At the time I was writing, and given my relative inexperience, any expectations on the part of the audience came a very distant second to trying to write a script good enough to prevent me from being fired. Mind you, with the arrogance of one who hasn't a clue what he's doing, I did hope to throw at least one curveball at the audience's expectations—specifically, a Bond girl [the thirteen-year-old paraplegic computer genius] who is his intellectual superior and who at the same time forces him into an unaccustomed paternal rather than a romantic role.

Can you talk about the invention of Erik Klebb, son of Rosa Klebb?

I mentioned in a previous question that much of *Silent Armageddon* was the result of inexperience and utter ignorance. I simply had no idea how mad some of the things I was proposing to do were. Erik is one of those things. It occurred to me that it might be fun if the famously-sapphic Rosa had a vodka-fueled one-night stand with a fellow agent, while in a boring and chilly Siberian posting, and that Erik was the result. I always assumed that Rosa killed Erik's father shortly after their liaison.

How was the look of your Bond settled on for *Shattered Helix*?

I had zero input on Bond's look in either of my stories, which is probably no bad thing, as I have *zero* talent as an artist. The chance to work on *Shattered Helix* with David Lloyd, co-creator of *V for Vendetta* (1988-1989) and a long-time hero of mine, was a particular treat. No one lays out a page or a cover like David. I own the artwork for his cover of *Shattered Helix #1* and, as far as I'm concerned, he nails Bond.

With the exception of the United States, Bond has been very popular in comic strip form all around the globe. Why do you think American's haven't embraced Bond in the comic book medium?

I suspect this has more to do with the irresistible rise of the superhero genre in the wake of the witch-hunt against the true crime and horror comics (which were far more popular at the time than superhero comics) of the late fifties, than with any active antipathy towards Bond comics. I wonder whether the US market simply wasn't yet ready to accept material outside the superhero norm.

Today, to the general anglophone reader, the words "comics" and "superheroes" have become practically synonymous, making the publication of non-superhero titles a riskier commercial proposition. In Europe and Asia, there hasn't been that concentration on a single genre and Bond stories sit comfortably alongside other espionage and thriller titles amongst the generally wider variety of material available to the European and Asian comics audiences.

I'm an infrequent comics buyer these days, but from my occasional visits to comic shops and browsing on a certain internet retail site, I get the impression that there's a wider spread of genres available to anglophone readers, nowadays, and a greater willingness among readers to look outside the superhero genre. Perhaps that is behind Dynamite's apparent success with Bond?

What's your favorite comic book Bond story?

I'm no scholar of Bond comics, but of those published by Dark Horse at the same time as *Shattered Helix* and *Silent Armageddon*, I'd go for *Serpent's Tooth* by Doug Moench and Paul Gulacy. Exuberant and ambitious, it drew largely from the gadget-heavy Roger Moore movie era—cloned dinosaurs! In a bio-dome on the ocean floor! On wheels! And took it further than even Cubby Broccoli could have budgeted for. I lost out to Doug and Paul in that year's Eagle Awards, which are the UK's comic Oscars. After the awards, one of the judges told me that while he considered *Shattered Helix* the better thriller, *Serpent's Tooth* was the better Bond story. I can live with that. [Doug Moench revealed to me that the image of Bond running from dinosaurs in *Serpent's Tooth* was inspired by Michael Crichton's 1990 novel *Jurassic Park* and not Steven Spielberg's 1993 film, which hadn't been released yet.]

What place does the illustrated Bond have in the character's rich legacy?

Like Sherlock Holmes, Bond is a character that has escaped both his creator and the medium—the novel—in which he first arose. Bond's readers and viewers are able to create their own version of Bond out of the various stories that have been told about him, pretty much regardless of medium. Illustrated Bond is a part of that ongoing legacy. What part it plays in any individual Bond fan's appreciation of the character is entirely down to the individual. And that's exactly as it should be.

What panel from either *Silent Armageddon* or *Shattered Helix* best sums up your Bond?

Yikes! Looking back through the issues, I can't find a single panel in either that sums up my interpretation. At the risk of sounding appallingly pretentious, I'd say that my interpretation of Bond was a work in progress. By the time I had completed both *Silent Armageddon* and *Shattered Helix*, I had approval on a short piece that set Bond against an 00 who had "gone rogue" as a result of being faced with the human suffering caused by the realpolitik, which he and Bond both served. Bond would be faced by a version of what he might become, should he allow himself to see the human consequences of his actions. I also had the go-ahead to outline a six-part story in which CERBERUS, in a bid for the ultimate in diplomatic immunity, would take over an entire country. Looking at my work from this distance, I'd venture that, while considering myself a Bond fan, as a writer, I looked for ways in which to challenge Bond's established worldview while still putting him through the high-octane action wringer. That said, I love the cover for the first issue of *Shattered Helix*.

I understand that you completed the script to issues three and four and that the artwork for issue three was finished. Instead of publishing issue three, Dark Horse canceled the series. What happened?

I'm afraid it came down to the artist (John Burns) missing the deadline for the third issue. This necessitated a last-minute rush to get the lettered art to Dark Horse, who then made the executive decision to hold back publication of issue three until they also had the completed issue four in-house to avoid delays once the issues had been re-solicited through the direct market. Delays to issues could have a seriously negative effect on sales, especially of limited series.

So, when the artist didn't deliver *any* art for issue four, Dark Horse decided to pull the plug. Ironically, the artist on *Silent Armageddon* is considered something of a legend in European comics. Sadly, given my experience working with him, I cannot subscribe to that opinion.

Looking back, with substantially more experience of publishing and broadcasting, it occurs to me that the originating editor of the Bond comics should have seen the problems coming and lined up a replacement. But that's twenty-twenty hindsight, right?

While the issues can be found on the second-hand market, none of the Dark Horse Bond comics are in print today. What are your feelings about having written a "lost" Bond comic?

The continued interest in *Silent Armageddon* and *Shattered Helix* has been a gratifying surprise in the years since I wrote them. It has been nice to get the chance to clear up the mystery that surrounded *Silent Armageddon*'s cancellation. I had no idea that it had become such a mystery among fans.

To be entirely honest, I'm not sure that *Silent Armageddon* has aged terribly well - computing technology and the internet has evolved at such a rate since I wrote it, back in the days of dial-up and MS-DOS, and the idea of a self-aware AI, embodied or not, has become such a standard trope. To me, it reads very much like an apprentice piece, one in which I started to get a real idea of how to write comics. I think *Shattered Helix* is the more successful of the two.

What other Bond stories were you working on when the series was canceled?

[I completed a] pitch/synopsis of "A Deadly Prodigal," a four-part short story that was going to appear in *Dark Horse Presents*, the anthology title that later saw the first appearance of Frank Miller's *Sin City*. The pitch had been approved and an artist (Peter Doherty) attached when Dark Horse closed Bond down.

At the time, I was developing a pitch for what I hoped would be a six-issue follow up to "A Deadly Prodigal," in which Cerberus set about destabilizing then taking over an entire country, to add diplomatic immunity as an extra layer of protection to their nefarious activities. Bond would find himself fighting side by side with the rogue 00 he encounters in "A Deadly Prodigal" and would be forced to face some of the consequences of the international realpolitik through which he has, until now, casually shot and shagged his way.

How would you like your Bond graphic novels to be remembered?

A prestige hardback collection would be nice. Seriously? I look back on them fondly and just hope that anyone who happens across them enjoys them. And if someone remembering them leads to a call from Dynamite? That would be fun, too!

* * *

Jowett shared with me his treatments for all four issues of Silent Armageddon *and "A Deadly Prodigal," his follow-up Bond comic. To read both treatments in their entirety, go to Appendix Three. Here is an expert of those treatments, which reveals how* Silent Armageddon *would have concluded:*

While Bond and his team fight off the CERBERUS militia, Terri taps into the power of ORPHEUS, CERBERUS's supercomputer. Entering cyberspace, she finds herself confronted by CERBERUS cybernauts, led by Penrose, who are as intent on finding Omega as she is. Bond enters cyberspace and runs interference while Terri follows a trail laid down by Omega, who appears glad to renew their acquaintance.

When he interposes himself between Terri and the attack of the last of the CERBERUS cybernauts, Bond 'dies' —his interface with cyberspace is destroyed. Suddenly back in the physical world, a chill wind of mortality whispering through him, he sees Terri press the button on her laptop that will activate the virus. Tense seconds tick by, the CERBERUS militia working ever closer to closing down their escape route, until Terri emerges from cyberspace, triumphant.

ORPHEUS overloads, taking most of the CERBERUS complex with it. Bond, Terri, and the team—down to two men as the result of two fatalities and one desertion—fight their way up through the city to the pre-arranged pick-up point. Angry, the city's inhabitants are as anxious for Bond's blood as CERBERUS. He and Terri make it to the pick-up by the narrowest of margins. Unknown to them both, Penrose clears the last obstacle – Klebb—from their path, before melting into the highly-risky cover of the city.

As the world staggers back to its feet, the inauguration of the OPTI-NET is delayed. A surge of distrust towards electronic devices casts the network's entire future in doubt—very good news, as far as Bond is concerned. Less good news is his reassignment. No trace of Omega can be found and Terri returns to Oxford to resurrect Garrard's project. Bond finds that he will miss her a great deal.

In Oxford, though she does miss Bond—her first half-decent father-figure – Terri
has a new friend: Program Omega. Not destroyed, contained within her lap-top, like a genie in a bottle, Omega is Terri's most precious secret.

Issue #1 of *Silent Armageddon*
Art by John M. Burns
© Dark Horse, 1993

Issue #1 of Shattered Helix
Art by David Lloyd
© Dark Horse, 1994

Art by John M. Burns

Unpublished pencil drawings for the third issue of *Shattered Helix.* Art by John M. Burns
Courtesy of Colin Brown. Used with permission of John M. Burns.

Unpublished pencil drawings for page three of *Shattered Helix #3*. Art by John M. Burns
Courtesy of Colin Brown. Used with permission of John M. Burns.

Unpublished pencil drawings for page 10 of *Shattered Helix #3*. Art by John M. Burns
Courtesy of Colin Brown. Used with permission of John M. Burns.

After my interview with John Burns concluded, the artist finished creating a panel for *Shattered Helix*. The first image is Burns's original pencil drawings. The second image is his inking, which was completed for this book. In the final image, Burns added color. He told me that he tried to complete the image in the same style that he originally used.

Unpublished pencil drawings for the fourth issue of *Shattered Helix*. Art by John M. Burns
Courtesy of John M. Burns

Unpublished inking for the fourth issue of *Shattered Helix*. Art by John M. Burns
Courtesy of John M. Burns

Unpublished final art for the fourth issue of *Shattered Helix.* Art by John M. Burns
Courtesy of John M. Burns

"Light of My Death"
Das Petrou

Launching a new James Bond graphic novel is often a major event for most comic book publishers. So when Dark Horse Comics published their Bond series in the 1990s, they signaled the import of the occasion by publishing the majority of their titles in their prestige format, with glossy hard card stock. As a result, Dark Horse's *Serpent's Tooth*, *A Silent Armageddon*, *Shattered Helix*, and *The Quasimodo Gambit* stood out from traditionally published comics.

Unfortunately, Dark Horse's "Light of My Death," written by Das Petrou and illustrated by John Watkiss, was not published with the same fanfare as their other titles. Instead, the comic was printed in four-parts in their anthology series that also featured storylines from other licensed properties, such as Godzilla, Alien, Predator, and RoboCop. As a result, the memorable comic went unnoticed by many Bond enthusiasts.

In "Light of My Death," in 1961, 007 investigates the death of a British intelligence agent who has been killed by a deadly assassin in the French Alps. Along the way, he reunites with his old flame Tatiana Romanova of *From Russia with Love* and, in Giza, he confronts and kills the assassin on top of the Great Sphinx. As Bond has accomplished his objective and eliminated the enemy, the story is apparently over. However, in the last two panels of the comic, Bond and M note that Mr. Amos, the apparent mastermind behind his colleague's murder, is still at large. In the final panel, M dismisses Bond, "Thank you, 007. That'll be all."[473]

After reading the comic numerous times, I started to question whether, in fact, that was all? I wondered if Petrou's dangling plot thread was a coda to "Light of My Death" or if he was laying the groundwork for another adventure that he intended to revisit in another story. To find out, I contacted Petrou and learned that he had even grander plans than I originally surmised.

* * *

Although Bond completes his mission, the story isn't quite complete. Mr. Amos, a Blofeld-like villain with a white cat, is still at large. Were their plans to continue the story?

Well observed. Yes. I was commissioned to write four twenty-page Bond stories, halfway through my writing of "Light of My Death." So I left things hanging a bit, with Amos still lurking and planning. I wanted a different title for the new, longer story, to follow. However, Richard Hansom, the UK editor at Dark Horse, didn't like any of the other titles I came up with. I can only remember one of the alternatives *Come Die With Me*.

What happened?

There were only two Bond projects that I was commissioned to do by Dark Horse. One was printed. The other didn't go to artwork or printing. This is what happened. On the strength of my series *Ring of Roses* [1992, in which the Church of England rules the country], Richard gave me a Bond project. So I came up with the loose idea and plot for "Light of My Death," which I intended to write as four full comics. However, Richard told me to take that idea and condense it to four six-page installments. Reluctantly, I did that. This is what came out as the four-part "Light of My Death," six-pages per installment. Then, Richard told me that Glidrose was happy for me to write four full comics, either twenty-four or thirty pages each comic. That was great. I agreed.

I thought I could round off some of the loose ends on the printed story with this and expand into other areas. This bigger story was going to be titled *Come Die With Me*, but Richard soon made me switch to the old title, for the shorter story, for this new story too. [As a result, both the published comic and its sequel would both have been called *Light of My Death*. "Light of My Death" (in quotes) refers to the 24-page comic. *Light of My Death* (in italics) refers to the 96-page (or more) follow-up.] I wrote all four comics for the bigger story and I was paid for all four. Then Dark Horse lost the Bond franchise and the project was canned.

Do you recall any restrictions you were given?

Richard would not let me declare outright that I had set the story in 1961, but I left plenty of clues. Also, I was not allowed to mention the true name of the villain Ernst Stavro Blofeld, because there were rights complications. So I changed the name to Amos. This came from a plot of a 1960s episode of *The Saint*, with Roger Moore, in which Simon Templar acts as a bodyguard for a fictional novelist Amos Klein who has written a series of Bond-type novels.

Most Bond comics take place in the present but "Light of My Death" is a period piece.

I read most of Fleming's books and concluded that to take Bond out of the Cold War and transpose him into the world of today, was like taking John Wayne out of Rio Grande and filming him sitting on a jumbo jet. It can't work. Bond is a creature of the Cold War. The stupid gadgets, flashy hi-tech, modernist interiors, and stupid, unbelievable plots had to give way to the mood and setting of the books. We needed to put Bond back into the real world. John Watkiss and I loved the early Connery films, especially *From Russia with Love*. It was closer to the book than most of the other films. We also liked the style, the period, and the setting.

I wanted Bond to live in the civil service offices of the late 1950s and early 1960s, with green linoleum floors, etc. I researched the year 1961 thoroughly, to find out what was happening in the world then. I discovered that there was a very important conference of non-aligned nations being held in Egypt that year. John Kennedy was settling into office as President. And the laser had been invented. So I focused on all that. After that, I wanted to concentrate on capturing some of the feeling of what it would have been like to have been working for British intelligence at the time, which is why I read some of John Le Carré's George Smiley books. Having said that, Ian Fleming did a good job of conveying some of the day to day life of working for MI6, but Le Carré gets much more into the nitty-gritty.

Anyway, this is the route I wanted to go down, and it paid off because I later discovered that Ian Fleming's widow, Ann, was really pleased with what I was doing, grounding Bond in the real world at a definite time period. I got nothing but positive responses, second-hand, of course, from her. The other guys were all continuing with the sci-fi adventurer version of Bond, common at the time. The artwork on those books was beautiful, and the comics looked great. But John and I ignored all that and concentrated on our version of the character. We did not want to be tempted away into that territory, even though we were ploughing a lonely furrow. No one since Fleming [in comics] had taken Bond back to the Cold War.

"Light of My Death" was serialized over four parts and included in an anthology comic with other licensed properties. That was not how the story was originally conceived. How did that affect your approach to the new version of the story?

I was very unhappy about having to tell my story in just four, six-page episodes. It restricted all the character development and most of the atmosphere I wanted to inject into the story. It was really hard to strip out all the different elements, including change of pace, dialogue, and of course, the plot development. I had envisaged it as four twenty-four-page comics. I found myself having to draw out the pages as a rough guide for what was possible, before sending the script off to the artist, John Watkiss, just to make sure it was possible to get across the story in such limited space. We didn't get a chance to express ourselves properly at all really. A lot of good stuff was left out.

I was paid in full for this, but just as I completed the task Dark Horse lost the Bond franchise. I don't know exactly what happened. But I can tell you that Ann loved everything I wrote for that. I remember very little about the longer story, even though I created it and gave it a lot of love. I've never actually even re-read it since Richard told me that Dark Horse was not able to do anything with it. I was shell-shocked. At the time, I was working in Paris, on a Walt Disney feature film, and it was a very stressful experience, a very difficult year. That was the early 1990s and I still haven't re-read those scripts. I'd put too much hard work, research, and planning into it, for nothing.

* * *

Upon further consideration, Petrou decided to revisit his original treatment for the continuing story of "Light of My Death." *After reading it, the artist shared his reaction to it with me.*

"By the way, I would have added a lot more dialogue and narration once John had drawn the comic. What I wrote was just to get the script approved, and to give John some direction. The way the scripts stand now, they are very light on dialogue balloons and narrative boxes. After John finished the pages, I would then write another layer of dialogue and narrative. That's how we worked on *Ring of Roses*. That way the language becomes more appropriate to the images. The bits I enjoyed reading were the banter between the other 00 agents [in their shared office] and the discussion with M. But, in general, I think I would have done things a little differently, given another bite of the cherry."

Petrou generously shared with me his various outlines, notes, and scripts for *Come Die With Me*, which would later be retitled *Light of My Death*. In the follow-up to "Light of My Death," set in the 1960s, Thomas McEwan, a reporter for Reuters who is trekking through the Amazon jungle, has uncovered information that he thinks will be of global interest. Before he can reveal what he has learned to anyone, McEwan is killed by a poison dart gun. [Note: During the Cold War, MI6 used journalists, including Fleming, to gather intelligence for them.[474]]

"Light of My Death," is ground-breaking for a variety of reasons. Petrou is the first comic book writer to take Bond back to Ian Fleming's Cold War setting. He also uses his knowledge of the period to build mood, tone, and atmosphere, as well as to drive the plot. For instance, after World War II, MI6 utilized journalists to gather intelligence for them. In his follow-up to "Light of My Death," Petrou considers what would happen if one of those journalists uncovered a nefarious scheme and was eliminated to prevent them from reporting it.

Back in London, an office-bound Bond is eager to get back into the field and out of the office that he shares with 008 and 0011. Bond is in M's bad graces after botching Operation Iceman, his previous mission. So, when Moneypenny summons Bond to M's office, the agent worries, "At best, I'm duty officer tonight (and I can't stand answering phones) and at worst it's goodbye to the secret service."[475] Bond is relieved when M informs Moneypenny that 008 will be the duty officer tonight and, after he's dressed down the contrite agent, M briefs Bond on his new mission.

M explains that McEwan had been investigating the whereabouts of art treasures that the Third Reich stole during World War II. The artwork is believed to be in the hands of the East Germans, a satellite state of the Soviet Union during the Cold War, who are selling them to wealthy Westerners to fund their nefarious activities. Bond's mission is to find out what happened to the reporter. Along the way, Bond encounters General Strasse, an ex-Nazi, who is selling his hoard of stolen art to "pay for his Aryan Army in South America"[476] and Mr. Amos, the villain from "Light of My Death," who is supplying Strasse with experimental laser weapons. In the explosive finale, Bond "foils the Nazi's attempt to invade Cuba by destroying its secret underground base in Mexico."[477]

Petrou sought to bring back familiar Bond allies. Appearing in the story are CIA Agent Felix Leiter and the head of Q Brand, Major Boothroyd, who supplies Bond with an attaché case that shoots a grappling-hook that Bond will eventually deploy to escape East German security officers who have cornered the spy on a rooftop. A handwritten note reveals that Petrou considered incorporating *Loelia Ponsonby, Bond's secretary from Fleming's novels, into the narrative.*

Petrou seemed to take joy in his approach to creating new characters for Bond to tangle with. The aforementioned Strasse, a fiendish villain with nearly translucent skin, uses a python to torture and kill his enemies. In one scene, Strasse slowly suffocates a prisoner with his snake. When a functionary tells Strasse that it will take hours before the man dies by this slow and painful method, Strasse replies with a big smile, "I know."[478]

In his first treatment, Petrou mischievously gives the Bond woman the name "Aurelle Sachs." Sachs would likely have been the first Jewish Bond woman.[479] Twelve years later, an important Bond ally would also be given a Jewish heritage.[480] In 2005's *The Moneypenny Diaries: Guardian Angel*, Samantha Weinberg revealed that Miss Moneypenny was Jewish and that her mother faced anti-Semitism. After being told the name Aurelle Sachs might be "too naughty for a comic book" but allowing that "something lightly less explicit"[481] would be acceptable, Petrou replaces it with the comparably suggestive Penelope Trait aka "Penny Trait."

Petrou's correspondences also reveal how the story evolved and how the writer incorporated notes from his editor and Glidrose. In one iteration of *Light of My Death*, Bond sneaks into Nazi headquarters in Italy that are "riddled with exotic traps" such as "roses that fire poison pellets, that spray toxic gas, and electric nets that suddenly sprint out from the tall grass."[482] Yet Glidrose states that the scene too closely recalls Blofeld's dangerous (and aptly named) Garden of Death that is filled with poisonous vegetation and lethal animals from Fleming's *You Only Live Twice*. In response, a pliable Petrou contends that he can turn the setting into a sculpture garden and alter the traps so that they include "a golden cupid that fires an explosive arrow, a fountain that sprays concentrated sulfuric acid," and a bust of Julius Caesar that tilts back to reveal a machine-gun.[483]

When coming up with the comic's title, Petrou took a page from Fleming's books. Fleming would take a well-known phrase and twist it. So "live and let live" becomes *Live and Let Die* and "you only live once" becomes *You Only Live Twice*. Thus, "light of my life" becomes *Light of My Death*. Petrou's hand and type-written notes reveal that he discussed different ways to incorporate the title into the narrative. For instance, among the options he considered are a laser gun and the villain's son, and in a possible exchange, General Strasse, an ex-Nazi, tells Bond that:

"'[She] was the light of my life, Mr. Bond.'

and then Bond looking at the laser gun says,

'And I suppose that contraption is going to be the light of my death.'"[484]

Petrou's handwritten notes also disclose that in another rendering he toyed with the notion that "'somebody might say, for example, 'Well Mr. Bond, I'd like to say that my son is the light of my life.'
Then Bond turns on the laser and kills him.
'And I'd like to say that I'm the light of your death.'"[485]

There is much to admire in Petrou's treatment. It's regrettable that he never had an opportunity to tell the story as he originally intended. The published version of "Light of My Death" is a gem of a short story but Petrou's complete *Light of My Death* could have been a more substantial Fleming-inspired (graphic) novel.

Unpublished drawing for "Light of My Death." Art by John Watkiss
Courtesy of Das Petrou

Unpublished drawing for "Light of My Death." Art by John Watkiss
Courtesy of Das Petrou

Unpublished drawing of James Bond for "Light of My Death." Art by John Watkiss
Courtesy of Das Petro

Unpub-
lished drawing of Bond for "Light of My Death." Art by John Watkiss
Courtesy of Das Petrou

Unpublished drawing of James Bond for "Light of My Death." Art by John Watkiss
Courtesy of Das Petrou

Unpublished drawing of Miss Moneypenny for "Light of My Death." Art by John Watkiss
Courtesy of Das Petrou

JAMES BOND
CHANGES TO 4 PART SERIES FORMERLY TITLED "COME DIE WITH ME"

1) Since we are carrying over the villain from LIGHT OF MY DEATH, and also tying up loose-ends from that story, and also as LIGHT OF MY DEATH was always very much intended to be an intro for this larger drama I agree with you Dick that it makes sense to keep this as the title for the whole saga. COME DIE WITH ME is therefore now redundant (so Frank Sinatra can now go ahead and use it as the title for his new album.)

2) Okay, I cave in. AURELLE SACHS is maybe just a little over-the-top as a name. I propose that the girl running the gallery is now an English, debutant-type called PENELOPE TRAIT (Penny Trait.)

While we are still on the subject of names, lets call the transparent-skinned, psychotic Nazi HEINRICH STRASSER. This retains the Germanic harshness of the name and offends no person, living or dead, apart from a founder member of the National Socialist Party (whose surname is still honoured in Germany in the naming of most of it's roads.)

3) PLOT POINTS

I am not worried about changing the Czech generals target for his nuclear missiles, but I don't feel that NATO headquarters carries the same sort of emotional value as a large, civilian area under nuclear threat. Your suggestion of the UN building in New York is a good one because whilst its destruction (by nuclear missile) would threaten the entire world order it would also end the lives of 5 million people.
We were discussing over the phone whether or not the UN Building existed in 1962. Just a few seconds after I put the phone down I recalled Alfred Hitchcocks NORTH BY NORTHWEST, which was made in 1956 and features (you guessed it) the UN Building. (Cary Grant goes there to find a delegate only to see the man in question fall into his arms with a knife in his back..)

AMOS'S MOTIVES
Having had his laucrative operation whereby he was syphoning off millions of dollars of western aid to non-aligned countries in South East Asia into his own coffers, Amos has had to turn to selling new technology (ilegally) to the East Bloc. But he still has his eye on the situation in Asia, and he feels that there's a lot of money to be had from a full blown war there. He is concerned that Kruschev and Kennedy are nudging towards an agreement on policy.
His wealth depends on ice-cold, East-West relations. His plan is to antagonise the East by engineerring a renegade invasion of Cuba, and to cause total chaos by encouraging a near-insane Czech general to launch a nuclear strike on the southern tip of Manhatten Island. This ensures the destruction of the UN Building at a time when Keneddy and Kruschev are present, which sets the world order into absolute chaos. In this situation Amos believes there is a lot of power, influence and (of course) capital to be gleaned.

THE ASSASINATION
As we discussed over the phone, I am now of the opinion that there is too much going on in the fourth issue. I really wanted to capture that side of Bond that Ian Fleming shows us in FROM A VIEW TO A KILL and FOR YOUR EYES ONLY. The Commando trained assasin. I was really interested in how Bond would get across the heavily fortified Czechoslovakian border from Austria across some dangerous mountain terain at night and then across a river, the north bank of which is crawling with tanks and troops. Furthermore all towns and villages from the southern border of Czechoslovakia to Prague itself were sealed off by troops. Trains were only allowed to stop within these fortified zones. Also all roads from the south were constantly under military surveillance. I like the

Unpublished outline for *Come Die With Me* by Das Petrou
Courtesy of Das Petrou

James Bond: 1942
Rahsan Ekedal

Dynamite Comics, as previously noted, has enjoyed an unprecedented run of original and adapted James Bond comics. However, despite Dynamite's prodigious output, not all of their ambitious plans have been realized.

Dynamite's *James Bond Origin* (2018-19) and *James Bond* (2019-20) were intended to be on-going series but both comics concluded their run prematurely. *Origin*, written by Jeff Parker, lasted twelve issues and *James Bond,* co-written by Vita Ayala and Danny Lore, ended publication after six installments. However, in both cases, it seems that the creators were aware that the respective series was ending and they wrapped-up their storylines accordingly.

In *Origin*, seventeen-year-old James learns the truth behind the death of his mentor Ronald Weldon, who also knew Monique and Andrew, Bond's deceased parents. In *James Bond*, 007 disrupts Mr. Big's operation and he conclusively declares that the "targets operations, funds, and resources have been dismantled." The last issue of *James Bond* includes 007's "final mission report, " a definitive-sounding communiqué.[486]

While the narratives were complete, neither series felt like the artist's ultimate statement about the spy and both comics hinted at further adventures. After all, Mr. Big is still on the loose in one series and James is still a teenager in the Royal Navy in the other.

Despite the unambiguous ending of *Origin*, Dynamite planned on creating a limited-series that would have brought Bond one step closer to becoming a Double-O agent. To that end, Dynamite paired artist Rahsan Ekedal and writer Jeff Parker together to create the sequel comic that was to be set the year after the events of *Origin*. However, their comic was put on hold.

In the following interview, Ekedal shares some of his memories about working on the unpublished Bond adventure.

* * *

What was the working title of your Bond comic?

While I was working the book, it was titled *James Bond: 1942* and it was a direct follow-up to *Origin*, which was the story of how James was first recruited into the intelligence service while he was just a kid.

Can you describe the basic premise of the series?

Yeah, essentially I'd describe the story as "young Bond learns hard lessons in Africa." The longer explanation would be that James is sent to Morocco on a secret op and quickly finds out that the politics of 1942 are extremely complicated. He is tasked with *protecting* a Nazi officer from a British assassin because the ramifications of this guy's death would be negative from the perspective of London, for byzantine reasons. From there, he gets entangled in further events playing out and there's a cool heist mission involving stealing an Italian merchant ship, getting lost in the desert, and other mischief.

It was a fun action story, but probably the one thing that appealed to me most was working in black characters, who are sorely underrepresented in spy fiction, generally. So as the artist, I was pushing that envelope wherever possible. One of my character designs was so popular with the rest of the team that he was elevated from minor character to co-star beside James. He was a Nigerian operative that appeared at the end of issue one and was a veteran of espionage. So I was proud that I managed to get James side by side with a black character who really shows him how ruthless you need to be to survive in the proxy wars between European powers in the colonized nations of Africa in this period.

Colonized nations often serve as colorful backdrops in spy fiction, but [writer] Jeff Parker and I were doing what we could to bring humanity and awareness to that trope, and I would have loved to explore that more.

How many issues was the mini-series intended to be?

I was asked to draw six issues. I think the idea was to continue the *James Bond Origin* series with follow-up miniseries, with mine being the first. But I don't know how much more was planned past my six issues.

Bond is a young intelligence officer at the start of James *Bond: 1942*. Is he recruited into the Double-O section by the story's end or otherwise hint at his future?

There was no appearance of the Double-O section in the scripts I read. But, there were certainly hints of the future, and Bond's meeting with a senior operative in the first two issues was showing the early experiences that would no doubt lead to his recruitment. There was also a cool scene at the end of issue two involving a certain famous Prime Minister, laying the groundwork

Describe the look of Bond and the look of the comic.

Bond is young in this series, thin but athletic. We were representing Ian Fleming's original version of the character and working directly with the Fleming estate. So, faithfully, I based his appearance on Hoagy Carmichael as Mr. Fleming described Bond in *Casino Royale*. But of course, a touch more handsome and square-jawed, and definitely with a fresh face since he's so young. He isn't as jaded or violent as his older self, so he has wider eyes, rounder cheeks, and a generally more optimistic physical attitude.

What was your take on the Bond character? Who was he for you?

Even though he's young, the reckless way he throws himself at danger is already there. So he is constantly forward and a bit aggressive in his mannerism. There's no fear in how Bond moves and how he looks at the world. I find that quality interesting in young James because it is not yet driven by the sort of fatalism that I see in the mature version of James Bond. Young Bond is driven by that extreme overconfidence that most young men have, that really is a form of naivete and bravado. A young, white, well-educated, athletic man thinks he knows everything and that he can do anything. In James's case, it's elevated higher by the fact that he has been chosen by older men he respects to be a weapon of war. And of course, by his innate talent for physicality and his naturally sharp wits and remarkable situational awareness.

For me, Bond isn't necessarily a good guy. He isn't a hero. He is the very sharp point of a spear propelled by the industrialized British Empire. He serves the agendas of other men. So his brilliance and his capacity for violence are literal weapons of war, and the destruction they can bring down on a person is pretty frightening, right? Because he just has to trust that his superiors are making the right choices. Bond as a young man is pretty much trying to follow orders and do the best he can. He has to make choices in seconds, hoping it works out, and people tend to live or die based on those choices.

In my brief time with the character, I realized one aspect of Bond that makes him so perennially popular. His character is elastic. It can be bent and stretched to fit every new era. He is an empty vessel into which each subsequent generation of writers and artists can pour the heady brew of contemporary ethical dilemmas. Through him, we explore the tension between morality and government. We know that our governments are sending men and women like Bond out there to kill, and we want to believe that it is all for the sake of good, ultimately. But if we acknowledge that this is not true, then we are forced to bear the moral weight of human suffering and death perpetrated in our names. James Bond is a catharsis for our collective conscience.

Richard Maibaum's Bond Essays

In his interview with me for my book *The Many Lives of James Bond*, three-time Bond screenwriter Bruce Feirstein said that if there were a Mount Rushmore for Bond movies, then Richard Maibaum, who wrote twelve of them, deserved to be on it. Richard Maibaum, second only to Ian Fleming, is widely considered to be the most important writer of the series. Maibaum was instrumental in helping to define the movie Bond and for imbuing Fleming's world-weary spy with his signature wit.

Bond's acidic wit is on display in a pair of scenes in *From Russia With Love*. In one, Bond reprimands himself for not realizing that Donald Grant (Robert Shaw), whom he'd thought was an ally, is an enemy agent. When Grant has his gun trained on the defenseless 007, Bond scoffs at the assassin's unsophisticated dinner order, "Red wine with fish. That should have told me something." And in another of Maibaum's classic quips, after he dispatches Rosa Klebb (Lotte Lenya), the poison-tipped-shoe wearing Russian operative, Bond offers this wry eulogy, "She's had her kicks."

Maibaum believed that the humor in the Bond films was a strategic departure from Fleming's novels. The screenwriter contended, "That was the thing we changed most about his books...We made Bond more humorous, throwing away those one-liners that are now obligatory in Bond films."[487]

Nevertheless, Maibaum was also careful to ensure that the humor in his scripts didn't undermine the tension. Maibaum said, "As a writer, I think one of my contributions to the Bonds is that I maintained a pretense of seriousness... Any time you are not serious about it, the picture suffers."[488]

Maibaum wrote or co-wrote some of the best films in the franchise: as well as the aforementioned *From Russia with Love*, he also wrote *Goldfinger*, *On Her Majesty's Secret Service*, *For Your Eyes Only*, and *The Living Daylights*. In addition to his prodigious screenwriting talents, Richard Maibaum also wrote a number of essays about the franchise. I found six of them among Maibaum's papers in the Special Collections Department at the University of Iowa's Libraries.[489]

The six articles are:
- "Deus ex Machina, 1965 Model"
- "No Title, or, 007's Secret Weapon"
- "James Bond Films"
- "James Bond and His Girls"
- "Writing the Bond films"
- "Cheers, 007!"

The first four pieces—"Deus ex Machina, 1965 Model," "No Title, or, 007's Secret Weapon," "James Bond Films," and "James Bond and His Girls"—were written in 1965 and were apparently designed to promote *Thunderball*. Each article looks at different aspects of the Bond phenomenon. "Deus ex Machina, 1965 Model" explores Bond's gadgets, "No Title, or, 007's Secret Weapon" concerns the writer's approach to adapting Bond into a cinematic hero and it analyzes the attributes of different Bond women, "James Bond Films" discusses the personalities and working methods of the producers Harry Saltzman and Albert Broccoli, and it examines why it's difficult to write a Bond script. "James Bond and His Girls," is a revised version of "No Title, or, 007's Secret Weapon." The fifth essay, "Writing the Bond films" appeared in the souvenir brochure *James Bond in Thunderball*.[490] The article describes Maibaum's writing process and his thoughts concerning what aspects of Fleming's writings should *not* be translated to film. The sixth essay, "Cheers, 007!" was published in 1987 in *The Hollywood Reporter* to commemorate the first 25 years of the franchise. These insightful and delightfully droll articles also provide an invaluable look into Maibaum's process of transforming Fleming's creation into screenplays.

* * *

"Deus ex Machina, 1965 Model"

The first draft of "Deus ex Machina, 1965 Model" is 5-pages long. The final draft is 6-pages. Neither draft bears a date.

"Deus ex Machina" is a full-throated defense of the many gadgets used in the films. Bond's reliance on technology was (and remains) a point of contention with some critics. But Maibaum gives no quarter on this point. He persuasively argues that Bond's use of Q's ingenious inventions to escape certain-death dates back to the Greeks. Maibaum writes that "Sophocles, Euripides, Aristophanes, et al, were no less gadget crazy than our present-day James Bond scriptwriters." He suggests that if trade papers like *Variety* wrote reviews of the classics, that they would still gripe about the "Greeks Gimmick Gaga."[491] Maibaum finds it comforting that the "old Greek masters who rocked the cradle of the drama were also not above resorting to mechanical devices."[492]

Maibaum elaborates that when the ancient heroes were in a "particularly sticky situation," the Greek and Roman writers would "fall back on the old mechane [Greek for machine]," a "kind of crane" that was used to "fly" an actor playing a God or Goddess across the stage in order to "extricate the hero from his predicament."[493] He explains that the Romans called this device the "'*deus ex machina*,' the God from The Machine." Maibaum maintains that *deus ex machina* is the "granddaddy of all the gadgets and gimmicks we dream up for the Bond films."[494]

Maibaum argues that unlike the classic heroes, Bond is a kind of super-being who therefore doesn't need to rely on divine intervention to save him. Instead, 007 "personally operates most of the machinery and usually rescues himself."[495]

In the "Deus ex Machine, 1965 Model," Maibaum discloses that the filmmakers hadn't yet decided which gadget will save Bond at the end of *Thunderball* when the film was in production. In the then-current draft of the script, Bond was to be pulled through a "blowhole of an otherwise sealed underwater cave."[496] According to Maibaum, the filmmakers had to decide whether Leiter "winches him out by helicopter" or if he should use a Skyhook, a new piece of equipment developed by the United States Army. In the film, Bond is saved by the Skyhook, but in a different setting.

Maibaum argues that technology also reflects the real world where "the struggle for power has become a contest between using all the marvelous machines made possible by technical progress."[497] Maibaum contends that the films didn't create that dynamic, they merely reflect it.

The scriptwriter contends that the gadgets used in the films improve on those in the books. He cites the laser beam in *Goldfinger* as a more effective choice than Fleming's more conventional circular buzz saw."[498] Maibaum also thinks that Bond's attaché case in *From Russia with Love* was superior to the gun hidden in a copy of *War and Peace*.

Maibaum also informs us that sometimes the filmmakers create scenarios in which Bond must use a gadget simply because it exists in the real world. For instance, the jetpack escape scene in *Thunderball* is "in the film only because there *is* such a device in existence, and it cried to be buckled onto James Bond's broad back."[499]

Although Maibaum personally researches the latest technology, he discloses that everyone in production is always on the lookout for cutting-edge innovations that will spice up the action. His job is to "integrate them effectively into the action."[500] He notes that ideas come from everywhere, including family members, and the filmmakers rely on the skilled technicians at Eon for translating the ideas so effectively and convincingly into the film. He also gives considerable credit to Albert Broccoli and Harry Saltzman for "spending the considerable sums required" to achieve the "most sensational thrills ever to be flashed upon the screen."[501]

Maibaum believes that the producers' approach is probably the "main reason they've captured a world audience of such rabid fans."[502] Maibaum concludes "Deus ex Machine," by presciently predicting that "James Bond and his gadgets will be with us for a long time."[503] It's worth noting that Connery was also against the franchise's increased emphasis on gadgetry.

Background Information: In the folder with the two drafts of "Deus ex Machine" is a letter to Maibaum from Tom Carlile who worked in the publicity department of Eon Productions. The correspondence provides some background details about the article. In the letter dated April 14, 1965, Carlile suggests that the proposed article should be about "how a screenwriter adapts the incredible scientific gadgets and newsworthy military devices to a Bond film."[504] Carlile also asks Maibaum to "concoct some good anecdotes about the equipment used" in *Thunderball*.[505]

The publicist hopes that "In addition to the *New York Times* I can place this extensively around the world." Carlile concludes the letter with the request that Maibaum finish the piece by May 5th, the date "we leave Nassau."[506] Carlile provides a mailing address to which Maibaum should send the article. Fittingly, it is Box 007.

Two other points that might be of minor interest to Bond aficionados. The letterhead of Harry Saltzman and Albert Broccoli's production company is rendered as "Eon Productions Ltd."[507] These days, Eon is usually written in all capital letters (EON). Additionally, someone, possibly Maibaum, scribbled a doodle of a head without a body on the letter. The simple drawing depicts a series of question marks coming out of the figure's head. The person might be a writer who is trying to come up with ideas. Or perhaps it represents the letter's recipient who is brooding over how to respond to Carlile's message.

"No Title, or, 007's Secret Weapon": "No Title, or, 007's Secret Weapon" is dated July 26, 1965, and is 15 pages long, including the cover page. The cover page indicates the piece is approximately 4,000 words long.

In the essay, Maibaum makes the case that there are two James Bonds—one from the novels and the other from the films. Maibaum argues that the cinematic Bond is the more popular one and he bolsters his argument with sales figures—40 million books sold vs. 100 million in movie ticket sales. Maibaum posits that when audiences of that time close their eyes, they think not of Fleming's Bond with his "thick black comma of hair falling over the right eyebrow" but of Connery's with his "ski-jump nose and pouting lips."[508]

Maibaum also believes that the voice of Bond no longer reflects Fleming's creation of the "cultivated accents of Eton and Sandhurst," but rather of the "faint but unmistakably less than upper-class Scotch burr."[509] Maibaum contends that whereas Fleming's Bond has the "assiduously-developed build" of a "gentleman-sportsman," the cinematic Bond has the physique of a "natural athlete who could have become a professional footballer."[510]

The screenwriter elaborates on the differences between the books and movie Bonds. Maibaum points out that Connery's Bond is "physically stronger' and "less introspective, never brooding, as Fleming's Bond does, about the moral issues involved in exercising his license to kill."[511] The book Bond is "somewhat subtler, sometimes, even romantic, gentler, more susceptible to personal involvement."[512] Maibaum notes that Fleming described Bond as being "lashed" but that in the films it's "Bond who does the lashing."[513]

Maibaum makes it clear that he doesn't consider the cinematic Bond "superior" to Fleming's: he is noting the deliberate "discrepancies" between the two.[514] The writer also contends that not only did Fleming not mind these differences but that he "approved of our irreverent, quasi-satirical approach."[515]

Maibaum adds that secret service agents "are not just icy killers, but also cold-blooded lovers."[516] A bit tongue-in-cheek, he marvels at Bond's sexual stamina and wonders if it was developed, at M's behest, as part of a "secret drill" or if the Q Branch provided a pharmaceutical boost.[517] Maibaum acknowledges that the movie Bond "is rather more of a cad than the other chap."[518]

A variation of Maibaum's line about "the other chap" was used two films later, in *On Her Majesty's Secret Service*, when George Lazenby's Bond laments that "This never happened to the other fella."

For years, I had believed that George Lazenby came up with this line. In many interviews, Lazenby convincingly made the claim. But while researching this book I came across a 1983 interview with Richard Maibaum who made the same assertion. Nevertheless, it's possible that both Maibaum and Lazenby share ownership of it. Jack Lugo, quoting from Charles Helfenstein's book *The Making of On Her Majesty's Secret Service*, reports that Maibaum's early screenplays for the film included different versions of the line, including "This never happened before to Double-O-Seven. Perhaps they ought to try again." and "This never happened to Sean Connery." It seems likely to me that Maibaum wrote a version of the line and Lazenby revised it.

Maibaum goes on to praise Fleming. He said that Fleming's character was an "intuitively brilliant concept, D'Artagnan and Don Juan combined in a single individual, believably and recognizably modernized."[519]

In "No Title, or, 007's Secret Weapon," Maibaum acknowledges Bond's frequent use of Q's equipment, but he believes that Bond's "most potent weapon is himself."[520]

Maibaum justifies Bond's occasional cold-bloodedness by asserting, "He is not a sadist, only a highly motivated public servant..."[521] Maibaum offers a hypothesis to explain why Bond and Miss Moneypenny never consummate their relationship. "Perhaps Moneypenny is an anachronistic virtue symbol which Bond unaccountably respects."[522]

He likens Ursula Andress's emerging from the ocean in *Dr. No* to the "birth of Venus."[523] He reveals that the filmmakers considered changing Pussy Galore's scandalous first name to the tamer Kitty. Maibaum also points out that Bond fails to convert enemy agent Fiona Volpe into an ally. "For once a playmate does not become a plaything."[524]

Maibaum also hypothesizes that Bond's seeming callous treatment of women may be necessary because "gallantry can only lead to disaster for a man in his vocation."[525] Although Bond enjoys the physical pleasures of a woman's company, as he does in the films, once the mission is over, their relationships will soon fizzle. "Bond the brute, will never look back."[526]

Another way in which the books and films are different is that the violence is toned down for the cinema. Maibaum incorrectly predicts that "No Reviewing Board" can be expected to pass the shocker in [the novel] *Casino Royale* involving Bond's testicles and a carpet-sweeper. Although the filmmakers might have been forced to tone down the scene in the sixties, the sequence was faithfully adapted in the 2006 version of *Casino Royale* to chilling effect.

Maibaum, who admired Terence Young, the director of the first two Bond films, thinks that *Goldfinger* created an "even surer, brisker, more sardonic Bond."[527]

"James Bond Films": Based on its content, I believe that "James Bond Films" was written in 1965, during the production of *Thunderball*. In this piece, Maibaum gives a potted biography of his pre-Bond professional life, including his work in theatre, television, and writing screenplays for Wallace Beery and Alan Ladd. He also touches on Fleming's dispute with Kevin McClory over the authorship of *Thunderball*. And he likens being a writer for Broccoli and Saltzman to being "both the anvil and one of the sledges."[528]

In "James Bond Films," Maibaum elaborates on what it's like to work for Albert Broccoli and Harry Saltzman. Maibaum praises them as "Socially affable, amusing, likable men," but on a professional level they are "savagely determined."[529] Maibaum says that Saltzman is "mercurial, quick-thinking, continually interrupting, spouts hot ideas like a geyser," and he calls Broccoli "volcanic" while granting that his "eruptions" are "infrequent."[530] He believes that Broccoli accepts other people's ideas "readily" and that Saltzman is "inclined to first reject ideas not his own can usually be persuaded."[531] Maibaum notes that Saltzman focuses on Bond's gadgets and Broccoli focuses on the women. Neither producer likes a screenplay to contain "too much dialogue" and they are both focused on "Bond's image as a super sleuth, super-brawler, super-lover."[532]

Maibaum suggested that Kevin McClory had "shrewdly maintained convictions" on the script and that he contributed a great deal to the underwater sequences.[533] Maibaum says that Guy Hamilton was focused on "Bondisms" and that he "dotes on sex-play, spectacle, refined variety of mayhem, and Bond's invaluable safety-valve quips."[534] Maibaum half-jokes that he and production designer Ken Adams debate whether "scripts are written to tell a story or to exhibit sets."[535]

Maibaum recounts that the production meetings (which he attended, along with all the producers, the director, and sometimes the production designer) involve lively discussions where the "wildest notion is encouraged."[536] He adds that the "floor belongs" to anyone with the best idea or the loudest shout.

He admits that the scripts are hard to write because it's hard to write a script with a "swift, more or less coherent story progression" while incorporating the "high jinx" that most fans demand.[537] Maibaum also contends that before a Bond movie is a blockbuster it is first a "brain-buster."[538]

Maibaum observes that each Bond script must have the perfect mixture of "suspense, action, comedy, satire... [and] unabashed sex."[539]

He observes that *Dr. No* is a "murder mystery," *From Russia with Love* and *Thunderball* "are suspense yarns," and that *Goldfinger* is a "man-to-man duel."[540]

It doesn't appear that the full article was preserved at the archives. "James Bond Films" ends in the middle of a paragraph where Maibaum posits the idea that Bond is afflicted with "satyriasis" or "excessively great sexual desire in the male."[541]

Of minor note, in the article, Maibaum repeatedly renders 007 as "Double 0-7."

"James Bond and His Girls": The incomplete typescript is dated August 3, 1965, and it is 16 pages long, including the cover. "James Bond and His Girls" is essentially a revision of "No Title, or, 007's Secret Weapon." However, instead of starting the article by comparing the cinematic Bond to the literary one, Maibaum refers to what he calls a "James Bond syndrome."[542] Maibaum explains that the syndrome, which often affects Bond fans, is "positively the latest sublimation" in which there is a "vicarious mass desire to achieve 007 status." He confesses to "sharing it" and "identifying" with Bond.[543] Maibaum reasons that most men long to be the "best dressed man, most sophisticated diner, luckiest gambler, top secret agent, and greatest lover of his generation all rolled into one."[544]

"No Title, or 007's Secret Weapon" concludes with a discussion of the women in *Thunderball*. In "James Bond and His Girls" Maibaum also discusses *On Her Majesty's Secret Service*, which he was writing at the time. He promises that a "devastatingly unexpected novelty" awaits filmgoers and that when Bond falls in love and gets married in the film" his "image is shattered, seemingly beyond repair."[545] Maibaum lets readers know that Bond will marry, in defiance of M. Maibaum also states that in Bond's section members are forbidden to marry and that by marrying Tracy it means "giving up his career."[546] He wonders if for true love Bond would be willing to defy M and sacrifice his career to become a "husband, a father?"[547] Maibaum knew that many Bond fans were familiar with the book, so he quickly provides the answers. He reveals that the filmmakers, like Fleming, kill off Tracy. Maibaum wraps-up the essay with a question about Bond: "Locating his heart, does he find it fractured?"[548]

"Writing the Bond films": As noted, this essay was included in *James Bond in Thunderball*, a lavishly illustrated 34-page souvenir program for the fourth Bond film. Its cover photo is a large color portrait of Maibaum. It depicts the salt and peppered haired author with a pipe clenched in his mouth as he works at his typewriter, the color of which almost matches his gray suit.

Maibaum begins his essay with the sentiment that "No one man writes the Bond films."[549] He describes the process of coming up with scenarios for the film in a lively conference room meeting with co-writers John Hopkins and Jack Whittingham, director Terence Young, production designer Ken Adams, editor Peter Hunt, and Harry Saltzman and Albert Broccoli. Maibaum explains that although the filmmakers are always looking to increase the stakes and excitement, they are also mindful that they don't want to avoid inadvertently creating a parody "out of a parody."[550]

Maibaum praises Fleming's creation for its "hair-raising situations" and its "magnificent flow of descriptive words"; but Maibaum notes that they don't always "translate" to the screen. Maibaum also believes that Fleming had an appealing "tongue-in-cheek attitude towards love, life, death, and violence..."[551] However, as effective as Fleming's writing is, Maibaum argued that his job as a screenwriter was to leave out a great deal of it from his screenplay.

As he did in other essays, Maibaum notes that Fleming's Bond "lacks any humour in print." Maibaum points out that the "jokes" are "necessary safety-valves; moments for relaxation" before the next suspenseful scene.[552]

Maibaum, who was an assistant writer on Alfred Hitchcock's *Foreign Correspondent* (1940), shares some advice that the Master of Suspense imparted to him, "Dear boy, don't be dull. I'm not interested in logic...Audiences should not have time to think about logic."[553] But Maibaum confidently rejects the great director's axiom and insists that today's audiences demand a certain degree of logic to suspend its disbelief, otherwise a film becomes a "farce."[554] Maibaum also points out that Hitchcock, who he appeared to admire, insisted that his films should have "13 bumps" which he defined as "shocks," "high-points," or "thrills."[555] Maibaum recalls that he and Broccoli didn't think 13 bumps were sufficient for a Bond movie; they always strived for "39 bumps."[556] One might assume that the number 39 was an arbitrary one and that Maibaum was merely picking a number greater than 13 to suggest that Bond films require a lot of excitement. But Maibaum has also used the "39 bumps" figure in other interviews, which leads me to think that he was being precise in his language.

This veteran writer also offers some advice to aspiring writers, "The first golden rule for any writer is to read... read anything and everything. Something picked up from glancing at a book or paper invariably proves useful later on."[557] Maibaum gives some insight into his writing habits. He works anywhere from 12 to 16 hours a day and his first draft is created in about 9 or 10 weeks. Maibaum explains that after he gives his first draft to the producers, the "group discussions" begin and then it takes him about four or five weeks to rewrite the script.[558] By today's standards, when rewrites can take months or even years, Maibaum was a remarkably quick and skillful writer. In those days, because the Bond films were released every one or two years, there was little time to squander.

"Cheers, 007!": Because "Cheers, 007!" was written to commemorate the first 25 years of the series, the tone is appropriately celebratory.[559] The article, including copious illustrations, is five pages long and it was published in the July 14, 1987 issue of *The Hollywood Reporter.*

"Cheers, 007!" begins with Maibaum's suggestion that for his toast to the franchise, it's time to "lift our martinis, shaken not stirred." He approvingly quotes the *New York Times* critic Richard Condon in whose estimation James Bond is the "ultimate anti-authoritarian in the sense that all authority is that which seeks to inhibit one's fantasies."[560]

But "Cheers, 007!" is not just a love note to the spy. Maibaum also includes Anthony Burgess's attack on the franchise. He notes that Burgess, who greatly prefers Fleming's Bond to the cinematic one, views the movie Bond as nothing more than a "harmless sensualist."

Maibaum also provides instances where he believes the movies improved upon the novels, sometimes by eliminating plot holes. He cites the novel *Goldfinger,* in which the villain intends to steal the money from Fort Knox. Maibaum points out that it "didn't occur to Fleming that such an operation would occupy hundreds of very strong men 12 days and nights. By then the army, navy, and marines would have arrived."[561] The filmmakers solve the problem by altering Goldfinger's impractical master plan. Now, instead of stealing the gold, Goldfinger intends to radiate it and make it "unusable for 58 years and his own considerable holding more valuable."[562] Identifying a problem can be simpler than solving it. Maibaum recalls that it "took us 10 days to figure that one out."[563]

Maibaum maintains that "the key to writing a Bond screenplay is to concoct the villain's caper." Once that is found the rest falls into place."[564] He observes that the films' plots are deliberately unfaithful to Fleming's books. "Of the 15 Broccoli-Bond films, 10 of the capers are not from Fleming. Five take only their titles and one or two incidents from his short stories."[565] According to Maibaum, the filmmaker's job is "to expand [Fleming's work] into properly constructed two-hour entertainments."[566]

Maibaum says that credit for Bond's one-liners belongs to the entire creative team, including producer Albert Broccoli, each director, all of whom he refers to by name, and to the many screenwriters. Maibaum also cites a few of his favorite killer quips and identifies the writers who dreamed them up. He praises Christopher Wood for the lines "Look after Mr. Bond. See that some harm comes to him" and Roald Dahl for the "drop in the ocean" rejoinder that 007 uses after disposing of a villain by dumping him into the sea. Maibaum also admires the threat written by Tom Mankiewicz that Bond delivers while aiming a rifle at the groin of a possible target, "Speak now or forever hold your piece."

Maibaum lauds some of the unsung Bond writers (whose work was sometimes uncredited). These include George MacDonald Fraser (*Octopussy*), Paul Dehn (Goldfinger), John Hopkins (*Thunderball*), Berkley Mather (*Dr. No, From Russia with Love,* and *Goldfinger*), Simon Raven (for providing additional dialogue for *On Her Majesty's Secret Service*), and Joanna Harwood (*Dr. No, From Russia with Love,* and *Goldfinger*). Maibaum also praises Michael Wilson, his writing partner for five Bond films, and he confides that although they sometimes argued over story ideas, he adds that "If collaborators don't fight, there's one collaborator too many."[567]

Maibaum concludes "Cheers, 007!" by praising Albert Broccoli who, for a quarter-of-a-century, "has held everything together."[568] Maibaum admiringly states that Broccoli leads with a simple but challenging command: "Amaze me."[569]

Final Thoughts: In most cases, only the final draft of the articles is kept in Maibaum's archives. Yet, the folder with his "Deus Ex Machine" article also contains an earlier draft, which includes typed and handwritten revisions. By examining Maibaum's corrections, we can better understand his writing process and observe his keen attention to detail. For instance, when describing the high-speed capabilities of Emilie Largo's yacht, Maibaum originally wrote that the vessel could "leave the U.S. Navy far behind."[570] Maibaum crossed out "far behind" and substituted "wallowing in its wake," a more dynamic description.[571]

When explaining the amount of comfort he felt in knowing that the Greeks also employed gadgetry to save their heroes from impending doom, Maibaum changed "kind of literary solace" to a "measure of literary balm," a slightly more optimistic assessment.[572] By eliminating "literary solace," Maibaum also avoids anyone's erroneous inference that he's alluding to Fleming's short story "Quantum of Solace" (1959).

In another instance, Maibaum's changes gave Bond greater agency. In the early draft Bond simply "purses" a hydrofoil, but in the rewrite, he "overtakes" the boat.[573] Perhaps this is an example of Maibaum making it clear that—as he writes in "No Title, or, 007's Secret Weapon"—it's "Bond who does the lashing."[574]

By reviewing his draft, we also find instances where Maibaum changed words for accuracy. When referring to Bond's use of gadgets, Maibaum originally wrote that 007 "operates the machinery" himself. In the final copy, Maibaum added "most of" to allow for the occasions where Bond relies on the help of his allies.[575] Maibaum also revised for clarity. For instance, he initially wrote that a gun was hidden in Tolstoy's *War and Peace*. After re-reading the draft, Maibaum made it clear that the weapon was hidden in "a volume of" the book.[576] Elsewhere, Maibaum explains that Fleming's original ending of *Thunderball* didn't have the "thrills" the filmmakers desired. When correcting the piece, Maibaum changed it to "shocks and thrills."[577] By adding the additional descriptor, Maibaum reminds the reader that the best Bond movies aren't just entertaining, sometimes they are shocking, positively shocking.

These five disparate articles have a few re-occurring ideas. In each of them, Maibaum is generous in praising his collaborators; he is exceptionally conversant in Fleming's Bond; and he possesses wide-ranging knowledge. Like Bond, Maibaum is erudite, urbane, and he displays a lethal wit.

Section 5 – Lost Bond Productions

Raymond Benson's Lost Bond Play

As a lifelong Bond fan, it's difficult for me not to be a little envious of Raymond Benson – a fellow enthusiast-turned-scholar-turned-writer. Benson wrote *The James Bond Bedside Companion* (1984), a comprehensive examination of the novels and the films. He then parlayed his feelings for and appreciation of Fleming's prose into success as a six-time Bond novelist: *Zero Minus Ten* (1997), *The Facts of Death*, (1998), *High Time to Kill* (1999), *Doubleshot* (2000), *Never Dream of Dying* (2001), and *The Man with the Red Tattoo* (2002).

Benson novelized the screenplays for *Tomorrow Never Dies* (1997), *The World Is Not Enough* (1999), and *Die Another Day* (2002) and published a trio of Bond short stories: "Blast from The Past" (1997), "Midsummer Night's Doom" (1999), a tongue-in-cheek piece for *Playboy*, where Bond encounters Hugh Hefner at one of the magazine founder's hedonistic parties, and "Live at Five" (1999) for *TV Guide*.

The Edgar Allan Poe Award nominee is the author of more than thirty-five books, including *The New York Time's* best sellers *Tom Clancy's Splinter Cell* (2004) and *Tom Clancy's Splinter Cell – Operation Barracuda* (2005), as well as five entries in his own *Black Stiletto* series (2011-15).

Benson's Bond bona fides extend beyond his books. He also wrote the role-playing game *You Only Live Twice II – Back of Beyond* (1986) and two text-based computer games: *A View to a Kill* (1985) and *Goldfinger* (1986).[578]

We begin the interview by talking about an interesting bit of Bond lore – Benson's unproduced *Casino Royale* play.

* * *

How did you turn the novel *Casino Royale* into a play?

It was autumn of 1985. I had written *The James Bond Bedside Companion*. When it was published, I was still doing theatre in New York as a director and music composer. I would also often work with playwrights, putting music to their lyrics. I was still mounting plays. Peter Janson-Smith was the chairman of Ian Fleming Publications, although at the time it was called Glidrose. He was in New York with a colleague. So we had lunch and I brought up the possibility. I asked, "Have you ever thought about a James Bond stage play?" He said, "No, I can't say that we have." I said, "What about *Casino Royale*? I think that would be a good stage play." He thought about it and said, "Well, that is the only title that we have the rights to." I said, "Because it's mostly an indoor Bond story it would work on the stage. He said, "You want to give it a shot?"

They paid me a fee to write the play. It took me about two months. When it was done, I mounted a staged reading here in New York. We used professional actors and performed it in front of an audience. It went very well. But a few weeks later the people at Ian Fleming Publications mysteriously decided that they didn't want to pursue putting James Bond on the stage. I don't know why.

Could you talk about the process of adapting it?

It's based on the novel *Casino Royale*. I used a lot of the dialogue verbatim. It was a period piece set in the nineteen-fifties. To make the card game visual, in the stage directions I wrote that screens would come down over the table that would project each player's hand of cards. Every time they drew a card, the slide could change. Of course, these days it would be animated but back then it was just slides.

A theatrical experience can't have the scope or action of a Bond movie.

In lieu of any kind of car chase, diving out of airplanes, explosions, or special effects, I concentrated on having really good fight scenes. I thought it would be exciting to show a well-choreographed fight scene with some brutal fighting on stage. I thought that would be thrilling. So I wrote that into the play as well.

In the novel, there's a scene in which Bond is stripped naked and tortured. Le Chiffre repeatedly bashes Bond's exposed groin with a "cane carpet beater."

I did adapt the torture scene pretty much verbatim. The way I described it in the stage directions is the chair would be specially built so that there would be a fake bottom. To the audience it would look like there was no bottom and that Bond was being hit. But there was a bottom. So when the paddle hit the bottom of the chair it would sound like it was hitting him. That's how it would've been done.

Would Bond have been nude as he was in the novel?

Yeah, he would've been naked. The actor playing Bond would have needed to have a really good physique. One that would make all the women go *oooh*. [Laughs]

Can you describe the structure?[579]

The play was in nine scenes. I don't remember if there was an intermission; probably was, either between scenes four-and-five or five-and-six.

Did the play begin with the equivalent of a pre-title sequence and end with the last line of the book – the bitch is dead?

The play begins with Bond coming into his hotel room and then getting a visit from Felix who doubles in the play as the Mathis character as well as Felix. I combined them into one person. It did end with "the bitch is dead."

What was the goal of the staged reading?

To see if the play worked. We wanted to hear it read by actors. We only staged it a little bit. The actors held the book while they did it and we had some movement. But it was minimal staging. There was no memorization of the lines. No real sets. But we had as much characterization and an indication of costumes as possible.

Who played Bond?

His name was Ed Clark. I don't know what happened to him but he was fine for the purposes of that stage reading. [Rounding out the cast was Elizabeth Huffman as Vesper Lynd, Stuart Laurence as Bond's ally Felix Leiter, and Robert Aberdeen as Le Chiffre. Aberdeen bears a striking resemblance to Mads Mikkelsen who played the villain in the 2006 film.]

Is the Bond you're writing for the play the same Bond that you're writing in your novels?

That's a good question. The Bond from the play was Fleming's Bond. There was no question about that. I was writing the Bond novels in the nineties. This was when Pierce Brosnan was James Bond. My directive from Ian Fleming Publications was trying to make the novels like the current movies. That means that they needed more action than Fleming's books.

However, I wanted to keep my Bond very much like Fleming's Bond. I wanted him to have his vices. I wanted him to smoke. I wanted him to drink a lot. I wanted him to womanize. They said, "That's fine. You can do that if you can make it work in today's world." A guy with those vices might be anachronistic in the nineties but I think it worked. He was a man out of place and out of time. It was as if I was taking Fleming's Bond and dropping him intact into the nineties and having him deal with a more modern world.

How would you describe Fleming's Bond?

I'll say right off that Sean Connery was my favorite Bond in the movies but the guy who I think was the most accurate to the literary Bond was Timothy Dalton. I think he nailed Fleming's Bond. Bond is serious. He's a brooder. He drinks a lot; he smokes a lot. He's a sensualist. He lives for sensual pleasures. He takes things to excess because he thinks he might die any day. He's not a happy person. He's probably not a nice guy. He doesn't have very many friends. The only friends he has in the books are Felix Leiter and Bill Tanner and, maybe some other guys in other countries like Tiger Tanaka. But those are more business friends and business relationships. The closest friendship he had was Felix Leiter in the books and they had a pretty good bonding. But I bet he wasn't a pleasant guy to be around. Take the moment in the book *The Spy Who Loved Me*, when Vivienne Michel first sees Bond—she thinks he's one of the bad guys. She goes, "God, it's another one of them!" because he looks like a mean, tough, dangerous guy. His personality *exudes* that.

What motivates him?

His patriotism. He is doing this for Queen and Country. He went into World War II at a very young age. He lied about his age to get into World War II and I think that was his element. We don't know much about Bond's childhood from the Fleming books. Later Charlie Higson would write about this period in his Young Bond novels. But from Fleming we only know that he was orphaned at age eleven and then we skip to the war years and we know that he was drafted into the secret service right after the war.

Doing something for Queen and Country is a very uncynical thing to do and what's interesting is that he's sort of a cynical person performing an uncynical act, a selfless act.

There have been all these claims that Bond was based on this particular spy or that guy or this guy. But I don't buy any of that. I think Bond was based on Ian Fleming. I think Fleming created a wish-fulfillment of what Fleming wanted to be. This was him because Bond's tastes in food and drink were Fleming's. What he smoked was Fleming's. What he liked to drive was what Fleming liked to drive. He liked the kind of woman that Fleming liked. So basically Fleming put his personality onto this blunt instrument and made him into an anti-hero.

I think Fleming himself had a very cynical view of the world. It was a more sardonic look conveyed with a dark sense of humor. But Bond didn't have a sense of humor until the very later books after the movies came out and then Fleming saw how they had treated Bond cinematically and, in the last two or three books, Bond gained a sense of humor. He didn't have it before those books. I don't mean to say the books did not have a sense of humor because they did. They definitely did. However, that was in the writing. That was Fleming's voice. But in most of the books *Bond* doesn't have a sense of humor.

There's another thing that the cinematic Bond did that the books didn't do. The films made Bond *sophisticated*. He knew all about wines and drinks and food and all that stuff. The Bond of the books was not that sophisticated. The writing was sophisticated and Fleming was sophisticated. Fleming made the world around Bond sophisticated and Bond enjoyed it. But Bond himself could not name all the special kinds of vintage, the temperature that you keep Dom Perignon and so on. The movies put Fleming's sophistication into the character of Bond. That was the main difference between the movie Bond and the literary Bond. The movies gave Bond sophistication and a sense of humor.

Why are the cinematic Bond and the book Bond so different?

Well if you go back to 1962 when the first movie came out the anti-hero was not really something that had happened in the movies. I mean you might have stray little examples here and there. For example, maybe Humphrey Bogart in *Casablanca* was an anti-hero. Maybe. An anti-hero is somebody who is a good guy but he's kind of a bad guy too. I think the Bond movies really opened that up. Bond was the first major cinematic anti-hero that was popular. I think Clint Eastwood's Man with No Name was next.

Before Daniel Craig, the movies didn't delve too deeply into Bond's head.

Fleming did that a lot with Bond. He got into Bond's head a lot. Bond would think to himself about the women or oh, this girl can't drive [as described in the novel *Thunderball*]. One of Bond's favorite expressions was, "What's the score?" You can count how many times he says that. The opening chapter of *Goldfinger* is nothing but Bond sitting in an airport. He's sitting there drinking bourbon and thinking about how he killed that Mexican and he's brooding about it, he's not happy about it. He's sitting there getting drunk and thinking about his job. But then [Junius] DuPont comes up and the novel starts. But that whole first chapter is his inner monologue.

Did you worry about the danger of revealing too much about Bond's character would dilute the mystery of him?

I didn't worry about it. I did my best at doing that kind of thing. I don't know if that was my strength. As far as my books are concerned, I think my strength was the plot. I'm very proud of my plots. As far as a "James Bond story," I think I did them pretty well.

When your books were first published, I don't know if we, the audience, were looking for you to delve deep into his psyche. I think we wanted Bond's adventures.

It's tricky with the Bond books because you have many ages and different generations of readers. The guys my age that grew up with reading Fleming were expecting a certain style of Bond. But then Ian Fleming Publications and the publishers wanted to attract younger readers. That's why they told me to make them like the Pierce Brosnan movies, with a lot of more action. My books have a lot more action than Fleming's books did. So they were trying to capture a younger audience with that approach. So they are different.

I think every author's Bond books exist in their own little alternate universe. Although Kingsley Amis' book *Colonel Sun* is sort of a continuation of Fleming's books and it does sort of happen in *The Man with the Golden Gun*, his last novel. But John Gardner's Bond books are not necessarily continuations after *Colonel Sun*. My books aren't necessarily continuations after John Gardner's books. The same holds true for the writers who followed me. They've taken Bond and created little universes of their own.

I think that's a discovery that we've only recently made. With the films, we often look for a unifying theory connecting all the actors – from Connery to Lazenby to Moore to Dalton to Brosnan to Craig. But you can make the case that they're not the same Bond. They're all so different.

Oh no, they're not alike at all. Back in the nineteen-eighties, Timothy Dalton was doing what Daniel Craig is doing but it didn't really fly at the time. I liked it and he was very popular in Europe but in the United States Dalton's movies did not do that well. I'm sorry that happened. After the Roger Moore era, audiences were not ready for a serious Bond. Some time had to pass. In the Two-Thousands and after the Jason Bourne movies and other movies, audiences were finally ready for a more tough, edgy, dark Bond. Daniel Craig is playing something like Fleming's original character.

***Licence to Kill* was a deliberate attempt to deviate from the Bond formula. They weren't trying to make the same old Bond movie.**

Yes, they tailored *Licence to Kill* to the way Timothy Dalton was playing Bond. The previous movie *The Living Daylights* was really a Roger Moore script. They wrote it as if Roger Moore was going to be in it. They didn't know who was going to be in *Living Daylights*, but it was going to be that sort of more fun and games romps that were typical of the Roger Moore films. Then Dalton came in and gave it this edge, and then they kind of went, okay, let's try doing a really serious, edgy Bond. *Licence to Kill* is very controversial. There are fans that love it and the fans that hate it. I love it. I think it's one of the best Bond movies because we really see Fleming's Bond in it. The plot was good and it uses a lot of *Live and Let Die* the novel as well as Fleming's short story "The Hildebrand Rarity" (1960). There's a lot of Fleming in that movie even though the title is not Fleming's.

When did you start writing *The James Bond Bedside Companion*? I started writing it in the fall of 1981.

How long did that take to write?

Three years.

Three years of writing and research?

Yeah, and waiting.

Waiting for?

Publishers and permissions.

Did you have a publisher when you started?

Yes. I got a contract right off the bat.

You broke new ground with *The Bedside Companion*. Not only were there few books about the Bond movies there were even fewer about Fleming's writing. Kingsley Amis' *James Bond Dossier* was a notable exception. Did you have a feeling that there was an appetite for your book?

I had no idea. It was a labor of love and I just wanted to do it. I thought it would be fun. I was a big Bond fan and I grew up with Bond. I saw the original Connery films on the big screen and read the books when I was nine, ten, and eleven. I just wanted to do it and I thought it would be a nice fun project. I had a day job at the time. I was doing theatre, so I had to work on it in between other projects. I went to England to do some research and I met some of Ian Fleming's friends and members of his family who were still alive at the time. I met the people at Glidrose and I went to the [Lilly] Library in Indiana where they have Fleming's manuscripts and I studied the manuscripts.

What do you think Fleming would have done with Bond if he had written another novel?

That's hard to say. Fleming was not well toward the end of his life. I think you can see that in *The Man with the Golden Gun* that his heart was not in it very much. It's a very weak book I'm afraid. It was only half there. I love *You Only Live Twice*, the book right before it.

In *You Only Live Twice*, Fleming does something interesting. Bond leaves Japan not realizing that Kissy Suzuki is pregnant. So there's a baby Bond somewhere...

I address that.

You address that in your short story "Blast from the Past." The notion that Bond was a father was a big plot point that was never fleshed out. Fleming introduced it in *You Only Live Twice*, but he died before his next novel was published. So it's possible that he would have picked up that thread later on. But who knows? How did "Blast from the Past" come about?

When I got asked to write the Bond novels I had gotten to know Hugh Hefner at *Playboy* and he liked my *Bedside Companion* because he's a Bond fan. In the sixties, *Playboy* published short stories and serializations of Fleming. So it was my idea. I suggested to Glidrose that we should ask *Playboy* if they want to do another Bond short story because they hadn't done one since the sixties and they said, oh that's a great idea. So I wrote to Mr. Hefner and said, "Hey, guess what I'm doing now? How would you like an exclusive short story?" and *Playboy* said, "Yes!" So I wrote the short story "Blast from the Past" before I wrote the first novel. It was sort of my trial run.

We couldn't include the character of James Suzuki as a living character because of the animated series *James Bond Jr.* [In Benson's universe, James Suzuki is the son of James Bond and Kissy Suzuki.] Also, because Eon had bought rights to any offspring of James Bond. So in my story, he had to be dead. Bond walks into the apartment and his son is dead on the floor. He's just a corpse and that's how we got around it.

Is Bond still a part of your life?

It's been over fifteen years since I wrote those novels. I feel like I've moved on. But my Bond books are still available and I'm still exploiting them. They get me in the door and they helped launch my career. But I've written a lot of other books. I think my five book *Black Stiletto* series is the best thing I've ever done and I'm more proud of that than any of the Bonds. But Bond will always be a part of me. I'm very proud of what I did.

PLAYWRIGHTS PREVIEW PRODUCTIONS

PLAYWRIGHTS PREVIEW PRODUCTIONS

presents a reading of

C A S I N O   R O Y A L E

A Play in Nine Scenes

by

RAYMOND BENSON

(Adapted from the novel by Ian Fleming)

CAST

JAMES BOND	ED CLARK
FELIX LEITER	STUART LAURENCE
VESPER LYND	ELIZABETH HUFFMAN
LE CHIFFRE	ROBERT ABERDEEN
MAN W/CREW CUT*BASIL*CHEF DE PARTIE*HUISSIER	JOE WHITE
VASSILI*CROUPIER*PROPRIETOR*SOMMELIER	SPIKE STEINGASSER
STAGE DIRECTIONS	FRAN BELLACH
DRAMATURG	STUART LAURENCE
STAGE MANAGER	ELAINE O'DONNELL

Please stay for a discussion with the playwright
immediately following the reading.

Thank you for supporting P.P.P.!!!

Program for the reading of Casino Royale
Courtesy of Raymond Benson

Raymond Benson at Goldeneye, Ian Fleming's home in Jamaica
Courtesy of Raymond Benson

Theme Park Ride: License to Thrill
Keith Melton

"For years he's risked his life to save the world. Now it's your turn." That was the tagline on one of the posters for the theme park ride *James Bond 007: License to Thrill*. Another poster posed the question: "Have you ever wanted to be James Bond?" The attraction gave Bond fans a chance to answer, *yes, please* and to discover how it would feel to see the world through Bond's eyes.

Making its debut at Paramount's Kings Dominion in Virginia in 1998, *License to Thrill* was directed by Keith Melton, written by Bond scribe Bruce Feirstein and theme-park creators Gary Goddard and Ty Granoroli and produced in conjunction with Eon. The now-defunct motion simulator.

In a waiting area, before visitors get to experience the action through James Bond's perspective in *James Bond 007: License to Thrill*, they are shown a short film featuring Judi Dench's M and Desmond Llewelyn's Q.[580] The four-minutes and four-seconds long presentation helped immerse audiences in Bond's thrilling world and imparted information critical to understanding the ride's unique premise.

M discloses that she is speaking "live from my headquarters in London. According to this dossier, you have applied for a position in our Double O section—that is agents who are licensed to kill. Your test today will be to accompany 007 as he goes on his latest mission." She explains that the nefarious terrorist Gunther Thorne is going to kidnap the brilliant seismologist Dr. Callie Reeve and use her technology to "trigger earthquakes." Bond is tasked with protecting Reeve and stopping Thorne "from carrying out his evil plans for worldwide domination."

"Trainees" (a.k.a. park guests) will be "able to accompany 007 on this assignment" with the help of cutting-edge technology that was developed by Q-branch. Q takes over and reveals that because Bond is wearing special glasses that transmit everything he sees, the ride-goers "get to experience the mission directly through his eyes." Q chuckles and observes, "Kind of like a high-tech view to a kill." Offering a quantum of solace he says, "I do hope you all come back in one piece."

[Note: In the pre-ride film, Llewelyn gets to play a rarely seen color of the quartermaster's personality – patience. While the Q of the feature films is perpetually exacerbated with Bond, the Q in the ride is slightly jovial and empathetic. Within the context of the conceit of the ride, this characterization is entirely appropriate and successful. After all, Q has no reason to rebuke the relatively inexperienced recruits, who are likely to be more respectful of his precious inventions than the perpetually impertinent 007.]

M returns and informs the recruits, "It's now time to find out if you have what it takes to be a Double O Agent like Commander Bond."

* * *

For those who didn't experience the attraction can you describe *License to Thrill*?

License to Thrill was an action-packed ride-film. The concept was that MI6 had placed a "recruiting station," concealed as a theme park attraction, in order to potentially find new Double O agents. Q has designed glasses that James wears that capture everything he sees. Q talks to James along the way, and at the end, we see and hear M as well. The ride would [purport to] record each viewer's reactions, from both a physical and emotional point of view, and this would help M in finding new agents.

What was the plot of the story within the ride?

The plot was simple. A gorgeous scientist is kidnapped and Bond takes chase to save her. All from Bond's POV.

It starts on a motorcycle, which jumps onto a moving train, then Bond has to run along the train, fighting bad guys. On the other side of a low tunnel, he sees the main bad guy Gunther Thorne climbing a dangling helicopter ladder. Bond runs along the top of the moving train, leaps for the ladder, and is carried away. The helicopter pilot tries knocking Bond loose by flying low over trees, but Bond hangs on, then he begins climbing.

Suddenly, Thorne, the kidnapped woman, and the pilot, all leap out of the helicopter as Thorne throws a hand grenade into the helicopter. Bond must free-fall away from the exploding helicopter, then dive towards and knock out the pilot midair. Bond pulls the ripcord of the parachute and floats down towards a lake.

We see Thorne and the woman just getting onto a boat, with two gun-toting henchmen on Jet Skis to protect them. Bond pulls out a gun and shoots both of the henchmen, and lands on one of the Jet Skis. The chase continues.

Thorne has a rocket launcher and starts firing at Bond. Bond dodges the oncoming rockets, which explode harmlessly in the water around him. As our bad guy reloads, Bond smashes the Jet Ski into the back of the boat. This knocks over our bad guys and gives the woman a chance to jump free into the water. Bond makes sure she's okay, then turns his attention back to Thorne. We see him starting to get up with his rocket launcher. Bond raises his arm, aims with a high-tech Q watch device, which shoots a mini-missile into the mouth of the rocket launcher. It explodes, taking out our bad guy.

This leaves Bond and the woman floating in the water together, with James already beginning to seduce our heroine. We hear a final weary comment from Q before the image fades to black.

How did you get involved in the creation of the ride?

I used to produce and direct media-based projects for Landmark Entertainment, among others. Gary Goddard from Landmark hired me to direct the project.

As the director what was your job?

I needed to take the challenging storyboards and find a way to create a Bond-level action sequence, seemingly without edits. So, I worked closely with a top stunt director to stage this carefully choreographed POV experience.

What did you hope to accomplish with the attraction?

The goal was to keep the level of the action "Bond-worthy," while at the same time not having the luxury and dynamic energy of multiple cuts or different angles. That's how a lot of action films build up their energy, with the use of editing and changing angles. We couldn't do that, so that was a huge challenge.

Can you describe the variety of stunts and how you handled them?

I worked closely with the stunt director to choreograph the action within the time allotted per sequence. We had to have a clean "in" and "out" so that editorially I could connect the various sequences so it appeared as though it was one continuous shot. We used various wipe/edit techniques to blend the sequences together. Ground, air, water, we did it all.

The pre-ride-film features scenes with Judi Dench as M and Desmond Llewelyn as Q. Did you direct those scenes?

I'd like to say I did, but it was done in London by someone else.

Not including that film with M and Q, how long was the ride itself?

About four-minutes and twenty-seconds.

The conceit of the attraction is that the person on the ride is seeing the world through Bond's eyes. Can you talk about that choice?

We stayed true to the idea of a POV ride-film. That way, the motion base seats could be programmed to match what the viewer was seeing, giving them a "you are there" feeling to the experience.

Because the ride is told through Bond's point of view, you don't see his face. But there are times when you see parts of him. During those moments, who played Bond?

It was a couple of different people. Mainly our camera operator, except for the aerial and motorcycle stunts.

Who provided the voice of Bond?

We listened to a lot of professional voice-over actors. We finally found one we liked that was a bit of a Roger Moore sound-alike.

How involved was Eon?

Eon had full approval story-wise but was not on the set as we shot.

Intellectual Properties like Star Wars, Marvel, Harry Potter, and, of course, Disney have successfully been translated into theme park attractions. But Bond skews to a more adult-minded audience. Is Bond well-suited to this kind of ride?

For the time, it worked very well. It was the most complicated live-action ride-film ever attempted at the time. The [entirely first-person POV feature] film *Hardcore Henry* (2015), was very similar to what we attempted, but much bigger in scope and scale. These days, most everything is done with CGI, but almost everything we did at the time were physical effects and stunts. I am still very proud of what we achieved. It was an honor to be a part of the Bond franchise, working with Eon, carrying the Bond tradition into a new path.

What were the technical and artistic challenges of allowing the audience to see the world through Bond's eyes?

We used many techniques and camera platforms to achieve all the sequences. We used various ATVs [All-Terrain Vehicles] and dune buggies for the ground sequences with the front end of a motorcycle in the frame to give the impression that we, as Bond, were riding a motorcycle. This included riding through a "laboratory" and using rocket launchers to blow open a closed roll-up door so that Bond could continue to chase after our main bad guy.

Then, for the jump onto the moving train, we brought in an experienced stunt motorcyclist and strapped a lightweight camera onto the motorcycle. This was the most dangerous stunt, as the jump happened the stuntman took off from the end of an earthen ramp and landed on the top of a moving train as it was just entering a metal bridge over a stream. If the motorcyclist erred, it could have had deadly results. On the day, however, after much practicing, he went for it and landed it in one take. I believe we did it one more time to be sure we really had it.

On top of the train, our camera operator Max Penner had a chest camera with a "heads up" display that he had created so that he could see what the camera was seeing, as well as see where he was going. We were shooting 8-perf, 65mm film, so not a small camera body. We had a safetyman, Tim Thomas, running behind him to keep him safe. Bond has to fight a couple of bad guys on the train top, and he is kicked down by one of them. A bad guy pulls out a knife to kill Bond but is taken out by a tunnel sign.

At the end of the passenger train section was a boxcar full of boxes. Above it was a helicopter that was "pacing" the train, with a breakaway rope dangling from below. Our operator literally jumped into the boxcar full of boxes as he grabbed the ladder. From the viewer's point of view, we see arms reach out and hands grabbing the ladder. A flash from the sun hides the other side of the edit, which now shows Bond's arms holding tight onto the rope ladder as he is being strafed by treetops below.

As he starts to climb, the bad guy leans out, throws in a live hand grenade, then takes the kidnapped woman with him and jumps out of the helicopter, closely followed by the pilot. A hidden cut [maintains the illusion that the ride is one continuation shot] now shows Bond releasing his grip and falling away from the helicopter. We see the helicopter explode in midair. Bond then turns around and sees the pilot below him. This sequence was shot by an aerial stunt-cameraman who had worked on Bond films before. With an 8-perf, 70mm camera strapped to his chest, he manages to fly to the stunt pilot, pretends to knock him out mid-flight, then pulls the pilot's ripcord. We see the parachute open.

On a hidden tilt down [to disguise another camera move], we now see Bond's legs dangling below him as he floats down towards a lake. He pulls out his gun and takes out the two henchmen on Jet Skis, then lands on one of them. This was achieved by putting our camera operator at the end of a large crane and "booming him down" towards the men and the lake. We timed explosives on the henchmen and one of the Jet Skis to make it more exciting. As our camera operator lands on the Jet Ski, the parachute covers him for a beat.

When he pulls the parachute away, that is our next hidden edit, and we are racing along on the Jet Ski after our main bad guy. The physical effects team had set up a course of explosions in the water that our Jet Ski stuntman had to maneuver around. It was pretty dangerous, and in fact, one explosion got a little too close and we thought we might have killed our operator! We did damage the Jet Ski, but the operator was okay.

A big water explosion hides the next edit, which has us ramming the bad guy's boat before he can reload his rocket launcher. We see the woman jump into the water. A swish pan to see if she's okay hides the next edit, then we turn back to the bad guy. Bond's arms lift into the frame and we see him push a button on his high-tech watch. CGI visual effects added a tiny missile that shoots out of the watch. We fly with the missile straight down the barrel of the bad guy's rocket launcher, which causes a huge explosion. Back to the girl in the water, and a catchy phrase or two to wrap things up, and the ride is over.

We tried putting in some of those double entendre lines that Bond is famous for, especially in the Sean Connery era. So, for instance, as Bond is chasing a moving train on a motorcycle while being shot at, Q suddenly pops up and starts talking to Bond. Bond cuts him off by saying "Sorry to cut you off Q, but I have a train to catch." Or, as he's hanging onto a knocked out pilot with a parachute, he says, "I hate flying economy class." Or at the end, he asks the woman, who is a tectonic plate specialist, "So Doctor, can you teach me how to make the earth move?" And she replies breathlessly, "Oh, Mr. Bond..."

Keith Melton, the director explains, "In this shot, we are shooting a test for a POV of 'Bond' holding on to the helicopter ladder, eventually being dragged along the treetops in an effort to knock him off."
Photo Courtesy of Keith Melton, © Keith Melton

Keith Melton: "We had many specialized rigs to give the illusion of Bond's 'continuous POV.' A special motorcycle stunt man was brought in to ride up a ramp and jumping up on to the top of a moving train, just before it gets to a metal bridge. This was a "must make" shot, and he could have been seriously injured or maimed if he didn't land the jump, with the extra weight of a film camera on the front handlebars. Fortunately, he landed it."
Photo Courtesy of Keith Melton, © Keith Melton

Keith Melton: "We had pre-rigged explosives in the water for the path that both boats would take. The back boat was the camera boat, and we had to time it just right so that the splash of the explosion would hide one of several "hidden edits" to make this seem like a continuous four-minute POV, full of big stunts and action."
Photo Courtesy of Keith Melton, © Keith Melton

Keith Melton: "After Bond is forced to jump away from an exploding helicopter, he has to free fall towards the pilot with the parachute, knock the pilot out, then float down towards the bad guys, who have landed in an awaiting boat in a lake below. This rig was to give the POV of Bond floating down towards the bad guys and the lake.
Photo Courtesy of Keith Melton, © Keith Melton

Melton: "As he's parachuting down, Bond fires at the two bad guys protecting the main bad guy and the beautiful kidnapped scientist. He explodes one boat, and commanders the other to give chase."
Photo Courtesy of Keith Melton, © Keith Melton

Keith Melton: "Bond makes a grand entrance on a motorcycle, shooting some of the bad guys and starting the chase sequence to save the captured scientist. This mini-sequence is cut film style (multiple angles) until Bond shows up. From then on, it's one supposedly continuous shot from Bond's POV."
Photo Courtesy of Keith Melton, © Keith Melton

Melton: "This is the train we used to shoot a moving fight scene on top of. After Bond takes out two bad guys, he runs to the helicopter just lifting off with the bad guy and beautiful scientist. He leaps and grabs onto the rope ladder as the helicopter pulls away. These are just some of the action moments of this complex ride film."
Photo Courtesy of Keith Melton, © Keith Melton

"The Chase"
Tom Kuntz

One of the secrets to the Bond franchise's longevity has been the producers' uncanny knack for casting the right actor for the period. Sean Connery's occasionally cruel but always cool James Bond was a product of the swinging sixties and Roger Moore's jokey and jovial Bond captured the zeitgeist of the disco nineteen-seventies and decadent -eighties. Daniel Craig's conflicted spy perfectly reflects the turbulence of the early twenty-first century. But what would happen if Craig's world-weary Bond were inserted into one of Moore's action-comedies? Could this mashup work?

"The Chase," a 2012 Heineken beer commercial tied to the release of *Spectre*, answers that question. In the Tom Kuntz-directed spot, Craig's Bond is chased by a trio of baddies. To evade capture, Bond steals a nearby powerboat. The villains follow suit and a boat chase on Lake Como ensues. Unbeknownst to Bond, a beautiful woman (Zara Prassinot) is preparing to water ski and is holding onto the tow rope that's attached to Bond's boat. So as Bond speeds away, the involuntary passenger is forced to ski behind him. As Bond's boat zigs, she zags. In a moment, reminiscent of *Live and Let Die*, she skis on dry land, interrupts a wedding in progress, and inadvertently steals the bride's bouquet along with the groom's top hat. During this sight gag, her tow rope goes over the head of an unlikely wedding guest, Bond villain Nick Nack. The posthumous appearance of Hervé Villechaize, who played the bad guy in *The Man with the Golden Gun* and died in 1993, was realized through the use of archival footage and digital trickery.

The high-spirited chase continues and the still-skiing heroine is pulled back onto the water. One of the villains jumps on Bond's boat. The two men fight, and during their scuffle, they bump into the boat's control panel and inadvertently turn off the engine. The woman jumps aboard the vessel. Realizing that Bond, who is struggling, needs help, she removes the top hat that she acquired at the wedding and, like Oddjob in *Goldfinger*, she throws it at the thug. The hat bounces harmlessly off the villain. Bond gives her a look that's incredulous and withering.

As the fight continues, Bond signals the woman with a head gesture. Intuitively understanding Bond's nonverbal instructions, she quickly attaches a nearby carabineer to the bad guy's belt. Bond starts the engine and the henchman, who is now attached to a parasail, flies off the boat. With the threat neutralized, Bond turns to his beautiful ally, and wryly inquires, "Lunch?"

"The Chase" marks Craig's third appearance as Bond in a Heineken beer commercial. Repurposed scenes from *Quantum of Solace* (2008) were cleverly integrated into 2008's "Enter the World of Bond" to make it appear that Craig was part of that ad's original storyline. However, Craig shot new material for his appearance in 2012's "Crack the Case." In the *Skyfall* tie-in, Craig's Bond flees from adversaries, boards a train, makes contact with Bond woman (Bérénice Marlohe), jumps off the speeding locomotive and, successfully repeating a feat from *The Spy Who Loved Me*, deploys his parachute, which displays the Union Jack.

In 2020's Heineken ad "Daniel Craig vs James Bond," which was made to promote *No Time to Die* (2021), a tuxedo-clad Craig is offered a martini by a bartender who refers to the drink as the "Double-O." Craig waves off the martini, orders a non-alcoholic beer, and explains "I'm working." In this instance, Craig is arguably appearing as himself and not Bond. In another version of the ad, it's explicitly made clear that Craig is appearing as himself and that fans and other well-wishers are playfully referring to him as Bond.

"The Chase" is a departure from those earlier commercials. In those ads, Craig's portrayal of Bond is in keeping with his cinematic Bond. But in "The Chase," Craig deviates slightly from his brooding Bond persona and successfully conveys 007's lighter side. Craig has said that he wouldn't be well-suited to making a Moore-era film. Although Craig's no-nonsense Bond would be out of place in outer space or driving a motorized gondola through the streets of Venice in a feature film, he fits nicely into this 90-second tonal experiment.

Kuntz, who has created digital shorts for the online satirical newspaper *The Onion* and who has directed many music videos and commercials, talked to me about his approach to making his sharply constructed "The Chase."

* * *

What did you want to accomplish with "The Chase?"

I get hired to direct commercials by the advertising agency [Wieden+Kennedy Amsterdam] and the client [Heineken]. *They* are the ones that had actual goals of the things they wanted to achieve. I can only assume it was to hype the latest film while also delivering the Heineken brand's message. They wanted to make a fun film people would find true to both voices.

There is a tradition of setting commercials in Bond's world. How did you want to continue the tradition and how did you want your commercial to be different from the previous ones?

Well, I'd have to say that any thinking like this would have happened more on a subconscious level. I think the prior Bond-Heineken commercial was my only real reference for what was possible for this brand and working within the Bond universe. When the basic story of a female hero and waterskiing came in, it was really about just trying to make sure the story played as fun. I think by default, I ended up in a more playful tone because that was what suited the narrative. It would have been hard—and probably wrong—to try to handle this too seriously. It was more of a romp – much less serious than the tone of the film we were tying into.

To me what's particularly interesting is that the commercial played with the notion of inserting Daniel Craig's Bond in the middle of a Roger Moore-era Bond film.

Aha, there you go! That's kind of what I was just getting at. I think when I got my hands on the setting and the textures—Lake Cuomo, Riva [high-end] boats, waterskiing, a female hero—it all just pointed to something a little more fun. Plus, this was a commercial we are talking about, so it had to entertain in a much shorter period of time. Daniel was very open to the tone change, but he was also very clear and very professional about how *his* Bond could operate in this universe. He was very smart and helpful in that way. He was very forthright about what he and *his* Bond *would* and *wouldn't* do.

How did you aim to balance those two quite difficult styles and tones?

Well, it wasn't easy. I think the balance was achieved by keeping Daniel's Bond consistent with the films. The rest of the story is a bit broader, a bit more retro, a bit more of a romp, a lot of suspension of disbelief that you could never get away with in a real film. But because Daniel stayed true to who he is in the films, it survives and doesn't cross over the line.

Describe your interpretation of Bond in "The Chase."

We tried to keep him Daniel's Bond and for him to be consistent with the character from the films. Doing this enabled us to let the world around him get a little wackier and more stylized.

He's not quite the Craig Bond we're accustomed to.

He was slightly more playful than the Bond in the corresponding films. He needed to be to deliver this story.

How was Daniel Craig to work with?

He was lovely. He was very professional and very respectful. He had clear notions of what his character would do, but none of it was rooted in anything but productivity and consistency.

Can you give an example of something Craig said his Bond *wouldn't* do?

When I shared my original rough storyboards with Daniel, there were some frames that I recall him responding to and saying, "I know what this is, I know what this look is here, that this moment wants, and I want you to know I just don't do this sort of look. Some actors do, but I can't and I don't." I don't recall the exact words he said but it was his way of being honest and clear about how he played Bond.

Do you recall a time that Craig offered an idea of what his Bond _would_ do?

It was about how his Bond would solve a problem in certain ways and not in others. I can't recall the exact details but one of our original solutions for the ending wasn't right for him.

These creative discussions between you and Daniel reveal how 007 gets reinvented by different artists.

To be candid, I was just a lowly commercial director. We made a little film that tied in with some beer. I don't think it was my place to have grand character conversations with Daniel. That was for Sam Mendes.

Do you consider the Bond in your commercial to be the cinematic Bond? Or is he a different Bond?

I don't personally see him much differently. For me, the hugest thing that happened in this film was that Bond played almost an accomplice instead of the hero. I mean, if you break it down, he sort of has her to thank for their success in the end [although Bond came up with the idea of how to dispatch the final villain], but she is the protagonist of the film.

There are numerous references to previous Bond films. There's a brief appearance by Nick Nack and an Oddjob-esque hat-throwing gag.

This was something the agency had established a bit in their prior ad, so it was offered to me to try to do it as well. Nick Nack was a great solution because, well, he was _short_ – and the idea of everyone having to duck to avoid the rope and him not having to suited us very well. We needed to find existing footage of him. So when we found a scene with him delivering quite a suitable performance, it all just came together. In terms of the hat throwing, I believe that was in the original agency script. I think everyone was keen to give Bond enthusiasts as many little Easter eggs as possible. We wanted to give them things to digest as inside jokes that only a true Bond fan would enjoy.

The first shot of the commercial evokes the opening shot of _Quantum of Solace_. The rest of the commercial evokes the _Live and Let Die_ boat chase. From a visual perspective, what were your references and influences for "The Chase?"

Interesting. I don't know. I wasn't aiming to reference any of those films. I looked at tons of boat chases and things from all sorts of films just to digest how they had been shot. I was keeping an eye out for what I liked and what I didn't. My biggest inspiration was the older European films that glamorized Italy and the French Riviera. It's a romantic setting and it's great to drop some chaos into it.

Talk about creating Bond's look for the commercial.

I wouldn't say I "created" his Bond look. I wanted him to be wearing something that suited the location, but beyond that, so much was established already from the movies. I just worked with his stylist to choose a suit that worked for our film.

"The Chase" ends with Bond dryly proposing "Lunch?" Did you shoot alternative lines?

Yes. This was one of our hardest tasks on this job. What the hell should he say at the end!? We wrote this line on our day shooting with him. I can't recall what the original line was, but it just felt contrived and we were craving something simple and clever. I hope we succeeded. It wasn't easy. Everything we wrote sounded horrible to us. It's a tricky thing to pull off. I think that line works and doesn't get in the way of the film. I hope I'm right.

"The Chase" poster
photo © Heineken, Danjaq LLC

Daniel Craig's stunt-double leaps into a "boat in a scene from "The Chase."
Courtesy of Tom Kuntz, © Tom Kuntz

Deadly assassins pursue James Bond in Kuntz's commercial.
Courtesy of Tom Kuntz, © Tom Kuntz

Bond woman Zara Parrisnot "skis" down the stairs.
Courtesy of Tom Kuntz, © Tom Kuntz

A stunt from "The Chase."
Courtesy of Tom Kuntz, © Tom Kuntz

Tom Kuntz directs Zara Parrisnot in a scene that recalls *Live and Let Die*.
Courtesy of Tom Kuntz, © Tom Kuntz

Lost Theme Song
"Never Say Never Again"

The history of Bond movies is filled with unused theme songs, recordings that for various reasons were not accepted by the producers. Some of the theme songs, like k.d. lang's "Tomorrow Never Dies," were created at Eon's behest but were not approved. Whereas, other compositions by popular recording artists, such as Blondie's rock version of "For Your Eyes Only" and Alice Cooper's guitar-heavy "The Man with the Golden Gun," were submitted for consideration but rejected.[581] Some of the discarded songs, including Dione Warwick's brassy "Mr. Kiss, Bang, Bang," would have enriched the Bond catalog, whereas others, such as Johnny Cash's country-infused "Thunderball," are simply confounding. There's even the rare instance where an artist agrees to sing a theme song but, for unknown reasons, never records one, as was the case with Frank Sinatra and "Moonraker."[582] However, the unused theme song for *Never Say Never Again* has an intriguing backstory.

Never Say Never Again featured the triumphant return of Sean Connery in his signature role. Under Irvin Kershner's direction, Connery shines as the weathered but still irresistible James Bond, Barbara Carrera steals every scene that she's in as the deliciously evil Fatima Blush, and Klaus Maria Brandauer delivers a chilling performance as the villainous Maximillian Largo. The screenplay by Lorenzo Semple, with uncredited rewrites by Dick Clement and Ian La Fernais, is witty and abounds with killer one-liners.

Because *Never Say Never Again* was not made by Eon, the filmmakers couldn't use certain signature elements of the series, including the opening gun barrel sequence and Monty Norman and John Barry's James Bond theme. Bond fans often criticize the movie's jazz-influenced score by composer Michel Legrand, and the soft-rock theme song, which was written by Legrand and lyricists Alan and Marilyn Bergman and sung by Lani Hall.

Part of the problem is that Legrand's song plays over an otherwise thrilling action set-piece. As a result, the placement of the pop song blunts the sequence's tension. Even Hall was disappointed by the results, "I didn't think it was the right music for that particular opening."[583] The song might have been more widely accepted had it played over the credits, as a Bond theme song usually is.

Although the results were disappointing, getting the Legrand and Bergman team was considered a coup at the time. The trio's previous effort, "The Windmills of Your Mind" for the *Thomas Crown Affair* (1968), won them an Oscar for best song.

However, Legrand and Bergman's theme song was not the only one written for the film. Stephen Forsyth and Jimmy Ryan submitted another tune, which was recorded by soul-singer and Tony-nominee Phyllis Hyman. Forsyth and Ryan's demo is more in keeping with the Bond theme songs at the time, including the Sheena Easton hit "For Your Eyes Only" (by Bill Conti and Mick Leeson) and the Rita Coolidge song "All Time High" (by John Barry and Tim Rice) for *Octopussy*.

The protagonist of the *Never Say Never Again* song is struggling with the idea of falling in love with Bond. She admits that he's the "perfect mastermind" who knows just how to "take this heart of mine." But she's also worried that "There was danger in your eyes" and she questions "Was I falling into hell or paradise?" By the song's end, she submits to Bond's charms and vows to "Never say never again."

Forsyth and Ryan submitted their song to Irvin Kershner, the film's director, who responded favorably to it and instructed Warner Bros., the film's distributor, to make a deal with the writing team. According to Forsyth, "Warner Bros. informed our attorney that the song was to be used as the title song in the picture." However, the songwriters' enthusiasm was short-lived. Forsyth remembered, "Shortly before its release, Warner Bros. informed us that the song could not be used because Michel Legrand, who wrote the score, threatened to sue them, claiming that contractually he had the right to the title song."[584] As a result, Forsyth and Ryan's song was not used in the movie, nor was it released as a single.

It would take more than two decades before the song was made public. In 2008, Forsyth made the song available on the internet. However, since its recording, Phyllis Hyman, who soulfully brought their song to life, died. Forsyth lamented, "Phyllis sadly took her own life in [1995]. The year before she died, she called me late one night and told me she felt that "Never Say Never Again" was 'her best and favorite recording.'"[585]

While Forsyth and Ryan's demo isn't as well-known as some of the other unused Bond songs, it does have its supporters. There's a fan-made video on YouTube that integrates the theme song into *Never Say Never Again*. In the video, Lani Hall's rock-ballad is stripped from the action-packed opening sequence and replaced with more appropriate suspense music from *Russia with Love* and *Thunderball*.[586] Forsyth and Ryan's theme song is given greater importance in the fan-cut, as it plays over Maurice Binder's water-themed title sequence from *Thunderball,* updated with the remake's credits.

As I mentioned, for proprietary reasons, *Never Say Never Again* could not include a gun barrel sequence. Nevertheless, a tech-savvy fan has found a way around this issue. Using face-swapping software, Connery's fifty-three-year-old face is superimposed over footage from one of Timothy Dalton's gun barrel sequences. The fan video gives viewers a convincing indication of how Forsyth and Ryan's song might have functioned in *Never Say Never Again*.

* * *

Thank you for agreeing to talk to me about your unused Bond song.

How can I resist? It's so out of left field. Only you and two other people know about the song.

No, the song has admirers. It's an interesting song with a fascinating backstory. How would you characterize it?

It's a pop ballad. It's in the tradition of a Celine Dion pop ballad [for *Titanic*] and in the tradition of David Foster [the songwriter and producer of many hits, including Whitney Houston's "I Will Always Love You."] It's that kind of song. But the theme songs were also characterizations of the movie itself. Like [*singing*] "Gold-fin-gah." So we had an eye towards that. We were aware that if it's a hit movie, then the theme song generally comes along for the ride. It can become a pop hit. Like Paul McCartney's "Live and Let Die."

Did you ever consider writing a rock song like "Live and Let Die"?

No, we didn't. We were trying to model it after "Goldfinger," a classy kind of pop ballad that had a classy sheen to it. We did this in the early nineteen-eighties when movie theme songs were not too raucous. We wanted to keep it in that pocket.

How did you come to write "Never Say Never Again"?

Steve Forsyth is my co-writer on this. I remember Steve came to me, and he was all excited. He said, "We have to write a Bond song." I said, "How?" He told me that he knew the director Irvin Kershner. Kershner suggested that we write a song, but it had to be cleared with James Horner, who was the composer of the movie at the time. James hadn't written a theme song yet. This was before *Titanic* [(1997) and the Celine Dion song "My Heart Will Go On."] In those days, he wasn't really a songwriter. So he said sure, go ahead and do it.

So you and Steve Forsyth sit down to try to write a Bond song. Where do you begin?

You analyze the previous Bond songs and you think about the wonderful vibe of the Bond theme. [*Hums the Bond theme*] "Du-du-du-dum." So we spent a couple of days going to each other's apartments, hanging out at the piano, and just pushing it through and throwing out lyric ideas. We'd say, "Does this lyric work? No? How about this?"

How much did you know about the movie other than Sean Connery was back as Bond?

Nothing. [Laughs] We didn't have a clue. But we know that the movies are about James Bond and he's half good guy and half bad guy. And all the Bond movies move in the same direction. They go through an hour and a half of blowing things up. It's a fabulous fantasy. But look at some of the popular movie theme songs at the time, like "To Sir, With Love" [1967]. I don't know if that song has anything to do with the movie. Even "Live and Let Die," not so much. "Goldfinger" named the guy. So that was different.

Our song was more of a seduction song. And the theme of seduction is in every Bond woman. We put the woman in a vulnerable position. [Singing] "We drank the wine, in the candlelight. My heart was crying, don't let go. There was danger in your eyes." I can't believe that I still remember the lyrics. We did it so long ago. I'm not even sure I have a copy of it. That was before DAT [digital audio tapes] and it was on reel-to-reel.

How did you come up with the character? Did you ever consider that the song could be told from Bond's point of view?

I don't recall making a conscious decision in that regard. It just seemed to go that way. Steve came up with the first two bars of the song and I picked up from there. It may have been his idea to do it from the woman's point of view. "Never say never" doesn't seem like something Bond would say. [Assuming a chastising voice] "Never say never again." Bond would say something like, "Fuck them, I'm going to blow their heads off." That's not Sean Connery or Daniel Craig or Roger Moore. Those guys are balls to the wall, with a bulldozer. "Never Say Never Again" is an "iffy title" where a person hasn't made up their mind. Does she want to trust this guy? He's a murderer. He's a secret agent. She's asking herself, "Am I going to get involved with a person like that?" That's what "never say never again" said to us. Otherwise, it's Bond singing, "I shot the plane down. I killed the bad guy." It wouldn't work.

You have a lyric "Behind the blue, your eyes are smiling." Is that about Bond's eye color?

Right. The idea was that he had steely blue eyes and behind those blue eyes, she probably saw something nice about him.

On the risk of being pedantic, Bond and Connery don't have blue eyes.

[Laughs] Which one? Which Bond?

Daniel Craig does. But you were writing for Connery.

Oops. Call it poetic license. Or maybe we can say the blue was about water.

It is a water-based film, so you have some cover there. Who is she addressing?

In parts of the song, she's not talking directly to Bond. She's reflecting.

That's an interesting distinction.

I think she's afraid. I think that much of the song is in her head. But it goes back and forth. "Night into day. So close together. Behind the blue, your eyes are smiling." It goes into the first person there. The first half seems to be in her head and in the second half she starts talking to him.

The next lyric is, "You're the perfect mastermind. You knew just the way to take this heart of mine." You rhymed "mastermind" and "heard of mine."

It's not a Cole Porter "perfect" rhyme but it's close enough. You get away with it by having words between and so the listener sort of forgets about it. I generally try to do perfect rhyme but sometimes the perfect rhyme is too dopey. If it's a dopey thought, I'll write an imperfect rhyme.

You wrote the song quickly.

We wrote it in just a couple of days. We had no time. We had to get it in. Steve got the tip well into production when they were looking for a composer. So the only way we had a shot is if we could get that envelope under the door as fast as possible. As I recall, Kirshner liked it; he liked it a lot. But unfortunately, when Michel Legrand was hired, he wanted to take the whole thing and do it himself. I don't blame him, but it was unfortunate for us. And the chips didn't fall our way.

Phyllis Hyman sang on the demo.

Phyllis Hyman was a great singer. She came in and nailed it. She's no longer with us. But she wasn't the first person to do our demo. The first person was a singer named Kasey Cisyk. She passed away from cancer. She was a studio singer who worked with me on a Carly Simon album called [*Carly Simon:*] *Live at Martha's Vineyard* (1988) She did a killer job and she was so excited about it. We did it on a little Fostex 8-track. But that's all there was in those days. We didn't have programs like GarageBand, Logic or Pro Tools. In those days, computers were not where they are now. So we did our best with what we had. It came out pretty good. I played the crappy piano on it and I tried to make it as good as I could.

Can you talk about the first recording with Kasey Cisyk?

I loved Kasey. She was so brutally honest. She came in and said [*in horrified voice*], "You are submitting for a movie theme and you're recording it on a Fostex 8-track?" But we were young writers with no budget and no money to do the thing. Kasey kind of reluctantly sang it. She did it for me as a favor. I won't say her heart wasn't into it, but it wasn't quite as impactful as we wanted it to be. Steve said, "We've got to get Phyllis Hyman." I said, "How we are going to get Phyllis Hyman." He said, "I am going to get on a train and go down to her house in Philadelphia. And I'm going to drag her ass up here." I said, "What?" He said, "Watch me." And damned if he didn't do it." Steve was a very convincing person. He's charming as can be and he's very good looking. He had a way of making people think he had the best ideas in the world, even if they weren't. [Laughs]

Tell me about the second session.

We did it at my apartment on 14th Street. She did it in my closet, which was kind of the perfect vocal booth. I had my clothes in the background. I had good equipment so what went into the Fostex 8-track was as good as any recording studio. But Phyllis was not used to working in an environment like that. She was a little weirded out. She said, "I don't know how I feel about singing in someone's closet." Phyllis required a great deal of soothing and calming down. Not in any weird way, not with an edge. She was just very insecure. And very lovable. She was a sweet woman. She just needed looking after. But Steve said, "Come on Phyllis, don't worry about it. You are going to be great." She got over it and she just killed it.

I originally thought Kasey was fine and I was ready to go with her. But Steve goes, "No, no, no. This is a once-in-a-lifetime thing. We have to get the best of the best of the best." I said, "Fine, what have you got?" But when Phyllis was done singing, I looked at Steve and said, "Oh, man. Were you right about this one?" We hugged her and she thanked us. She said, "Would you please send it to me, I want to put it on one of my albums." But unfortunately, she passed away, so it never happened.

So, you do the recording with her and give it to Kershner who likes it. But then they tell you that they were not going to use it? Do you remember that feeling?

I do remember that feeling. I remember it right now. [Laughs] After James Horner left, Steve called me and said that Michel Legrand was going to write the score. I said, "Okay, great." But then he called me a few days later and said, "You're not going to believe this. He also wants to write the theme." I said, "Really, what about the lyrics?" He said, "He writes with the Bergmans." It sounded like a winning team, but I was incredibly disappointed. They are incredibly talented, but I don't think their song was their best shot.

We weren't Hollywood. We weren't in those circles. We lived in New York and if you want to work in Hollywood you have to live there so that the director can come over to your studio on five minutes' notice to sit down with you and play you the dailies. I had so many connections in New York that I felt like I would be starting from scratch if I moved there. So I never felt like "We got it. We got it. We got it. Oh, we don't got it." We "don't got it" was always sitting in the corner.

Do you ever wonder what might have happened if they used your song?

Hell, yeah. My career would have taken a very different turn. If Steve and I hit with "Never Say Never Again," we would have been very much in demand for songwriters for movie themes. A hit song from a James Bond movie is a ticket to ride.

Section 6—Lost Bond Performances

Toby Stephens is James Bond

Name the performer who has played James Bond the greatest number of times. Who comes to mind? Perhaps it's Roger Moore who portrayed Bond in seven movies produced by Eon. Or maybe you first thought of Sean Connery, whose performances in six Eon Bond films, in the non-Eon film *Never Say Never Again*, and in the 2005 video game *From Russia with Love* brings his total to eight appearances. Still, even many Bond fans might have overlooked Toby Stephens, who has played the spy nine times (so far) in a series of radio dramas for the BBC.

Stephens has starred as Bond on radio in *Dr. No* (2008), *Goldfinger* (2010), *From Russia with Love* (2012), *On Her Majesty's Secret Service* (2014), *Diamonds are Forever* (2015), *Thunderball* (2016), *Moonraker* (2018), *Live and Let Die* (2019), and *The Man with the Golden Gun* (2020). The productions are directed by Martin Jarvis, who also serves as the voice of Ian Fleming, the show's narrator, and they are produced with Rosalind Ayres, an actress and Jarvis's wife, through their company Jarvis & Ayers. Hugh Whitemore adapted *Dr. No*, the first radio play, and Archie Scottney is credited with writing the following eight adaptations, which all run approximately 90 minutes. Unfortunately, none of these splendid productions are commercially available. However, they can routinely be found on BBC Radio 4's website and on YouTube.

Celebrated actors often perform alongside Stephens, among them Sir Ian McKellen (Auric Goldfinger), Alfred Molina (Ernst Stavro Blofeld), and Tom Conti (Emile Largo). The productions sometimes draw familiar faces from the movie franchise. Joanna Lumley, who played one of Blofeld's Angels of Death in *On Her Majesty's Secret Service*, plays their handler and SPECTRE agent, Irma Bunt, and Rosamund Pike, who appeared as the cool Miranda Frost in *Die Another Day*, voices Pussy Galore.

The stock company consists of John Standing (M), Danie Dee (Moneypenny), Josh Stamberg (Felix Leiter), and Julian Sands (Q). Ian Ogilvy, who is said to have been considered as a possible replacement for Roger Moore and who narrated four Bond novels in 1981, plays Colonel Smithers in *Goldfinger*. Peter Capaldi, who would go on to play the twelfth doctor in *Doctor Who*, is cast as the Armourer in *Dr. No*. In the same production, Lucy Fleming, the niece of Ian Fleming and the co-head of Ian Fleming Publications, appears in a cameo role as the librarian in a winking nod to the author.

Before playing Double-O Seven, Stephens's most visible contribution to the Bond franchise was his performance as Gustav Graves, Bond's antagonist in *Die Another Day*. Stephens also narrated the audiobook *From Russia with Love* and Jeffrey Deaver's Bond continuation novel *Carte Blanche*. According to Jarvis, Toby Stephens was a shoo-in for the role of the hero in the radio plays. Jarvis told the Bond fan site Artistic License Renewed, that Stephens "was our first choice and in fact, he was Eon's too."[587]

While he might have been Eon's first choice, Stephens is not the first actor to play Bond on the radio. Bob Holness played the role in the South African Broadcast Company's adaptation of *Moonraker* in 1958. Unfortunately, the production has been lost to time; it was performed live and it was never recorded. Thirty-two years later, Michael Jayston played 007 in the BBC's 1990 production of *You Only Live Twice*. [For more information about both productions, read *The Many Lives of James Bond*, my previous book about the franchise.] It would take another eighteen years before Bond would return to the radio in *Dr. No*, a production that was well-received by many Bond aficionados and the general public.

The original intention was for Stephens to play Bond only once, in *Dr. No*. In an interview conducted for Ian Fleming's official website, Jarvis explained that the dramatization was initiated by Lucy Fleming, as a way to commemorate her uncle's centenary. However, *Dr. No* was so successful that Eon, who holds the performance rights, suggested that additional programs could be produced.[588] According to Jarvis, "We have had great support and encouragement on every level from Lucy Fleming and from Eon who recognize that our 'movies in the mind' are authentic and entertaining."

Jarvis and Ayers's productions are successful because they capture the spirit of Fleming's novels and, no less, due to Stephen's effective performances. Jarvis told me that "We stay as close as we can to the action and character of the original novels. We are guided by his creator, Ian Fleming. In the novels, James Bond is vulnerable, decent, romantic, and, crucially, has a conscience." Stephens's 007 is not an impervious hero. Instead, he's both physically and emotionally vulnerable. Although he displays many heroic traits and remains courageous, Stephens's Bond is also fallible and occasionally frightened; and he is not always ready with the perfect quip.

Jarvis also elaborated on the qualities that Stephens brings to Bond, "Toby Stephens brings great truth and humanity to the role. He is blessed with a terrific acting imagination. Audiences believe he is living within the situation and actually in the various locations, whether being grilled by M, chasing villains in a scary Vegas car chase, confronting Blofeld on a Swiss mountain top, or pursuing the evil Largo in an underwater showdown."

The radio format, where Stephens's voices Bond's intimate thoughts, gives listeners a unique insight into Bond's character. As Ayers told the *Independent*, "Although people are used to the spectacular visuals of the James Bond movies, the dramatization allows the listener to hear Bond's inner thoughts, his vulnerability and his strength, which is what you read in the original book too."[589]

Jarvis persuasively contends that Bond's interior monologues are faithful to Fleming's novels while simultaneously providing a unique experience to the audience. For Jarvis, "The listener experiences Bond's inner attitudes and reactions as they are happening. We derive these directly from Fleming's graceful in-the-moment prose. Sometimes, where it seems useful to paint a further picture, we'll hear from our narrator himself—the voice of Ian Fleming. Fleming and Bond's thoughts sometimes run in tandem. A line from Fleming, then a line from Bond. Back and forth. For example, 007's escape from Dr. No's lair via a ventilation shaft, where the combo of narrative and Bond's desperate thinking, as he hauls himself upwards, makes for a truthful, adventurous cliff-hanging scenario."

The dramatizations also feature elements of Fleming's novels that are unexplored in Eon's films. During Bond's encounters with M in the movies, 007 is often defiant or rebellious. But in the radio dramas, the two colleagues have a much more cordial, even occasionally paternal, relationship. While delivering the requisite thrills, the radio plays also allow for idiosyncratic moments, such as in *On Her Majesty's Secret Service* when M invites 007 to "pull a cracker, James" and to take part in a light-hearted Christmas holiday tradition. The informal request catches Bond off guard and M must prod James before the agent accepts his superior's offer.[590] The production also features Aileen Mowat in *From Russia with Love*, as the first and, to date, only actor to portray Bond's Scottish housekeeper, May.

Fans might be surprised to discover how humorous the radio dramas sometimes are. The first quarter of *Thunderball*, where M sends 007 to the Shrublands health clinic to detox, is a bit of a romp. But for Jarvis, the humor is compatible with Fleming. Jarvis admits, "We are not above inventing a few extra jokes. But always, we hope, serving the original. There's plenty of humor in the books. And in our productions."

Even when the Eon films adapt elements of Fleming's novels, they never retain the period setting. The radio dramas take a different approach. The director posits, "It's fascinating for us to preserve the period in which each novel was written. They range from the fifties into the sixties. No updating. So the Cold War, Cuban crisis, Russia's relationship with the United States all feature a great deal. And curiously, it's still completely recognizable and relevant. Bond lives on."

Before he was cast as Bond and while he was promoting *Die Another Day*, Stephens spoke about the spy's appeal. "As a kid, I used to wish I was 007 because I wanted to be that cool and debonair. And that kind of lone-wolf figure who's completely self-sufficient. That appeals to the male psyche, especially when you're young and reliant on other people's affection."[591]

Until now, Stephens has publicly said very little about playing Bond and his unique contribution to the character's rich legacy.

* * *

When acting in radio dramas, what do you want to bring to the character of James Bond? What is your goal?

I want to be as faithful to the storytelling as I possibly can. I don't want to impose too much of my own character on top of Bond's. I want to do what Ian Fleming wants and what Fleming described, as efficiently as possible. As a character, Bond is very efficient. I don't think that there is anything extraneous about him.

What motivates your Bond?

I think Bond loves doing his job. I think he enjoys it. It comes to him naturally. He's instinctive to it. Sometimes the people who are best at things are so because they're right for that particular job. And I think James Bond is right for his job. He's qualified for it in every way. He's got the right kind of mind for it. He's got the right kind of body for it. He has a very high tolerance for pain. And I think he can think clearly under very difficult circumstances. It's rather like Special Forces, who vet people to get the men that have the highest tolerance for all of those things. Yet, they can still think clearly and they aren't completely at the whim of their own fight or flight instincts. Bond is very cool under fire. He's a natural at being a spy. I think he takes pride in his job. He loves what he does.

By using aspects of their own personality, each Bond actor has found a way to make the part their own. What aspects of your personality did you use for the role?

You see, I don't agree with that. I don't agree with bringing myself to the part. Beyond actually just doing my job and telling the story as clearly as possible, I don't think I have anything to offer the role. I try not to imbue Bond with too many of my own traits. I want to keep him almost neutral and let the audience read into him what they want to. Because Bond is everyone's fantasy persona, especially men, I don't want to give him too much of my own character. That way people can project onto him what they want. [Stephen's thoughts about Bond seem to mirror Fleming's who, in *Moonraker*, describes Bond as a "silhouette."[592]]

When you are narrating a Bond book, who is the Bond that you are thinking about?

I'm honestly saying I don't think of any of the Bonds that I've seen. I'm trying to go back to a much more pared-down version, which is Fleming's version of Bond.

In addition to playing Bond in the radio dramas, you also narrated the audiobook versions of *From Russia with Love* and the continuation novel *Carte Blanche*. For me, there is a subtle but key difference in your approach to playing Bond in the two different mediums. When you are a narrator, you sound deliberately closer to a "composite Bond" or to the Bond of our collective dreams. Your radio Bond is your "take" on the character. Can you comment on the difference between your two Bonds?

When reading the books, one becomes far more embedded in the narrative than just playing Bond in the radio dramas. So I think there is a difference because the Bond I'm reading in the novels is much more embedded in Fleming's books in the narrative. Whereas playing him on the radio dramas, you're purely playing an adapted version in dramatic scenes. So it just has a different quality. I'm flattered that you picked up the difference.

What I love about doing the dramas on the radio is the difference between doing the scenes. And then these kinds of soliloquy versions. Martin Jarvis very cleverly gave Bond interior monologues. It's not only a handy device for telling the story and letting the audience know what's going on, but it also lets them know how Bond is coping with it.

What scene in any of the radio dramas best sums up your Bond and why?

There's a scene in *Dr. No*, which is the first one that we did, where he's on the bed and there is a [deadly] centipede climbing up the bedsheets. And you hear his inner monologue, where he is just dealing with the situation. [In the scene, we hear Bond's analytic mind evaluate the threat and, as his terror intensifies, the best way to neutralize it. It's a tour-de-force performance for Stephens, who delivers a three-minute soliloquy.] It sums him up. He's un-flamboyant, practical, cool, calm, rational, thinking this through, and getting in control of the fear that is creeping up. He manages to get out of the situation because he can think in a way that most people just really couldn't under pressure.

What place do the radio plays have in the Bond franchise? How do you think they contribute to the Bond legacy?

I think the radio Bond plays contribute because they are a sort of halfway house between the films and the books. They are not the books because they are dramatized. But I think they are closer to the books than the movies are. I also think they're pretty faithful to the books. We've had to change some of the more unpleasant and racist aspects of the books that reflected a different time. But the radio plays are unlike the movies, where everything is imagined for you. I think you get the best experience by reading the book. Then you can imagine everything your-self. The radio play does a little bit for you, but you can still bring your imagination to it.

What does it mean to you personally to play Bond?

He's one of the fantasy personas of every boy and man. So it's great to have actually inhabited him in some way. The films glamorize Bond and make him this fantasy creature. They often also stretch the bounds of reality. What I like about the radio dramas and especially the books is that he's a bit more earthbound; he's more believable. He's fallible; he's human. And he doesn't always get it right. There is also something gritty about him, which I like about the books and about the dramatized versions that we've done. The films can't dwell too much on those aspects of his personality. Perhaps they feel that it would be boring if they don't up the ante all the time. But I prefer the gritty version of the character in the books.

Toby Stephens is James Bond.
Illustration by Pat Carbajal

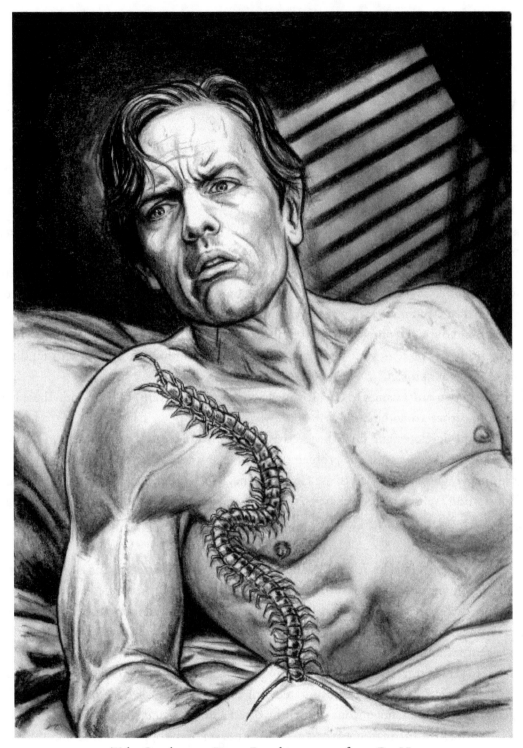

Toby Stephens as James Bond in a scene from *Dr. No*.
Illustration by Pat Carbajal

Bond Dance Performance:
Blair Farrington is (almost) James Bond

The list of actors who almost played James Bond is seemingly countless. The list includes actors who were considered (Trevor Howard), reportedly offered the part but turned it down (Clint Eastwood, Burt Reynolds, and Adam West), screen tested but not hired (Sam Neil, James Brolin, and Henry Cavill), and options from the rumor mill (Clive Owen and Michael Fassbender).

The list also includes John Gavin, who was cast to play Bond in *Diamonds Are Forever* but was released from his contract when Sean Connery was convinced to return to the role. Before his death in 2019, I reached out to John Gavin, who by then had also become the president of the Screen Actors Guild and the United States Ambassador to Mexico, and sought to interview him about his brief association with Bond. Gavin graciously declined my request. He wrote me: "I appreciate your interest in wanting to speak to me for your book. I must point out to you, however, that I did not play Bond during my time in the entertainment field and that, with all respect, I have no interest in discussing hypotheticals. My place in your story is but a footnote — nothing more. Notwithstanding, I wish you the utmost success with your project."

I would like to add two other names to the growing list of actors who were almost Bond. These names aren't as familiar as some of the other would-be Bonds.

In 2007, video game developer and publisher Activision planned to create a game based on Daniel Craig's first Bond film *Casino Royale*. There was just one problem; the film's star was reluctant to take part in the project. While Activision was ultimately given permission to use Craig's likeness, they still needed to cast an actor to mimic Craig's voice. David Houston, an aspiring voice-over artist, thought he was getting his lucky break when his agent told him that he landed the part.[593] But plans for the game were eventually scrapped and Houston's hopes of being the voice of Bond were dashed.

In an interview with me, Houston recalled, "The day before I was to leave for Los Angeles [to record Bond's lines], I got a call from my agent saying that the recording sessions were being postponed and would be rescheduled. My agent assured me that she'd stay on top of things and that I'd be informed immediately once the go-ahead was given. Even the casting director told me not to worry, the job was mine. Weeks went by and turned into months, with calls to my agent returning no news. Eight months later, I got an email from the editor of a James Bond fan website. He wanted to get my reaction to the news that Daniel Craig had finally agreed to voice Bond in the upcoming game [*007: Quantum of Solace*, which incorporated elements of the cancelled *Casino Royale* title]. It was from him not my agent, not Activision, not anyone directly involved with the game that I got the news."

Like David Houston, Blair Farrington was cast as 007 but never got the opportunity to play the role. Farrington was originally selected to play James Bond in the elaborate tribute to the franchise at the 54th Academy Awards in 1982 in Los Angeles.[594] However, Farrington was injured while rehearsing the production number and was not able to perform the physically demanding part during the live show. His understudy, Joseph Malone, went on instead.

***

How were you cast as James Bond?

I was brought in for a private audition with choreographer Walter Painter. It went well and Walter told me I was perfect for this role. I received a call that evening confirming I had the job.

What did the show's producers tell you about their concept for the production number?

The director, Marty Passetta explained this was a tribute to James Bond films and its most famous villains.[595] It was to be performed with Sheena Easton singing her then-current Bond tune "For Your Eyes Only" and that I would battle all the iconic villains and ultimately save Ms. Easton's life.

What were you told about how they wanted you to portray Bond?

They wanted me to be a believable, strong, and dashing Bond and to treat the role as an actor and action hero. This would be more about stunts than dancing.

What did you hope to convey about Bond and his character through your dance moves?

I found myself absorbed in the character and the responsibility that I felt playing one of the world's most famous film action heroes. I approached it as an actor, and let the dance and stunts just happen organically.

Joseph Malone told me that he was given the note to be careful not to move like Robin Hood—that is, they wanted something more virile and less balletic. What were the biggest possible pitfalls and how did you plan to sidestep them?

They wanted me to be tough and masculine. My single objective was to protect and save Sheena Easton from one perilous scene to the next. There was a bit of Bruce Lee in how I took out groups of bad guys and featured villains.

Were you at all concerned that a dancing Bond might not work?

Not at all. I was at my peak as a dancer and felt confident in my intent as an actor. I used my athletic ability to bring Bond to life in a live stage production and wasn't concerned about the perception of being a dancer. I was Bond.

You felt like Bond. Can you expand on that thought?

I did feel like Bond. At that point, Sean Connery was the Bond character I most admired and the one that got me hooked on the Ian Fleming character. He was the role model by which all other Bonds to follow were tasked to live up to. It was a lofty goal, but I knew I needed to power through and find the inner strength and smarts to persevere. I knew I needed to have cat-like reflexes and be unfazed by the many attempts by the villains to kill me as they jointly held Sheena captive.

What do you remember about working with Richard Kiel and Harold Sakata, who played Jaws and Oddjob, respectively?

We shared a dressing room, which I was honored and humbled by. It felt surreal to me as they were bigger than life characters in my perception of them from their Bond films. They helped me believe in this role, as they were the real deal and I knew I needed to counter their cunning as only the real James Bond would. They were true gentlemen and very kind to me.

What were the biggest challenges of the production?

This was at the time the largest live TV production number ever produced, including a specialty automobile that Bond arrived in, with an enormous and complex set, tons of special effects, complicated camera moves, and timing that required me to hit my marks with precision.

You suffered a very severe injury during rehearsals that made it impossible for you to appear in the production number." That must have been enormously disappointing.

It was nothing short of devastating.

What did you take away from the experience?

I hold no ill feelings towards anyone. What happened is in the past, and because of the injury—I had severed three of the four major cruciate ligaments—I retired from performing a few years later after two years of rehab, I created a production company in Las Vegas, Farrington Productions. I went on to produce, direct and choreograph for *The Merv Griffin Show* (1962-86), as well as for multi-million-dollar entertainment attractions, headliners, television commercials, and productions in Vegas and around the world. I continue to produce and create shows and entertainment.

This experience and heartbreak contributed to shaping who I am today and forced me to turn lemons into lemonade. I received a letter from the director a few days after the show, which I will always remember. Marty said, "You are the Baryshnikov of Hollywood. No one can ever take that away from you." What more could I ask for?

Sean Connery is James Bond

With a wink and a smile, I offer one final lost Bond performance.

When Sean Connery played James Bond in 1983's *Never Say Never Again,* it appeared that it would be the last time that the actor would utter the signature phrase, "Bond, James Bond" in front of a movie camera. Yet fifteen years later, Connery stood on a set as the cameras rolled on the set of a big-budget motion picture while cameras rolled and he introduced himself in the spy's distinctive manner.

The unexpected moment took place during the filming of the 1998 spy action-adventure *The Avengers,* based on the British sixties television series that featured several actors who would later appear in the Bond film franchise, such as Diana Rigg (*On Her Majesty's Secret Service*), Honor Blackman (*Goldfinger*), and Patrick Macnee (*A View to a Kill*). Given the show's influence on Eon's series, casting Connery as its Bondesque villain was a considerable coup.

In the adaptation, Connery played the evil scientist Sir August de Wynter, who is scheming to control the weather. In it, a kilt-wearing Connery threatens, "The weather is no longer in God's hands but in mine." His performance as de Wynter is the closest fans would ever get to seeing the actor playing a Bond villain, albeit a parodic one. Later, Connery nearly anticipates the title of the twenty-fifth Eon film when he snarls, "Time to die."

During the production of *The Avengers,* the movie's director Jeremiah S. Chechik asked Connery to record a birthday message to his co-star, and future M, Ralph Fiennes. But Chechik didn't want to deliver a traditional birthday message – he wanted Connery to perform the greeting in character as James Bond.

For this book, Chechik chronicled how he convinced Connery to play Bond one more time:

The shoot for *The Avengers* at Pinewood and Shepperton [Studios, in England] was

smooth and completely delightful. We were oblivious, me most of all, to the studio political machinations that were going on in Los Angeles. Problems between me and an executive, who eventually took over when I returned to finish the film became clear, as he was never a proponent of the film to begin with.

The eventual version [that was released] had so much cut out and the music was changed from dark to "fun" that it crushed my dreams. But the shooting was a pleasure. One day on Rafe's [Ralph Fiennes] birthday, we were shooting with Sean in an interior storm that we had created on a soundstage. Soaked as we all were during this odd sword fight, we were in great spirits. Sean was having fun, no easy feat for that curmudgeon, as it was not golf-related. Rafe and I occasionally winked and nodded at each other amazed that we were both working with the icon. Throughout the shoot, Sean and I shared a lot more than a single whiskey together and had a pretty good relationship on and off stage.

During the day, I approached him when Rafe was off set, to film a small birthday greeting from the James Bond of old (something Sean rarely does/did). So cameras on, rolling, action and out of the mythic Sean Connery's mouth came the perfectly rendered and captured greeting which included the famous, "Happy Birthday greeting, from Bond...James Bond."

After reading Chechik's account, I wanted to clarify how Connery delivered the line. I asked the director, "When Connery said 'Bond, James Bond,' was he saying it in character as Bond? Was he *performing* it, and not merely saying it? I'm asking about that indefinable but immediately recognizable moment when an actor fills his soul and fully embodies a part." To my delight, Chechik replied, "Yes, yes, and yes. In character. That's what made the moment."

Unfortunately, Connery's performance has never been seen by the public and it is probably lost to time. Chechik explained that he "never knew what happened to that clip." Somewhere, there is footage of the first movie Bond uttering the iconic line from a character that changed the cinematic landscape.

Appendix One:
James Bond Stories

The following is a list of James Bond stories that have been told in various mediums, including novels, short stories, films, television, comics, video games, and radio dramas. However, it is not a complete account. Instead, is it intended to demonstrate the massive scope of the franchise and the generative power of Ian Fleming's malleable creation.

A few notes about the list. The tiles of comic books and video games are often preceded with the branding "James Bond 007." To avoid repetition and to emphasize the titles of individual projects, I have usually omitted the labeling. So the graphic novel *James Bond 007: Service* appears as *Service*. I have listed only the English-language comic books and I have omitted unlicensed works, such as the text-based video game *Shaken But Not Stirred* (1982), the novels *The Killing Zone*, which was self-published in the mid-nineteen-eighties, 2015's *Licence Expired: The Unauthorized James* and *Bond*, 2018's *Bond Unknown*, as well as the 2019 opera *James Bond: A Convenient Lie*. I have also excluded unpublished works, such as Geoffrey Jenkin's *Per Fine Ounce*, Raymond Benson's short story "The Heart of Erzulie" and his "Casino Royale" stage play. I haven't included songs, audiobooks, and video games that aren't story driven, such as 2006's *James Bond Trivia*. What remains are hundreds of stories featuring Bond's enthralling missions.

* * *

Novels
Casino Royale, 1953
Live and Let Die, 1954
Moonraker, 1955
Diamonds Are Forever, 1956
From Russia with Love, 1957
Dr. No, 1958
Goldfinger, 1959
For Your Eyes Only (short story collection), 1960
"From a View to a Kill" (originally published 1959)
"For Your Eyes Only"
"Quantum of Solace" (originally published 1959)
"Risico"
"The Hildebrand Rarity"
Thunderball, 1961
The Spy Who Loved Me, 1962
On Her Majesty's Secret Service, 1963
You Only Live Twice, 1964
The Man with the Golden Gun, 1965
Octopussy and The Living Daylights (short story collection), 1966
"Octopussy" (originally published 1965)
"The Living Daylights" (originally published 1962)

"The Property of a Lady" (originally published 1963 and not originally part of this collection)

"007 in New York" (originally published 1963)

Colonel Sun, 1968

James Bond: The Authorized Biography of 007, 1973

James Bond, The Spy Who Loved Me (novelization), 1977

James Bond and Moonraker (novelization), 1979

Licence Renewed, 1981

For Special Services, 1982

Icebreaker, 1983

Role of Honour, 1984

Nobody Lives for Ever, 1986

No Deals, Mr. Bond, 1987

Scorpius, 1988

Win, Lose or Die, 1989

Licence to Kill (novelization), 1989

Brokenclaw, 1990

The Man from Barbarossa, 1991

Death is Forever, 1992

Never Send Flowers, 1993

SeaFire, 1994

GoldenEye (novelization), 1995

Cold, 1996

"Blast from the Past" (short story), 1997

Zero Minus Ten, 1997

Tomorrow Never Dies (novelization), 1997

The Facts of Death, 1998

"Midsummer Night's Doom" (short story), 1999

"Live at Five" (short story), 1999

The World Is Not Enough (novelization), 1999

High Time to Kill, 1999

DoubleShot, 2000

Never Dream of Dying, 2001

The Man with the Red Tattoo, 2002

Die Another Day (novelization), 2002

Devil May Care, 2008

Carte Blanche, 2011

Solo, 2013

Trigger Mortis, 2015

Forever and a Day, 2018

Young Bond Books

SilverFin, 2005

Blood Fever, 2006

Double or Die, 2007

Hurricane Gold, 2007

By Royal Command, 2008

"A Hard Man to Kill" (short story), 2009

Shoot to Kill, 2014

Heads You Die, 2016

Strike Lightning, 2016

Red Nemesis, 2017

Find Your Fate Interactive Game Books

Win, Place, or Die, 1985

Strike It Deadly, 1985

Programmed For Danger, 1985

Barracuda Run, 1985

Read Along Books

A View to a Kill, 1985

Moonraker, 1985

The Spy Who Loved Me, 1985

The Living Daylights, 1987

James Bond Jr. Books

003½: *The Adventures of James Bond Junior*, 1967

A View to a Thrill, 1992

The Eiffel Target, 1992

Live and Let's Dance, 1992

Sandblast, 1992

Sword of Death, 1992

High Stakes, 1992

Tunnel of Doom, 1993

Barbella's Revenge, 1993

Freeze Frame, 1993

Dangerous Games, 1993

As Good As Gold (interactive gamebook), 1993

The Moneypenny Diaries Books

Guardian Angel, 2005

Secret Servant, 2006

"For Your Eyes Only, James," (short story), 2006

"Moneypenny's First Date with James Bond," (short story), 2006

Final Fling, 2008

Films

Dr. No, 1962

From Russia with Love, 1963

Goldfinger, 1964

Thunderball, 1965

Casino Royale, 1967

You Only Live Twice, 1967

On Her Majesty's Secret Service, 1969

Diamonds Are Forever, 1971

Live and Let Die, 1973

The Man with the Golden Gun, 1974

The Spy Who Loved Me, 1977

Moonraker, 1979

For Your Eyes Only, 1981 *Octopussy*, 1983

Never Say Never Again, 1983

A View to a Kill, 1985

The Living Daylights, 1987 *Licence to Kill*, 1989

GoldenEye, 1995

Tomorrow Never Dies, 1997

The World Is Not Enough, 1999 *Die Another Day*, 2002

Casino Royale, 2006

Quantum of Solace, 2008

Skyfall, 2012

Spectre, 2015

No Time to Die, 2021

Radio Dramas

Moonraker, 1956

You Only Live Twice, 1990

Dr. No, 2008

Goldfinger, 2010

From Russia with Love, 2012

On Her Majesty's Secret Service, 2014

Diamonds Are Forever, 2015

Thunderball, 2016

Moonraker, 2018

Live and Let Die, 2019

The Man with the Golden Gun, 2020

Television

Casino Royale, 1954

James Bond Jr. 1991

(Episode titles)

"The Beginning," 1991

"Earth Cracker," 1991

"The Chameleon," 1991

"Shifting Sands," 1991

"Plunder Down Under," 1991

"A Chilling Affair," 1991

"Nothing to Play With," 1991

"Location: Danger," 1991

"The Eiffel Missile," 1991

"A Worm in the Apple," 1991
"Valley of the Hungry Dunes," 1991
"Pompeii and Circumstance," 1991
"Never Give a Villain a Fair Shake," 1991
"City of Gold," 1991
"Never Lose Hope," 1991
"No Such Loch," 1991
"Appointment in Macau," 1991
"Lamp of Darkness," 1991
"Hostile Takeover," 1991
"Cruise to Oblivion," 1991
"A Race Against Disaster," 1991
"The Inhuman Race," 1991
"Live and Let's Dance," 1991
"The Sword of Power," 1991
"It's All in the Timing," 1991
"Dance of the Toreadors," 1991
"Fountain of Terror," 1991
"The Emerald Key," 1991
"Ship of Terror," 1991
"Deadly Recall," 1991
"Red Star One," 1991
"Scottish Mist," 1991
"The Art of Evil," 1991
"The Heartbreak Caper," 1991
"Mindfield," 1991
"Leonardo da Vinci's Vault," 1991
"Far Out West," 1991
"Avalanche Run," 1991
"Queen's Ransom," 1991
"Barbella's Big Attraction," 1991
"There But For Ms. Fortune," 1991
"Invaders from S.C.U.M.," 1991
"Going for the Gold," 1991
"A Deranged Mind," 1991
"Catching the Wave," 1991
"The Last of the Tooboos," 1991
"S.C.U.M. on the Water," 1991
"Goldie's Gold Scam," 1991
"Canine Caper," 1991
"Weather or Not," 1991
"Ol' Man River," 1991
"Between a Rock and a Hard Place," 1991
"Sherlock IQ," 1991

"Killer Asteroid," 1991

"Danger Train," 1991

"Quantum Diamonds," 1991

"Rubies Aren't Forever," 1991

"Garden of Evil," 1991

"The Thing in the Ice," 1991

"Goldie Finger at the End of the Rainbow," 1991

"Dutch Treat," 1991

"No Time to Lose," 1991

"Monument to S.C.U.M.," 1991

"Northern Lights," 1991

"Thor's Thunder," 1991

Short Films/Television Commercials

Visa Commercial, possibly titled "Bond (Coming to theatres everywhere)," 1997

"Crack the Case," 2012

"Happy & Glorious," 2012

"The Chase," 2015

"Daniel Craig vs James Bond," 2020

Comic Strips

Casino Royale, 1958

Live and Let Die, 1958

Moonraker, 1959

Diamonds Are Forever, 1959

From Russia with Love, 1960

Dr. No, 1960

Goldfinger, 1960

Risico, 1961

From a View to a Kill, 1961

For Your Eyes Only, 1961

Thunderball, 1961

On Her Majesty's Secret Service, 1964

You Only Live Twice, 1965

The Man with the Golden Gun, 1966

The Living Daylights, 1966

Octopussy, 1966

The Hildebrand Rarity, 1967

The Spy Who Loved Me, 1968

The Harpies, 1968

River of Death, 1969

Colonel Sun, 1969

The Golden Ghost, 1970

Fear Face, 1971

Double Jeopardy, 1971

Starfire, 1971

Trouble Spot, 1971

Isle of Condors, 1972

The League of Vampires, 1972

Die with My Boots On, 1973

The Nevsky Nude, 1974

The Phoenix Project, 1974

The Black Ruby Caper, 1975

Till Death Do Us Apart, 1975

The Torch-Time Affair, 1975

Hot-Shot, 1976

Nightbird, 1976

Ape of Diamonds, 1976

When the Wizard Awakes, 1977

Sea Dragon, 1977

Death Wing, 1977

The Xanadu Connection, 1978

Shark Bait, 1978

Doomcrack, 1981

The Paradise Plot, 1981

Deathmask, 1982

Flittermouse, 1983

Polestar, 1983

The Scent of Danger, 1983

Snake Goddess, 1983

Double Eagle, 1984

Comic Books: English Language

Dr. No, (film adaptation), 1962

For Your Eyes Only, (film adaptation), 1981

Octopussy, (film adaptation), 1983

Licence to Kill, (film adaption), 1989

Permission to Die, 1991

Serpent's Tooth, 1992

A Silent Armageddon, 1993

Light of My Death, 1993

Shattered Helix, 1994

"Minute of Midnight," 1994

GoldenEye, (film adaptation), 1995

The Quasimodo Gambit, 1995

SilverFin, 2008

VARGR, 2015

Eidolon, 2016

Black Box, 2017

Hammerhead, 2016

Service, 2017

Kill Chain, 2017
Solstice, 2017
The Body, 2018
Casino Royale, 2018
James Bond Origin, 2019
James Bond 007, 2019
Live and Let Die, 2019
Reflections of Death, (anthology comic book), 2020
"The Broker"
"The Rare Dinner"
"The Oddest Job"
"One Pistol, Three Silencers"
"Men Without a Country"
"The Hook"

Comic Book Spin-offs:
Felix Leiter, 2017
Moneypenny, 2017
M, 2018

James Bond Jr. Comics
The Beginning, 1992
The Eiffel Missile, 1992
Earthcracker, 1992
Plunder Down Under, 1992
Dance of the Toreadors, 1992
The Gilt Complex, 1992
Sure As Eggs Is Eggs, 1992
Wave Goodbye to the USA, 1992
Absolute Zero, 1992
Friends Like These, 1992
Indian Summer, 1992
Homeward Bound, 1992

James Bond Jr. mini comics
"V.I.P. Treatment," 1993
"Dressed to Kill," 1993
"Close Encounters of the S.C.U.M. Kind!," 1993
"Thunder in The Congo!," 1993
"Venetian Bind!," 1993
"Slay Bells in the Snow," 1993
"Peak Performance!," 1994

"Race to the Finish!," 1994[596]

Video Games
James Bond 007, 1983
A View to a Kill, 1985
A View to a Kill: The Computer Game, (text game), 1985

Goldfinger, (text game), 1986

The Living Daylights, 1987

Live and Let Die, 1988

Licence to Kill, 1989

James Bond 007: Action Pack, 1989

The Spy Who Loved Me, 1990

The Stealth Affair, 1990

James Bond Jr., 1991

The Duel, 1993

GoldenEye 007, 1997

James Bond 007, 1998

Tomorrow Never Dies, 1999

The World Is Not Enough, 2000

007 Racing, 2000

Agent Under Fire, 2001

007 Ice Racer, 2002

Nightfire, 2002

007 Hover Chase, 2003

Everything or Nothing, 2003

GoldenEye: Rogue Agent, 2004

From Russia with Love, 2005

SilverFin (mobile phone game), 2006

Casino Royale (mobile phone game), 2006

Young Bond: Avenue of Death, 2007

James Bond: Top Agent, 2008

The Shadow War, (Young James Bond), 2008

Quantum of Solace, 2008

Blood Stone, 2010

GoldenEye 007, 2010

GoldenEye 007: Reloaded, 2011

007: License to Drive, 2011

007 Legends, 2012

James Bond: World of Espionage (mobile phone game), 2015

Theme Park Rides

James Bond 007: A License To Thrill, 1998

Appendix Two:
The Big List of Bond Actors

I have attempted to assemble a comprehensive list of actors who so far have played James Bond, but with a couple of exceptions. I have not included the stuntmen who have doubled for Bond in the movies or the actors and voice artists who have narrated numerous editions of Bond audiobooks. I have also omitted almost-Bond actors like John Gavin, who was hired to play Bond in *Diamonds Are Forever* but was released from the contract when Sean Connery agreed to reprise the role, or others like Sam Neill and James Brolin, who shot extensive screen tests but were not cast.

* * *

Barry Nelson played Jimmy Bond in the television production of *Casino Royale* (1954). Even though 007 is re-ferred to as "Jimmy Bond" throughout the live broadcast, the end credits identify the character as "James Bond."

Bob Holness provided the voice of James Bond in the South African radio adaption of *Moonraker* (1956).

Bob Simmons played Bond in the gun barrel sequence that begins the films *Dr. No* (1962), *From Russia with Love* (1963), and *Goldfinger* (1964).

Sean Connery starred as 007 in *Dr. No* (1962), *From Russia with Love* (1963), *Goldfinger* (1964), *Thunderball* (1965), *You Only Live Twice* (1967), *Diamonds Are Forever* (1971), and *Never Say Never Again* (1983). He also provided Bond's voice for the video game *James Bond 007: From Russia with Love* (2005). [Connery also played Bond in a recorded birthday message to Ralph Fiennes when they were filming the spy film *The Avengers* (1998).]

David Niven appeared as Sir James Bond in *Casino Royale* (1967).

Peter Sellers played Evelyn Tremble who, in an effort to confuse the opposition, is given the code-name James Bond in *Casino Royale*.

Terrence Cooper was cast as agent Cooper, who is also given the code-name "James Bond, 007" in *Casino Royale*.

Ursula Andress appeared as Vesper Lynd who is also called "James Bond" in *Casino Royale*.

Joanna Pettet played Bond's daughter Mata Bond who is also called "James Bond" in *Casino Royale*.

Daliah Lavi played The Detainer whose alias is 007 in *Casino Royale*.

Woody Allen starred as 007's nephew Jimmy Bond in *Casino Royale*.

George Lazenby starred as James Bond in *On Her Majesty's Secret Service* (1967). He has also played other characters, which are thinly veiled versions of 007, including "J.B." in the TV film *The Return from the Man from U.N.C.L.E.* (1983), and "James" in the revival of *Alfred Hitchcock Presents* in the episode "Diamonds Aren't Forever" (1989). Lazenby played aging spy "Double-O-Seventy" in a comedic sketch on *This Hour Has 22 Minutes* (2012).[597]

George Baker dubbed Lazenby's dialogue in *On Her Majesty's Secret Service* (1969) during the scenes in which Bond poses as genealogist Sir Hilary Bray. (Nineteen-years before Eon's space-themed *Moonraker*, Baker starred in the non-Bond film *The Moonraker* (1958) as the eponymous smuggler.)

Roger Moore starred as James Bond in *Live and Let Die* (1973), *The Man with the Golden Gun* (1974), *The Spy Who Loved Me* (1977), *Moonraker* (1979), *For Your Eyes Only* (1981), *Octopussy* (1983), and *A View to a Kill* (1985). He first played James Bond in 1964, in a seven-minute sketch on the variety show *Mainly Millicent*.

Christopher Cazenove played Bond in the BBC documentary show *Omnibus: The British Hero* (1973), in which he appeared in recreations of scenes from Ian Fleming's novels.[598]Cazenove was also the narrator for the audiobook of John Gardener's 007 continuation novel *Sea Fire*.[599]

Alexander Scourby narrated ABC's 1976 broadcast of *On Her Majesty's Secret Service* as James Bond. When ABC aired the movie, they made significant changes, including rearranging the order of scenes and dividing the film into two parts. In order to make sense of the now-jumbled plot, the network added a narrator who identifies himself as Bond and is voiced by Scourby.[600]

Joseph Malone played James Bond in 1982 during the 54th Academy Awards ceremony in a production number paying tribute to Bond movies as Sheena Easton performed the Oscar-nominated song "For Your Eyes Only."

Ed Clark was cast as James Bond in the staged reading of Raymond Benson's theatrical adaptation of *Casino Royale* (1986).

Timothy Dalton played 007 in both *The Living Daylights* (1987) and *Licence to Kill* (1989).

Michael Jayston voiced the part of James Bond in the radio adaption of *You Only Live Twice* (1990).

Corey Burton played James Bond Jr. in sixty-five episodes of the children's cartoon series *James Bond Jr.* (1991).

Pierce Brosnan starred as Bond in *GoldenEye* (1995), *Tomorrow Never Dies* (1997), *The World Is Not Enough* (1999), and *Die Another Day* (2002). Brosnan also played Bond in the video games *James Bond 007: Everything or Nothing* (2003), and in a 1997 commercial for Visa. [Note: Using footage from *Tomorrow Never Dies*, he was also featured in a 1997 Heineken advertisement in which real people who share the secret agent's name also appear.]

An unidentified actor provided the voice of James Bond for the theme-park attraction *James Bond 007: License to Thrill* (1998).

Stephen Critchlow played Bond in the video game adaption of *Tomorrow Never Dies* (1997).[601]

Tim Bentick supplied the voice of 007 in the video game version of *The World Is Not Enough* (2000) and *007 Racing* (2002). Bentick voiced some of Bond's lines in *Everything or Nothing* when Brosnan, who recorded the vast majority of the game, was not available to record the additional dialogue.

Andrew Bicknell provided the dialogue for Bond for the video game *007: Agent Under Fire* (2001).

Maxwell Caulfield voiced the part of James Bond for the video game *007: Nightfire* (2002).

Jason Carter supplied the voice of the secret agent in the video game *GoldenEye: Rogue Agent* (2004).

Geoffrey Rush played Peter Sellers playing James Bond in the biopic *The Life and Death of Peter Sellers* (2004), during scenes reenacting the making of 1967's *Casino Royale*.

Daniel Craig played James Bond in *Casino Royale* (2006), *Quantum of Solace* (2008), *Skyfall* (2012), *Spectre* (2015), and *No Time to Die* (2021). Craig provided the voice of Bond for the video games *007: Quantum of Solace* (2008), *GoldenEye 007* (2010), and *James Bond 007: Blood Stone* (2010). Craig also played 007 in the Heineken commercials 'Crack the Case' (2012), 'The Chase' (2015), and in "Happy & Glorious" (2012), the short film that opened the 2012 Olympics and featured Bond and Queen Elizabeth II. [Note: Craig also appeared as Bond in a 2008 Heineken ad but that commercial simply repurposed scenes from *Quantum of Solace* and integrated them into the ad. In the Heineken ad "Daniel Craig vs James Bond" (2020), a tuxedo-clad Craig is offered a martini by a bartender who refers to the drink as the "Double-O." Craig waves off the martini, orders a non-alcoholic beer, and explains "I'm working." In this instance, Craig is arguably appearing as himself and not Bond. In another version of the ad, it's explicitly stated that Craig is appearing as himself and not as 007.]

An unidentified actor supplied the voice of Bond in "Waiter," a 2006 commercial for Heineken. In the advertisement, an off-screen Bond says, "Darling, if you see room service, I ordered you a Heineken." The promo was directed by the Academy Award-winning writer Stephen Gaghan and features Eva Green reprising her role from *Casino Royale* as Vesper Lynd.

Toby Stephens played the spy in a series of radio dramas for BBC's Radio 4, including *Dr. No* (2008), *Goldfinger* (2010), *From Russia with Love* (2012), *On Her Majesty's Secret Service* (2014), *Diamonds Are Forever* (2015), *Moonraker* (2018), *Live and Let Die* (2019), and *The Man with the Golden Gun* (2020). He played Bond while giving dramatic readings from Fleming's novels at a 2008 benefit event for the British Heart Foundation at the London Palladium called "The Story of James Bond—A Tribute to Ian Fleming"[602] and narrated the 2012 edition of the *From Russia with Love* audiobook.

Timothy Watson gave a convincing imitation of Daniel Craig's Bond when he played the spy in the video game *007 Legends* (2012).

Josh Lawson played James Bond in the documentary *Becoming Bond* (2017), in scenes where George Lazenby, whose life he was portraying, was making *On Her Majesty's Secret Service*.

[Redacted] will play James Bond in Eon's 26th James Bond film.

Appendix Three:
Simon Jowett's Bond Comic Treatments

During my interview with Simon Jowett, I asked him to describe the plot of issues three and four of *A Silent Armageddon* and "A Deadly Prodigal," a 24-page Bond story that would be told in four-parts. Instead of briefly summarizing them, he sent me the complete outlines for both unpublished stories. With Jowett's permission, I present both treatments.

* * *

JAMES BOND: A SILENT ARMAGEDDON

SYNOPSIS

BOOK ONE

Ten years ago, deep and secure in a Minuteman silo in the American Midwest, a spot check of the missile launch programs uncovers a minor discrepancy. Further investigation shows that entire programs have been rewritten, by hands unknown. These new instructions would deposit warheads on American cities, those of friendly and enemy nations, apparently without discrimination, as well as upon areas of no strategic worth whatsoever. The culprit is never found.

In New York, James Bond participates in a quiet raid upon an amusement arcade. The arcade is believed to be the front for a SPECTRE-run drugs operation. It is also believed to be a waystation for computer software stolen from Western governmental contractors. Despite some resistance from thugs one would not normally expect to possess the brain power to play 'Space Invaders', the backroom of the arcade—the supposed drugs den—is empty. There is a closed-circuit camera mounted in one high corner of the room, and a large bomb concealed in the shadows to the rear of the room. Bond barely escapes the blast. Sifting through the rubble, he finds no evidence of this trap having been set by SPECTRE. He does, however, find an enamel lapel pin in the shape of a three-headed dog.

(At this point, it might be worth pointing out that, despite the use of the name SPECTRE in the above paragraph, the comic will contain no mention of the name. The organization will be referred to in a veiled fashion by Bond as "The Competition" or "Our ghostly friends" or some other oblique but appropriate euphemism. The purpose of this part of the scene is to indicate that there is a new gang in town, potentially more cunning and dangerous than the old one.)

Eight-and-a-half years later, Eddie Byle, software cowboy and smack addict, is run to the ground by enforcers sent by his supplier, Troy Baines. Byle owes Baines a great deal of money and has been dodging him for weeks. He has been feeding his habit by hacking into health centre computers, arranging for open prescriptions from a number of addiction treatment centres. His attempts at dealing, in the hope of paying off Baines, have all failed. Cornered by Baines and his heavies, he offers a trade.

Byle is not a great hacker; his successes have all been due to his use of Program Omega. Stumbled upon during a hack that was going badly, Omega seems able to go anywhere, do anything that is asked of it. Unaware of its true nature, Byle believes Omega to be only semi-autonomous, somehow mislaid by its original programmer. In order to preserve his kneecaps, Byle offers Omega to Baines.

Eighteen months later, Byle brings Baines some potentially bad news. A NATO-sponsored team of research scientists, based in Oxford, are ready to test their own semi-autonomous program—a crude form of Program Omega.

Baines has done very well out of Omega. It has given him access to financial institutions across the globe. He has taken their money without them having the slightest idea that it is gone. He is very rich. He intends to become richer still. He has no intention of tolerating any competition.

Baines turns to CERBERUS for help. A relative newcomer to the field of international terror and espionage, the organization has three main areas of interest: espionage, extortion, and enforcement. Each area is overseen by a different leader, giving rise to the three-headed power structure symbolized by Cerberus, the mythical three-headed dog which guarded the gates of Hades. Always ready to explore new avenues of potential income, CERBERUS dispatches to Oxford an assault team, led by the late Rosa Klebb's precociously sadistic 19-year-old bastard, Erik. With brutal efficiency, it wipes out the research team, led by Professor Garrard, and destroys their laboratory and records. Then it returns to Chicago, demanding Omega in return.

In Oxford, Bond is assigned to protect the only survivor of the CERBERUS attack. Terri Li is a 13-year-old orphan, born into the most extreme poverty in Hong Kong, where she contracted the potentially fatal disease Poliomyelitis. As a result of the care she received in a religious order's orphanage, she survived the infection, but is confined to a wheelchair. A mathematical prodigy with an almost preternatural affinity for computers, she was the lynchpin of Garrard's project. The murders of the other project members bear the hallmarks of a CERBERUS job and there are fears of another attempt on Terri's life. Apparently in shock, she is surly and uncommunicative when she is given into Bond's custody.

Not in shock, but suspicious of all around her, Terri is determined to protect what she knows. An almost pathological secrecy was her main survival strategy in the orphanage. Secretly, she continues her work. As she does so, she is surprised to find that someone is waiting for her in cyberspace, someone who wants to talk to her: Omega.

* * *

BOOK TWO

The OPTI-NET will revolutionize communications: a global digital optical-fibre network, it will allow instantaneous exchange of immense amounts of information. The 'Global Village' will have arrived. Anyone able to bend the network to their will would become a truly unstoppable, invisible world power. CERBERUS has been hard at work to that end.

Hong Kong's 'Walled City' is a criminal ghetto of such savagery and maze-like complexity that it is a no-go area for law enforcement agents. At its heart, one of CERBERUS's main communications centres is devoted to the task of cracking the security protocols which protect the OPTI-NET, now only weeks from inauguration.

Byle has been brought here, memories of Baines' slow death at the hands of Erik Klebb fresh in his mind. H has been assigned the task of finding Omega. Not waiting for Klebb to start work on him, Byle offered to give CERBERUS the program, only to find that it was no longer his to give. It had vanished from the memory chip on which Byle believed he had it imprisoned. Talking for his life, making grand claims about his genius, he promised to find the program, or else design a new one, from scratch.

Byle arrives in time to witness another failure to beat the NET's security systems. In awe of the amount of equipment and expertise CERBERUS commands, he begins to realize that he is way out of his depth.

In the UK, Bond's renowned charm has failed to draw Terri out of herself or make her more than sullenly cooperative. Compared to the Faustian dialogue that is developing between Terri and Omega, Bond has no chance.

Bond's charm works more successfully upon Dr. Jessica Penrose, an American cyberneticist who worked briefly with Garrard and Terri. She and Terri seemed to get on, so Bond's superiors brought her in to apply 'a woman's touch' to the girl's rehabilitation. However, their choice of woman causes problems—Penrose works for CERBERUS.

By chance, Bond discovers evidence of the correspondence between Terri and Omega. Both he and Penrose assume that it is controlled by a human operator. Terri, grown even more sullen in the face of Bond's censure, keeps the fact of the program's autonomy to herself, even though she agrees to 'trace' it for them.

BABEL Centre, New York, houses the world's most powerful computer. It will be a major nexus in the OPTI-NET. Bond's plan is to use BABEL to trace Omega's operator. The plan is a spectacular failure: Terri warns Omega of the trap; To cover its tracks, Omega causes BABEL and its ancillary systems—the building's lights, heating, elevators – to overload. In the midst of the darkness and confusion, CERBERUS attempts to snatch Terri.

Bond is wounded thwarting CERBERUS's efforts. Their methods of information retrieval from humans are notoriously unpleasant. Penrose's cover is blown and Terri is forced to choose between her and Bond. She chooses Bond and they use her hacking talents to skip the U.S. under assumed names using illegally-booked airline tickets.

Omega's reaction to the trap and its ability to manipulate the several systems within the BABEL complex breed in Bond a nasty suspicion of its true nature. What Terri is now willing to tell him confirms this. Omega has no controller. It is a creature of almost pure will, staggering in its constantly evolving complexity and limitless in potential.

The reason for CERBERUS's interest is clear: they would use Omega to gain access to the OPTI-NET ahead of its official inauguration. Even if CERBERUS was unable to harness Omega, should the program access the network, it would gain immediate, invisible control over world affairs. Humanity would become enslaved without realizing it.

Bond sees his only option to be the destruction of Omega. Unable to trust the security of the Secret Service, he is far from sure how this might be achieved.

* * *

BOOK THREE

A wall-mounted cash dispenser begins to vomit notes onto the street. In the ensuing chaos, three people die, and traffic is held up for a day.

The electronic security system of a modern prison seems to act of its own volition. Cell locks are frozen open. The inmates take over.

Paris, Marseilles, Berlin, Rome. Bond and Terri hide in perpetual motion as they travel across Europe, tracking down men who have fought against and alongside Bond at various times in the past and for various reasons.

While Bond risks his life for his country, his vision of the world, these men do so for reasons very much their own. Adrenalin junkies, borderline psychotics, men whose philosophy of life demands that they live always on the edge of losing it. Impossible to trust, they are the only men Bond can turn to.

Living in a succession of hotel rooms, Terri is at work on a new program. Using parts bought on rare shopping trips with Bond, she is modifying her lap-top computer and designing a virus which, she tells Bond, will destroy Omega. Bond's careful perusal of the hotel bills for use of the telephone while he is out prevents her from renewing her correspondence with Omega. She aches to slip back into the cool mathematical half-light of cyberspace and the embrace of her first love.

Omega has a new correspondent. Penrose arrived in the Walled City armed with a copy of Terri's communications with the program. Contact with Omega is achieved and negotiations begin. Byle, fearful of what Penrose's success means for his continued well-being, sabotages the contact. This is discovered and Byle is executed. Herself an unwilling pawn in CERBERUS's game, Penrose is continually appalled by her masters' chill savagery and fearful of what her fate may be. Independent of any human agency, Omega continues to grow, to explore the interfaces between his world and ours. Every time he does so, the electronic glue that holds together the global financial/industrial complex pulls a little further apart.

In Berlin, Klebb's team catches up with Bond. Klebb has always blamed Bond for his mother's death. After narrowly escaping death at Klebb's hands, thanks to the presence of the latest member of his own small assault team, Bond brings forward his plan. He will foil both Omega's and CERBERUS's wishes regarding the OPTI-NET by taking the battle to the Walled City, infecting Omega with Terri's virus and destroying the communications centre.

With CERBERUS at his heels, Terri's virus as yet incomplete and no guarantee as to how far his five-man assault team can be trusted, Bond sets the final wheels in motion.

***

BOOK FOUR

When the numbers on the screens of Wall Street's dealing computers start to move around of their own accord, billions of dollars are wiped off share values. In a panic, the systems are shut down. In other cities, trading comes to a halt as people can no longer trust the information they are being given.

Nuclear material due for treatment and disposal is diverted to urban landfill sites and dumped among piles of household refuse that are scavenged over by hordes of the cities' poor. Some wars end and others begin because military commanders do not know whether to believe what they see on their radar screens. Terri barely completes the modifications to her lap-top, to a second deck, to be used by Bond in case of an emergency, and to her virus program, before the doors to the Walled City are opened to them. One of Bond's team is a former native of the ghetto. Terri was also, for a brief period, an inhabitant of this vast slum; ghosts from her past scream at her as she struggles to control the motorized exo-skeleton into which she is strapped and which enables her to stand and walk. The team moves as swiftly and as stealthily as possible through the city's three-dimensional maze toward the CERBERUS complex, painfully aware that their presence will already have been whispered ahead of them. They encounter sudden stiff resistance as they near the complex, but not enough to prevent their entry.

While Bond and his team fight off the CERBERUS militia, Terri taps into the power of ORPHEUS, CERBERUS's supercomputer. Entering cyberspace, she finds herself confronted by CERBERUS cybernauts, led by Penrose, who are as intent on finding Omega as she is. Bond enters cyberspace and runs interference while Terri follows a trail laid down by Omega, who appears glad to renew their acquaintance.

When he interposes himself between Terri and the attack of the last of the CERBERUS cybernauts, Bond 'dies' —his interface with cyberspace is destroyed. Suddenly back in the physical world, a chill wind of mortality whispering through him, he sees Terri press the button on her laptop that will activate the virus. Tense seconds tick by, the CERBERUS militia working ever closer to closing down their escape route, until Terri emerges from cyberspace, triumphant.

ORPHEUS overloads, taking most of the CERBERUS complex with it. Bond, Terri, and the team—down to two men as the result of two fatalities and one desertion—fight their way up through the city to the pre-arranged pick-up point. Angry, the city's inhabitants are as anxious for Bond's blood as CERBERUS. He and Terri make it to the pick-up by the narrowest of margins. Unknown to them both, Penrose clears the last obstacle – Klebb—from their path, before melting into the highly-risky cover of the city.

As the world staggers back to its feet, the inauguration of the OPTI-NET is delayed. A surge of distrust towards electronic devices casts the network's entire future in doubt - very good news, as far as Bond is concerned. Less good news is his reassignment. No trace of Omega can be found and Terri returns to Oxford to resurrect Garrard's project. Bond finds that he will miss her a great deal. In Oxford, though she does miss Bond—her first half-decent father-figure – Terri has a new friend: Program Omega. Not destroyed, contained within her lap-top, like a genie in a bottle, Omega is Terri's most precious secret.

***

JAMES BOND: A DEADLY PRODIGAL a proposal for a 24-page story.

OVERVIEW

Assigned to protect a man he despises, Bond discovers that, to successfully complete his mission, he will have to kill a former colleague and friend.

Former communist apparatchik, Konstantin Kolovsky, rose to power in the former Soviet satellite state of Estovia on a wave of rabid nationalism and ethnic intolerance. He swept aside the fragile democracy that had been formed in the wake of the Eastern Bloc's collapse and installed a new dictatorship. Making his first visit to the West, he is pressing the British Government to extradite members of the ousted democratic government who now live in exile in the U.K. and agitate against him. He is also living the high life, staying in the best hotels, eating in the best restaurants and attending high-profile social functions. He has been making it very difficult for the normal diplomatic security measures to be enforced. Bond is assigned to keep a close eye on him. Bond finds Kolovsky to be an intolerable character: personally boorish and egocentric, politically cynical, and ruthless. Despite a rueful sympathy with anyone who might want to remove Kolovsky from the scene, Bond does his duty.

Bond's adherence to duty comes into direct confrontation with his admiration and friendship for William ('Bill') Sinclair, a former member of the Double-0 Section who went missing in Estovia during the chaos unleashed by Kolovsky's drive for power. Sinclair, it transpires, was deeply affected by what he saw during the putsch and has thrown in his lot with the democratic underground. He has returned to Britain to kill Kolovsky.

The former friends clash as one seeks to kill Kolovsky while the other has been ordered to protect the dictator. The certainties of duty and loyalty upon which Bond has built his career suddenly appear to be less than solid in the face of Sinclair, who is now willing to risk his life for an ideal, a cause. Meanwhile, Kolovsky presses ahead with his own hidden agenda: the deaths of the exiled democrats.

Friends, enemies, or both? Bond struggles to come to terms with the contradictions of the situation in a maelstrom of betrayal and danger that erupts across the polo fields of the Home Counties and the derelict wharves of London's East End.

* * *

PART ONE (six pages)

Bond has accompanied Kolovsky to the finals of a high-profile polo tournament at a ground in the Home Counties. Kolovsky's original request that he be guarded by his own militia was turned down in favour of the Diplomatic Security Squad, headed, in this instance, by Bond. Kolovsky is accompanied by one other Estovian national, his personal assistant, Katarinya Rikov.

Tall, possessed of striking features and a well-trained physique, Rikov attracted Bond's attention almost immediately. Unfortunately, she seems interested only in Kolovsky's safety. She is by his side almost every minute of the day. Rebuffed but not down-hearted, Bond diverts himself with one of the polo grooms while the third chukka gets under way.

As the spectators return to their seats having taken part in the half-time ritual of "treading in"—treading divots of earth, dug up by the ponies' hooves, back into place—the match takes a deadly turn. Instead of riding out onto the pitch to join the other players, a player whom no one has seen before steers his pony across the pitch, towards Kolovsky who is walking back towards his seat in the members' enclosure. Knocking aside the surprised security men, the rider is about to deliver a fatal blow to the dictator when Bond, also on horseback, intervenes.

Galloping towards the melee on one of the horses being groomed by his young Partner-in-dalliance, he draws his Walther PPK and takes aim at the would-be assassin.

The face he sees along the barrel of his pistol causes him, for what may be the first time in his career as a Double-0 agent, to hesitate in the pursuance of his duty. The horseback assassin is Bill Sinclair.

Having fought and worked his way out of the poverty of his East End childhood via scholarships to public schools and to Cambridge, Sinclair's ability to combine hard work with imagination and a flair that bordered on the cavalier had won him a place in the Double-0 Section in record time. It had also earned him Bond's friendship and admiration. He had disappeared while on a mission in Estovia, believed killed during the violent clashes between Kolovsky's supporters and those of the democratic government. That he is alive is a surprise, albeit a pleasant one. That he is now attempting to kill the man Bond has been charged to protect is a much greater and far less pleasant shock.

Sinclair takes advantage of Bond's moment of inaction. Knocking the Walther from Bond's grasp, he makes his escape across the surrounding fields, leaving a shaken Bond to explain to an outraged Kolovsky that Sinclair is a consummate professional—an 'agent's agent'—who could never be counted out of a fight and who never gave up on a mission. Kolovsky's chances of leaving Britain alive have just lengthened and Bond's mission has just become much harder because, without a doubt, Sinclair will try again.

* * *

PART TWO (six pages)

Despite Bond's warning, Kolovsky is determined to continue with his itinerary. Bond appeals to M to have Kolovsky forcibly restrained from his high-profile tour about the country. M informs him that Her Majesty's Government has no intention of spending over the odds on the security of a Penny-ante dictator whose future usefulness to British interests is liable to be quite limited. Bond is surprised to discover that his report of Sinclair's attempt on Kolovsky's life serves only to confirm rumours of the former agent's continued health and involvement in the Estovian resistance movement. Bond is informed that his job is to keep Kolovsky alive until he leaves British soil, by any means necessary. He is also informed that, given Sinclair's effectiveness in situations of this kind, Bond is probably the only person with a hope of stopping him, or at least of holding him at bay.

While all his training tells him to suppress any personal feelings he may have towards a job, Bond finds it impossible to feel anything but used, by his government, by M. The fact that he knows Sinclair, his temperament and methodology, the fact that they were friends, are what make him, in the eyes of his superiors, the best man to stop the rogue agent. And he is all too aware that, if Sinclair crosses his path again, there will be only one way of stopping him. Never has duty weighed more heavily upon Bond as he rejoins Kolovsky, now in London.

Kolovsky is scheduled to attend the gala opening of a new production of the opera GOTTERDAMMERUNG at the Royal Opera House, Covent Garden, and is determined to do so. The leader of the Estovian democrats-in-exile, a former music critic and samizdat activist before the collapse of the Soviet-backed regime, will also be in attendance. Bond is Kolovsky's reluctant chaperone. Rikov, however, does not accompany them to the opera house.

During the interval, Bond believes he catches sight of Sinclair. He follows him into the maze of backstage passages, only to lose sight of him. Instead of re-locating Sinclair, Bond finds himself watching the Estovian democrats' leader, Vasili Hartog, who appears to be waiting for somebody.

The somebody that appears is not the one Hartog was waiting for. This somebody wants him dead. Bond intervenes to protect the political exile. The would-be killer bolts and Bond finds himself ploughing through the backstage clutter, dodging around ropes and wires that would garotte the unwary and ducking bullets and chunks of scenery thrown at him by his quarry.

When a piece of scenery strikes him a glancing blow, Bond is momentarily disoriented. The would-be killer takes the opportunity to double back and move in for the kill. Bond shakes off his dizziness to find himself staring at the business end of a stiletto blade.

* * *

PART THREE (six pages)

The assassin is cut down by a shot from the shadows. Bond's rescuer steps

into the light: Sinclair. Lifting away the now-limp assassin's mask, Sinclair reveals Katarinya Rikov to have been Hartog's would-be killer. Covering Bond with the gun he used to save his life, Sinclair tells the story of his conversion from 'agents' agent' to fighter for a cause.

Sinclair had been sent to Estovia as an observer. He was to assess the situation and recommend which side—the democrats' or Kolovsky's – would offer Britain the most benefits in exchange for official recognition. However, the sight of the atrocities committed by Kolovsky's para-military supporters in the name of "persuasion", made it increasingly difficult to maintain his neutrality. When the family of a man who had been his guide, and, latterly, his friend, suffered at the hands of Kolovsky's men, he gave up trying.

Dropping out of sight of his controllers in British Intelligence, he joined

the democratic resistance movement, advising the rebels on guerrilla tactics and leading some of the raids. He devised the plan to kill Kolovsky while the dictator was out of the country and away from the tight security he enjoyed inside Estovia and was here to carry it out.

By explaining this to Bond and by revealing that Kolovsky has plans of his own to wipe out the exiled democrats under cover of his Western diplomatic tour, evidenced by Rikov's attempt on Hartog's life, Sinclair had hoped to convince Bond to turn a blind eye long enough for Sinclair to kill Kolovsky. If Bond had agreed, Sinclair would have been more than a little surprised. As it is, he nods his unhappy understanding and shoots Bond.

* * *

PART FOUR (six pages)

By the time Bond recovers from the powerful tranquilizer carried by the darts in Sinclair's gun, his former colleague is long gone. Sinclair left Rikov, tied and hung from one of the scenery lifting ropes, as a parting gift.

Although both Kolovsky and Rikov enjoy diplomatic immunity from prosecution, the British Government has no intention of tolerating their presence any longer than is absolutely necessary. While a decoy police-and-limousine convoy heads for Heathrow Airport, Bond escorts Kolovsky to a safe house in the East End. The dictator will be flown out from the Docklands Heliport in the early hours of the following morning.

When Bond is informed that the convoy reached Heathrow unmolested and that Rikov had been put aboard the first plane to Estovia, he knows that Sinclair is on his way east, if he's not already there.

He's there. Firing off star-shells and concussion grenades to disorientate those inside the safe house, Sinclair also gives away his position to Bond in an apparent lapse of professionalism. Bond takes advantage of it and, leaving Kolovsky in the care of two other agents, heads after him.

The grenades and star-shells were a ploy to draw Bond from the house. Sinclair intended to make sure Bond was clear of the house before detonating the powerful bomb he had planted outside it. Either Kolovsky would be killed in the blast or would be reduced to running through the streets, looking for shelter as Sinclair tracked him down. Bond figured this out while he disarmed the bomb before heading after Sinclair and taking the bomb's detonator – a powerful explosive package in its own right – with him.

On a derelict wharf on the bank of the once-bustling River Thames, Bond comes face-to-face with Sinclair. He berates his former friend for his willingness to kill the two other agents with the bomb meant for Kolovsky. Is he so sure of his own righteousness that he can justify committing atrocities of his own? As Sinclair pauses for troubled thought, Bond makes his move. In the ensuing scuffle, Sinclair gains possession of the detonator and presses the trigger.

Caught at the edge of the explosion, Bond receives cuts, bruises, and concussion. Sinclair, much closer to the explosion, is believed to have been killed, his body blown into the Thames by the blast. This is the second time Sinclair has been declared 'missing, believed dead.' Bond believes he knows enough about his former friend to reserve judgement.

Kolovsky's death, shot as he stepped from a car to enter a New York hotel, while on the last leg of his Western tour, by a man riding a high-powered motorcycle, who then successfully evaded Kolovsky's FBI escort, would seem to lend weight to Bond's suspicions.

Acknowledgments

One of the great pleasures of writing *The Many Lives of James Bond*, my first book on 007, was how the Bond community opened up their arms and embraced the book and me. I was more than a little nervous about how passionate Bond fans would react to the book and I was gratified by their response. I would like to thank Tom Sears and Chris Wright at *James Bond Radio*, David Zaritsky from *The Bond Experience*, Joseph Darlington from *Being Bond*, Anders Frejdh from *From Sweden with Love*, Nicolas Suszczyk of *The Bond of the Millennium*, Tom Cull of Artistic Licence Renewed, Alan J. Porter of *The Illustrated* 007, Dr. Lisa Funnell of *For His Eyes Only: The Women of James Bond*, Matt Spaiser of Bond Suits, Ajay Chowdhury of *Some Kind of Hero*, Mark O'Connell of *Catching Bullets*, Lee Pfeiffer of Cinema Retro, Remmert van Braam of the Bond Lifestyle, Archivo 007, Steven Jay Rubin of *The James Bond Films*, Richard Schenkman of *Bondage*, Lee Pfeiffer of *The Incredible World of 007* and *Cinema arRetro*, James Chapman of *Licensed to Thrill*, Andy Lane of *The Bond Files*, Bruce Scivally of *James Bond: The Legacy*, Mike White of *The Projection Booth*, Thomas Nixdorf of The Nixdorf Collection, Llewella Chapman of *Fashioning James Bond*, Phil Noble Jr., *Archivo 007*, Greg Bechtlof of *MI6*, Bill Koenig of *The Spy Command*, Peter Lorenz of the *Illustrated 007* and Calvin Dyson, who helped "discover" the uncredited actor who played James Bond in a video game.

I'd also like to thank all the readers who expressed their enthusiasm for my last book. Their comments, to quote Ian Fleming, "warmed my heart." Some of those wonderful people include Mark Ashby, William Kanas, Cal David, Glenn Hewett, Darren Noble, David Stephens, Brian Dobson, Oscar Rubio, Martin Hrdr, Michael Gallipo, David Stephens, Victor Tapia, Howard Pieratt, Steve Brock, Sean Hannam, Marc Hernandez, and Anagnostis Karras,

My heartfelt thanks to all the artists who agreed to be interview. They were all generous with their time and I'm grateful that they shared their memories and experiences with me.

My appreciation also goes to Audrey Sperano DiSpigna, Anne Reingold, Maria Vassilopoulos, Emma Lowe, Sarah M. Kelly, Colin Brown, Carol Ives, and Jane Wenning, for her help in editing the book.

I'm overjoyed that Sean Longmore has designed the cover for this book. I am thrilled to include artist Pat Carbajal's striking illustrations in this volume.

Deepest thanks also go to Jack Lugo of *James Bond Radio*, Brian McKaig of *The Bondologist Blog*, and Clinton Rawls of *Comics Royale*. Their insights, support, and knowledge of Bond were invaluable, as was their kindness and friendship.

I want to thank my friends Jerry Kolber, Adam Davis, John Rawles, Johanna Gendelman, Sara Blumenthal, Chris Van Cleef, and Jim Graham.

Additional appreciation must go the team at RKO—Ted Hartley, Mary Beth O'Connor, Brian Anderson, Steven Tolman, Amy McMillan, and Celia Castevens.

I also want to thank my family for all of their support. For my dear and beloved uncle Elliot Ravetz, who is always so generous with his time, advice, and love. This book is immeasurably improved by his contributions. For my mom the honorable Sandra Edlitz, who always believes in me. I'd also like to thank my wonderful sister Tracy, who is also a great aunt. Additional love and thanks go to Gail Ravetz, Mark Visceglia, Doctor Joan Shapiro, and Doctor Irving Shapiro. I also want to remember my late father, Robert Edlitz.

Above all I must thank Doctor Susan Shapiro, my wise and beautiful wife, and Sophie and Ben, my two amazing, interesting, and idiosyncratic children.

Notes

[1] Phil Nobile Jr. "You Only Live Thrice," *Birth.Movies.Death.com*, October 5, 2012, http://birthmovies-death.com/2012/10/05/you-only-live-thrice

[2] Scott Meslow, "Timothy Dalton opens up about Penny Dreadful, leaving James Bond, and the demon in all of us," *The Week*, "May 12, 2014, http://theweek.com/articles/447045/timothy-dalton-opens-about-penny-dread-ful-leaving-james-bond-demon-all

[3] Michael G. Wilson and Alfonse Ruggiero, "Bond 17 Outline," May 8, 1990

[4] Michael G. Wilson and Alfonse Ruggiero, p1

[5] Michael G. Wilson and Alfonse Ruggiero, p1

[6] Michael G. Wilson and Alfonse Ruggiero, p1

[7] Michael G. Wilson and Alfonse Ruggiero, p1

[8] Michael G. Wilson and Alfonse Ruggiero, p1

[9] Michael G. Wilson and Alfonse Ruggiero, p1

[10] Michael G. Wilson and Alfonse Ruggiero, p1

[11] Michael G. Wilson and Alfonse Ruggiero, p2

[12] Michael G. Wilson and Alfonse Ruggiero, p2

[13] Michael G. Wilson and Alfonse Ruggiero, p3

[14] Michael G. Wilson and Alfonse Ruggiero, p3

[15] Michael G. Wilson and Alfonse Ruggiero, p3

[16] Michael G. Wilson and Alfonse Ruggiero, p3

[17] Michael G. Wilson and Alfonse Ruggiero, p3

[18] Michael G. Wilson and Alfonse Ruggiero, p4

[19] Michael G. Wilson and Alfonse Ruggiero, p4

[20] Michael G. Wilson and Alfonse Ruggiero, p5

[21] Michael G. Wilson and Alfonse Ruggiero, p5

[22] Michael G. Wilson and Alfonse Ruggiero, p5

[23] Michael G. Wilson and Alfonse Ruggiero, p5

[24] Michael G. Wilson and Alfonse Ruggiero, p5

[25] Michael G. Wilson and Alfonse Ruggiero, p5

[26] Michael G. Wilson and Alfonse Ruggiero, p6

[27] Michael G. Wilson and Alfonse Ruggiero, p6

[28] Michael G. Wilson and Alfonse Ruggiero, p6

[29] Michael G. Wilson and Alfonse Ruggiero, p7

[30] Michael G. Wilson and Alfonse Ruggiero, p7

[31] Michael G. Wilson and Alfonse Ruggiero, p7

[32] Michael G. Wilson and Alfonse Ruggiero, p7

[33] Michael G. Wilson and Alfonse Ruggiero, p8

[34] Michael G. Wilson and Alfonse Ruggiero, p8

[35] Michael G. Wilson and Alfonse Ruggiero, p8

[36] Michael G. Wilson and Alfonse Ruggiero, p8

[37] Michael G. Wilson and Alfonse Ruggiero, p9

[38] Michael G. Wilson and Alfonse Ruggiero, p9

[39] Michael G. Wilson and Alfonse Ruggiero, p10

[40] Michael G. Wilson and Alfonse Ruggiero, p11

[41] Michael G. Wilson and Alfonse Ruggiero, p11

[42] Michael G. Wilson and Alfonse Ruggiero, p11

[43] Michael G. Wilson and Alfonse Ruggiero, p11

[44] Michael G. Wilson and Alfonse Ruggiero, p12

[45] Michael G. Wilson and Alfonse Ruggiero, p13

[46] Michael G. Wilson and Alfonse Ruggiero, p13

[47] Michael G. Wilson and Alfonse Ruggiero, p13

[48] Michael G. Wilson and Alfonse Ruggiero, p13

[49] Michael G. Wilson and Alfonse Ruggiero, p13

[50] Michael G. Wilson and Alfonse Ruggiero, p14

[51] Michael G. Wilson and Alfonse Ruggiero, p14

[52] Michael G. Wilson and Alfonse Ruggiero, p14

[53] Michael G. Wilson and Alfonse Ruggiero, p15

[54] Michael G. Wilson and Alfonse Ruggiero, p15

[55] Michael G. Wilson and Alfonse Ruggiero, p15

[56] Michael G. Wilson and Alfonse Ruggiero, p16

[57] Michael G. Wilson and Alfonse Ruggiero, p16

[58] Michael G. Wilson and Alfonse Ruggiero, p17

[59] John Culhane, *The Los Angeles Times*, "'Broccoli . . . Cubby Broccoli': How a Long Island vegetable farmer became the man who produced all of the real James Bond movies," July 9, 1989, http://articles.latimes.com/1989-07-09/entertainment/ca-5205_1_james-bond-pictures

[60] Michael G. Wilson and Alfonse Ruggiero, p15

[61] Michael G. Wilson and Alfonse Ruggiero

[62] Matthew Field and Ajay Chowdhury, *Some Kind of Hero: The Remarkable Story of the James Bond Films*, The History Press, 2015

[63] Matthew Field and Ajay Chowdhury, *Some Kind of Hero: The Remarkable Story of the James Bond Films*, The History Press, 2015

[64] William Davies, William Osborne, Al Ruggiero and Michael Wilson, "*Bond XVIII*," January 2, 1991.

[65] William Davies, William Osborne, Al Ruggiero, and Michael Wilson, "*Bond XVIII*," January 2, 1991, p2.

[66] William Davies, William Osborne, Al Ruggiero, and Michael Wilson, p2

[67] William Davies, William Osborne, Al Ruggiero, and Michael Wilson, p3

[68] William Davies, William Osborne, Al Ruggiero, and Michael Wilson, p3

[69] William Davies, William Osborne, Al Ruggiero, and Michael Wilson, p4

[70] William Davies, William Osborne, Al Ruggiero, and Michael Wilson, p6

[71] William Davies, William Osborne, Al Ruggiero, and Michael Wilson, p6

[72] William Davies, William Osborne, Al Ruggiero, and Michael Wilson, p8

[73] William Davies, William Osborne, Al Ruggiero, and Michael Wilson, p8

[74] William Davies, William Osborne, Al Ruggiero, and Michael Wilson, p8

[75] William Davies, William Osborne, Al Ruggiero, and Michael Wilson, p11

[76] William Davies, William Osborne, Al Ruggiero, and Michael Wilson, p11

[77] William Davies, William Osborne, Al Ruggiero, and Michael Wilson, p12

[78] William Davies, William Osborne, Al Ruggiero, and Michael Wilson, p12

[79] William Davies, William Osborne, Al Ruggiero, and Michael Wilson, p16

[80] William Davies, William Osborne, Al Ruggiero, and Michael Wilson, p16

[81] William Davies, William Osborne, Al Ruggiero, and Michael Wilson, p16

[82] William Davies, William Osborne, Al Ruggiero, and Michael Wilson, p16

[83] William Davies, William Osborne, Al Ruggiero, and Michael Wilson, p18

[84] William Davies, William Osborne, Al Ruggiero, and Michael Wilson, p18

[85] William Davies, William Osborne, Al Ruggiero, and Michael Wilson, p19

[86] William Davies, William Osborne, Al Ruggiero, and Michael Wilson, p19

[87] William Davies, William Osborne, Al Ruggiero, and Michael Wilson, p21

[88] William Davies, William Osborne, Al Ruggiero, and Michael Wilson, p23

[89] William Davies, William Osborne, Al Ruggiero, and Michael Wilson, p24

[90] William Davies, William Osborne, Al Ruggiero, and Michael Wilson, p27

[91] William Davies, William Osborne, Al Ruggiero, and Michael Wilson, p27

[92] William Davies, William Osborne, Al Ruggiero, and Michael Wilson, p29

[93] William Davies, William Osborne, Al Ruggiero, and Michael Wilson, p31

[94] William Davies, William Osborne, Al Ruggiero, and Michael Wilson, p32

[95] William Davies, William Osborne, Al Ruggiero, and Michael Wilson, p32

[96] William Davies, William Osborne, Al Ruggiero, and Michael Wilson, p36

[97] William Davies, William Osborne, Al Ruggiero, and Michael Wilson, p37

[98] William Davies, William Osborne, Al Ruggiero, and Michael Wilson, p43

[99] William Davies, William Osborne, Al Ruggiero, and Michael Wilson, p47

[100] William Davies, William Osborne, Al Ruggiero, and Michael Wilson, p51

[101] William Davies, William Osborne, Al Ruggiero, and Michael Wilson, p62

[102] William Davies, William Osborne, Al Ruggiero, and Michael Wilson, p69

[103] William Davies, William Osborne, Al Ruggiero, and Michael Wilson, p69

[104] William Davies, William Osborne, Al Ruggiero, and Michael Wilson, p71

[105] William Davies, William Osborne, Al Ruggiero, and Michael Wilson, p75

[106] William Davies, William Osborne, Al Ruggiero, and Michael Wilson, p76

[107] William Davies, William Osborne, Al Ruggiero, and Michael Wilson, p76

[108] William Davies, William Osborne, Al Ruggiero, and Michael Wilson, p76

[109] William Davies, William Osborne, Al Ruggiero, and Michael Wilson, p77

[110] William Davies, William Osborne, Al Ruggiero, and Michael Wilson, p78

[111] William Davies, William Osborne, Al Ruggiero, and Michael Wilson, p78

[112] William Davies, William Osborne, Al Ruggiero, and Michael Wilson, p79

[113] William Davies, William Osborne, Al Ruggiero, and Michael Wilson, p80

[114] William Davies, William Osborne, Al Ruggiero, and Michael Wilson, p84

[115] William Davies, William Osborne, Al Ruggiero, and Michael Wilson, p88

[116] William Davies, William Osborne, Al Ruggiero, and Michael Wilson, p88

[117] William Davies, William Osborne, Al Ruggiero, and Michael Wilson, p89

[118] William Davies, William Osborne, Al Ruggiero, and Michael Wilson, p89

[119] William Davies, William Osborne, Al Ruggiero, and Michael Wilson, p89

[120] William Davies, William Osborne, Al Ruggiero, and Michael Wilson, p92

[121] William Davies, William Osborne, Al Ruggiero, and Michael Wilson, p92

[122] William Davies, William Osborne, Al Ruggiero, and Michael Wilson, p92

[123] William Davies, William Osborne, Al Ruggiero, and Michael Wilson, p92

[124] William Davies, William Osborne, Al Ruggiero, and Michael Wilson, p93

[125] William Davies, William Osborne, Al Ruggiero, and Michael Wilson, p93

[126] William Davies, William Osborne, Al Ruggiero, and Michael Wilson, p96

[127] William Davies, William Osborne, Al Ruggiero, and Michael Wilson, p97

[128] William Davies, William Osborne, Al Ruggiero, and Michael Wilson, p97

[129] William Davies, William Osborne, Al Ruggiero, and Michael Wilson, p99

[130] William Davies, William Osborne, Al Ruggiero, and Michael Wilson, p99

[131] William Davies, William Osborne, Al Ruggiero, and Michael Wilson, p100

[132] William Davies, William Osborne, Al Ruggiero, and Michael Wilson, p100

[133] William Davies, William Osborne, Al Ruggiero, and Michael Wilson, p101

[134] William Davies, William Osborne, Al Ruggiero, and Michael Wilson, p107

[135] William Davies, William Osborne, Al Ruggiero, and Michael Wilson, p107

[136] William Davies, William Osborne, Al Ruggiero, and Michael Wilson, p108

[137] William Davies, William Osborne, Al Ruggiero, and Michael Wilson, p113

[138] William Davies, William Osborne, Al Ruggiero, and Michael Wilson, p117

[139] William Davies, William Osborne, Al Ruggiero, and Michael Wilson, p117

[140] William Davies, William Osborne, Al Ruggiero, and Michael Wilson, p118

[141] William Davies, William Osborne, Al Ruggiero, and Michael Wilson, p118

[142] William Davies, William Osborne, Al Ruggiero, and Michael Wilson, p118

[143] William Davies, William Osborne, Al Ruggiero, and Michael Wilson, p118

[144] William Davies, William Osborne, Al Ruggiero, and Michael Wilson, p119

[145] William Davies, William Osborne, Al Ruggiero, and Michael Wilson, p119

[146] William Davies, William Osborne, Al Ruggiero, and Michael Wilson, p120

[147] William Davies, William Osborne, Al Ruggiero, and Michael Wilson, p120

[148] William Davies, William Osborne, Al Ruggiero, and Michael Wilson, p121

[149] William Davies, William Osborne, Al Ruggiero, and Michael Wilson, p121

[150] William Davies, William Osborne, Al Ruggiero, and Michael Wilson, p121

[151] William Davies, William Osborne, Al Ruggiero, and Michael Wilson, p121

[152] William Davies, William Osborne, Al Ruggiero, and Michael Wilson, p89

[153] William Davies, William Osborne, Al Ruggiero, and Michael Wilson, p11

[154] William Davies, William Osborne, Al Ruggiero, and Michael Wilson, p69

[155] William Davies, William Osborne, Al Ruggiero, and Michael Wilson, p11

[156] William Davies, William Osborne, Al Ruggiero, and Michael Wilson, p32

[157] Matthew Field and Ajay Chowdhury, *Some Kind of Hero*, The History Press, 2015

[158] William Davies, William Osborne, Al Ruggiero and Michael G. Wilson, p32

[159] William Davies, William Osborne, Al Ruggiero, and Michael Wilson, p107

[160] Mark Edlitz, The Many Lives of James Bond

[161] William Davies, William Osborne, Al Ruggiero and Michael Wilson, p30

[162] William Davies, William Osborne, Al Ruggiero, and Michael Wilson, p97

[163] William Davies, William Osborne, Al Ruggiero, and Michael Wilson, p92

[164] William Davies, William Osborne, Al Ruggiero, and Michael Wilson, p26

[165] William Davies, William Osborne, Al Ruggiero, and Michael Wilson, p51

[166] William Davies, William Osborne, Al Ruggiero, and Michael Wilson, p21

[167] Matthew Field and Ajay Chowdhury, *Some Kind of Hero*, The History Press, 2015

[168] BoxOfficeMojo.com

[169] David McClintick, and Anne Fairlcoth, "The Predator How an Italian Thug Looted MGM, Brought Credit Lyonnais to Its Knees, And Made the Pope Cry," *Fortune*, July 8, 1996, http://archive.fortune.com/magazines/fortune/fortune_archive/1996/07/08/214344/index.htm

[170] Suzan Ayscough, "Danjaq on bond wagon with two script deals," *Variety*, May 26, 1993, http://variety.com/1993/film/news/danjaq-on-bond-wagon-with-two-script-deals-107186/

[171] Suzan Ayscough, "Danjaq on bond wagon with two script deals," *Variety*, May 26, 1993

[172] Suzan Ayscough, "Danjaq on bond wagon with two script deals," *Variety*, May 26, 1993

[173] Athena Stamos, "The John Cork CBn Interview," *CommanderBond.net*, November 14, 2005, http://commanderbond.net/2992/the-john-cork-cbn-interview.html

[174] Suzan Ayscough, "Danjaq on bond wagon with two script deals," *Variety*, May 26, 1993 http://variety.com/1993/film/news/danjaq-on-bond-wagon-with-two-script-deals-107186/

[175] Carl Nolte, "Richard Burget Smith, 48, author and screenwriter, *SF Gate*, July 7, 2011, http://www.sfgate.com/bayarea/article/Richard-Burges-Smith-48-author-and-screenwriter-2355665.php

[176] Richard Smith, Reunion with Death, December 14, 1993, p1

[177] Richard Smith, p2

[178] Richard Smith, p2

[179] Richard Smith, p2

[180] Richard Smith, p2

[181] Richard Smith, p2

[182] Richard Smith, p2

[183] Richard Smith, p2

[184] Richard Smith, p2

[185] Richard Smith, p3

[186] Richard Smith, p3

[187] Richard Smith, p3

[188] Richard Smith, p3

[189] Richard Smith, p3

[190] Richard Smith, p3

[191] Richard Smith, p4

[192] Richard Smith, p4

[193] Richard Smith, p4

[194] Richard Smith, p4

[195] Richard Smith, p5

[196] Richard Smith, p5

[197] Richard Smith, p5

[198] Richard Smith, p5

[199] Richard Smith, p5

[200] Richard Smith, p5

[201] Richard Smith, p5

[202] Richard Smith, p5

[203] Richard Smith, p5

[204] Richard Smith, p5

[205] Richard Smith, p6

[206] Richard Smith, p6

[207] Richard Smith, p6

[208] Richard Smith, p6

[209] Richard Smith, p6

[210] Richard Smith, p6

[211] Richard Smith, p7

[212] Richard Smith, p7

[213] Richard Smith, p7

[214] Richard Smith, p8

[215] Richard Smith, p8

[216] Richard Smith, p8

[217] Richard Smith, p8

[218] Richard Smith, p9

[219] Richard Smith, p9

[220] Richard Smith, p9

[221] Richard Smith, p9

[222] Richard Smith, p9

[223] Richard Smith, p10

[224] Richard Smith, p10

[225] Richard Smith, p10

[226] Richard Smith, p10

[227] Richard Smith, p12

[228] Richard Smith, p12

[229] Richard Smith, p12

[230] Richard Smith, p13

[231] Richard Smith, p13

[232] Richard Smith, p13

[233] Richard Smith, p13

[234] Richard Smith, p13

[235] Richard Smith, p14

[236] Richard Smith, p14

[237] Richard Smith, p14

[238] Richard Smith, p15

[239] Richard Smith, p15

[240] Richard Smith, p15

[241] Richard Smith, p15

[242] Richard Smith, p16

[243] Richard Smith, p16

[244] Richard Smith, p17

[245] Richard Smith, p17

[246] Richard Smith, p18

[247] Richard Smith, p18

[248] Richard Smith, p18

[249] Richard Smith, p19

[250] Richard Smith, p20

[251] Richard Smith, p20

[252] Richard Smith, p20

[253] Richard Smith, p21

[254] Richard Smith, p21

[255] Richard Smith, p21

[256] Richard Smith, p21

[257] Richard Smith, p23

[258] Richard Smith, p23

[259] Richard Smith, p23

[260] Richard Smith, p24

[261] Richard Smith, p26

[262] Richard Smith, p26

[263] Richard Smith, p26

[264] Richard Smith, p27

[265] Richard Smith, p27

[266] Richard Smith, p30

[267] Richard Smith, p30

[268] Richard Smith, p31

[269] Richard Smith, p31

[270] Richard Smith, p31

[271] Richard Smith, p32

[272] Richard Smith, p32

[273] Richard Smith, p32

[274] Richard Smith, p32

[275] John Brosnan, *James Bond in the Cinema*, The Tantivy Press, 1972

[276] Richard Smith, p33

[277] Richard Smith, p33

[278] Richard Smith, p34

[279] Richard Smith, p35

[280] Richard Smith, p36

[281] Richard Smith, p36

[282] Richard Smith, p37

[283] Dan Cox, "Dalton bails out as Bond," *Variety*, April 12, 1994. https://variety.com/1994/film/news/dalton-bails-out-as-bond-120067/

[284] Matthew Field and Ajay Chowdhury, *Some Kind of Hero*, History Press, 2015

[285] Suzan Ayscough, "Danjaq on bond wagon with two script deals," *Variety*, May 26, 1993

[286] Paul Rowlands, "John Cork Talks To Paul Rowlands," Money Into Light.com http://www.money-into-light.com/2012/12/john-cork-talks-to-paul-rowlands-part-1.html

[287] Ian Fleming, *Moonraker*, page 4, Jonathan Cape, 1955

[288] Richard Smith, page 8

[289] Richard Smith, page 4

[290] Richard Smith, page 3

[291] Richard Maibaum and Michael Wilson, Bond XV Treatment, November 8, 1985, Cover Page

[292] Richard Maibaum Papers, The University of Iowa Libraries, Iowa City, Iowa.

[293] Richard Maibaum and Michael Wilson, Bond XV Treatment, November 8, 1985, p1

[294] Richard Maibaum and Michael Wilson, Bond XV Treatment, November 8, 1985, p1

[295] Richard Maibaum and Michael Wilson, Bond XV Treatment, November 8, 1985, p1

[296] Richard Maibaum and Michael Wilson, Bond XV Treatment, November 8, 1985, p2

[297] Richard Maibaum and Michael Wilson, Bond XV Treatment, November 8, 1985, p2

[298] Richard Maibaum and Michael Wilson, Bond XV Treatment, November 8, 1985, p2

[299] Richard Maibaum and Michael Wilson, Bond XV Treatment, November 8, 1985, p2

[300] Richard Maibaum and Michael Wilson, Bond XV Treatment, November 8, 1985, p3

[301] Richard Maibaum and Michael Wilson, Bond XV Treatment, November 8, 1985, p3

[302] Richard Maibaum and Michael Wilson, Bond XV Treatment, November 8, 1985, p3

[303] Richard Maibaum and Michael Wilson, Bond XV Treatment, November 8, 1985, p3

[304] Richard Maibaum and Michael Wilson, Bond XV Treatment, November 8, 1985, p3

[305] Richard Maibaum and Michael Wilson, Bond XV Treatment, November 8, 1985, p3

[306] Richard Maibaum and Michael Wilson, Bond XV Treatment, November 8, 1985, p3

[307] Richard Maibaum and Michael Wilson, Bond XV Treatment, November 8, 1985, p3

[308] Richard Maibaum and Michael Wilson, Bond XV Treatment, November 8, 1985, p4

[309] Richard Maibaum and Michael Wilson, Bond XV Treatment, November 8, 1985, p4

[310] Richard Maibaum and Michael Wilson, Bond XV Treatment, November 8, 1985, p5

[311] Richard Maibaum and Michael Wilson, Bond XV Treatment, November 8, 1985, p5

[312] Richard Maibaum and Michael Wilson, Bond XV Treatment, November 8, 1985, p5

[313] Richard Maibaum and Michael Wilson, Bond XV Treatment, November 8, 1985, p5

[314] Richard Maibaum and Michael Wilson, Bond XV Treatment, November 8, 1985, p5

[315] Richard Maibaum and Michael Wilson, Bond XV Treatment, November 8, 1985, p5

[316] Richard Maibaum and Michael Wilson, Bond XV Treatment, November 8, 1985, p5

[317] Richard Maibaum and Michael Wilson, Bond XV Treatment, November 8, 1985, p5

[318] Richard Maibaum and Michael Wilson, Bond XV Treatment, November 8, 1985, p6

[319] Richard Maibaum and Michael Wilson, Bond XV Treatment, November 8, 1985, p7

[320] Richard Maibaum and Michael Wilson, Bond XV Treatment, November 8, 1985, p7

[321] Richard Maibaum and Michael Wilson, Bond XV Treatment, November 8, 1985, p13

[322] Richard Maibaum and Michael Wilson, Bond XV Treatment, November 8, 1985, p13

[323] Richard Maibaum and Michael Wilson, Bond XV Treatment, November 8, 1985, p14

[324] Richard Maibaum and Michael Wilson, Bond XV Treatment, November 8, 1985, p14

[325] Richard Maibaum and Michael Wilson, Bond XV Treatment, November 8, 1985, p15

[326] Richard Maibaum and Michael Wilson, Bond XV Treatment, November 8, 1985, p16

[327] Richard Maibaum and Michael Wilson, Bond XV Treatment, November 8, 1985, p17

[328] Richard Maibaum and Michael Wilson, Bond XV Treatment, November 8, 1985, p17

[329] Richard Maibaum and Michael Wilson, Bond XV Treatment, November 8, 1985, p18

[330] Richard Maibaum and Michael Wilson, Bond XV Treatment, November 8, 1985, p22

[331] Richard Maibaum and Michael Wilson, Bond XV Treatment, November 8, 1985, p23

[332] Richard Maibaum and Michael Wilson, Bond XV Treatment, November 8, 1985, p24

[333] Richard Maibaum and Michael Wilson, Bond XV Treatment, November 8, 1985, p25

[334] Richard Maibaum and Michael Wilson, Bond XV Treatment, November 8, 1985, p25

[335] Richard Maibaum and Michael Wilson, Bond XV Treatment, November 8, 1985, p26

[336] Richard Maibaum and Michael Wilson, Bond XV Treatment, November 8, 1985, p28

[337] Richard Maibaum and Michael Wilson, Bond XV Treatment, November 8, 1985, p31

[338] Richard Maibaum and Michael Wilson, Bond XV Treatment, November 8, 1985, p31

[339] Richard Maibaum and Michael Wilson, Bond XV Treatment, November 8, 1985, p31

[340] Richard Maibaum and Michael Wilson, Bond XV Treatment, November 8, 1985, p34

[341] Richard Maibaum and Michael Wilson, Bond XV Treatment, November 8, 1985, p35

[342] Richard Maibaum and Michael Wilson, Bond XV Treatment, November 8, 1985, p35

[343] Richard Maibaum and Michael Wilson, Bond XV Treatment, November 8, 1985, p35

[344] Maibaum and Wilson, Undated and incomplete 19-Page Treatment, p5

[345] Maibaum and Wilson, Undated and incomplete 19-Page Treatment, p5

[346] Maibaum and Wilson, Undated and incomplete 19-Page Treatment, p7

[347] Maibaum and Wilson, Undated and incomplete 19-Page Treatment, p7

[348] Maibaum and Wilson, Undated and incomplete 19-Page Treatment, p8

[349] Maibaum and Wilson, Undated and incomplete 19-Page Treatment, p9

[350] Maibaum and Wilson, October 25, 1986, p3

[351] Maibaum and Wilson, Undated and incomplete 19-Page Treatment, p9

[352] Maibaum and Wilson, Undated and incomplete 19-Page Treatment, p10

[353] Maibaum and Wilson, Undated and incomplete 19-Page Treatment, p10

[354] Maibaum and Wilson, Undated and incomplete 19-Page Treatment, p11

[355] Maibaum and Wilson, Undated and incomplete 19-Page Treatment, p17

[356] Maibaum and Wilson, Undated and incomplete 19-Page Treatment, p10

[357] Maibaum and Wilson, Undated and incomplete 19-Page Treatment, p8

[358] Maibaum and Wilson, Undated and incomplete 19-Page Treatment, p14

[359] Maibaum and Wilson, Undated and incomplete 19-Page Treatment, p15

[360] Maibaum and Wilson, Undated and incomplete 19-Page Treatment, p15

[361] Maibaum and Wilson, Undated and incomplete 19-Page Treatment, p2

[362] Maibaum and Wilson, Undated and incomplete 19-Page Treatment, p2

[363] Maibaum and Wilson, Undated and incomplete 19-Page Treatment, p2

[364] Maibaum and Wilson, October 25, 1986, p18

[365] Maibaum and Wilson, November 8, 1985 5-page addendum, p1

[366] Maibaum and Wilson, October 25,1986, p15

[367] Maibaum and Wilson, November 8, 1985, p3

[368] Maibaum and Wilson, November 8, 1985, p3

[369] Maibaum and Wilson, Undated and incomplete 19-Page Treatment, p6

[370] Maibaum and Wilson, Undated and incomplete 19-Page Treatment, p5

[371] Maibaum and Wilson, Undated incomplete 19-Page Treatment, p5

[372] Maibaum and Wilson, Undated and incomplete 19-Page Treatment, p5

[373] Maibaum and Wilson, Undated and incomplete 19-Page Treatment, p4

[374] Maibaum and Wilson, Undated and incomplete 19-Page Treatment, p4

[375] Maibaum and Wilson, Undated and incomplete 19-Page Treatment, P. 10

[376] Maibaum and Wilson, Undated and incomplete 19-Page Treatment, P. 10

[377] Maibaum and Wilson, Undated and incomplete 19-Page Treatment, p5

[378] Licence to Kill Treatment with holograph revisions. [abandoned storyline] Earlier title *Bond XVI* p7

[379] Maibaum and Wilson, October 25, 1986, p14

[380] Maibaum and Wilson, November 8, 1985

[381] Matthew Field and Ajay Chowdhury, *Some Kind of Hero: The Remarkable Story of the James Bond Films*, The History Press, 2015

[382] Licence to Kill Treatment with holograph revisions. [abandoned storyline] Earlier title *Bond XVI* p2

[383] Licence to Kill Treatment with holograph revisions. [abandoned storyline] Earlier title *Bond XVI* p8-9

[384] Licence to Kill Treatment with holograph revisions. [abandoned storyline] Earlier title *Bond XVI* p33

[385] Licence to Kill Treatment with holograph revisions. [abandoned storyline] Earlier title *Bond XVI* p23

[386] Maibaum and Wilson, incomplete 19-Page Treatment, P. 5

[387] Maibaum and Wilson, November 8, 1985, p27

[388] Maibaum and Wilson, November 8, 1985, p16

[389] Maibaum and Wilson, November 8, 1985, p1

[390] Maibaum and Wilson, Undated and incomplete 19-Page Treatment, p1

[391] Daniela Bianchi appears as herself in the 2012 film *Noi non siamo come James Bond* (*We're nothing like James Bond*). In the quasi-documentary, longtime friends Mario Balsamo and Guido Gabrielli confront their mortality, reminisce about life, revel in their shared passion for Bond and, with the help of Bianchi, contact Sean Connery by phone. Connery's voice is briefly heard telling the filmmakers "Sorry chaps" but they've caught him at an inopportune moment.

[392] James Bond Jr Show Bible, unsigned, p1

[393] James Bond Jr Show Bible, unsigned, p1

[394] James Bond Jr Show Bible, unsigned, p1

[395] James Bond Jr Show Bible, unsigned, p1

[396] James Bond Jr Show Bible, unsigned, p2

[397] James Bond Jr Show Bible, unsigned, p1

[398] James Bond Jr Show Bible, unsigned, p11

[399] James Bond Jr Show Bible, unsigned, p10

[400] James Bond Jr Show Bible, unsigned, p22

[401] James Bond Jr Show Bible, unsigned, p31

[402] James Bond Jr Show Bible, unsigned, p6

[403] James Bond Jr Show Bible, unsigned, p32

[404] James Bond Jr Show Bible, unsigned, p32

[405] James Bond Jr Show Bible, unsigned, p32

[406] James Bond Jr Show Bible, unsigned, p33

[407] James Bond Jr Show Bible, unsigned, p33

[408] James Bond Jr Show Bible, unsigned, p27

[409] James Bond Jr Show Bible, unsigned, p27

[410] James Bond Jr Show Bible, unsigned, p34

[411] James Bond Jr Show Bible, unsigned, p34

[412] James Bond Jr Show Bible, unsigned, p34

[413] James Bond Jr Show Bible, unsigned, p35

[414] James Bond Jr Show Bible, unsigned, p35

[415] James Bond Jr Show Bible, unsigned, p27

[416] JamesBondJrOnline.Angelfire.com

[417] JamesBondJrOnline.Angelfire.com/books.html

[418] John Peel, *A View to a Thrill*, p1, Fantail Books, 1991

[419] John Peel, *A View to a Thrill*, p1, Fantail Books, 1991

[420] John Peel, *A View to a Thrill*, p48, Fantail Books, 1991

[421] John Peel, *A View to a Thrill*, p6, Fantail Books, 1991

[422] John Peel, *A View to a Thrill*, p6, Fantail Books, 1991

[423] John Peel, *A View to a Thrill*, p6, Fantail Books, 1991

[424] John Peel, *Sword of Death*, p67, Fantail Books, 1991

[425] Dave Morris, *As Good As Gold*, Mammoth, 1993, p11

[426] Dave Morris, *As Good As Gold*, Mammoth, 1993

[427] Dave Morris, *As Good As Gold*, Mammoth, 1993, p55

[428] Dave Morris, *As Good As Gold*, Mammoth, 1993, p55

[429] Dave Morris, *As Good As Gold*, Mammoth, 1993, p55

[430] Richard Schickel, *Happy Birthday 007: 25 Years of James Bond*, ABC, 1987. I was reminded of the Roger Moore quote while watching Calvin Dyson's YouTube video "Roger Moore as Bond in 1987? The Strange 'Happy Anniversary 007' TV Special."

[431] History of James Bond 007 Games (1983 – 2020), YouTube, https://youtu.be/j8kB68DGwO0, May 2, 2020

[432] Nick Kincaid, 007Forever.com, "The Search for RD Mascott (James Bond Junior 003 ½)" web.archive.org/web/20060617134228/http:/www.007forever.com/books/investigativereports004.html

[433] Jake Rossen, Mental Floss.com "No One Knows Who Wrote his James Bond Novel," November 6, 2015 https://www.mentalfloss.com/article/70751/no-one-knows-who-wrote-james-bond-novel

[434] R.D. Mascott, *003½: The Adventures of James Bond Junior*, Glidrose Productions ltd., Random House, 1968, p208

[435] Ian Fleming, *On Her Majesty's Secret Service*, Thomas & Mercer edition, 2012, p58

[436] Ian Fleming, *You Only Live Twice*, Thomas & Mercer edition, 2012, p206

[437] R.D. Mascott, *003½: The Adventures of James Bond Junior*, Glidrose Productions ltd., Random House, 1968, p6

[438] R.D. Mascott, *003½: The Adventures of James Bond Junior*, Glidrose Productions ltd., Random House, 1968, p6

[439] Andy Lane and Paul Simpson, *The Bond Files*, Virgin Publishing, 2002, p127

[440] Unknown author, *The Bookseller*, July 22, 1967. I first learned about Saltzman's plans from Sean Egan "James Bond: The Secret History," John Blake Publishing, 2016, p192

[441] Sean Egan "James Bond: The Secret History," John Blake Publishing, 2016, p193

[442] Andy Lane and Paul Simpson, *The Bond* Files, Virgin Books, 2002, p63

[443] Alan Hager, editor *Encyclopedia of British* Writers, *1800 to Present*, DWJ Books, 2009, p88

[444] John Cox, The Book Bond.com, http://www.thebookbond.com/2009/04/find-your-fate-with-james-bond.html

[445] R.L. Stine "James Bond in Win, Place, or Die," Ballantine Books, p67, 1985

[446] R.L. Stine "James Bond in Win, Place, or Die," Ballantine Books, p93

[447] R.L. Stine "James Bond in Win, Place, or Die," Ballantine Books, p90

[448] R.L. Stine "James Bond in Win, Place, or Die," Ballantine Books, p28

[449] Steve Oftinoski, Barracuda Run, Publisher, 1985

[450] Oftinoski, p.1

[451] Oftinoski, p.91

[452] Oftinoski, p.111

[453] Clinton Rawls, Comic Royale, Comics Royale.com

[454] Alan J Porter, *James Bond: The History of the Illustrated 007*, Hermes Press, 2008

[455] Clinton Rawls, Comic Royale, Comics Royale.com

[456] Clinton Rawls translation of Germán Gabler. "Operación Riesgo," April 1968, Comics Royale.

[457] Ian Fleming, "Risico" from *For Your Eyes Only*, Thomas & Mercer edition, 2012

[458] Germán Gabler, "Sabotaje," Zig-Zag, July 1969

[459] Germán Gabler, "La Reina de las Abejas," Zig-Zag, January 1970

[460] Germán Gabler, "La Reina de las Abejas," Zig-Zag, January 1970

[461] Germán Gabler, "La Reina de las Abejas," Zig-Zag, January 1970

[462] Germán Gabler, "Los Condenados," Zig-Zag, April 1971

[463] Germán Gabler, "La Reina de las Abejas," Zig-Zag, January 1970

[464] Germán Gabler, "La Playa de las Flores," Zig-Zag, April 1970

[465] Germán Gabler, "La Playa de las Flores," Zig-Zag, April 1970

[466] Germán Gabler, "La Reina de las Abejas," Zig-Zag, January 1970

[467] Unidentified Author, "Zig Zag "007" James Bond Comic Books, MI6-HQ.com, May 13, 2007, https://www.mi6-hq.com/sections/comics/zigzag.php3?s=comics

[468] Simon Jowett and John Burns, *A Silent Armageddon* #2, p8, 1993

[469] Alan J. Porter, *James Bond: The History of the Illustrated 007*, Hermes Press, 2008 p146

[470] Simon Jowett and David Lloyd, *Shattered Helix* #2, p7, 1994

[471] Simon Jowett and David Lloyd, *Shattered Helix* #2, p17, 1994

[472] John Pearson, *The Life of Ian Fleming*, Bloomsbury Reader, 2011. First published in 1966.

[473] Das Petrou, "James Bond: Light of My Death" Dark Horse Comics, 1993

[474] Jeremy Duns, *Diamonds in the Rough*, 2015, as reported by Anthony on the podcast The 00 Files by in episode "0050 Interview Jeremy Duns," April 15, 2020

[475] Das Petrou, "Light of My Death, Issue 1," p12

[476] Das Petrou, "Come Die With Me, Notes," p10

[477] Das Petrou, "Plot Changes 2"

[478] Das Petrou, "Come Die With Me Notes" p5

[479] Das Petrou, "Come Die With Me: Part 2," p2

[480] Colin Burnett, "Video Lecture: "Theorizing Threaded Media; Or Why James Bond Isn't Just a Failed Attempt at Star Wars," September 2, 2019, https://colinatthemovies.wordpress.com/2019/09/02/video-lecture-theorizing-threaded-media-or-why-james-bond-isnt-just-a-failed-attempt-at-star-wars/

[481] "COME DIE WITH ME," p1

[482] Das Petrou, "James Bond: Come Die With Me: Part 2," p2

[483] Das Petrou, "Plot Changes 2"

[484] "COME DIE WITH ME," p10

[485] Das Petrou, "Editor's Decision," p2

[486] Vita Ayala and Danny Lorre, *James Bond*, Dynamite Entertainment, 2019

[487] Patrick McGilligan, *Backstory: Interviews with Screenwriters of Hollywood's Golden* Age, University of California Press, p286.

[488] Patrick McGilligan, *Backstory: Interviews with Screenwriters of Hollywood's Golden* Age, University of California Press, p288.

[489] Richard Maibaum Papers, The University of Iowa Libraries, Iowa City, Iowa.

[490] I first learned about the essay while reading *Some Kind of Hero: The Remarkable Story of the James Bond Films Remarkable Story of the James Bond Films* by Mattew Field and Ajay Chowdhury, The History Press, 2015

[491] "Deus ex Machina, 1965 Model" Article by Richard Maibaum . Typescript with holograph revisions, together with correspondence, April - 1965, p1

[492] "Deus ex Machina, 1965 Model" Article by Richard Maibaum . Typescript with holograph revisions, together with correspondence, April - 1965, p1

[493] "Deus ex Machina, 1965 Model" Article by Richard Maibaum . Typescript with holograph revisions, together with correspondence, April - 1965, p1

[494] "Deus ex Machina, 1965 Model" Article by Richard Maibaum . Typescript with holograph revisions, together with correspondence, April - 1965, p1

[495] "Deus ex Machina, 1965 Model" Article by Richard Maibaum . Typescript with holograph revisions, together with correspondence, April - 1965, p2

[496] "Deus ex Machina, 1965 Model" Article by Richard Maibaum . Typescript with holograph revisions, together with correspondence, April - 1965, p2

[497] "Deus ex Machina, 1965 Model" Article by Richard Maibaum . Typescript with holograph revisions, together with correspondence, April - 1965, p3

[498] "Deus ex Machina, 1965 Model" Article by Richard Maibaum . Typescript with holograph revisions, together with correspondence, April - 1965, p3

[499] "Deus ex Machina, 1965 Model" Article by Richard Maibaum . Typescript with holograph revisions, together with correspondence, April - 1965, p5

[500] "Deus ex Machina, 1965 Model" Article by Richard Maibaum . Typescript with holograph revisions, together with correspondence, April - 1965, p5

[501] "Deus ex Machina, 1965 Model" Article by Richard Maibaum . Typescript with holograph revisions, together with correspondence, April - 1965, p6

[502] Deus ex Machina, 1965 Model" Article by Richard Maibaum . Typescript with holograph revisions, together with correspondence, April - 1965, p6

[503] "Deus ex Machina, 1965 Model" Article by Richard Maibaum . Typescript with holograph revisions, together with correspondence, April - 1965, p6

[504] Tom Carlile letter to Maibaum. April 14, 1965. Richard Maibaum Archives.

[505] Tom Carlile letter to Maibaum. April 14, 1965. Richard Maibaum Archives.

[506] Tom Carlile letter to Maibaum. April 14, 1965. Richard Maibaum Archives.

[507] Tom Carlile letter to Maibaum. April 14, 1965. Richard Maibaum Archives.

[508] "No Title, or, 007's Secret weapon." Article by Richard Maibaum; typescript. July 26 - 1965, p1

[509] No Title, or, 007's Secret weapon." Article by Richard Maibaum; typescript. July 26 - 1965, p1

[510] No Title, or, 007's Secret weapon." Article by Richard Maibaum; typescript. July 26 - 1965, p2

[511] No Title, or, 007's Secret weapon." Article by Richard Maibaum; typescript. July 26 - 1965, p3

[512] No Title, or, 007's Secret weapon." Article by Richard Maibaum; typescript. July 26 - 1965, p3

[513] No Title, or, 007's Secret weapon." Article by Richard Maibaum; typescript. July 26 - 1965, p3

[514] No Title, or, 007's Secret weapon." Article by Richard Maibaum; typescript. July 26 - 1965, p1

[515] No Title, or, 007's Secret weapon." Article by Richard Maibaum; typescript. July 26 - 1965, p1

[516] No Title, or, 007's Secret weapon." Article by Richard Maibaum; typescript. July 26 - 1965, p4

[517] No Title, or, 007's Secret weapon." Article by Richard Maibaum; typescript. July 26 - 1965, p4

[518] No Title, or, 007's Secret weapon." Article by Richard Maibaum; typescript. July 26 - 1965, p4

[519] No Title, or, 007's Secret weapon." Article by Richard Maibaum; typescript. July 26 - 1965, p2

[520] No Title, or, 007's Secret weapon." Article by Richard Maibaum; typescript. July 26 - 1965, p3

[521] No Title, or, 007's Secret weapon." Article by Richard Maibaum; typescript. July 26 - 1965, p4

[522] No Title, or, 007's Secret weapon." Article by Richard Maibaum; typescript. July 26 - 1965, p7

[523] No Title, or, 007's Secret weapon." Article by Richard Maibaum; typescript. July 26 - 1965, p7

[524] No Title, or, 007's Secret weapon." Article by Richard Maibaum; typescript. July 26 - 1965, p14

[525] No Title, or, 007's Secret weapon." Article by Richard Maibaum; typescript. July 26 - 1965, p8

[526] No Title, or, 007's Secret weapon." Article by Richard Maibaum; typescript. July 26 - 1965, p11

[527] No Title, or, 007's Secret weapon." Article by Richard Maibaum; typescript. July 26 - 1965, p11

[528] "James Bond films." James Bond article by Richard Maibaum. Untitled typescript, p3

[529] "James Bond films." James Bond article by Richard Maibaum. Untitled typescript, p4

[530] "James Bond films." James Bond article by Richard Maibaum. Untitled typescript, p4

[531] "James Bond films." James Bond article by Richard Maibaum. Untitled typescript, p4

[532] "James Bond films." James Bond article by Richard Maibaum. Untitled typescript, p4

[533] "James Bond films." James Bond article by Richard Maibaum. Untitled typescript, p5

[534] "James Bond films." James Bond article by Richard Maibaum. Untitled typescript, p5

[535] "James Bond films." James Bond article by Richard Maibaum. Untitled typescript, p6

[536] "James Bond films." James Bond article by Richard Maibaum. Untitled typescript, p6

[537] "James Bond films." James Bond article by Richard Maibaum. Untitled typescript, p6-7

[538] "James Bond films." James Bond article by Richard Maibaum. Untitled typescript, p7

[539] "James Bond films." James Bond article by Richard Maibaum. Untitled typescript, p2

[540] "James Bond films." James Bond article by Richard Maibaum. Untitled typescript, p7

[541] "James Bond films." James Bond article by Richard Maibaum. Untitled typescript, p10

[542] "James Bond and His Girls." Article by Richard Maibaum; incomplete typescript. August 3 - 1965

[543] "James Bond and His Girls." Article by Richard Maibaum; incomplete typescript. August 3 - 1965

[544] "James Bond and His Girls." Article by Richard Maibaum; incomplete typescript. August 3 - 1965, p1

[545] "James Bond and His Girls." Article by Richard Maibaum; incomplete typescript. August 3 - 1965, p14

[546] "James Bond and His Girls." Article by Richard Maibaum; incomplete typescript. August 3 - 1965, p15

[547] "James Bond and His Girls." Article by Richard Maibaum; incomplete typescript. August 3 - 1965, p15

[548] "James Bond and His Girls." Article by Richard Maibaum; incomplete typescript. August 3 - 1965, p15

[549] Richard Maibaum, "Writing the Bond films," Sackville Publishing, p27, 1965

[550] Richard Maibaum, "Writing the Bond films," Sackville Publishing, p27, 1965

[551] Richard Maibaum, "Writing the Bond films," Sackville Publishing, p27, 1965

[552] Richard Maibaum, "Writing the Bond films," Sackville Publishing, p27, 1965

[553] Richard Maibaum, "Writing the Bond films," Sackville Publishing, p27, 1965

[554] Richard Maibaum, "Writing the Bond films," Sackville Publishing, p27, 1965

[555] Richard Maibaum, "Writing the Bond films," Sackville Publishing, p27, 1965

[556] Richard Maibaum, "Writing the Bond films," Sackville Publishing, p27, 1965

[557] Richard Maibaum, "Writing the Bond films," Sackville Publishing, p27, 1965

[558] Richard Maibaum, "Writing the Bond films," Sackville Publishing, p27, 1965

[559] Richard Maibaum, "Cheers, 007!" Hollywood Reporter, July 14, 1987, p3

[560] Richard Maibaum, "Cheers, 007!" Hollywood Reporter, July 14, 1987, p3

[561] Richard Maibaum, "Cheers, 007!" Hollywood Reporter, July 14, 1987, p4

[562] Richard Maibaum, "Cheers, 007!" Hollywood Reporter, July 14, 1987, p4

[563] Richard Maibaum, "Cheers, 007!" Hollywood Reporter, July 14, 1987, p4

[564] Richard Maibaum, "Cheers, 007!" Hollywood Reporter, July 14, 1987, p5

[565] Richard Maibaum, "Cheers, 007!" Hollywood Reporter, July 14, 1987, p5

[566] Richard Maibaum, "Cheers, 007!" Hollywood Reporter, July 14, 1987, p5

[567] Richard Maibaum, "Cheers, 007!" Hollywood Reporter, July 14, 1987, p6

[568] Richard Maibaum, "Cheers, 007!" Hollywood Reporter, July 14, 1987, p6

[569] Richard Maibaum, "Cheers, 007!" Hollywood Reporter, July 14, 1987, p6

[570] "Deus ex Machina, 1965 Model" Article by Richard Maibaum. Undated original draft. Page 1

[571] "Deus ex Machina, 1965 Model" Article by Richard Maibaum. Undated original draft. Page 1

[572] Deus ex Machina, 1965 Model" Article by Richard Maibaum. Undated original draft. Page 1

[573] "Deus ex Machina, 1965 Model" Article by Richard Maibaum. Undated original draft. Page 2

[574] No Title, or, 007's Secret weapon." Article by Richard Maibaum; typescript. July 26 - 1965, p3

[575] "Deus ex Machina, 1965 Model" Article by Richard Maibaum. Undated original draft. Page 1

[576] "Deus ex Machina, 1965 Model" Article by Richard Maibaum. Typescript with holograph revisions, together with correspondence, April - 1965, p4

[577] "Deus ex Machina, 1965 Model" Article by Richard Maibaum. Undated original draft. Page 4

[578] RaymondBenson.com

[579] The majority of the interview was conducted live. However, the following two responses about the play were sent via email and, later, edited.

[580] Filmmaker and Bond fan Paul Scrabo videotaped the pre-ride film. It can be found at his website Scrabo.com.

[581] Owen Williams "License Denied: The Bond Themes You Didn't Get to Hear," Empire Online, September 9, 2015

[582] Jon Burlingame, The Music of James Bond, Oxford University Press, 2012

[583] James Bond's Greatest Hits, https://www.youtube.com/watch?v=bVAi3XJogz4

[584] Tim Lucas, "The Bond Theme You Never Heard," Video Watchdog.com, April 21, 2008

[585] Tim Lucas, "The Bond Theme You Never Heard," Video Watchdog.com, April 21, 2008

[586] Jonathan J, "Never Say Never Again intro sung by Phyllis Hyman (James Bond 007), https://www.youtube.com/watch?v=9uU4j84VKoE

[587] Tom Cull, "The Man with the Golden Microphone: Exclusive Interview with Martin Jarvis," Artistic License Renewed, December 14, 2016, https://literary007.com/2016/12/14/the-man-with-the-golden-microphone-exclusive-interview-with-martin-jarvis/

[588] "Agent in the Field: Martin Jarvis," IanFleming.com, http://www.ianfleming.com/agent-field-martin-jarvis/

[589] Ian Burrell, "Inside Story: Radio that's licensed to thrill," Independent, December 3, 2007, https://www.independent.co.uk/news/media/inside-story-radio-thats-licensed-to-thrill-761427.html

[590] Not all Bond aficionados responded favorably to M suggestions that Bond "pull a cracker." Edward Biddulph of the website James Bond Memes, who enjoyed the On Her Majesty's Secret Service adaptation overall, believes that the conversation was "very out of character" for the admiral. Despite the departure from the source material, I found the amusing exchange to be consistent with the relationship between M and Bond that was established in the radio dramas. Edward Biddulph, "OHMSS on the BBC – a review," May 3, 2014,
https://jamesbondmemes.blogspot.com/2014/05/ohmss-on-bbc-review.html?fbclid=IwAR36Rm-SL_MGAFiRxZ2ATEdGT37AbRFBGWdJZlKTkoWs6Wn64z6AzBU7u_v4

[591] James Inverne, "Villain with a Past," Sunday Telegraph, December 2002.

[592] Ian Fleming, Moonraker, Thomas & Mercer edition, 2012, p244

[593] "David Houston to Provide Voice for James Bond in New Videogame," MI6-HQ.com, November 22, 2007, Retrieved from https://www.mi6-hq.com/news/index.php?itemid=5596

[594] Jon Burlingame, The Music of James Bond, p.154, Oxford University Press, November 1, 2012

[595] Marty Passetta directed 17 Oscars, including the telecast where one-time James Bond David Niven quipped that the male nude-streaker was getting laughs by "stripping off and showing his shortcomings." YouTube Channel, "The Streaker: 1974 Oscars," March 30, 2015, https://www.youtube.com/watch?v=EWBc-ir6IFM

[596] "James Bond Jr. (very) rare UK comics, Commander Bond.net, April 2019, https://quarterdeck.commanderbond.net/t/james-bond-jr-very-rare-uk-comics/1265

[597] *This Hour Has 22 Minutes*, 2012, http://www.cbc.ca/22minutes/videos/clips-season-20/james-bond-spoof

[598] "Who Played James Bond: A Complete History," 007James.com, https://www.007james.com/articles/who_played_james_bond_part_2.php

[599] Dan Gale, "*Tape Secret! The Audiobooks of James Bond*," James Bond Radio.com, November 4, 2016. http://jamesbondradio.com/tape-secret-audiobooks-james-bond-documentary/

[600] Unknown writer, "OHMSS – 1976 ABC TV Version," The 007 Dossier.com, http://www.the007dossier.com/007dossier/post/2013/06/18/OHMSS-The-1976-ABC-TV-Version

[601] I started researching 007 voice over actor Stephen Critchlow at the suggestion of Calvin Dyson, a Bond expert who provides insight and commentary on all aspects of the Bond phenomena at his YouTube channel, which used to be called *Calvin Dyson Reviews Bond*.

[602] https://www.timeout.com/london/theatre/the-story-of-james-bond-a-tribute-to-ian-fleming

ABOUT THE BOOK COVER DESIGNER

Sean Longmore is a graphic designer and digital artist who specializes in using Photoshop to create key art with a cinematic style. Sean has worked in theatre design, producing work for numerous touring and Off-West End pro-ductions and has worked with multiple arts education charities. He also works freelance. Sean has a first-class honors degree in Media and Performance and is a huge fan of all aspects of film production. He has been exploring late 20th century movie posters, with a focus on posters created specifically for the Japanese film market, by creating his own adaptations of James Bond posters. He first became a Bond fan at age seven when he fell in love with *The Spy Who Loved Me*; he cannot imagine his life without 007 and regrets that he has yet to become a secret agent who wears a bright yellow ski suit.

Sean lives in Manchester in the UK.

ABOUT THE ILLUSTRATOR

Artist Pat Carbajal started as a political cartoonist at various national newspapers in Argentina. He then moved on to portrait art, illustrations, children's books, comic books, and storyboards for commercials.

Pat started producing art for the American market in 2007 when he illustrated covers for *Timeline of The Planet of the Apes* by Rich Handley for Hasslein Books. In 2009, he painted covers for the Bluewater Productions biography series, which were based on the lives of influential American women. Rock stars were the next subject for Pat. Bob Dylan, Jim Morrison, and Jimi Hendrix were the legends that were featured in *Rock and Roll Comics: The Sixties*, followed by Ozzy Osborne, AC/DC, and Guns N' Roses in *Rock and Roll Comics: Rock Heroes*.

The first graphic novel that Pat completely illustrated was *Allan Quartermain*, which was written by Clay and Susan Griffith and was published by Bluewater. Together with Clay and Susan Griffith, he created the character of The Raven for Bluewater's *Vincent Price Presents*, a classic horror comic book that starred Hollywood screen legend Vincent Price. Pat made his debut as a writer in the following issue of the comic.

For Hasslein Books, Pat illustrated the covers and interior art for *Lexicon of The Planet of the Apes, Back in Time, The Back to the Future Lexicon, A Matter of Time, Back to the Future Chronology*, and *Total Immersion, The Red Dwarf Encyclopaedia*.

Pat also creates exclusive designs for t-shirts with Rotten Cotton. He also produces comic book and cover artwork for Eibon press, with a series of horror graphic novels based on cult movies, including *Maniac,* Lucio Fulci's *Zombie,* and *The Beyond*.

Pat lives in Argentina.

ABOUT THE AUTHOR

Mark Edlitz has worked as a writer and producer for ABC News, NBC-Uni, CNBC, Discovery ID, and for National Geographic Channel's *Brain Games*.

Edlitz's writings about pop culture have appeared in *The Huffington Post*, *Los Angeles Times Hero Complex*, *Moviefone*, and *Empire* magazine online.

He wrote and directed the award-winning independent film *The Eden Myth* and directed *Jedi Junkies*, a documentary about extreme Star Wars fans.

Edlitz's book *How to Be a Superhero* includes interviews with actors who have played superheroes over the past seven decades.

His book *The Many Lives of James Bond* consists of original interviews with artists who have created James Bond movies, novels, television, radio dramas, comic books, and video games. It also includes a large collection of interviews who have played 007 in different media.

Edlitz lives in New York with his wife and two children.

CPSIA information can be obtained
at www.ICGtesting.com
Printed in the USA
LVHW020509121220
674004LV00009B/116

9 781735 461625